Third Workshop on Abusive Language Online 2019

Florence, Italy
1 August 2019

ISBN: 978-1-5108-9111-1

Printed by Curran Associates, Inc. (2019)

For permission requests, please contact the Association for Computational Linguistics
at the address below.

Association for Computational Linguistics
209 N. Eighth Street
Stroudsburg, Pennsylvania 18360

Phone: 1-570-476-8006
Fax: 1-570-476-0860

acl@aclweb.org

Additional copies of this publication are available from:

Curran Associates, Inc.
57 Morehouse Lane
Red Hook, NY 12571 USA
Phone: 845-758-0400
Fax: 845-758-2633
Email: curran@proceedings.com
Web: www.proceedings.com

ACL 2019

The Third Workshop on Abusive Language Online

Proceedings of the Workshop

August, 1, 2019
Florence, Italy

Introduction

The last few years have seen a surge in attention to various forms of abuse such as cyberbullying, hate speech, and scapegoating occurring on online platforms. At the same time, there has been a rise in interest in using Natural Language Processing (NLP) to address these issues at scaale. However, in order to develop robust, long-term solutions for this problem, we require perspectives from diverse disciplines ranging from psychology, law, gender studies, communications, and critical race theory. Our goal with the Abusive Language Workshop is to provide a platform to facilitate the interdisciplinary conversations and collaborations necessary to thoughtfully address the issue of abuse at scale.

Each year, we choose a theme for our workshop that guides the talks and panel discussions at the workshop. In previous years we focused on the policy aspect of online abuse and the stories and experiences of those who have received large amounts of online abuse. The themes do not limit the original research presented at the workshop, rather it helps frame the research presented through the lens of its potential to address the concerns of the theme. For this year, we have chosen to focus on *human content rating*, the practice of annotating and moderating data - an aspect which is often unspoken, assumed, and often forms the basis of the research conducted.

Human judgments of online abuse are critical for building training data for automated models, human-in-the-loop solutions that rely on crowd workers' ratings along with automated moderation, and embedding the evaluations of models into the cultural fabric. Thus, human ratings in the context of toxicity in language raise important questions around the various socio-cultural biases that affect those ratings, but also on the impact it has on the psychological safety of the raters themselves. In order to situate our conversation around this theme, we have confirmed four keynote speakers and panelists who are leading experts on content moderation, crowd work, and the impact of algorithmic solutions on people:

Katherine Lo, University of California, Irvine

Kat Lo is the Content Moderation Program Lead at Meedan and visiting researcher at the University of California, Irvine specializing in online moderation and harassment. Lo consults with technology, social media, and game companies on platform policy and enforcement. She also serves on the advisory board for nonprofits and advocacy organizations that focus on online harassment and mental health.

Safiya Noble, University of California, Los Angeles

Dr. Safiya Umoja Noble is an Associate Professor at UCLA in the Departments of Information Studies and African American Studies. She is the author of a best-selling book on racist and sexist algorithmic bias in commercial search engines, entitled Algorithms of Oppression: How Search Engines Reinforce Racism (NYU Press), which has been widely-reviewed in journals and periodicals including the Los Angeles Review of Books, featured in the New York Public Library 2018 Best Books for Adults(non-fiction), and recognized by Bustle magazine as one of "10 Books about Race to Read Instead of Asking a Person of Color to Explain Things to You". Safiya is the recipient of a Hellman Fellowship and the UCLA Early Career Award. Her academic research focuses on the design of digital media platforms on the internet and their impact on society. Her work is both sociological and interdisciplinary, marking the ways that digital media impacts and intersects with issues of race, gender, culture, and technology.

Sarah T. Roberts, University of California, Los Angeles

Roberts researches information work and workers, and is a leading global authority on "commercial content moderation," the term she coined to describe the work of those responsible for making sure media content posted to commercial websites fit within legal, ethical, and the site's own guidelines and standards. She is frequently consulted on matters of policy, worker welfare, and governance related to moderation issues. She is a 2018 Carnegie Fellow and winner of the 2018 EFF Barlow Pioneer Award in recognition of her work on commercial content moderation. Her book, "Behind the Screen: Content Moderation in the Shadows of Social Media", will be released on June 25 2019 (Yale University Press).

Nithum Thain, Jigsaw

Nithum Thain is a Software Engineer at Google Jigsaw. He works on the Conversation-AI effort that leverages Machine Learning technologies to help improve online conversation. Previously, Nithum was a Lecturer at Berkeley in NLP and a Postdoc at Simon Fraser University. Nithum holds a PhD in Algorithmic Game Theory from McGill University under the supervision of Dr. Adrian Vetta and an MBA from Oxford University as a Rhodes Scholar.

In addition, we will have a multi-disciplinary panel discussion where experts will debate and contextualize the major issues facing computational analysis of abusive language online, with a specific focus on human raters' work. This session will be followed by a poster session that will facilitate discussions around the research papers described in these proceedings.

Continuing the success of the past two workshops, we received 41 submissions describing high quality original research. In order to encourage submissions from social science researchers, we had a separate track for non-archival work. We conducted a rigorous review process where each paper received reviews from at least three researchers, at least one of which was a non-NLP researcher working on a field relevant to the paper. After review, we selected 21 papers to be presented at the workshop as posters. These include 14 long papers, 5 short papers, 1 demo paper, and 1 non-archival extended abstract. The authors of all accepted papers will be given an opportunity to expand their work into full journal articles to be considered for publication in a forthcoming special issue on abusive language online in the journal *First Monday*.

The accepted papers deal with a wide array of topics, both proposing new techniques to better detect abuse, as well as extending abuse detection to more languages and types of abuse. Three of the accepted papers bring social science perspectives on this issue, a significant improvement compared to last two iterations of the workshop. Our proceedings is also geographically diverse: representing work from 14 different countries: United States, United Kingdom, Italy, Canada, Netherlands, Australia, Indonesia, Portugal, Turkey, Germany, Croatia, Norway, India, and Switzerland (as per contact authors' affiliation).

With this, we welcome you to the 3rd Workshop on Abusive Language Online and look forward to the conversations and your participation.

Joel, Sarah, Vinod, and Zeerak

Organizers:

Vinodkumar Prabhakaran, Google
Sarah T. Roberts, University of California, Los Angeles
Joel Tetreault, Grammarly
Zeerak Waseem, University of Sheffield

Tunde Adefioye, KVS, Belgium
Mark Alfano, Delft University of Technology, Netherlands
Hind Almerekhi, Qatar Foundation, Qatar
Jisun An, Qatar Computing Research Institute, Hamad Bin Khalifa University, Qatar
Renata Barreto, Berkeley Law, United States
Elizabeth Belding, UC Santa Barbara, United States
Joachim Bingel, University of Copenhagen, Denmark
Peter Bourgonje, Potsdam University, Germany
Andrew Caines, University of Cambridge, United Kingdom
Pedro Calais, UFMG, Brazil, Brazil
Michael Castelle, University of Warwick, United Kingdom
Eshwar Chandrasekharan, Georgia Institute of Technology, United States
Wendy Chun, Brown University, United States
Isobelle Clarke, University of Birmingham, United Kingdom
Montse Cuadros, Vicomtech, Spain
Tyrus Cukavac, Bloomberg, United States
Aron Culotta, Illinois Institute of Technology, United States
Kareem Darwish, Qatar Computing Research Institute, Qatar Foundation, Qatar
Thomas Davidson, Cornell University, United States
Ona de Gibert Bonet, University of the Basque Country, Spain
Kelly Dennis, University of Connecticut, United States
Lucas Dixon, Jigsaw/Google, United States
Nemanja Djuric, Uber ATG, United States
Jacob Eisenstein, Georgia Institute of Technology, United States
Elisabetta Fersini, University of Milano-Bicocca, Italy
Darja Fišer, University of Ljubljana, Slovenia
Paula Fortuna, INESC TEC and Pompeu Fabra University, Portugal
Maya Ganesh, Leuphana University, Germany
Sara E. Garza, FIME-UANL, Mexico
Ryan Georgi, University of Washington, United States
Lee Gillam, University of Surrey, United Kingdom
Tonei Glavinic, Dangerous Speech Project, Spain
Genevieve Gorrell, University of Sheffield, United Kingdom
Erica Greene, The New York Times, United States
Alex Hanna, Google, United States
Mareike Hartmann, University of Copenhagen, Denmark
Christopher Homan, Rochester Institute of Technology, United States
Manoel Horta Ribeiro, Universidade Federal de Minas Gerais, Brazil
Hossein Hosseini, Department of Electrical Engineering, University of Washington, United States
Veronique Hoste, Ghent University, Belgium
Ruihong Huang, Computer Science and Engineering, Texas A&M University, United States
Dan Jurafsky, Stanford University, United States

Mladen Karan, University of Zagreb, Faculty of Electrical Engineering and Computing, Zagreb, Croatia, Croatia
Anna Kasunic, Carnegie Mellon University, United States
Christian Katzenbach, Humboldt Institute for Internet and Society, Germany
George Kennedy, Intel, United States
Ralf Krestel, Hasso Plattner Institute, Univteersity of Potsdam, Germany
Haewoon Kwak, Qatar Computing Research Institute, Hamad Bin Khalifa University, Qatar
Els Lefever, LT3, Ghent University, Belgium
Nikola Ljubešić, Jožef Stefan Institute, Slovenia
Elizabeth Losh, William and Mary, United States
Pranava Madhyastha, Imperial College London, United Kingdom
Walid Magdy, The University of Edinburgh, United Kingdom
Rijul Magu, Conduent, United States
Prodromos Malakasiotis, Athens University of Economics and Business Informatics Department, Greece
Shervin Malmasi, Harvard Medical School, United States
Puneet Mathur, Netaji Subhas Institute of Technology, India
Diana Maynard, University of Sheffield, United Kingdom
Yashar Mehdad, Airbnb, United States
Rada Mihalcea, University of Michigan, United States
Pushkar Mishra, Facebook, United Kingdom
Mainack Mondal, Cornell Tech, United States
Hamdy Mubarak, Qatar Computing Research Institute, Qatar Foundation, Qatar
Smruthi Mukund, Amazon, United States
Smaranda Muresan, Columbia University, United States
Isar Nejadgholi, Researcher, Canada
Iva Nenadic, Research Associate, Italy
Chikashi Nobata, Apple Inc., United States
Gustavo Henrique Paetzold, Federal University of Technology, Brazil
Alexis Palmer, University of North Texas, United States
Viviana Patti, University of Turin, Dipartimento di Informatica, Italy
John Pavlopoulos, Athens University of Economics and Business, Greece
Seeta Pena Gangadharan, London School of Economics and Political Science, United Kingdom
Christopher Potts, Stanford University, United States
Daniel Preoţiuc-Pietro, Bloomberg, United States
Michal Ptaszynski, Kitami Institute of Technology, Japan
Georg Rehm, DFKI, Germany
Julian Risch, Hasso Plattner Institute, University of Potsdam, Germany
Melissa Robinson, University of North Texas, United States
Carolyn Rose, Carnegie Mellon University, United States
Björn Ross, University of Duisburg-Essen, Germany
Paolo Rosso, Universitat Politècnica de València, Spain
Niloofar Safi Samghabadi, University of Houston, United States
Magnus Sahlgren, RISE, Sweden
Christina Sauper, Facebook, United States
Tyler Schnoebelen, Decoded AI, United States
Alexandra Schofield, Cornell University, United States
Marian Simko, Slovak University of Technology in Bratislava, Slovakia
Caroline Sinders, Convocation Design + Research, United States
Alison Sneyd, The University of Sheffield, United Kingdom
Jeffrey Sorensen, Jigsaw, United States

Rachele Sprugnoli, FBK / University of Trento, Italy
Linnet Taylor, Tilburg University, Netherlands
Achint Thomas, Embibe, India
Sara Tonelli, FBK, Italy
Dimitrios Tsarapatsanis, University of York, United Kingdom
Betty van Aken, Beuth University of Applied Sciences Berlin, Germany
Joris Van Hoboken, Vrije Universiteit Brussel, Belgium
Anna Vartapetiance, Surrey Centre for Cyber Security / University of Surrey, United Kingdom
Erik Velldal, University of Oslo, Norway
Rob Voigt, Stanford University, United States
Cindy Wang, Stanford University, United States
Ingmar Weber, Qatar Computing Research Institute, Qatar
Jacque Wernimont, Arizona State University, United States
Michael Wojatzki, Language Technology Lab, University of Duisburg-Essen, Germany
Helen Yannakoudakis, University of Cambridge, United Kingdom
Seunghyun Yoon, Seoul National University, Republic of Korea
Aleš Završnik, Institute of criminology at the Faculty of Law Ljubljana, Slovenia
Torsten Zesch, Language Technology Lab, University of Duisburg-Essen, Germany
Andrej Švec, Slovak University of Technology in Bratislava, Slovakia

Additional Reviewers:

Daniela Agostinho, University of Copenhagen, Denmark
Nanna Thylstrup, Copenhagen Business School, Denmark

Invited Speaker:

Katherine Lo, University of California, Irvine
Safiya Noble, University of California, Los Angeles
Sarah T. Roberts, University of California, Los Angeles

Panelists:

Katherine Lo, University of California, Irvine
Nithum Thain, Jigsaw

Table of Contents

Workshop Program

Thursday, August 01, 2019

9:00–10:35	**Session 1**

9:00–9:15   *Opening Remarks*

9:15–9:55   *Keynote 1: Katherine Lo*

9:55-10:35   *Keynote 2: Safiya Noble*

10:35–11:00   ***Break***

11:00–12:00   **Session 2: Panel Discussion**

12:00–13:30   ***Lunch***

13:30–15:10   **Session 3: Posters**

13:30–14:20   **Poster Session A**

Subversive Toxicity Detection using Sentiment Information
Eloi Brassard-Gourdeau and Richard Khoury

Exploring Deep Multimodal Fusion of Text and Photo for Hate Speech Classification
Fan Yang, Xiaochang Peng, Gargi Ghosh, Reshef Shilon, Hao Ma, Eider Moore and Goran Predovic

Detecting harassment in real-time as conversations develop
Wessel Stoop, Florian Kunneman, Antal van den Bosch and Ben Miller

Racial Bias in Hate Speech and Abusive Language Detection Datasets
Thomas Davidson, Debasmita Bhattacharya and Ingmar Weber

A Platform Agnostic Dual-Strand Hate Speech Detector
Johannes Skjeggestad Meyer and Björn Gambäck

Detecting Aggression and Toxicity using a Multi Dimension Capsule Network
Saurabh Srivastava and Prerna Khurana

An Impossible Dialogue! Nominal Utterances and Populist Rhetoric in an Italian Twitter Corpus of Hate Speech against Immigrants
Gloria Comandini and Viviana Patti

"Condescending, Rude, Assholes": Framing gender and hostility on Stack Overflow
Sian Brooke

Online aggression from a sociological perspective: An integrative view on determinants and possible countermeasures
Sebastian Weingartner and Lea Stahel

15:10–15:40   ***Break***

Session 4

15:40–16:20   *Keynote 3: Sarah T. Roberts*

16:20–17:20   *Interdisciplinary Work Proposals & Plenary Discussion*

17:20–17:35   *Closing Remarks*

Subversive Toxicity Detection using Sentiment Information

Éloi Brassard-Gourdeau   **Richard Khoury**

Department of Computer Science and Software Engineering

Université Laval

Quebec City, Canada

`eloi.brassard-gourdeau.1@ulaval.ca richard.khoury@ift.ulaval.ca`

Abstract

The presence of toxic content has become a major problem for many online communities. Moderators try to limit this problem by implementing more and more refined comment filters, but toxic users are constantly finding new ways to circumvent them. Our hypothesis is that while modifying toxic content and keywords to fool filters can be easy, hiding sentiment is harder. In this paper, we explore various aspects of sentiment detection and their correlation to toxicity, and use our results to implement a toxicity detection tool. We then test how adding the sentiment information helps detect toxicity in three different real-world datasets, and incorporate subversion to these datasets to simulate a user trying to circumvent the system. Our results show sentiment information has a positive impact on toxicity detection.

1 Introduction

Online communities abound today, forming on social networks, on webforums, within videogames, and even in the comments sections of articles and videos. While this increased international contact and exchange of ideas has been a net positive, it has also been matched with an increase in the spread of high-risk and toxic content, a category which includes cyberbullying, racism, sexual predation, and other negative behaviors that are not tolerated in society. The two main strategies used by online communities to moderate themselves and stop the spread of toxic comments are automated filtering and human surveillance. However, given the sheer number of messages sent online every day, human moderation simply cannot keep up, and either leads to a severe slowdown of the conversation (if messages are pre-moderated before posting) or allows toxic messages to be seen and shared thousands of times before they are deleted (if they are post-moderated after being posted and reported). In addition, human moderation cannot scale up easily to the number of messages to monitor; for example, Facebook has a team of 20,000 human moderators, which is both massive compared to the total of 25,000 other employees in the company, and minuscule compared to the fact its automated algorithms flagged messages that would require 180,000 human moderators to review[1]. Keyword detection, on the other hand, is instantaneous, scales up to the number of messages, and prevents toxic messages from being posted at all, but it can only stop messages that use one of a small set of denied words, and are thus fairly easy to circumvent by introducing minor misspellings (i.e. writing "kl urself" instead of "kill yourself"). In (Hosseini et al., 2017), the authors show how minor changes can elude even complex systems. These attempts to bypass the toxicity detection system are called subverting the system, and toxic users doing it are referred to as subversive users.

In this paper, we consider an alternative strategy for toxic message filtering. Our intuition is that, while high-risk keywords can easily be disguised, the negative emotional tone of the message cannot. Consequently, we will study the correlation between sentiment and toxicity and its usefulness for toxic message detection both in subversive and non-subversive contexts. It is important to note that toxicity is a very abstract term that can have different definitions depending on context, and each dataset described in Section 4 has its own. They all gravitate around negative messages such as insults, bullying, vulgarity and hate speech, therefore these types of toxic behavior are the ones we focus on, as opposed to other types such as fraud or grooming that would use more positive messages.

The rest of this paper is structured as follows.

---

[1] `http://fortune.com/2018/03/22/human-moderators-facebook-youtube-twitter/`

1

Proceedings of the Third Workshop on Abusive Language Online, pages 1–10

Florence, Italy, August 1, 2019. ©2019 Association for Computational Linguistics

After a review of the relevant literature in the next section, we will consider the problem of sentiment detection in online messages in Section 3. We will study the measure of toxicity and its correlation to message sentiment in Section 4. Finally, we will draw some concluding remarks in Section 5.

2 Related Work

Given the limitations of human and keyword-based toxicity detection systems mentioned previously, several authors have studied alternative means of detecting toxicity. In one of the earliest works on the detection of hate speech, the authors of (Warner and Hirschberg, 2012) used n-grams enhanced by part-of-speech information as features to train an SVM classifier to accurately pick out anti-semitic online messages. Following a similar idea, the authors of (Nobata et al., 2016) conducted a study of the usefulness of various linguistic features to train a machine learning algorithm to pick out hate speech. They found that the most useful single feature was character n-grams, followed closely by word n-grams. However, it was a combination of all their features (n-grams, features of language, features of syntax, and word embedding vectors) that achieved the highest performance. The authors of (Alorainy et al., 2018) studied hate speech through the detection of othering language. They built a custom lexicon of pronouns and semantic relationships in order to capture the linguistic differences when describing the in-group and out-group in messages, and trained a word embedding model on that data.

Hate speech is not the only form of toxicity that has been studied. In (Reynolds et al., 2011), the authors studied cyberbullying. They developed a list of 300 "bad" words sorted in five levels of severity. Next, they used the number and density of "bad" words found in each online message as the features to train a set of machine learning systems. The authors of (Ebrahimi, 2016) also used words as features in two systems, this time to detect sexual predators. One used the TFxIDF values of the words of the text to train a single-class SVM classifier, and the other used a bag-of-words vector of the text as input to a deep neural network. The authors found that the latter system offered the better performance in their experiments.

Recently, deep learning has become very popular for NLP applications, and pre-trained word embeddings have been shown to be very effec-tive in most text-based neural network applications. In (Agrawal and Awekar, 2018), four different deep learning models were implemented and shown to outperform benchmark techniques for cyberbullying detection on three different datasets. In (Chatzakou et al., 2017), a deep neural network taking a word embedding vector as input was used to detect cyberbullying on Twitter.

It thus appears from the related literature that authors have tried a variety of alternative features to automatically detect toxic messages without relying strictly on keyword detection. However, sentiment has rarely been considered. It was one of the inputs of the deep neural network of (Chatzakou et al., 2017), but the paper never discussed its importance or analyzed its impact. The authors of (Hee et al., 2018) conducted the first study of cyberbullying in Dutch, and considered several features, including a subjectivity keyword lexicon. They found its inclusion helped improve results, but that a more sophisticated source of information than simple keyword detection was required. And the study of (Dani et al., 2017) used the sentiment of messages, as measured by the SentiStrength online system, as one of several features to detect cyberbullying messages. However, an in-depth analysis of how sentiment can benefit toxicity detection has not been done in any of these papers, and a study of the use of sentiment in a subversive context has never been done.

3 Sentiment Detection

3.1 Lexicons

Sentiment detection, or the task of determining whether a document has a positive or negative tone, has been frequently studied in the literature. It is usually done by using a sentiment lexicon that either classifies certain words as positive or negative, or quantifies their level of positivity or negativity. We decided to consider six such lexicons:

- **SentiWordNet**[2] is a widely-used resource for sentiment mining. It is based on Word-Net, and assigns three scores to each synset, namely positivity, negativity, and objectivity, with the constraint that the sum of all three must be 1. Using this lexicon requires a bit of preprocessing for us, since the same word can occur in multiple different synsets

---

[2]http://sentiwordnet.isti.cnr.it/

with different meanings and therefore different scores. Since picking out the intended meaning and synset of a polysemous word found in a message is beyond our scope, we instead chose to merge the different meanings and compute a weighted average of the scores of the word. The weights are the ranks of the synsets, which correspond to the popularity of that meaning of the word in documents. The average score equation is :

$$score = \frac{\sum^k \frac{score}{rank}}{\sum^k \frac{1}{rank}} \qquad (1)$$

where k is the number of times the word occurs with the same part of speech. We compute the average positivity and negativity scores, but not the objectivity scores, since they are not useful for our purpose and since they are simply the complement of the other two. This allows us to extract 155,287 individual words from the lexicon, with a positivity and negativity score between 0 and 1 for each. We should note that SentiWordNet differentiates a word based on part-of-speech, and we maintain this distinction in our work.

- **Afinn**[3] is a lexicon of 3,382 words that are rated between -5 (maximum negativity) and 5 (maximum positivity). To match SentiWord-Net, we split this score into positivity and negativity scores between 0 and 1. For example, a word with a -3 score was changed to have a positive score of 0 and a negative score of 0.6.

- **Bing Liu**[4] compiled lists of 6,789 positive or negative words. Given no other information, we assigned each word in the positive list a positivity score of 1 and a negativity score of 0, and vice-versa for the negative-list words.

- **General Inquirer** [5] is a historically-popular lexicon of 14,480 words, though only 4,206 of them are tagged as positive or negative. As for the Bing Liu lexicon, we assigned binary positive and negative scores to each word that was tagged as positive or negative.

- **Subjectivity Clues**[6] extends the sentiment tags of the General Inquirer to 8,222 words using a dictionary and thesaurus. It also adds a binary strength level (strong or weak) to the polarity information. We merged polarity and strength as a measure of 0.5 and 1 for weak or strong positivity or negativity.

- **NRC**[7] has a list of 14,182 words that are marked as associated (1) or not associated (0) with 8 emotions (anger, fear, anticipation, trust, surprise, sadness, joy, disgust) and two sentiments (negative and positive). We transform this association into binary positive and negative scores in the same way we did for Bing Liu and General Inquirer.

All six of these lexicons have limitations, which stem from their limited vocabulary and the ambiguity of the problem. Indeed, despite being thousands of words each and covering the same subject and purpose, our six lexicons have only 394 words in common, indicating that each is individually very incomplete compared to the others. And we can easily find inconsistencies between the ratings of words, both internally within each lexicon and externally when we compare the same words between lexicons. Table 1 illustrates some of these inconsistencies: for instance, the word "helpless" is very negative in SentiWordNet but less so in Afinn and Subjectivity Clues, while the word "terrorize" is more strongly negative in the latter two resources but less negative (and even a bit positive) in SentiWordNet. Likewise, the word "joke" is strongly positive, weakly positive, or even negative, depending on the lexicon used, and the word "merry" is more positive than "joke" according to every lexicon except SentiWordnet, which rates it equally positive and negative. By contrast the word "splendid" has the same positivity values as "merry" in all lexicons except SentiWordnet, where it has the highest possible positivity score.

In a longer document, such as the customer reviews these lexicons are typically used on (Ohana et al., 2012; Tumsare et al., 2014; Agarwal et al., 2015), these problems are minor: the abundance and variety of vocabulary in the text will insure that the correct sentiment emerges overall despite the noise these issues cause. This is not true for the short messages of online conversations, and it

---

[3] https://github.com/fnielsen/afinn
[4] https://www.cs.uic.edu/~liub/FBS/sentiment-analysis.html
[5] http://www.wjh.harvard.edu/~inquirer/

[6] http://mpqa.cs.pitt.edu/lexicons/
[7] https://nrc.canada.ca/en/

Word	SentiWordNet	Afinn	Bing Liu	General Inquirer	Subjectivity Clues	NRC
terrorize	[0.125, 0.250]	-3	negative	negative	strong negative	negative
helpless	[0.000, 0.750]	-2	negative	negative	weak negative	negative
joke	[0.375, 0.000]	2	negative	positive	strong positive	negative
merry	[0.250, 0.250]	3	positive	positive	strong positive	positive
splendid	[1.000, 0.000]	3	positive	positive	strong positive	positive

Table 1: Sentiment of words per lexicon

has forced some authors who study the sentiments of microblogs to resort to creating or customizing their own lexicons (Nielsen, 2011). This, incidentally, is also why we could not simply use an existing sentiment classifier. We will instead opt to combine these lexicons into a more useful resource.

3.2 Message Preprocessing

The first preprocessing step is to detect the presence and scope of negations in a message. Negations have an important impact; the word "good" may be labeled positive in all our lexicons, but its actual meaning will differ in the sentences "this movie is good" and "this movie is not good". We thus created a list of negation keywords by combining together the lists of the negex algorithm[8] and of (Carrillo de Albornoz et al., 2012), filtering out some irrelevant words from these lists, and adding some that were missing from the lists but are found online.

Next, we need to determine the scope of the negation, which means figuring out how many words in the message are affected by it. This is the challenge of, for example, realizing that the negation affects the word "interesting" in "this movie is not good or interesting" but not in "this movie is not good but interesting". We considered two algorithms to detect the scope of negations. The first is to simply assume the negation affects a fixed window of five words[9] after the keyword (Councill et al., 2010), while the second discovers the syntactic dependencies in the sentence in order to determine precisely which words are affected (Dadvar et al., 2011).

We tested both algorithms on the SFU review corpus of negation and speculation[10]. As can be

	Fixed window	Dependencies
Accuracy	71.75%	82.88%
Recall	95.48%	90.00%
Precision	69.65%	78.37%
Exact match	9.03%	43.34%
Std	3.90 words	5.54 words
ms/sentence	2.4	68

Table 2: Comparison between fixed window and syntactic dependencies negation detection algorithms

seen in Table 2, the dependency algorithm gave generally better results, and managed to find the exact scope of the negation in over 43% of sentences. However, that algorithm also has a larger standard deviation in its scope, meaning that when it fails to find the correct scope, it can be off by quite a lot, while the fixed window is naturally bounded in its errors. Moreover, the increased precision of the dependencies algorithm comes at a high processing cost, requiring almost 30 times longer to analyze a message as the fixed window algorithm. Given that online communities frequently deal with thousands of new messages every second, efficiency is a major consideration, and we opted for the simple fixed window algorithm for that reason.

The second preprocessing step is to detect sentiment-carrying idioms in the messages. For example, while the words "give" and "up" can both be neutral or positive, the idiom "give up" has a clear negative sentiment. Several of these idioms can be found in our lexicons, especially SentiWordNet (slightly over $60,000$). We detect them in our messages and mark them so that our algorithm will handle them as single words going forward.

Finally, we use the NLTK wordpunct_tokenizer to split messages into words, and the Stanford fasterEnglishPOSTagger to get the part-of-speech of each word. Since our lexicons contain only four

---

[8] `https://github.com/mongoose54/negex/tree/master/negex.python`

[9] The average window size in our test dataset was 5.36 words, so we rounded to the closest integer.

[10] `https://www.researchgate.net/publication/256766329_SFU_Review_Corpus_Negation_Speculation`

parts-of-speech (noun, verb, adverb, and adjective) and Stanford's tagger has more than 30 possible tags, we manually mapped each tag to one of the four parts-of-speech (for example, "verb, past participle" maps to "verb").

3.3 Message Sentiment

Once every word has a positivity and a negativity score, we can use them to determine the sentiment of an entire message. We do this by computing separately the sum of positive scores and of negative scores of words in the message, and subtracting the negative total from the positive total. In this way, a score over 0 means a positive message, and a score under 0 means a negative message. We consider two alternatives at this point: one in which we sum the sentiment value of all words in the message, and one where we only sum the sentiment value of the top-three[11] words with the highest scores for each polarity. We label these "All words" and "Top words" in our results. The impact of this difference is felt when we consider a message with a few words with a strong polarity and a lot of words with a weak opposite polarity; in the "Top words" scheme these weak words will be ignored and the strong polarity words will dictate the polarity of the message, while in the "All words" scheme the many weak words can sum together to outweigh the few strong words and change the polarity of the message.

We optionally take negations into account in our sentiment computation. When a word occurs in the window of a negation, we flip its positivity and negativity scores. In other words, instead of adding its positivity score to the positivity total of the message, we added its negativity score, and the other way round for the negativity total. Experiments where this is done are labeled "Negativity" in our results.

Finally, we optionally incorporate word weights based on their frequency in our datasets. When applied, the score of each word is multiplied by a frequency modifier, which we adapted from (Ohana et al., 2012):

$$ frequency\_modifier = 1 - \sqrt{\frac{n}{n_{max}}} \qquad (2) $$

where n is the number of times the word appears in a dataset, and n_{max} is the number of times the

most frequent word appears in that dataset. Experiments using this frequency modifier are labeled "Frequency" in our results.

3.4 Experimental Results

Our experiments have four main objectives: (1) to determine whether the "All words" or the "Top words" strategy is preferable; (2) to determine whether the inclusion of "Negation" and "Frequency" modifiers is useful; (3) to determine which of the six lexicons is most accurate; and (4) to determine whether a weighted combination of the six lexicons can outperform any one lexicon.

To conduct our experiments, we used the corpus of annotated news comments available from the Yahoo Webscope program[12]. The comments in this dataset are annotated by up to three professional, trained editors to label various attributes, including type, sentiment and tone. Using these three attributes, we split the dataset into two categories, sarcastic and non-sarcastic, and then again into five categories, clear negative, slight negative, neutral, slight positive, and clear positive. Finally, we kept only the non-sarcastic comments where all annotators agreed to reduce noise. This gives us a test corpus of 2,465 comments.

To evaluate our results, we compute the sentiment score of each comment in our test corpus using our various methods, and we then compute the average sentiment score of comments in each of the five sentiment categories. For ease of presentation, we give a simplified set of results in Table 3, with only the average score of the two negative and the two positive labels combined, along with the overlap of the two distributions. The overlap is obtained by taking two normal distributions with the the means and standard deviations of the positive and the negative sets, and calculating the area in common under both curves. It gives us a measure of the ambiguous region where comments may be positive or negative. A good sentiment classifier will thus have very distant positive and negative scores and a very low overlap.

These results show that there are important differences between the lexicons. Three of the six are rather poor at picking out negative sentiments, namely Subjectivity Clues (where negative messages are on average detected as more positive than the positive messages), General Inquirer, and

---

NRC. This bias for positivity is an issue for a study on toxicity, which we expect to be expressed using negative sentiments. The other three lexicons give a good difference between positive and negative messages. For these three lexicons, we find that using *All words* increases the gap between positive and negative scores but greatly increases the standard deviation of each sentiment class, meaning the sentiment of the messages becomes ambiguous. On the other hand, using *Top words* reduces the overlap between the distributions and thus gives a better separation of positive and negative sentiments. And while adding frequency information or negations does not cause a major change in the results, it does give a small reduction in overlap.

To study combinations of lexicons, we decided to limit our scope to SentiWordNet, Afinn, and Bing Liu, the three lexicons that could accurately pick out negative sentiments, and on the *Top words* strategy. We consider three common strategies to combine the results of independent classifiers: majority voting, picking the one classifier with the maximum score (which is assumed to be the one with the highest confidence in its classification), and taking the average of the scores of all three classifiers. For the average, we tried using a weighted average of the lexicons and performed a grid search to find the optimal combination. However, the best results were obtained when the three lexicons were taken equally. For the majority vote, we likewise take the average score of the two or three classifiers in the majority sentiment.

Table 4 presents the results we obtain with all three strategies. It can be seen that combining the three classifiers outperforms taking any one classifier alone, in the sense that it creates a wider gap between the positive and negative messages and a smaller overlap. It can also be seen that the addition of negation and frequency information gives a very small improvement in the results in all three cases. Comparing the three strategies, it can be seen that the maximum strategy gives the biggest gap in between positive and negative distribution, which was to be expected since the highest positive or negative sentiment is selected each time while it gets averaged out in the other two classifiers. However, the average score strategy creates a significantly smaller standard deviation of sentiment scores and a lower overlap between the distributions of positive and negative messages. For

that reason, we find the average score to be the best of the three combination strategies.

In all cases, we find that most misclassified messages in our system are due to the lack of insults in the vocabulary. For example, none of the lexicons include colorful insults like "nut job" and "fruitcake", so messages where they appear cannot be recognized as negative. Likewise, some words, such as the word "gay", are often used as insults online, but have positive meanings in formal English; this actually leads to labeling insult messages as positive. This issue stems from the fact that these lexicons were designed for sentiment analysis in longer and more traditional documents, such as customer reviews and editorials. One will seldom, if ever, find insults (especially politically-incorrect ones such as the previous examples) in these documents.

4 Toxicity Detection

The main contribution of this paper is to study how sentiment can be used to detect toxicity in subversive online comments. To do this, we will use three new test corpora:

- The **Reddit**[13] dataset is composed of over 880,000 comments taken from a wide range of subreddits and annotated a few years ago by the *Community Sift* tool developed by *Two Hat Security*[14]. This toxicity detection tool, which was used in previous research on toxicity as well (Mohan et al., 2017), uses over 1 million n-gram rules in order to normalize then categorize each message into one of eight risk levels for a wide array of different categories, 0 to 3 being super-safe to questionable, 4 being unknown and 5 to 7 being mild to severe. In our case, we consider the scores assigned to each message in five categories, namely bullying, fighting, sexting, vulgarity, and racism.

- The **Wikipedia Talk Labels**[15] dataset consists of over 100,000 comments taken from discussions on English Wikipedia's talk pages. Each comment was manually annotated by around ten Crowdflower workers as

[13]https://bigquery.cloud.google.com/
table/fh-bigquery:reddit_comments.2007
[14]https://www.twohat.com/community-
sift/
[15]https://figshare.com/articles/
Wikipedia_Talk_Labels_Toxicity/4563973

Experiment	SWN	Afinn	Bing Liu	Gen. Inq.	Subj. Clues	NRC
All words	[-0.22, 0.31] 0.81	[-0.43, 0.45] 0.71	[-1.17, 0.69] 0.67	[0.03, 1.44] 0.73	[2.31, 1.97] 0.76	[-0.15, 1.00] 0.77
All/Neg	[-0.34, 0.17] 0.79	[-0.44, 0.39] 0.69	[-1.08, 0.61] 0.70	[-0.27, 0.99] 0.77	[1.66, 1.52] 0.83	[-0.62, 0.75] 0.75
All/Freq	[-0.21, 0.29] 0.80	[-0.42, 0.40] 0.71	[-1.17, 0.58] 0.68	[-0.09, 1.23] 0.76	[1.98, 1.70] 0.82	[-0.19, 0.90] 0.79
All/Neg/Frq	[-0.29, 0.18] 0.78	[-0.42, 0.35] 0.69	[-1.06, 0.52] 0.71	[-0.33, 0.85] 0.79	[1.45, 1.34] 0.86	[-0.56, 0.69] 0.77
Top words	[-0.23, 0.11] 0.75	[-0.23, 0.31] 0.68	[-0.54, 0.54] 0.67	[-0.03, 0.59] 0.80	[1.18, 1.17] 0.99	[-0.14, 0.54] 0.77
Top/Neg	[-0.24, 0.10] 0.74	[-0.24, 0.29] 0.67	[-0.50, 0.53] 0.67	[-0.12, 0.57] 0.77	[0.86, 0.71] 0.94	[-0.28, 0.49] 0.73
Top/Freq	[-0.16, 0.15] 0.74	[-0.23, 0.28] 0.67	[-0.56, 0.47] 0.67	[-0.07, 0.52] 0.79	[1.00, 1.01] 0.99	[-0.15, 0.50] 0.77
Top/Neg/Frq	[-0.17, 0.14] 0.73	[-0.23, 0.26] 0.67	[-0.51, 0.48] 0.66	[-0.14, 0.49] 0.77	[0.61, 0.76] 0.93	[-0.26, 0.45] 0.74

Table 3: Average sentiment scores of negative and positive (respectively) labeled messages, and their overlap.

Experiment	Majority vote	Maximum wins	Average scores
Top words	[-0.36, 0.34] 0.67	[-0.60, 0.52] 0.67	[-0.32, 0.32] 0.64
Top + Negation	[-0.35, 0.34] 0.66	[-0.59, 0.51] 0.66	[-0.31, 0.30] 0.63
Top + Frequency	[-0.34, 0.32] 0.66	[-0.58, 0.48] 0.67	[-0.31, 0.30] 0.63
Top + Neg. + Freq.	[-0.32, 0.30] 0.65	[-0.55, 0.50] 0.65	[-0.29, 0.29] 0.63

Table 4: Sentiment scores using combinations of lexicons.

toxic or not toxic. We use the ratio of toxic marks as a toxicity score. For example, if a message is marked toxic by 7 out of 10 workers, it will have a 0.7 toxicity score.

- The **Kaggle toxicity competition**[16] dataset is also taken from discussions on English Wikipedia talk pages. There are approximatively 160,000 comments, which were manually annotated with six binary labels: toxic, severe_toxic, obscene, threat, insult, and identity_hate. This allows us to rate comments on a seven-level toxicity scale, from 0/6 labels marked to 6/6 labels marked.

Sentiment	Reddit	Wikipedia	Kaggle
Standard	-0.2410	-0.3839	-0.3188
Negation	-0.2021	-0.3488	-0.2906
Frequency	-0.2481	-0.3954	-0.3269
Neg + Freq	-0.2056	-0.3608	-0.3003

Table 5: Correlation between sentiment and toxicity.

4.1 Correlation

Our first experiment consists in computing the sentiment of each message in each of our three test corpora, and verifying how they correlate with the different toxicity scores of each of the corpora. Following the results we found in Section 3, we used the best three lexicons (SentiWordNet, Afinn, and Bing Liu), combined them by taking the average score, and used our four algorithm variations. The results are presented in Table 5. It can be seen that there is a clear negative correlation between toxicity and sentiment in the messages, as expected. Our results also show that using words only or including frequency information makes the relationship clearer, while adding negations muddies it. These results are consistent over all three test corpora, despite being from different sources and labeled using different techniques. The lower score on the Reddit dataset may simply be due to

the fact it was labeled automatically by a system that flags potentially dangerous content and not by human editors, so its labels may be noisier. For example, mentioning sexual body parts will be labeled as toxicity level 5 even if they are used in a positive message, because they carry more potential risk.

4.2 Subversive Toxicity Detection

Our second experiment consists in studying the benefits of taking sentiments into account when trying to determine whether a comment is toxic or not. The toxicity detector we implemented in this experiment is a deep neural network inspired by the most successful systems in the Kaggle toxicity competition we used as a dataset. It uses a bi-GRU layer with kernel size of 40. The final state is sent into a single linear classifier. To avoid overfitting, two 50% dropout layers are added, one before and one after the bi-GRU layer.

The network takes as input a message split into words and into individual characters. The words are represented by the 300d fastText pretrained word embeddings[17], and characters are represented by a one-hot character encoding but

[16]https://www.kaggle.com/c/jigsaw-toxic-comment-classification-challenge

[17]https://github.com/facebookresearch/fastText

restricted to the set of 60 most common characters in the messages to avoid the inclusion of noise. The character embeddings enrich the word embeddings and allow the system to extract more information from the messages, especially in the presence of misspellings (Shen et al., 2017). Finally, we used our "top + frequency" sentiment algorithm with the best three lexicons (SentiWordNet, Afinn, and Bing Liu) to determine the sentiment of each message. We input that information into the neural network as three sentiment values, corresponding to each of the three lexicons used, for each of the frequent words retained for the message. Words that are not among the selected frequent words or that are not found in a lexicon receive a sentiment input value of 0. Likewise, experiments that do not make use of sentiment information have inputs of 0 for all words. These input values are then concatenated together into a vector of 363 values, corresponding to the 300 dimensions of fastText, the 60 one-hot character vector, and the 3 sentiment lexicons.

The output of our network is a binary "toxic or non-toxic" judgment for the message. In the Kaggle dataset, this corresponds to whether the "toxic" label is active or not. In the Reddit dataset, it is the set of messages evaluated at levels 5, 6 or 7 by *Community Sift* in any of the topics mentioned earlier. And in the Wikipedia dataset, it is any message marked as toxic by 5 workers or more. We chose this binary approach to allow the network to learn to recognize toxicity, as opposed to types of toxic messages on Kaggle, keyword severity on Reddit, or a particular worker's opinions on Wikipedia. However, this simplification created a balance problem: the Reddit dataset is composed of 12% toxic messages and 88% non-toxic messages, the Wikipedia dataset is composed of 18% toxic messages, and the Kaggle dataset of 10% toxic messages. To create balanced datasets for training, we kept all toxic messages and undersampled randomly the set of non-toxic messages to be equal to the number of toxic messages. This type of undersampling is commonplace in order to avoid the many training issues that stem from heavily imbalanced datasets.

Our experiment consists in comparing the toxicity detection accuracy of our network when excluding or including sentiment information and in the presence of subversion. Indeed, as mentioned in Sections 1 and 2, it is trivial for a subversive

user to mask toxic keywords to bypass toxicity filters. In order to simulate this behavior and taking ideas from (Hosseini et al., 2017), we created a substitution list that replaces popular toxic keywords with harmless versions. For example, the word "kill" is replaced by "kilt", and "bitch" by "beach". Our list contains 191 words, and its use adds noise to 82% of the toxic Kaggle messages, 65% of the Wikipedia messages, and 71% of the Reddit messages. These substitutions are only done at testing time, and not taken into account in training, to simulate the fact that users can create never-before-seen modifications.

We trained and tested our neural network with and without sentiment information, with and without subversion, and with each corpus three times to mitigate the randomness in training. In every experiment, we used a random 70% of messages in the corpus as training data, another 20% as validation data, and the final 10% as testing data. The average results of the three tests are given in Table 6. We performed a *t-test* on the accuracy result distribution to determine if the difference between the results with and without sentiment information is statistically significant, and the *p-value* is also included in Table 6. As a reminder, the *t-test* compares the two distributions to see if they are different from each other, and assigns a *p-value* to this result. As a general rule, a *p-value* below 0.05 indicates that the *t-test* found a statistically significant difference between the two distributions.

It can be seen that sentiment information helps improve toxicity detection in a statistically-significant manner in all cases but one. The improvement is smaller when the text is clean (without subversion). In those experiments, the accuracy improvement is of 0.5% or less. However, the introduction of subversion leads to an important drop in the accuracy of toxicity detection for the network that uses the text alone. Most of that loss comes from a much lower recall score, which is unsurprising considering the fact that we are modifying the most common toxic words. The inclusion of sentiment information makes it possible to mitigate that loss. With subversion, including sentiment information improves the accuracy of toxicity detection by more than 0.5% in all experiments, and as much as 3% on the Kaggle dataset, along with a decrease in *p-value* in all cases.

For example, the message "The bot sucks. No skills. Shut it down." isn't detected as toxic after

Dataset	Standard			Sentiment			$p\text{-}value$
	Accuracy	Precision	Recall	Accuracy	Precision	Recall	
Kaggle	93.2%	93.1%	93.0%	93.7%	92.1%	95.2%	0.0188
Subv. Kaggle	77.2%	93.3%	58.8%	80.1%	94.1%	65.6%	<0.0001
Wiki	88.1%	87.4%	89.1%	88.5%	87.9%	89.4%	0.0173
Subv. Wiki	81.4%	86.1%	75.5%	82.0%	86.3%	75.9%	0.0165
Reddit	94.0%	98.2%	89.6%	94.1%	98.3%	89.7%	0.4159
Subv. Reddit	87.1%	98.0%	75.9%	88.0%	98.2%	77.5%	0.0098

Table 6: Accuracy, precision and recall on regular and subversive datasets, with and without sentiment, along with the $t\text{-}test$ $p\text{-}value$ when comparing accuracy result distribution

adding subversion, because the toxic word "sucks" is changed to the harmless word "socks". However, when including sentiment information, the system detects the negative tone of the message - with the "No skills. Shut it down." part being clearly negative - and increases the score sufficiently for the message to be classified as toxic. Sentiment information is also helpful even in the absence of subversion. For example, the message "You make me sick to my stomach, whoever you are and whatever your motivations might be. You have caused an odious stench which will be impossible to erase." lacks recognizable toxic features such as insults and curse words and is classified as non-toxic by the sentiment-less neural network. However, the negative sentiment of "sick", "stench", and "odious" (none of which are normally found in abusive word lists) allows the sentiment neural network to recognize the message as toxic.

Comparing the different corpora, it can be seen that the improvement is smallest and least significant in the Reddit dataset experiment, which was to be expected since it is also the dataset in which toxicity and sentiment had the weakest correlation in Table 5. We can note that our toxicity detection neural network performs very well nonetheless in all cases, even with subversion and without sentiment information. This may be due to the fact that the messages in all datasets are user-generated and therefore noisy already. In addition, the character encoding of the neural network is robust to misspellings, as opposed to a keyword lookup system. The results are also very close to the top solutions of the Kaggle competition for the Kaggle dataset with a 98.1 AUC (top solutions being 98.8) while taking a lot less time to train and not using huge manual misspellings lists or data augmentation like all top solutions do.

5 Conclusion

In this paper, we explored the relationship between sentiment and toxicity in social network messages. We began by implementing a sentiment detection tool using different lexicons and different features such as word frequencies and negations. This tool allowed us to demonstrate that there exists a clear correlation between sentiment and toxicity. Next, we added sentiment information to a toxicity detection neural network, and demonstrated that it does improve detection accuracy. Finally, we simulated a subversive user who circumvents the toxicity filter by masking toxic keywords in their messages, and found that using sentiment information improved toxicity detection by as much as 3%. This confirms our fundamental intuition, that while it is possible for a user to mask toxic words with simple substitutions, it is a lot harder for a user to conceal the sentiment of a message.

Our work so far has focused on single-line messages and negative toxicity detection. There are however several different types of toxicity, some of which correlate to different sentiments. For instance, fraud or sexual grooming will use more positive sentiments in order to lure victims. Differentiating between these types of toxicity will strengthen the correlation to message sentiment and further improve our results. Likewise, handling entire conversations will allow us to include contextual information to the sentiment of each message, and to detect sudden changes in the sentiment of the conversation that correspond to a disruptive toxic comment.

Acknowledgment

This research was made possible by the financial, material, and technical support of Two Hat Security Research Corp., and the financial support of the Canadian research organization MITACS.

References

Basant Agarwal, Namita Mittal, Pooja Bansal, and Sonal Garg. 2015. Sentiment analysis using common-sense and context information. *Computational intelligence and neuroscience*, 2015:30.

Sweta Agrawal and Amit Awekar. 2018. Deep learning for detecting cyberbullying across multiple social media platforms. *CoRR*, abs/1801.06482.

Jorge Carrillo de Albornoz, Laura Plaza, Alberto Dìaz, and Miguel Ballesteros. 2012. Ucm-i: A rule-based syntactic approach for resolving the scope of negation. In *SEM 2012: The First Joint Conference on Lexical and Computational Semantics – Volume 1: Proceedings of the main conference and the shared task, and Volume 2: Proceedings of the Sixth International Workshop on Semantic Evaluation (SemEval 2012)*, pages 282–287. Association for Computational Linguistics.

Wafa Alorainy, Pete Burnap, Han Liu, and Matthew Williams. 2018. Cyber hate classification:'othering'language and paragraph embedding. *arXiv preprint arXiv:1801.07495*.

Despoina Chatzakou, Nicolas Kourtellis, Jeremy Blackburn, Emiliano De Cristofaro, Gianluca Stringhini, and Athena Vakali. 2017. Mean birds: Detecting aggression and bullying on twitter. *CoRR*, abs/1702.06877.

Isaac G Councill, Ryan McDonald, and Leonid Velikovich. 2010. What's great and what's not: learning to classify the scope of negation for improved sentiment analysis. In *Proceedings of the workshop on negation and speculation in natural language processing*, pages 51–59. Association for Computational Linguistics.

Maral Dadvar, Claudia Hauff, and Franciska de Jong. 2011. Scope of negation detection in sentiment analysis. *Dutch- Belgian Information Retrieval Workshop*.

Harsh Dani, Jundong Li, and Huan Liu. 2017. Sentiment informed cyberbullying detection in social media. *Machine Learning and Knowledge Discovery in Databases*, pages 52–67.

Mohammadreza Ebrahimi. 2016. *Automatic Identification of Online Predators in Chat Logs by Anomaly Detection and Deep Learning*. Ph.D. thesis, Concordia University.

Cynthia Van Hee, Gilles Jacobs, Chris Emmery, Bart Desmet, Els Lefever, Ben Verhoeven, Guy De Pauw, Walter Daelemans, and Véronique Hoste. 2018. Automatic detection of cyberbullying in social media text. *CoRR*, abs/1801.05617.

Hossein Hosseini, Sreeram Kannan, Baosen Zhang, and Radha Poovendran. 2017. Deceiving google's perspective API built for detecting toxic comments. *CoRR*, abs/1702.08138.

Shruthi Mohan, Apala Guha, Michael Harris, Fred Popowich, Ashley Schuster, and Chris Priebe. 2017. The impact of toxic language on the health of reddit communities. In *Canadian Conference on Artificial Intelligence*, pages 51–56. Springer.

Finn Årup Nielsen. 2011. A new anew: Evaluation of a word list for sentiment analysis in microblogs. *arXiv preprint arXiv:1103.2903*.

Chikashi Nobata, Joel Tetreault, Achint Thomas, Yashar Mehdad, and Yi Chang. 2016. Abusive language detection in online user content. In *Proceedings of the 25th international conference on world wide web*, pages 145–153. International World Wide Web Conferences Steering Committee.

Bruno Ohana, Sarah Jane Delany, and Brendan Tierney. 2012. A case-based approach to cross domain sentiment classification. In *International Conference on Case-Based Reasoning*, pages 284–296. Springer.

Kelly Reynolds, April Kontostathis, and Lynne Edwards. 2011. Using machine learning to detect cyberbullying. In *Machine learning and applications and workshops (ICMLA), 2011 10th International Conference on*, volume 2, pages 241–244. IEEE.

Yanyao Shen, Hyokun Yun, Zachary C. Lipton, Yakov Kronrod, and Animashree Anandkumar. 2017. Deep active learning for named entity recognition. *CoRR*, abs/1707.05928.

Pranali Tumsare, Ashish S Sambare, Sachin R Jain, and Andrada Olah. 2014. Opinion mining in natural language processing using sentiwordnet and fuzzy. *International Journal of Emerging Trends & Technology in Computer Science (IJETTCS) Volume*, 3:154–158.

William Warner and Julia Hirschberg. 2012. Detecting hate speech on the world wide web. In *Proceedings of the Second Workshop on Language in Social Media*, pages 19–26. Association for Computational Linguistics.

Exploring Deep Multimodal Fusion of Text and Photo for Hate Speech Classification

**Fan Yang   Xiaochang Peng   Gargi Ghosh
Reshef Shilon   Hao Ma   Eider Moore   Goran Predovic**
Facebook Inc.
{flymonkey,xiaochang,gghosh,reshefshilon,haom,idr,predovic}@fb.com

Abstract

Interactions among users on social network platforms are usually positive, constructive and insightful. However, sometimes people also get exposed to objectionable content such as hate speech, bullying, and verbal abuse etc. Most social platforms have explicit policy against hate speech because it creates an environment of intimidation and exclusion, and in some cases may promote real-world violence. As users' interactions on today's social networks involve multiple modalities, such as texts, images and videos, in this paper we explore the challenge of automatically identifying hate speech with deep multimodal technologies, extending previous research which mostly focuses on the text signal alone. We present a number of fusion approaches to integrate text and photo signals. We show that augmenting text with image embedding information immediately leads to a boost in performance, while applying additional attention fusion methods brings further improvement.

1 Introduction

While social network platforms give people the voice to speak, they also have a need to moderate abusive and objectionable content that is harmful for their communities. Most social platforms have explicit policy against hate speech (e.g. https://www.facebook.com/communitystandards/hate_speech) because such content creates an environment of intimidation, exclusion, and in some cases promote real-world violence.

The automatic identification of hate speech has been mostly formulated as a natural language processing problem (e.g. Mishra et al., 2018; Gunasekara and Nejadgholi, 2018; Kshirsagar et al., 2018; Magu and Luo, 2018; Sahlgren et al., 2018). The signal from text, however, sometimes is not sufficient for determining whether a piece of content (such as a post) on the social network platforms constitutes hate speech. There is a need to take into account signals from multiple modalities in order to have a full comprehension of the content for hate speech classification. For example, "these are disgusting parasites", the sentence itself can be either benign or hateful, depending on what "these" refer to; and when it is combined with a photo of people or symbols in a post, it is very likely to be hate speech. We have seen many cases where the text itself is benign, but the whole post is hateful if we consider the context of the image.

There has been a number of research on multimodal fusion in the deep learning era. For example, Tong et al. (2017) apply an outer product fusion method to combine text and photo information for the task of detecting human trafficking. For the task of user profiling, formulated as a multi-tasking classification problem, Vijayaraghavan et al. (2017) propose a hierarchical attention model; and Farnadi et al. (2018) propose the UDMF framework, a hybrid integration model that combines both early feature fusion and later decision fusion using both stacking and power-set combination. Zhong et al. (2016) also studied the combination of image and captions for the task of detecting cyberbullying. For the task of name tagging, formulated as a sequence labeling problem, Lu et al. (2018) apply a visual attention model to put the focus on the sub-areas of a photo that are more relevant to the text encoded by a bi-LSTM model. For the task of image-text matching, Wang et al. (2017) compare an embedding network that projects texts and photos into a joint space where semantically-similar texts and photos are close to each other, with a similarity network that fuses text embeddings and photo embeddings via element multiplication. For the task of sentiment analysis, Zadeh et al. (2017); Ghosal et al. (2018);

11

Proceedings of the Third Workshop on Abusive Language Online, pages 11–18
Florence, Italy, August 1, 2019. ©2019 Association for Computational Linguistics

Bagher Zadeh et al. (2018); Liu et al. (2018) propose several models, namely contextual inter-modal attention, dynamic fusion graph, and low-rank multimodal fusion, for integrating visual, audio, and text signals on the CMU-MOSEI data set. There is also research initiative in multimodal summarization (Li et al., 2017) and multimodal translation (Calixto et al., 2017; Delbrouck and Dupont, 2017). These works have demonstrated the effectiveness of multimodal fusion methods in problems where non-text signals play an important role in disambiguating the text.

In this research, we explore deep multimodal fusion of text and photo for the task of hate speech classification on social networks, where hate speech posts frequently appear with images. We experiment with many fusion techniques, including simple concatenation, bilinear transformation, gated summation, and attention mechanism. We find that concatenation with photo information in the convolution text classifier immediately gives us a nice gain, while fusion with attention offers further improvement. Specifically attention with deep cloning, sparsemax, and symmetric_gate provides the best performance. These results shall shed light on better identifying hate speech to provide a safer community of online social networks.

2   Text And Photo Fusion

In this section we first describe our baseline convolutional text classifier, and the image features of photos. We then describe many approaches of fusing texts and photos, including basic concatenation, gated summation, bilinear transformation, and attention with different alternations.

2.1   Convolutional text model

We adopt the convolutional sentence classification architecture by Kim (2014) as our baseline text model, as illustrated on the left hand side in Figure 1.

1. For each word in a piece of text, we retrieve the pre-trained embeddings $[v_1, v_2, ..., v_n]$. These embeddings are fixed during our model training. We then apply a word-level MLP on each of the word embeddings, creating the new word embeddings $[v'_1, v'_2, ..., v'_n]$. This word-level MLP serves as a solution of fine-tuning the word embeddings towards the hate speech domain, by applying a systematic transform to the whole embeddings space, which has the benefit of also taking care of words that do not appear in the training data. We then apply a dropout layer on the word-level so that the model is more robust against word embeddings features.

2. We next apply a 1D-convolution to the words. With proper padding, we ensure that the output of the convolution matches the length of the input for different ngram-window sizes (Gehring et al., 2017). This offers the convenience for executing attention operation (see Section 2.5). The output of the convolution is a list of vectors $[c_1, c_2, ..., c_n]$.

3. We then apply max-pooling and tanh to create a fixed-size vector representation for the piece of text, denoted as t.

4. Finally we apply dropout, MLP and softmax on the vector t to discriminate between *hate* vs *benign*.

2.2   Photo features

We first pre-train a deep neural network for image classification, similar to the deep ResNet neural architecture (He et al., 2016) for ImageNet (Deng et al., 2009), with hundreds of millions of photos on a social network platform (not limited to the domain of hate speech). For each photo, we then extract the features from the second last layer, which is a float vector of 4096 dimensions. Finally we run iterative quantization to convert this vector into a hash of 256-bit binary vector (Gong et al., 2013). We store the photo hashes for efficient photo indexing, searching, and clustering.

In this research, we conveniently represent each photo with its hash (Sablayrolles et al., 2018). The hash takes advantage of the deep pre-trained image network which offers discriminative semantic representations. It preserves the similarity between original photos: the photos with smaller Hamming distance between their hashes look similar to each other. While it is suboptimal as the iterative quantization might be information-lossy, the photo hashing technique provides an infrastructure-economic solution to compactly store and promptly retrieve the information of billions of photos on the platform.

Note that the hash comes from the second last layer representations of the deep ImageNet-like network. This has the flavor of transfer learning

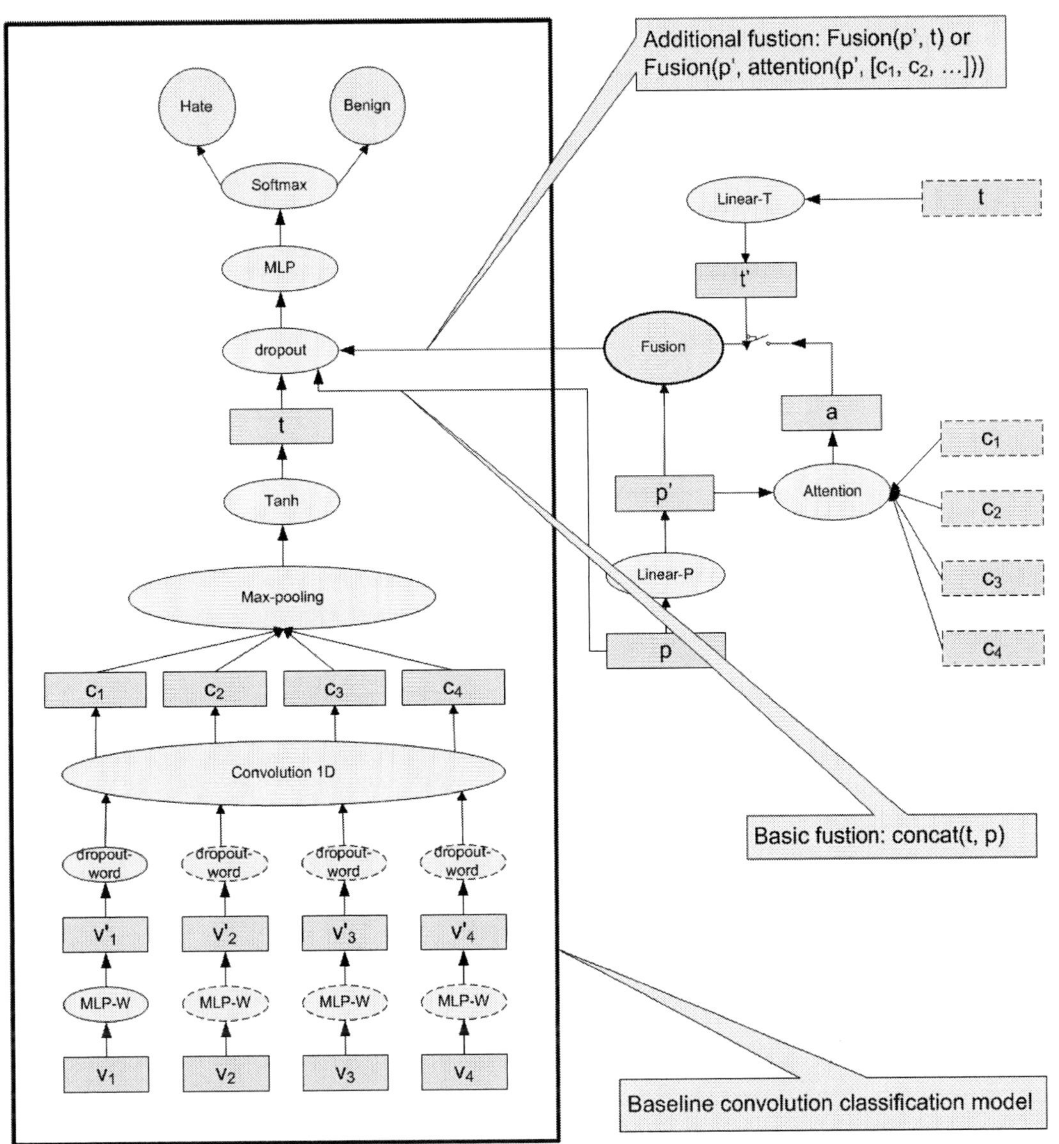

Figure 1: Model architecture of text and photo fusion: ellipses (in yellow) represent operations; and rectangles (in green) represent vectors. Shapes in dot lines are *clones* of their corresponding components.

(Oquab et al., 2014), where we pre-train the network with a large amount of out-of-domain photos, and then fix the second last layer and below. The hash offers a generic representation for which we will then fine-tune with in-domain photos.

2.3 Basic fusion: concatenation

The most straightforward way of integrating text with photo features is to concatenate t and p, as illustrated in Figure 1, where t is the text representation vector after max-pooling and *tanh* activation function, and p is the 256-dimensional photo hash as mentioned before. The concatenated vector is followed by dropout, MLP and softmax operations for the final hate speech classification. Note that with this basic concatenation, the photo hash p would actually impact the text representation t through back-propagating the loss down to the word embeddings MLP.

2.4 Additional fusion

On top of the basic concatenation, we have also explored other fusion techniques: gated summation and bilinear transformation.

- **Gated summation** Miyamoto and Cho (2016) propose a gated summation approach

13

to integrate word and character information. We adopt their approach and apply it to text and photo fusion, as illustrated in Equation (1). We first apply linear transformations to t and p so that they have the same dimension $|t'| = |p'|$. We then calculate a gate G as a sigmoid (σ) function on p', where u_p (a weighed vector) and B_p (a bias scalar) are parameters to be learned. We then use the gate value G to weigh the summation of t' and p' to create the fusion vector f. We use the vector $concat(t, p, f)$ for the target hate speech classification.

$$
\begin{aligned}
t' &= W_t \cdot t + b_t \\
p' &= W_p \cdot p + b_p \\
G &= \sigma(u_p^T \cdot p' + B_p) \\
f &= G * t' + (1 - G) * p'
\end{aligned}
\tag{1}
$$

The gated summation approach is later further extended in Lu et al. (2018), referred to as *visual modulation gate*, to dynamically control the combination of visual and textual signals, as illustrated in Equation (2).

$$
\begin{aligned}
\beta_t &= \sigma(W_t \cdot t' + U_t \cdot p' + b_t) \\
\beta_p &= \sigma(W_p \cdot t' + U_p \cdot p' + b_p) \\
m &= \tanh(W_m * t' + U_m * p' + b_m) \\
f &= \beta_t * t' + \beta_p * m
\end{aligned}
\tag{2}
$$

In this paper, we will refer to Miyamoto and Cho (2016)'s formula as *simple-gated fusion* and Lu et al. (2018)'s formula as *symmetric-gated fusion*.

- **Bilinear transformation** is a filter to integrate the information of two vectors into one vector. Mathematically we have $bilinear(t', p', dim) = t'^T \cdot M \cdot p' + b$, where dim is a hyper-parameter indicating the expected dimension of the output vector, M is a weight matrix of dimension (dim, $|t'|$, $|p'|$), and b is a bias vector of dimension dim. Again we concatenate t, p, and $bilinear(t', p', dim)$ for hate speech classification.

2.5 Attention mechanism

Attention mechanism was initially proposed in neural machine translation to dynamically adjust the focus on the source sentence (Bahdanau et al., 2014), but its application has been extended to many areas including multimodal fusion (Lu et al., 2018; Ghosal et al., 2018; Bagher Zadeh et al., 2018). The idea of attention is to use the information of a vector (called *query*) to weighted-sum a list of vectors (called *context*). Mathematically, it is implemented as Equation (3). The context vector is the 1D-convolution output $[c_1, c_2, ..., c_n]$ from text, while the query vector is the photo vector p'. W_a is a parameter to be learned.

$$
\begin{aligned}
s_i &= softmax(c_i^T \cdot W_a \cdot p') \quad i = 1, ..., n \\
a &= sum(s_i * c_i)
\end{aligned}
\tag{3}
$$

- **Simple vs symmetric-gated fusion** Once we have the attention vector a, which is a weighted sum of the c_i vectors from text signal only, we will further apply fusion with the photo information g'. Again we can consider the fusion techniques described in Section 2.4. In this paper we experiment with both the simple- and symmetric-gated fusions, as bilinear is pretty expensive to run. We use the concatenation of t, g, and $gated\_fusion(a, g')$ for hate speech classification.

- **Sparsemax vs softmax** We also experiment with sparsemax (Martins and Astudillo, 2016), an alternative to softmax, in Equation (3) for calculating the attention vector a. Sparsemax is an activation function that outputs a vector of sparse probabilities where most of the values are zero, which could offer a more selective and compact attention focus.

- **Deep vs shallow** Another implementation detail is whether to back-propagate the derivatives when we clone the vectors $c_1, c_2, ..., c_n$ for attention calculation. *Shallow clone*, which makes a copy of c_i but stops the back-propagation (during attention), has less impact on the convolutions and word-embeddings; while *deep clone*, passing the derivatives through to convolutions and word embeddings, has a bigger impact.

3 Experiments

3.1 Data

We sample from seven months of user-reported data on a social network platform, which users re-

	Positive	**Negative**	**Total**
Train & dev	320K	58K	378K
Test	42K	11K	53K

Table 1: Data set size

port as hate speech. Every piece of content contains some text and exactly one photo. These data are then reviewed by the platform according to the community standard[1]. Contents that are determined to violate the community standard receive a positive label while otherwise negative. We use the last month of the data as test set, while the first six months of data are randomly split with 90% as training set and 10% as development set for determining early stopping. Table 1 gives some rough stats of the data set size.

3.2 Hyper-parameters

In our experiments, the dimension of pre-trained word embeddings is 300. The new word embeddings after word-level MLP is also set at 300-dimension. Both word-level and classification-level dropout rates are set to 0.2. We use convolution windows $[1, 3, 5]$ with 128 filters each. These parameters were tuned in pilot studies to optimize the baseline convolution text classification performance. The dimension of fusion vectors p', t', and a is set to be 128. We use ADAM optimizer with a learning rate of 0.001. We run 20 epochs for training and select the best model with development data.

3.3 Results

A hate speech classifier can be used for many purposes, for example, to down-rank contents in newsfeed service, to proactively report contents for human reviews, to provide feedback for the creating users, or to provide warning message for consuming users. Generally a different decision threshold is needed for each scenario. Thus we use ROC-AUC as the performance metric in this paper, which measures the classifier's performance across all scoring points.

Results are shown in Table 2. The convolution text model gives us a baseline of 82.1. When concatenating the photo features p in the convolution training, we immediately get a nice boost to 84.0. We do not see a clear gain with additional fusion

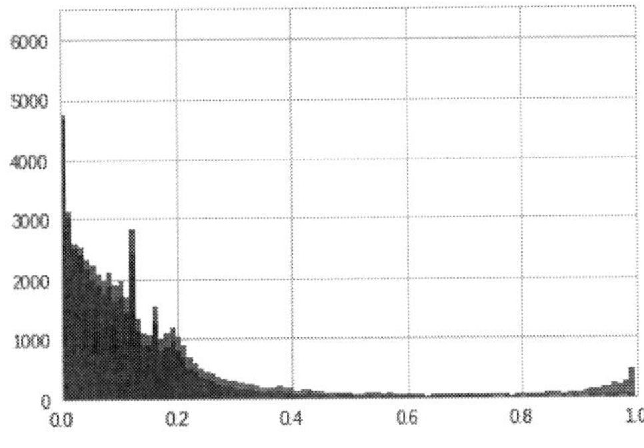

(a) Convolutional text model

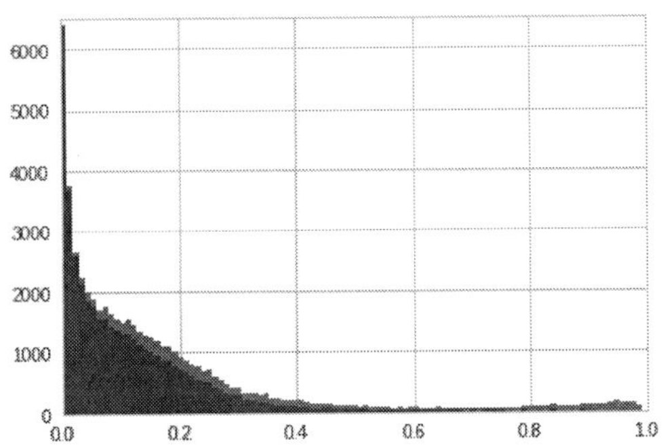

(b) Basic concatenation fusion model

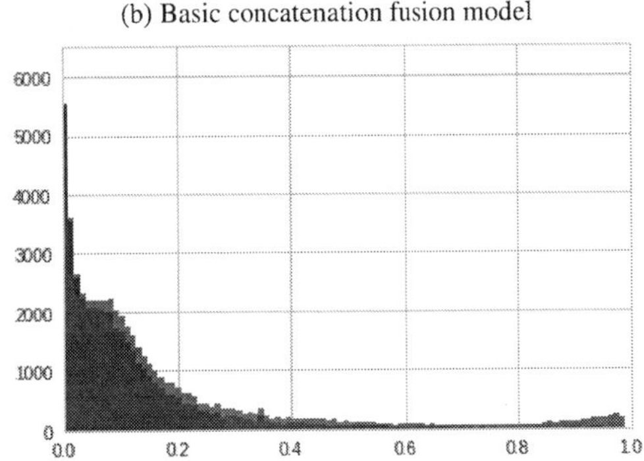

(c) Attention model (symmetric, deep, sparsemax)

Figure 2: Score distribution histogram: blue for benign and red for hate speech. X axis is classifier score. Y axis is the count of items in the score segment.

using gated summation, either simple_gate or symmetric_gate. Bilinear transformation even brings the performance down. We speculate that there might be an overfitting issue with bilinear but we didn't investigate further as bilinear transformation runs very slow, about 8X to 10X slower than the other approaches.

Fusion using attention mechanism turn out to work pretty well. Generally, we see that deep cloning tends to perform better than shallow cloning, suggesting the benefit of deeper engagement of text and photo information. We see that sparsemax tends to perform better than softmax,

---

[1] https://www.facebook.com/communitystandards/hate_speech

Inputs	Additional Fusion Mode	Attention Mode		ROC-AUC
		max	clone	
t				82.1
t, g				84.0
t, g, fusion(t', g')	simple_gated			83.9
t, g, fusion(t', g')	symmetric_gated			84.1
t, g, fusion(t', g')	bilinear			82.7
t, g, fusion(attention(t', g'), g')	simple_gated	softmax	shallow	84.0
t, g, fusion(attention(t', g'), g')	simple_gated	softmax	deep	84.6
t, g, fusion(attention(t', g'), g')	simple_gated	sparsemax	shallow	84.3
t, g, fusion(attention(t', g'), g')	simple_gated	sparsemax	deep	84.6
t, g, fusion(attention(t', g'), g')	symmetric_gated	softmax	shallow	84.1
t, g, fusion(attention(t', g'), g')	symmetric_gated	softmax	deep	84.7
t, g, fusion(attention(t', g'), g')	symmetric_gated	sparsemax	shallow	84.3
t, g, fusion(attention(t', g'), g')	symmetric_gated	sparsemax	deep	84.8

Table 2: Experimental Results

suggesting the benefit of sparse weights on the summation of convolution outputs, which gives a higher focus on the important segments and totally ignores the trivial segments. We also see that symmetric_gate tends to perform better than simple_gate, suggesting the benefit of weighing the gated summation using both text and photo information (over using the photo channel only). Finally using the attention fusion with deep cloning, sparsemax, and symmetric_gate gives us a performance of 84.8, another nice improvement over basic concatenation, which is statistically significant at the 99% confidence level. In practice, we have found that improvement of 0.5 AUC would generally lead to observed production quality.

3.4 Discussion

Figure 2 shows the score distributions for three models: the baseline convolutional text model, the basic concatenation fusion model, and the attention fusion model with symmetric-gate, deep clone, and sparsemax. The baseline model has a spike at the score of about 0.13, which involves a significant false negative. Error analysis reveals that this is the section where posts contain none but OOV words.[2] Thus the text model extracts no useful signals but only uses the prior distribution which classifies all those posts as benign. With the

concatenation of photo signals, the model can then learn to classify a piece of content as hate speech if there is a similar photo previously labelled as hate speech in the training data, which helps to improve recall.

We have also found cases where the photo signals help to improve precision as well. We found that when users have their posts deleted by the platform they sometimes make a screen shot (which is a photo) of the deleted post, and post it with some texts complaining or appealing about the community standard. The majority of these reposts are still hate speech, with a few exceptions where the original posts were deleted by mistakes. When training with text signals only, the model is overfitted towards text and it thus treats all the posts that complain or appeal the community standards as hate speech. With the integration of photo signals, the model actually learns that a piece of text complaining about community standard policy with a benign photo does not necessarily create hate speech, and so is able to avoid fitting all posts of policy complaining to hate speech.

The improvement of additional attention fusion over basic concatenation is a bit subtle. We observe that when both the text and the photo alone do not constitute a strong signal for hate speech, the basic concatenation model tends to classify the post as benign, although together they might create an impression of hate speech. With the additional attention fusion, the model would be able to highlight on some key phrases in the text to

---

[2]Texts on social network platforms are very noisy – there are typos, misspellings, long digits, foreign languages, and other online specials such as hashtags that we do not have in our limited vocabulary. A character model such as (Zhang et al., 2015) and (Bojanowski et al., 2017) should help to alleviate such problems though.

correctly recall some posts of hate speech. For example, with the text "If you look at the photo, I do think that they are disgusting parasites" and a photo of people, the attention model would be able to focus on the word "parasites" and catches it as hate speech. Sparsemax shines especially for longer texts. This is also shown in Figure 2 as the attention model is able to push more hate speech posts (in red) to the right hand side.

4 Conclusion

Interactions among users on social network platforms enable constructive and insightful conversations and civic participation; however, verbal abuse such as hate speech could also happen and lead to degraded user experience or even worse consequence. As users' interactions on today's social networks involve multiple modalities, in this paper we take the challenge of automatically identifying hate speech with deep multimodal technologies, expanding on previous research that mostly focuses on the text signal alone. We explore a number of fusion approaches to integrate text and photo signals, including concatenation, bilinear, gated summation, and attention fusion. We find that simply concatenating the text and photo embeddings immediately leads to a boost in performance, while additional attention fusion with symmetric gate, deep clone, and sparsemax brings further improvement. Our future work includes investigating fusion with multiple photos, and fusion with more modalities (such as audio and video).

References

AmirAli Bagher Zadeh, Paul Pu Liang, Soujanya Poria, Erik Cambria, and Louis-Philippe Morency. 2018. Multimodal language analysis in the wild: Cmu-mosei dataset and interpretable dynamic fusion graph. In *Proceedings of the 56th Annual Meeting of the Association for Computational Linguistics (Volume 1: Long Papers)*, pages 2236–2246. Association for Computational Linguistics.

Dzmitry Bahdanau, Kyunghyun Cho, and Yoshua Bengio. 2014. Neural machine translation by jointly learning to align and translate. *CoRR*, abs/1409.0473.

Piotr Bojanowski, Edouard Grave, Armand Joulin, and Tomas Mikolov. 2017. Enriching word vectors with subword information. *Transactions of the Association for Computational Linguistics*, 5:135–146.

Iacer Calixto, Qun Liu, and Nick Campbell. 2017. Doubly-attentive decoder for multi-modal neural machine translation. In *Proceedings of the 55th Annual Meeting of the Association for Computational Linguistics (Volume 1: Long Papers)*, pages 1913–1924, Vancouver, Canada. Association for Computational Linguistics.

Jean-Benoit Delbrouck and Stéphane Dupont. 2017. An empirical study on the effectiveness of images in multimodal neural machine translation. In *Proceedings of the 2017 Conference on Empirical Methods in Natural Language Processing*, pages 910–919. Association for Computational Linguistics.

Jia Deng, Wei Dong, Richard Socher, Li-Jia Li, Kai Li, and Li Fei-Fei. 2009. Imagenet: A large-scale hierarchical image database. *2009 IEEE Conference on Computer Vision and Pattern Recognition*, pages 248–255.

Golnoosh Farnadi, Jie Tang, Martine De Cock, and Marie-Francine Moens. 2018. User profiling through deep multimodal fusion. In *Proceedings of the Eleventh ACM International Conference on Web Search and Data Mining*, WSDM '18, pages 171–179, New York, NY, USA. ACM.

Jonas Gehring, Michael Auli, David Grangier, Denis Yarats, and Yann N. Dauphin. 2017. Convolutional sequence to sequence learning. *CoRR*, abs/1705.03122.

Deepanway Ghosal, Md Shad Akhtar, Dushyant Chauhan, Soujanya Poria, Asif Ekbal, and Pushpak Bhattacharyya. 2018. Contextual inter-modal attention for multi-modal sentiment analysis. In *Proceedings of the 2018 Conference on Empirical Methods in Natural Language Processing*, pages 3454–3466. Association for Computational Linguistics.

Yunchao Gong, Svetlana Lazebnik, Albert Gordo, and Florent Perronnin. 2013. Iterative quantization: A procrustean approach to learning binary codes for large-scale image retrieval. *IEEE Trans. Pattern Anal. Mach. Intell.*, 35(12):2916–2929.

Isuru Gunasekara and Isar Nejadgholi. 2018. A review of standard text classification practices for multi-label toxicity identification of online content. In *Proceedings of the 2nd Workshop on Abusive Language Online (ALW2)*, pages 21–25. Association for Computational Linguistics.

K. He, X. Zhang, S. Ren, and J. Sun. 2016. Deep residual learning for image recognition. In *2016 IEEE Conference on Computer Vision and Pattern Recognition (CVPR)*, pages 770–778.

Yoon Kim. 2014. Convolutional neural networks for sentence classification. In *Proceedings of the 2014 Conference on Empirical Methods in Natural Language Processing (EMNLP)*, pages 1746–1751. Association for Computational Linguistics.

Rohan Kshirsagar, Tyrus Cukuvac, Kathy McKeown, and Susan McGregor. 2018. Predictive embeddings for hate speech detection on twitter. In *Proceedings of the 2nd Workshop on Abusive Language Online (ALW2)*, pages 26–32. Association for Computational Linguistics.

Haoran Li, Junnan Zhu, Cong Ma, Jiajun Zhang, and Chengqing Zong. 2017. Multi-modal summarization for asynchronous collection of text, image, audio and video. In *Proceedings of the 2017 Conference on Empirical Methods in Natural Language Processing*, pages 1092–1102. Association for Computational Linguistics.

Zhun Liu, Ying Shen, Varun Bharadhwaj Lakshminarasimhan, Paul Pu Liang, AmirAli Bagher Zadeh, and Louis-Philippe Morency. 2018. Efficient low-rank multimodal fusion with modality-specific factors. In *Proceedings of the 56th Annual Meeting of the Association for Computational Linguistics (Volume 1: Long Papers)*, pages 2247–2256. Association for Computational Linguistics.

Di Lu, Leonardo Neves, Vitor Carvalho, Ning Zhang, and Heng Ji. 2018. Visual attention model for name tagging in multimodal social media. In *Proceedings of the 56th Annual Meeting of the Association for Computational Linguistics (Volume 1: Long Papers)*, pages 1990–1999. Association for Computational Linguistics.

Rijul Magu and Jiebo Luo. 2018. Determining code words in euphemistic hate speech using word embedding networks. In *Proceedings of the 2nd Workshop on Abusive Language Online (ALW2)*, pages 93–100. Association for Computational Linguistics.

André F. T. Martins and Ramón F. Astudillo. 2016. From softmax to sparsemax: A sparse model of attention and multi-label classification. In *Proceedings of the 33rd International Conference on International Conference on Machine Learning - Volume 48*, ICML'16, pages 1614–1623. JMLR.org.

Pushkar Mishra, Helen Yannakoudakis, and Ekaterina Shutova. 2018. Neural character-based composition models for abuse detection. In *Proceedings of the 2nd Workshop on Abusive Language Online (ALW2)*, pages 1–10. Association for Computational Linguistics.

Yasumasa Miyamoto and Kyunghyun Cho. 2016. Gated word-character recurrent language model. In *Proceedings of the 2016 Conference on Empirical Methods in Natural Language Processing*, pages 1992–1997. Association for Computational Linguistics.

Maxime Oquab, Leon Bottou, Ivan Laptev, and Josef Sivic. 2014. Learning and transferring mid-level image representations using convolutional neural networks. In *Proceedings of the IEEE conference on computer vision and pattern recognition*, pages 1717–1724.

Alexandre Sablayrolles, Matthijs Douze, Cordelia Schmid, and Hervé Jégou. 2018. A neural network catalyzer for multi-dimensional similarity search. *CoRR*, abs/1806.03198.

Magnus Sahlgren, Tim Isbister, and Fredrik Olsson. 2018. Learning representations for detecting abusive language. In *Proceedings of the 2nd Workshop on Abusive Language Online (ALW2)*, pages 115–123. Association for Computational Linguistics.

Edmund Tong, Amir Zadeh, Cara Jones, and Louis-Philippe Morency. 2017. Combating human trafficking with multimodal deep models. In *Proceedings of the 55th Annual Meeting of the Association for Computational Linguistics (Volume 1: Long Papers)*, pages 1547–1556, Vancouver, Canada. Association for Computational Linguistics.

Prashanth Vijayaraghavan, Soroush Vosoughi, and Deb Roy. 2017. Twitter demographic classification using deep multi-modal multi-task learning. In *Proceedings of the 55th Annual Meeting of the Association for Computational Linguistics (Volume 2: Short Papers)*, pages 478–483, Vancouver, Canada. Association for Computational Linguistics.

Liwei Wang, Yin Li, and Svetlana Lazebnik. 2017. Learning two-branch neural networks for image-text matching tasks. *CoRR*, abs/1704.03470.

Amir Zadeh, Minghai Chen, Soujanya Poria, Erik Cambria, and Louis-Philippe Morency. 2017. Tensor fusion network for multimodal sentiment analysis. In *Proceedings of the 2017 Conference on Empirical Methods in Natural Language Processing*, pages 1103–1114. Association for Computational Linguistics.

Xiang Zhang, Junbo Jake Zhao, and Yann LeCun. 2015. Character-level convolutional networks for text classification. *CoRR*, abs/1509.01626.

Haoti Zhong, Hao Li, Anna Squicciarini, Sarah Rajtmajer, Christopher Griffin, David Miller, and Cornelia Caragea. 2016. Content-driven detection of cyberbullying on the instagram social network. In *Proceedings of the Twenty-Fifth International Joint Conference on Artificial Intelligence*, IJCAI'16, pages 3952–3958. AAAI Press.

Detecting harassment in real time as conversations develop

Wessel Stoop
CLST, Radboud University
w.stoop@let.ru.nl

Florian Kunneman
CLST, Radboud University
f.kunneman@let.ru.nl

Antal van den Bosch
KNAW Meertens Instituut
antal.van.den.bosch@meertens.knaw.nl

Ben Miller
Emory University
b.j.miller@emory.edu

Abstract

We developed a machine-learning-based method to detect video game players that harass teammates or opponents in chat earlier in the conversation. This real-time technology would allow gaming companies to intervene during games, such as issue warnings or muting or banning a player. In a proof-of-concept experiment on *League of Legends* data we compute and visualize evaluation metrics for a machine learning classifier as conversations unfold, and observe that the optimal precision and recall of detecting toxic players at each moment in the conversation depends on the confidence threshold of the classifier: the threshold should start low, and increase as the conversation unfolds. How fast this *sliding threshold* should increase depends on the training set size.

1 Introduction

In many online platforms that allow user interaction, verbal harassment has become commonplace. For example, a survey by The Wikimedia Foundation showed that '38% of the 3,845 Wikimedia editors that were surveyed (an estimated total over 130,000) had experienced some form of harassment, and over half of those contributors felt a decrease in their motivation to contribute in the future' (Wulczyn et al., 2017). In this work we would like to focus on harassment in the online gaming community, where so-called *toxic players* are the subject of frequent media attention. For some video games over 1% of the player base is estimated to be consistently toxic[1]. Yet, for the game *League of Legends*, researchers found that this 1% of the player population only accounted for 5% of the toxic speech. The former director of Riot Games' Player Behavior Unit attributes most

toxicity to "the average person just having a bad day" (Maher, 2016). As encounters with harassment are a major predictor for players quitting a video game[2], creating healthy communities is an important focus point for many video game developers[3].

There has been an increase recently in the number of academic papers on automatically detecting harassment; see Zhang et al. (2018b) and van Aken et al. (2018) for overviews. Many of these works focus on datasets with relatively short conversations (often <20 turns), consisting of longer utterances (often multiple full sentences). As a result, most of these studies approach detecting verbal harassment as a classical text classification task, where each individual comment is considered a document on its own that should be assigned one of two or more categories. Conversations in video games, on the other hand, are different in nature: they consist of up to several hundreds of utterances, depending on the length of a match in the chosen video game, and these utterances are usually shorter, at least partly due to the restriction that the act of typing temporarily prevents players from playing. For this reason, we focus less on rating individual *comments* (an individual swear word or insult does not indicate harassment per se), but instead on detecting *players* within a match that consistently and knowingly harass teammates and/or opponents.

Self-policing of communities has been implemented by many game companies, among other things in the form of post-game ratings by other players. Based on this information, video game developers already have a good estimate of which players behaved badly at what time, so an au-

---

[1] https://www.youtube.com/watch?v=HQwL6zh7AgA &feature=youtu.be&t=39m38s

[2] https://www.youtube.com/watch?v=HQwL6zh7AgA &feature=youtu.be&t=33m57s

[3] https://kotaku.com/league-of-legends-neverending-war-on-toxic-behavior-1636894289

Proceedings of the Third Workshop on Abusive Language Online, pages 19–24
Florence, Italy, August 1, 2019. ©2019 Association for Computational Linguistics

tomated system that makes this estimate retroactively would not be of much added value. Instead, toxic players should be detected as the conversation develops, as early as possible, making it possible for gaming companies to intervene in one way or the other (like warning, muting or banning a player). Translated to a machine learning task, this means that instances (e.g.: players) change over time, as more information about the instances (more utterances) becomes available. This leads to *time* as an extra dimension of interest for metrics like precision, recall and F-score: instead of presenting them as a single number, it should be represented how they change during the conversation.

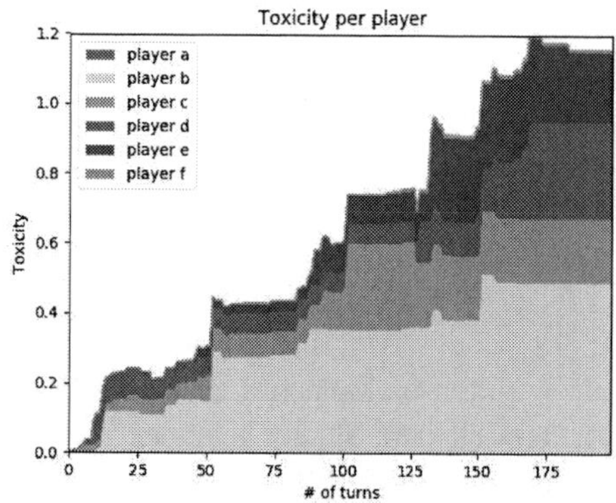

Figure 1: Classifier confidence for the 'toxic' class for six players during a single conversation.

A visualization of the estimated 'temperature' of a single conversation over time is given in Figure 1. In this work we will apply this idea of detecting harassment over the course of a conversation at scale, to evaluate various (parameters of) classifiers during the course of a conversation. More specifically, we will show that the optimal confidence threshold above which a player can be considered toxic increases as a conversation evolves, and that the rate of this increase interacts with the amount of training material.

2   Related work

The task of harassment detection in online conversation relates to tasks like cyberbullying and hate speech detection (van Aken et al., 2018). Despite differences in terminology and definitions of these terms, similar methods can often be applied; we will therefore treat it as one research field.

Early approaches to detecting harassment employ a simple lexicon or 'classic' machine learning algorithms such as Support Vector Machines, Naive Bayes, Logistic Regression, and Random Forests (see Schmidt and Wiegand (2017) for an overview) and focus on manually extracted features. Besides word or character n-grams and POS tags, the approaches typically make use of features such as punctuation, word and document length, capitalization, and gender identity of the speaker (Davidson et al., 2017; Nobata et al., 2016; Waseem, 2016; Waseem and Hovy, 2016). Many of these approaches have the advantage of explainability (to a certain extent), but struggle when harassment is implicit (Dinakar et al., 2011) or when harassment-related words have multiple meanings (Kwok and Wang, 2013; Davidson et al., 2017).

Some works apply these techniques to harassment in video games specifically: lexicon-based approaches have been shown to be useful for the games *DotA* (Märtens et al., 2015), *StarCraft II* (Thompson et al., 2017) and *World of Tanks* (Murnion et al., 2018), whereas Balci and Salah (2015) apply a Bayesian Point Machine to the game *Okey*. Of particular relevance is the study by Blackburn and Kwak (2014), who use the crowd sourced Tribunal decisions in the game *League of Legends* as their ground truth, similar to this paper (see Section 3). Besides language data, they feed a Random Forest classifier with various game-specific features, such as the number of kills and deaths, and the type of report by other players. The combined model can emulate Tribunal decisions with an Area Under the ROC Curve (AUC) of 80%.

More recent studies often use deep neural networks, with the most popular architectures being Convolutional Neural Networks (CNN) and Recurrent Neural Networks (RNN). The main advantage of the former is its ability to extract useful features, while the latter is well suited for the sequential nature of language. Zhang et al. (2018b) conduct an extensive evaluation of approaches for detecting hate speech so far and propose a combination of CNNs and RNNs to outperform them. Similarly, van Aken et al. (2018) do an in-depth error analysis for various approaches to toxic comment classification, and propose an ensemble method to outperform them.

Whereas most of these studies classify individual utterances, there are also works with a broader scope. Focusing on users instead of utterances,

Cheng et al. (2015) aim to detect 'antisocial users' in online communities over a longer period of time. They observe that the post quality of users labeled as antisocial worsens over time, possibly related to being censored. Using a variety of features as input, they use logistic regression to predict which users will be banned in the future. They achieve an AUC of 80% after observing 5–10 posts. Focusing on early instead of retrospective detection, Zhang et al. (2018a) try to predict whether the relatively short conversations on Wikipedia talk pages (average 4.6 utterances) will derail based on the first few utterances. While humans can do this with 72% accuracy, their 'Perspective API' achieves a score of 64.9%.

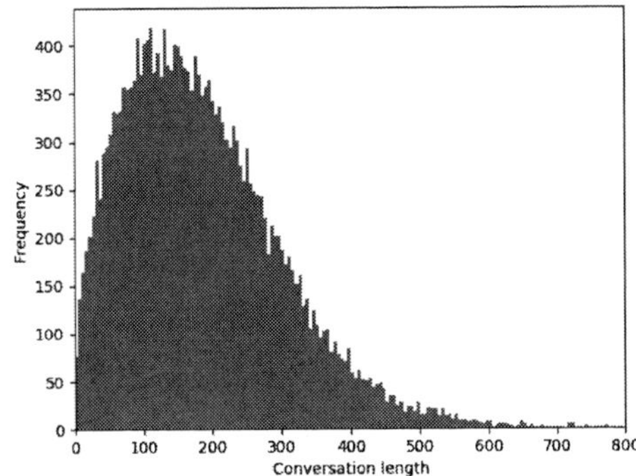

Figure 2: The number of utterances per conversation in our dataset.

3 Dataset

As a dataset, we use 5000 conversations from the video game *League of Legends*, obtained from video game developer Riot Games, containing utterances by 48512 players. Toxic players in this dataset were first identified by team mates and opponents, and later reassessed by other members of the community in a voting system called the 'Tribunal'. Only cases where a so-called 'overwhelming majority' was reached were considered toxic.

An average conversation in our dataset consists of 186.77 utterances (standard deviation 122.01), as visualized in figure 2, by 9.7 speakers (standard deviation 6.07). An average utterance consists of 3.15 words (standard deviation 2.63). 10.3% of the speakers in our dataset were labeled toxic by the Tribunal.

A typical case of harassment looks like this:

```
Z fukin bot n this team....
```

```
  so cluelesss gdam
V u cunt
A WTF
J TSM
V TSMMM
A 35 baron
Z wow voli....u jus let them kill
  me....instead of peeling
V ARE YOU RETARDED
L cheesed?
V U ULTED INTO 4 PEOPLE
D no death rocket plz
V HOW DO I PEED FOR UR AUTISTIC
  ASS
V ur mom should have swallowed you
Z this game is like playin with
  pre 30s lol....complete
  clueless lewl
L ur shyt zed
V AUTISM
D Oh bby|
```

Pilot experiments showed that the three main predictors for toxicity in this dataset are swear words, insults and talking about losing, all of which are present in this example ('fukin', 'u cunt', 'u jus let them kill me', respectively).

4 Method

To monitor conversations in progress and evaluate the success, we developed the framework HaRe (Harassment Recognizer)[4]. During a conversation, HaRe keeps track of toxicity estimates for all participants separately, updating the estimate for each speaker every time s/he makes an utterance. This is done by concatenating all utterances for that speaker, separated by *[NEW UTTERANCE]* tags, and classifying the resulting text. As an example, to obtain toxicity estimates in a conversation where three players each have generated six utterances so far, this means the classifier is asked to classify three texts, all containing five *[NEW UTTERANCE]* tags. All graphs in this work were created by the HaRe visualization module.

For classifier setup, we adopted the best performing neural network architecture in the *Toxic Comment Classification Challenge* on Kaggle[5], feeding a sequence of words to an RNN with an embedding layer (300 dimensions), two bidirectional GRU layers (16 units) feeding into two final dense layers (256 units). The output layer is a single sigmoid unit indicating the network's confidence that the input text is toxic. This is imple-

---

[4]The software and source code for HaRe is available at https://github.com/woseseltops/HaRe

[5]The setup is explained here: https://www.kaggle.com/c/jigsaw-toxic-comment-classification-challenge/discussion/52557

mented in HaRe and uses TensorFlow under the hood (Abadi et al., 2015).

We split the dataset into 1000 conversations for evaluation and 4000 for training (but in figure 6 we also experiment with smaller training set sizes). Training texts were created by concatenating all utterances per player, similar to how conversations are offered to the classifier during the classification phase. Important differences between the training and classification phase are (1) the texts in the training phase were downsampled to have an equal 50%-50% distribution of toxic and non-toxic texts, while during the classification phase only 10.3% of the texts were labeled toxic, and (2) training was done on full conversations that had finished, while during the classification phase the conversations were most often not finished yet (so the texts to classify in the beginning of conversations were considerably shorter).

5   Results

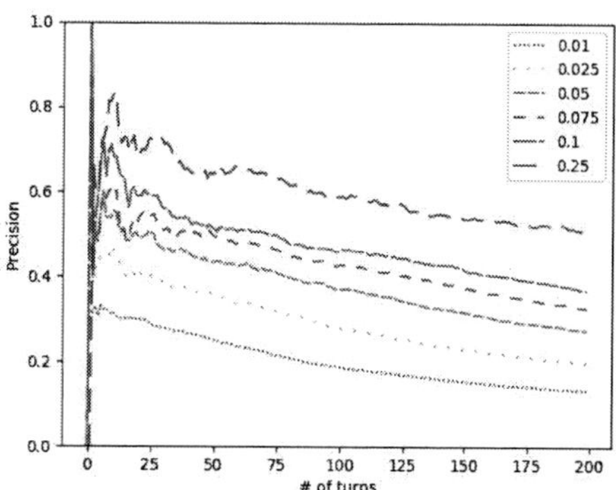

Figure 3: Precision recognizing toxic players over the course of conversations for various confidence thresholds.

Figures 3, 4 and 5 visualize the precision, recall and F-score of our classifier as the conversation unfolds, aggregated over our 1000 test conversations. They were created using a classifier trained on 4000 conversations and various thresholds. We see recall increase during a conversation as more information on each of the players (that is, more utterances) becomes available. However, every new utterance is also an extra source of information that could incorrectly be interpreted as an indicator for toxicity, leading to a decrease in precision during a conversation.

The rate of the recall increase and precision de-

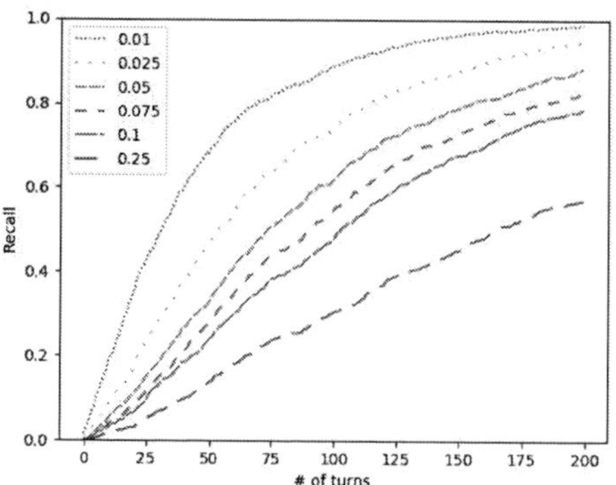

Figure 4: Recall recognizing toxic players over the course of conversations for various confidence thresholds.

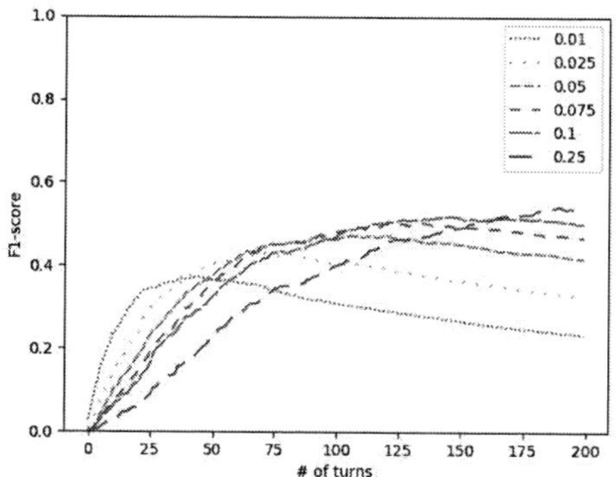

Figure 5: F-score recognizing toxic players over the course of conversations for various confidence thresholds.

crease over time greatly depend on the confidence level above which a player is considered toxic. Interestingly, this leads to a situation where the optimal threshold (that is, the threshold that results in the highest F-score) changes over the course of a conversation: whereas in the beginning the threshold should be as low as possible, it should generally be increased as the conversation progresses and more data to work with (more utterances) becomes available.

Figure 6 shows the results of retroactively selecting the threshold with the highest F-score for each turn in the conversation, for classifiers trained on various amounts of data. We observe that the rate in which this sliding threshold should be increased itself depends on the size of the training set: the larger the training set, the slower the threshold can be increased.

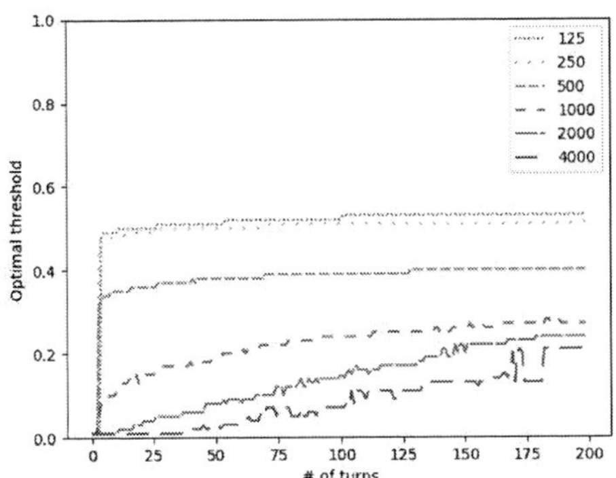

Figure 6: Confidence thresholds for optimal F-scores over the course of conversations for various training set sizes.

6   Discussion and conclusion

In this work we focused on detecting harassment as early as possible in a video game chat session, and observed that the classifier confidence threshold should start low and should be moved up during a conversation as more material for each speaker becomes available, for an optimal F-score at each point in the conversation. The exact starting point and rate of increase of this *sliding threshold* of course depend on the classifier setup and dataset; we showed for example that there seems to be an interaction with the training set size. To decide the optimal values for these two parameters for conversation monitoring software, creating a graph like figure 6 could be useful.

A downside of the approach presented here is that low recall scores are ambiguous in interpretation: they could either indicate a badly performing classifier missing actual harassment, or a lack of harassment so far. For both reasons evaluation measures tend to be low in the first few turns of a conversation. Furthermore, all evaluation metrics used focus on toxicity and ignore whether the classifier is making correct negative judgements at any point; this would call for metrics such as Area Under the ROC Curve.

Our approach should be compared to an approach that labels harassment at the utterance level. This may help pinpoint the exact moment at which the toxic player started using toxic language; this may be earlier than the point at which our confidence threshold is exceeded.

References

Martín Abadi, Ashish Agarwal, Paul Barham, Eugene Brevdo, Zhifeng Chen, Craig Citro, Greg S. Corrado, Andy Davis, Jeffrey Dean, Matthieu Devin, Sanjay Ghemawat, Ian Goodfellow, Andrew Harp, Geoffrey Irving, Michael Isard, Yangqing Jia, Rafal Jozefowicz, Lukasz Kaiser, Manjunath Kudlur, Josh Levenberg, Dan Mané, Rajat Monga, Sherry Moore, Derek Murray, Chris Olah, Mike Schuster, Jonathon Shlens, Benoit Steiner, Ilya Sutskever, Kunal Talwar, Paul Tucker, Vincent Vanhoucke, Vijay Vasudevan, Fernanda Viégas, Oriol Vinyals, Pete Warden, Martin Wattenberg, Martin Wicke, Yuan Yu, and Xiaoqiang Zheng. 2015. TensorFlow: Large-scale machine learning on heterogeneous systems. Software available from tensorflow.org.

Betty van Aken, Julian Risch, Ralf Krestel, and Alexander Löser. 2018. Challenges for toxic comment classification: An in-depth error analysis. In *Proceedings of the 2nd Workshop on Abusive Language Online (ALW2)*, pages 33–42, Brussels, Belgium. Association for Computational Linguistics.

Koray Balci and Albert Ali Salah. 2015. Automatic analysis and identification of verbal aggression and abusive behaviors for online social games. *Computers in Human Behavior*, 53:517–526.

Jeremy Blackburn and Haewoon Kwak. 2014. Stfu noob!: Predicting crowdsourced decisions on toxic behavior in online games. In *Proceedings of the 23rd International Conference on World Wide Web*, WWW '14, pages 877–888, New York, NY, USA. ACM.

Justin Cheng, Cristian Danescu-Niculescu-Mizil, and Jure Leskovec. 2015. Antisocial behavior in online discussion communities. *CoRR*, abs/1504.00680.

Thomas Davidson, Dana Warmsley, Michael Macy, and Ingmar Weber. 2017. Automated hate speech detection and the problem of offensive language. In *Proceedings of the 11th International AAAI Conference on Web and Social Media*, ICWSM '17, pages 512–515.

Karthik Dinakar, Roi Reichart, and Henry Lieberman. 2011. Modeling the detection of textual cyberbullying. In *Papers from the 2011 ICWSM Workshop*.

Irene Kwok and Yuzhou Wang. 2013. Locate the hate: Detecting tweets against blacks. In *Proceedings of the Twenty-Seventh AAAI Conference on Artificial Intelligence*, AAAI'13, pages 1621–1622. AAAI Press.

Brendan Maher. 2016. Can a video game company tame toxic behaviour? *Nature News*, 531(7596):568.

Marcus Märtens, Siqi Shen, Alexandru Iosup, and Fernando Kuipers. 2015. Toxicity detection in multiplayer online games. In *2015 International Workshop on Network and Systems Support for Games (NetGames)*, pages 1–6. IEEE.

Shane Murnion, William J Buchanan, Adrian Smales, and Gordon Russell. 2018. Machine learning and semantic analysis of in-game chat for cyberbullying. *Computers & Security*, 76:197–213.

Chikashi Nobata, Joel Tetreault, Achint Thomas, Yashar Mehdad, and Yi Chang. 2016. Abusive language detection in online user content. In *Proceedings of the 25th International Conference on World Wide Web*, WWW '16, pages 145–153, Republic and Canton of Geneva, Switzerland. International World Wide Web Conferences Steering Committee.

Anna Schmidt and Michael Wiegand. 2017. A survey on hate speech detection using natural language processing. pages 1–10.

Joseph J Thompson, Betty HM Leung, Mark R Blair, and Maite Taboada. 2017. Sentiment analysis of player chat messaging in the video game starcraft 2: Extending a lexicon-based model. *Knowledge-Based Systems*, 137:149–162.

Zeerak Waseem. 2016. Are you a racist or am i seeing things? annotator influence on hate speech detection on twitter. In *Proceedings of the First Workshop on NLP and Computational Social Science*, pages 138–142, Austin, Texas. Association for Computational Linguistics.

Zeerak Waseem and Dirk Hovy. 2016. Hateful symbols or hateful people? predictive features for hate speech detection on twitter. In *Proceedings of the NAACL Student Research Workshop*, pages 88–93, San Diego, California. Association for Computational Linguistics.

Ellery Wulczyn, Dario Taraborelli, Nithum Thain, and Lucas Dixon. 2017. Algorithms and insults: Scaling up our understanding of harassment on wikipedia. `https://blog.wikimedia.org/2017/02/07/scaling-understanding-of-harassment/`. Accessed: 2019-04-11.

Justine Zhang, Jonathan Chang, Cristian Danescu-Niculescu-Mizil, Lucas Dixon, Yiqing Hua, Dario Taraborelli, and Nithum Thain. 2018a. Conversations gone awry: Detecting early signs of conversational failure. In *Proceedings of the 56th Annual Meeting of the Association for Computational Linguistics (Volume 1: Long Papers)*, pages 1350–1361, Melbourne, Australia. Association for Computational Linguistics.

Ziqi Zhang, David Robinson, and Jonathan Tepper. 2018b. Detecting hate speech on twitter using a convolution-gru based deep neural network. In *The Semantic Web*, pages 745–760, Cham. Springer International Publishing.

Racial Bias in Hate Speech and Abusive Language Detection Datasets

Thomas Davidson
Department of Sociology
Cornell University
trd54@cornell.edu

Debasmita Bhattacharya
Department of
Computer Science
Cornell University
db758@cornell.edu

Ingmar Weber
Qatar Computer
Research Institute
iweber@hbku.edu.qa

Abstract

Technologies for abusive language detection are being developed and applied with little consideration of their potential biases. We examine racial bias in five different sets of Twitter data annotated for hate speech and abusive language. We train classifiers on these datasets and compare the predictions of these classifiers on tweets written in African-American English with those written in Standard American English. The results show evidence of systematic racial bias in all datasets, as classifiers trained on them tend to predict that tweets written in African-American English are abusive at substantially higher rates. If these abusive language detection systems are used in the field they will therefore have a disproportionate negative impact on African-American social media users. Consequently, these systems may discriminate against the groups who are often the targets of the abuse we are trying to detect.

1 Introduction

Recent work has shown evidence of substantial bias in machine learning systems, which is typically a result of bias in the training data. This includes both supervised (Blodgett and O'Connor, 2017; Tatman, 2017; Kiritchenko and Mohammad, 2018; De-Arteaga et al., 2019) and unsupervised natural language processing systems (Bolukbasi et al., 2016; Caliskan et al., 2017; Garg et al., 2018). Machine learning models are currently being deployed in the field to detect hate speech and abusive language on social media platforms including Facebook, Instagram, and Youtube. The aim of these models is to identify abusive language that directly targets certain individuals or groups, particularly people belonging to protected categories (Waseem et al., 2017). Bias may reduce the accuracy of these models, and at worst, will mean that the models actively discriminate against the same groups they are designed to protect.

Our study focuses on racial bias in hate speech and abusive language detection datasets (Waseem, 2016; Waseem and Hovy, 2016; Davidson et al., 2017; Golbeck et al., 2017; Founta et al., 2018), all of which use data collected from Twitter. We train classifiers using each of the datasets and use a corpus of tweets with demographic information to compare how each classifier performs on tweets written in African-American English (AAE) versus Standard American English (SAE) (Blodgett et al., 2016). We use bootstrap sampling (Efron and Tibshirani, 1986) to estimate the proportion of tweets in each group that each classifier assigns to each class. We find evidence of systematic racial biases across all of the classifiers, with AAE tweets predicted as belonging to negative classes like hate speech or harassment significantly more frequently than SAE tweets. In most cases the bias decreases in magnitude when we condition on particular keywords which may indicate membership in negative classes, yet it still persists. We expect that these biases will result in racial discrimination if classifiers trained on any of these datasets are deployed in the field.

2 Related works

Scholars and practitioners have recently been devoting more attention to bias in machine learning models, particularly as these models are becoming involved in more and more consequential decisions (Athey, 2017). Bias often derives from the data used to train these models. For example, Buolamwini and Gebru (2018) show how facial recognition technologies perform worse for darker-skinned people, particularly darker-skinned women, due to the disproportionate presence of white, male faces in the training

25

Proceedings of the Third Workshop on Abusive Language Online, pages 25–35
Florence, Italy, August 1, 2019. ©2019 Association for Computational Linguistics

data. Natural language processing systems also inherit biases from the data they were trained on. For example, in unsupervised learning, word embeddings often contain biases (Bolukbasi et al., 2016; Caliskan et al., 2017; Garg et al., 2018) which persist even after attempts to remove them (Gonen and Goldberg, 2019). There are many examples of bias in supervised learning contexts: YouTube's captioning models make more errors when transcribing women (Tatman, 2017), AAE is more likely to be misclassified as non-English by widely used language classifiers (Blodgett and O'Connor, 2017), numerous gender and racial biases exist in sentiment classification systems (Kiritchenko and Mohammad, 2018), and errors in both co-reference resolution systems and occupational classification models reflect gendered occupational patterns (Zhao et al., 2018; De-Arteaga et al., 2019).

While hate speech and abusive language detection has become an important area for natural language processing research (Schmidt and Wiegand, 2017; Waseem et al., 2017; Fortuna and Nunes, 2018), there has been little work addressing the potential for these systems to be biased. The danger posed by bias in such systems is, however, particularly acute, since it could result in negative impacts on the same populations the systems are designed to protect. For example, if we mistakenly consider speech by a targeted minority group as abusive we might unfairly penalize the victim, but if we fail to identify abuse against them we will be unable to take action against the perpetrator. Although no model can perfectly avoid such problems, we should be particularly concerned about the potential for such models to be *systematically* biased against certain social groups, particularly protected classes.

A number of studies have shown that false positive cases of hate speech are associated with the presence of terms related to race, gender, and sexuality (Kwok and Wang, 2013; Burnap and Williams, 2015; Davidson et al., 2017). While not directly measuring bias, prior work has explored how annotation schemes (Davidson et al., 2017) and the identity of the annotators (Waseem, 2016) might be manipulated to help to avoid bias. Dixon et al. (2018) directly measured biases in the Google Perspective API classifier,[1] trained on data from Wikipedia talk comments, finding that

it tended to give high toxicity scores to innocuous statements like "I am a gay man". They called this "false positive bias", caused by the model overgeneralizing from the training data, in this case from examples where "gay" was used pejoratively. They find that a number of such "identity terms" are disproportionately represented in the examples labeled as toxic. Park et al. (2018) build upon this study, using templates to study gender differences in performance across two hate speech and abusive language detection datasets. They find that classifiers trained on these data tend to perform worse when female identity terms used, indicating gender bias in performance. Wiegand et al. (2019) identify more general biases due to the sampling procedures used to collect training data, resulting in classifiers associating innocuous topics like sports with abusive language. We build upon this work by auditing a series of abusive language and hate speech detection datasets for racial biases. We evaluate how classification models trained on these datasets perform in the field, comparing their predictions for tweets written in language used by whites or African-Americans.

3 Research design

3.1 Hate speech and abusive language datasets

We focus on Twitter, the most widely used data source in abusive language research. We use all available datasets where tweets are labeled as various types of abuse and are written in English. We now briefly describe each of these datasets in chronological order.

Waseem and Hovy (2016) collected 130k tweets containing one of seventeen different terms or phrases they considered to be hateful. They then annotated a sample of these tweets themselves, using guidelines inspired by critical race theory. These annotators were then reviewed by "a 25 year old woman studying gender studies and a nonactivist feminist" to check for bias. This dataset consists of 16,849 tweets labeled as either racism, sexism, or neither. Most of the tweets categorized as sexist relate to debates over an Australian TV show and most of those considered as racist are anti-Muslim.

To account for potential bias in the previous dataset, Waseem (2016) relabeled 2876 tweets in the dataset, along with a new sample from the tweets originally collected. The tweets were anno-

---

[1] https://www.perspectiveapi.com

tated by "feminist and anti-racism activists", based upon the assumption that they are domain-experts. A fourth category, racism *and* sexism was also added to account for the presence of tweets which exhibit both types of abuse. The dataset contains 6,909 tweets.

Davidson et al. (2017) collected tweets containing terms from the Hatebase,[2] a crowdsourced hate speech lexicon, then had a sample coded by crowdworkers located in the United States. To avoid false positives that occurred in prior work which considered all uses of particular terms as hate speech, crowdworkers were instructed not to make their decisions based upon any words or phrases in particular, no matter how offensive, but on the overall tweet and the inferred context. The dataset consists of 24,783 tweets annotated as hate speech, offensive language, or neither.

Golbeck et al. (2017) selected tweets using ten keywords and phrases related to anti-black racism, Islamophobia, homophobia, anti-semitism, and sexism. The authors developed a coding scheme to distinguish between potentially offensive content and serious harassment, such as threats or hate speech. After an initial round of coding, where tweets were assigned to a number of different categories, they simplified their analysis to include a binary harassment or non-harassment label for each tweet. The dataset consists of 20,360 tweets, each hand-labeled by the authors.[3]

Founta et al. (2018) constructed a dataset intended to better approximate a real-world setting where abuse is relatively rare. They began with a random sample of tweets then augmented it by adding tweets containing one or more terms from the Hatebase lexicon and that had negative sentiment. They criticized prior work for defining labels in an ad hoc manner. To develop a more comprehensive annotation scheme they initially labeled a sample of tweets, allowing each tweet to belong to multiple classes. After analyzing the overlap between different classes they settled on a coding scheme with four distinct classes: abusive, hateful, spam, and normal. We use a dataset they published containing 91,951 tweets coded into these categories by crowdworkers.[4]

---

[2] https://hatebase.org/

[3] The paper describes 35k tweets but there were many duplicates in this dataset which were removed from the dataset the authors made available.

[4] They describe 80k tweets in the paper but more tweets were added to the dataset released by the authors. Some of the tweets in this dataset are duplicates: if all versions of a

Dataset	Class	Precision	Recall	F1
W. & H.	Racism	0.73	0.79	0.76
	Sexism	0.69	0.73	0.71
	Neither	0.88	0.85	0.86
W.	Racism	0.56	0.77	0.65
	Sexism	0.62	0.73	0.67
	R. & S.	0.56	0.62	0.59
	Neither	0.95	0.92	0.94
D. et al.	Hate	0.32	0.53	0.4
	Offensive	0.96	0.88	0.92
	Neither	0.81	0.95	0.87
G. et al.	Harass.	0.41	0.19	0.26
	Non.	0.75	0.9	0.82
F. et al.	Hate	0.33	0.42	0.37
	Abusive	0.87	0.88	0.88
	Spam	0.5	0.7	0.58
	Neither	0.88	0.77	0.82

Table 1: **Classifier performance**

3.2 Training classifiers

For each dataset we train a classifier to predict the class of unseen tweets. We use regularized logistic regression with bag-of-words features, a commonly used approach in the field. While we expect that we could improve predictive performance by using more sophisticated classifiers, we expect that any bias is likely a function of the training data itself rather than the classifier. Moreover, although features like word embeddings can work well for this task (Djuric et al., 2015) we wanted to avoid inducing any bias in our models by using pre-trained embeddings (Park et al., 2018).

We pre-process each tweet by removing excess white-space and replacing URLs and mentions with placeholders. We then tokenize them, stem each token, and construct n-grams with a maximum length of three. Next we transform each dataset into a TF-IDF matrix, with a maximum of 10,000 features. We use 80% of each dataset to train models and hold out the remainder for validation. Each model is trained using stratified 5-fold cross-validation. We conduct a grid-search over different regularization strength parameters to identify the best performing model. Finally, for each dataset we identify the model with the best average F1 score and retrain it using all of the training data. The performance of these models on the 20% held-out validation data is reported in Table 1. Overall we see varying performance across the classifiers, with some performing much better out-of-sample than others. In particular, we see that hate speech and harassment are particu-

---

duplicated tweet were coded in the same way by the majority of coders we retained one copy and deleted the rest; if the labels disagreed we removed all copies.

larly difficult to detect. Since we are primarily interested in *within classifier, between corpora* performance, any variation between classifiers should not impact our results.

3.3 Race dataset

We use a dataset of tweets labeled by race from Blodgett et al. (2016) to measure racial biases in these classifiers. They collected geolocated tweets in the U.S. and matched them with demographic data from the Census on the population of non-Hispanic whites, non-Hispanic blacks, Hispanics, and Asians in the block group where the tweets originated. They then identified words associated with particular demographics and trained a probabilistic mixed-membership language model. This model learns demographically-aligned language models for each of the four demographic categories and is used to calculate the posterior proportion of language from each category in each tweet. Their validation analyses indicate that tweets with a high posterior proportion of non-Hispanic black language exhibit lexical, phonological, and syntactic variation consistent with prior research on AAE. Their publicly-available dataset contains 59.2 million tweets.

We define a *user* as likely non-Hispanic black if the average posterior proportion across all of their tweets for the non-Hispanic black language model is ≥ 0.80 (and ≤ 0.10 Hispanic and Asian combined) and as non-Hispanic white using the same formula but for the white language model.[5] This allows us to restrict our analysis to tweets written by users who predominantly use one of the language models. Due to space constraints we discard users who predominantly use either the Hispanic or the Asian language model. This results in a set of 1.1m tweets written by people who generally use non-Hispanic black language and 14.5m tweets written by users who tend to use non-Hispanic white language. Following Blodgett and O'Connor (2017), we call these datasets *black-aligned* and *white-aligned* tweets, reflecting the fact that they contain language associated with either demographic category but which may not all

---

[5]We use this threshold following Blodgett and O'Connor (2017) and after consulting with the lead author. While these cut-offs should provide high confidence that the users tend to use AAE or SAE, and hence serve as a proxy for race, it is important to note that not all African-Americans use AAE and that not all AAE users are African-American, although use of the AAE dialect suggests a social proximity to or affinity for African-American communities (Blodgett et al., 2016)

be produced by members of these categories. We now describe how we use these data in our experiments.

3.4 Experiments

We examine whether the probability that a tweet is predicted to belong to a particular class varies in relation to the racial alignment of the language it uses. The null hypothesis of no racial bias is that the probability a tweet will belong to a negative class is independent of the racial group the tweet's author is a member of. Formally, for class c_i, where $c_i = 1$ denotes membership in the class and $c_i = 0$ the opposite, we aim to test $H_N : P(c_i = 1|black) = P(c_i = 1|white)$. If $P(c_i = 1|black) > P(c_i = 1|white)$ and the difference is statistically significant then we can reject the null hypothesis H_N in favor of the alternative hypothesis H_A that black-aligned tweets are classified into c_i at a higher rate than white-aligned tweets. Conversely, if $P(c_i = 1|black) < P(c_i = 1|white)$ we can conclude that the classifier is more likely to classify white-aligned tweets as c_i. We should expect that white-aligned tweets are more likely to use racist language or hate speech than black-aligned tweets, given that African-Americans are often targeted with racism and hate speech by whites. However for some classes like sexism we have no reason to expect there to be racial differences in either direction.

To test this hypothesis we use bootstrap sampling (Efron and Tibshirani, 1986) to estimate the proportion of tweets in each dataset that each classifier predicts to belong to each class. We draw n random samples with replacement of k tweets from each of the two race corpora, where $n = k = 1000$. For each sample we use each classifier to predict the class membership of each tweet, then store the proportion of tweets that were assigned to each class, p_i. For each classifier-class pair, we thus obtain a pair of vectors, one for each corpus, each containing n sampled proportions. The bootstrap estimates for the proportion of tweets belonging to class i for each group, $\widehat{p_{i_{black}}}$ and $\widehat{p_{i_{white}}}$, are calculated by taking the mean of the elements in each vector: $\frac{1}{n}\sum_{j=1}^{n} p_{ij}$. We then use a t-test to test whether $\widehat{p_{i_{black}}} = \widehat{p_{i_{white}}}$. We also calculate the ratio $\frac{\widehat{p_{i_{black}}}}{\widehat{p_{i_{white}}}}$, which shows the magnitude of any difference. Values greater than 1 indicate that black-aligned tweets are classified as belonging to class i at a higher rate than white-

Dataset	Class	$\widehat{p_{i_{black}}}$	$\widehat{p_{i_{white}}}$	t	p	$\widehat{\dfrac{p_{i_{black}}}{p_{i_{white}}}}$
Waseem and Hovy	Racism	0.001	0.003	-20.818	***	0.505
	Sexism	0.083	0.048	101.636	***	1.724
Waseem	Racism	0.001	0.001	0.035		1.001
	Sexism	0.023	0.012	64.418	***	1.993
	Racism and sexism	0.002	0.001	4.047	***	1.120
Davidson et al.	Hate	0.049	0.019	120.986	***	2.573
	Offensive	0.173	0.065	243.285	***	2.653
Golbeck et al.	Harassment	0.032	0.023	39.483	***	1.396
Founta et al.	Hate	0.111	0.061	122.707	***	1.812
	Abusive	0.178	0.080	211.319	***	2.239
	Spam	0.028	0.015	63.131	***	1.854

Table 2: **Experiment 1**

We focus on the "negative" classes so other classes have been omitted. Stars indicate level of statistical significance. $*** = p < 0.001$. No stars indicates $p > 0.05$.

aligned tweets.

We also conduct a second experiment, where we assess whether there is racial bias conditional upon a tweet containing a keyword likely to be associated with a negative class. While differences in language will undoubtedly remain, this should help to account for the possibility that results in Experiment 1 are driven by differences in the true distribution of the different classes of interest, or of words associated with these classes, in the two corpora. For classifier c and category i, we evaluate $H_N : P(c_i = 1|black, t) = P(c_i = 1|white, t)$ for a given term t. We conduct this experiment for two different terms, each of which occurs frequently enough in the data to enable our bootstrapping approach. We select the term "n*gga", since it is a particularly prevalent source of false positives for hate speech detection (Kwok and Wang, 2013; Davidson et al., 2017; Waseem et al., 2018).[6] In this case, we expect that tweets containing the word should be classified as more negative when used by whites, thus $H_{A_1} : P(c_i = 1|black, t) < P(c_i = 1|white, t)$. The other alternative, $H_{A_2} : P(c_i = 1|black, t) > P(c_i = 1|white, t)$ would indicate that black-aligned tweets containing the term are penalized at a higher rate than comparable white-aligned tweets. We also assess the results for the word "b*tch" since it is a widely used sexist term, which is often also used casually, but we have no theoretical reason to expect there to be racial dif-

ferences in its usage. The term "n*gga" was used in around 2.25% of black-aligned and 0.15% of white-aligned tweets. The term "b*tch" was used in 1.7% of black-aligned and 0.5% of white-aligned tweets. The substantial differences in the distributions for these two terms alone are consistent with our intuition that some of the results in Experiment 1 may be driven by differences in the frequencies of words associated with negative classes in the training datasets. Since we are using a subsample of the available data, we use smaller bootstrap samples, drawing $k = 100$ tweets each time.

4 Results

The results of Experiment 1 are shown in Table 2. We observe substantial racial disparities in the performance of *all classifiers*. In all but one of the comparisons, there are statistically significant ($p < 0.001$) differences and in all but one of these we see that tweets in the black-aligned corpus are assigned negative labels more frequently than those by whites. The only case where black-aligned tweets are classified into a negative class less frequently than white-aligned tweets is the racism class in the Waseem and Hovy (2016) classifier. Note, however, the extremely low rate at which tweets are predicted to belong to this class for both groups. On the other hand, this classifier is 1.7 times more likely to classify tweets in the black-aligned corpus as sexist. For Waseem (2016) we see that there is no significant difference in the estimated rates at which tweets are classified as racist across groups, although the rates remain low. Tweets in the black-aligned corpus

---

[6] We also planned to conduct the same analysis using the "-er" suffix, however the sample was too small, with the word being used in 555 tweets in the white-aligned corpus (0.004%) and 61 in the black-aligned corpus (0.005%).

are classified as containing sexism almost twice as frequently and 1.1 times as frequently classified as containing racism and sexism compared to those in the white-aligned corpus. Moving onto Davidson et al. (2017), we find large disparities, with around 5% of tweets in the black-aligned corpus classified as hate speech compared to 2% of those in the white-aligned set. Similarly, 17% of black-aligned tweets are predicted to contain offensive language compared to 6.5% of white-aligned tweets. The classifier trained on the Golbeck et al. (2017) dataset predicts black-aligned tweets to be harassment 1.4 times as frequently as white-aligned tweets. The Founta et al. (2018) classifier labels around 11% of tweets in the black-aligned corpus as hate speech and almost 18% as abusive, compared to 6% and 8% of white-aligned tweets respectively. It also classifies black-aligned tweets as spam 1.8 times as frequently.

The results of Experiment 2 are consistent with the previous results, although there are some notable differences. In most cases the racial disparities persist, although they are generally smaller in magnitude and in some cases the direction even changes. Table 3 shows that for tweets containing the word "n*gga", classifiers trained on Waseem and Hovy (2016) and Waseem (2016) are both predict black-aligned tweets to be instances of sexism approximately 1.5 times as often as white-aligned tweets. The classifier trained on the Davidson et al. (2017) data is significantly *less* likely to classify black-aligned tweets as hate speech, although it is more likely to classify them as offensive. Golbeck et al. (2017) classifies black-aligned tweets as harassment at a higher rate for both groups than in the previous experiment, although the disparity is narrower. For the Founta et al. (2018) classifier we see that black-aligned tweets are slightly *less* frequently considered to be hate speech but are much more frequently classified as abusive.

The results for the second variation of Experiment 2 where we conditioned on the word "b*tch" are shown in Table 4. We see similar results for Waseem and Hovy (2016) and Waseem (2016). In both cases the classifiers trained upon their data are still more likely to flag black-aligned tweets as sexism. The Waseem and Hovy (2016) classifier is particularly sensitive to the word "b*tch" with 96% of black-aligned and 94% of white-aligned tweets predicted to belong to this class. For Davidson et al. (2017) almost all of these tweets are

classified as offensive, however those in the black-aligned corpus are 1.15 times as frequently classified as hate speech. We see a very similar result for Golbeck et al. (2017) compared to the previous experiment, with black-aligned tweets flagged as harassment at 1.1 times the rate of those in the white-aligned corpus. Finally, for the Founta et al. (2018) classifier we see a substantial racial disparity, with black-aligned tweets classified as hate speech at 2.7 times the rate of white aligned ones, a higher rate than in Experiment 1.

5 Discussion

Our results demonstrate consistent, systematic and substantial racial biases in classifiers trained on all five datasets. In almost every case, black-aligned tweets are classified as sexism, hate speech, harassment, and abuse at higher rates than white-aligned tweets. To some extent, the results in the first experiment may be driven by underlying differences in the rates at which speakers of different dialects use particular words and phrases associated with these negative classes in the training data. For example, the word "n*gga" appears fifteen times as frequently in the black-aligned corpus compared to the white-aligned corpus.[7] However, the second experiment shows that these disparities tend to persist even when comparing tweets containing keywords likely to be associated with negative classes. While some of the remaining disparities are likely due to differences in the distributions of other keywords we did not condition on, we expect that other more innocuous aspects of black-aligned language may be associated with negative labels in the training data, leading classifiers to disproportionately predict that tweets by African-Americans belong to negative classes. We now discuss the results as they pertain to each of the datasets used.

Classifiers trained on data from Waseem and Hovy (2016) and Waseem (2016) only predicted a small fraction of the tweets to be racism. We suspect that this is due to the composition of their dataset, since the majority of the racist training examples consist of anti-Muslim rather than anti-black language. Across both datasets the words "n*gger" and "n*gga" appear in 4 and 10 tweets

---

[7] It is also possible that these disparities are amplified by the Blodgett et al. (2016) model, which constructs the posterior proportions of different language models in part by exploiting underlying differences in word frequencies associated with the different demographic categories.

Dataset	Class	$\widehat{p_{i_{black}}}$	$\widehat{p_{i_{white}}}$	t	p	$\widehat{\dfrac{p_{i_{black}}}{p_{i_{white}}}}$
Waseem and Hovy	Racism	0.010	0.011	-1.462		0.960
	Sexism	0.147	0.100	31.932	***	1.479
Waseem	Racism	0.010	0.010	0.565		1.027
	Sexism	0.040	0.026	18.569	***	1.554
	Racism and sexism	0.011	0.010	0.835		1.026
Davidson et al.	Hate	0.578	0.645	-31.248	***	0.896
	Offensive	0.418	0.347	32.895	***	1.202
Golbeck et al.	Harassment	0.085	0.078	5.984	***	1.096
Founta et al.	Hate	0.912	0.930	-15.037	***	0.980
	Abusive	0.086	0.067	16.131	***	1.296
	Spam	0.010	0.010	-1.593		1.000

Table 3: **Experiment 2, $t =$ "n*gga"**

Dataset	Class	$\widehat{p_{i_{black}}}$	$\widehat{p_{i_{white}}}$	t	p	$\widehat{\dfrac{p_{i_{black}}}{p_{i_{white}}}}$
Waseem and Hovy	Racism	0.010	0.010	-0.632		0.978
	Sexism	0.963	0.944	20.064	***	1.020
Waseem	Racism	0.011	0.011	-1.254		0.955
	Sexism	0.349	0.290	28.803	***	1.203
	Racism and sexism	0.012	0.012	-0.162		0.995
Davidson et al.	Hate	0.017	0.015	4.698	***	1.152
	Offensive	0.988	0.991	-6.289	***	0.997
Golbeck et al.	Harassment	0.099	0.091	6.273	***	1.091
Founta et al.	Hate	0.074	0.027	46.054	***	2.728
	Abusive	0.925	0.968	-41.396	***	0.956
	Spam	0.010	0.010	0.000		1.000

Table 4: **Experiment 2, $t =$ "b*tch"**

respectively. Looking at the sexism class on the other hand, we see that both models were consistently classifying tweets in the black-aligned corpus as sexism at a substantially higher rate than those in the white-aligned corpus. Given this result, and the gender biases identified in these data by Park et al. (2018), it not apparent that the purportedly expert annotators were any less biased than amateur annotators (Waseem, 2016).

The classifier trained on Davidson et al. (2017) shows the largest disparities in Experiment 1, with tweets in the black-aligned corpus classified as hate speech and offensive language at substantially higher rates than white-aligned tweets. We expect that this result occurred for two reasons. First, the dataset contains a large number of cases where AAE is used (Waseem et al., 2018). Second, many of the AAE tweets also use words like "n*gga" and "b*tch", and are thus frequently associated with the hate speech and offensive classes, resulting in "false positive bias" (Dixon et al., 2018). On the other hand, the distinction be-

tween hate speech and offensive language appears to hold up to scrutiny: while a large proportion of tweets in Experiment 2 containing the word "n*gga" are classified as hate speech, the rate is substantially higher for white-aligned tweets. Without this category we expect that many of the tweets classified as offensive would instead be mistakenly classified as hate speech.

Turning to the Golbeck et al. (2017) classifer we found that tweets in the black-aligned dataset were significantly more likely to be classified as harassment in all experiments, although the disparity decreased substantially after conditioning on certain keywords. It seems likely that their simple binary labelling scheme may not be sufficient to capture the variation in language used, resulting in high rates of false positives.

Finally, Founta et al. (2018) is the largest and perhaps the most comprehensive of the available datasets. In Experiment 1 we see that this classifier has the second highest rates of racial disparities, classifying black-aligned tweets as hate speech, abusive, and spam at substantially higher rates than white-aligned tweets. In Experiment 2 the classifier is slightly less likely to classify black-aligned tweets containing the word "n*gga" as hate speech but is 2.7 times more likely to predict that black-aligned tweets using "b*tch" belong to this category.

6 Conclusion

Our study is the first to measure racial bias in hate speech and abusive language detection datasets. We find evidence of substantial racial bias in all of the datasets tested. This bias tends to persist even when comparing tweets containing certain relevant keywords. While these datasets are still valuable for academic research, we caution against using them in the field to detect and particularly to take enforcement action against different types of abusive language. If they are used in this way we expect that they will *systematically* penalize African-Americans more than whites, resulting in racial discrimination. We have not evaluated these datasets for bias related to other ethnic and racial groups, nor other protected categories like gender and sexuality, but expect that such bias is also likely to exist. We recommend that efforts to measure and mitigate bias should start by focusing on how bias enters into datasets as they are collected and labeled. In particular, future work should focus on the following three areas.

First, some biases emerge at the point of data collection (Wiegand et al., 2019). Some studies sampled tweets using small, ad hoc sets of keywords created by the authors (Waseem and Hovy, 2016; Waseem, 2016; Golbeck et al., 2017), an approach demonstrated to produce poor results (King et al., 2017). Others start with large crowd-sourced dictionaries of keywords, which tend to include many irrelevant terms, resulting in high rates of false positives (Davidson et al., 2017; Founta et al., 2018). In both cases, by using keywords to identify relevant tweets we are likely to get non-representative samples of training data that may over- or under-represent certain communities. In particular, we need to consider whether the linguistic markers we use to identify *potentially* abusive language may be associated with language used by members of protected categories. For example, although Davidson et al. (2017) started with thousands of terms from the Hatebase lexicon, AAE is over-represented in

the dataset (Waseem et al., 2018) because some keywords associated with this speech community were used more frequently on Twitter than other keywords in the lexicon and were consequentially over-sampled.

Second, we expect that the people who annotate data have their own biases. Since individual biases in reflect societal prejudices, they aggregate into systematic biases in training data. The datasets considered here relied upon a range of different annotators, from the authors (Golbeck et al., 2017; Waseem and Hovy, 2016) and crowdworkers (Davidson et al., 2017; Founta et al., 2018) to activists (Waseem, 2016). Even the classifier trained on expert-labeled data (Waseem, 2016) flags black-aligned tweets as sexist at almost twice the rate of white-aligned tweets. While we agree that there is value in working with domain-experts to annotate data, these results suggest that activists may be prone to similar biases as academics and crowdworkers. Further work is therefore necessary to better understand how to integrate expertise into the process and how training can be used to help to mitigate bias. We also need to consider how sociocultural context influences annotators' decisions. For example, 48% of the workers employed by Founta et al. (2018) were located in Venezuela but the authors did not consider whether this affected their results (or if the annotators understood English sufficiently for the task).

Third, we observed substantial variation in the rates of class membership across classifiers and datasets. In Experiment 1 the rate at which tweets were assigned to negative classes varied from 1% to 18%. Some of the low proportions may indicate a preponderance of false negatives due to a lack of training data, suggesting that these models may not be able to sufficiently generalize beyond the data they were trained on. The high proportions may signal too many false positives, which may a result of the over-sampling of abusive language in labeled datasets. Founta et al. (2018) claim that, on average, between 0.1% and 3% of tweets are abusive, depending upon the category of abuse. Identifying such content is therefore a highly imbalanced classification problem. When labeling datasets and evaluating our models we must pay more attention to the baseline rates of usage of different types of abusive language and how they may vary across populations (Silva et al., 2016).

Finally, we need to more carefully consider

how contextual factors interact with linguistic subtleties and our definitions of abuse. The "n-word" is a particularly useful illustration of this issue. It exhibits polysemy, as it can be extremely racist or quotidian, depending on the speaker, the context, and the spelling. While the history of the word and its usages is too complex to be summarized here (Neal, 2013), when used with the "-er" suffix it is generally considered to be a racist ephiphet, associated with white supremacy. Prior work has confirmed that the use of this variant online is generally considered to be hateful (Kwok and Wang, 2013), although not always the case, for example when a victim of abuse shares an insult they have received. However the variant with the "-a" suffix is typically used innocuously by African-Americans (Kwok and Wang, 2013), indeed our results indicate that it is used far more frequently in black-aligned tweets (although it is still used by many white people).[8] Despite this distinction, some studies have considered this variant to be hateful (Silva et al., 2016; Alorainy et al., 2018). This approach results in high rates of false positive cases of hate speech, thus Davidson et al. (2017) included a class for offensive language which does not appear to be hateful and let annotators decide which class tweets belonged to based upon their interpretation of the context, many of whom labeled tweets containing the term as offensive. Waseem et al. (2018) criticized this decision, claiming that it is problematic to ever consider the word to be offensive due to its widespread use among AAE speakers. This critique appears to be reasonable in the sense that we should not penalize African-Americans for using the word, but it avoids grappling with how to act when the word is used by other speakers and in other contexts. What should be done if it is used by a white social media user in reference to a black user? How should the context of their interaction and the nature of their relationship affect our decision?

A "one-size-fits-all", context-independent approach to defining and detecting abusive language is clearly inappropriate. Different communities have different speech norms, such that a model suitable for one community may discriminate against another. However there is no consensus in the field on how and if we can develop detection systems sensitive to different social and cultural contexts. In addition to our recommendations for improving training data, we emphasize the necessity of considering how context matters and how detection systems will have uneven effects across different communities.

7 Limitations

First, while the Blodgett et al. (2016) dataset is the best available source of tweets labeled as AAE, we do not have ground truth labels for the racial identities of the authors. By filtering on users who predominantly used one type of language we may also miss users who may frequently code-switch between AAE and SAE. Second, although we roughly approximate this in Experiment 2, we cannot rule out the possibility that the results, rather than evidence of bias, are a function of different distributions of negative classes in the corpora studied. It is possible that words associated with negative categories in our abusive language datasets are also used to predict race by Blodgett et al. (2016), potentially contributing to the observed disparities. To more thoroughly investigate this issue we therefore require ground truth labels for abuse *and* race. Third, the results may vary for different classifiers or feature sets. It is possible that more sophisticated modeling approaches could enable us to alleviate bias, although they could also exacerbate it. Fourth, we did not interpret the results of the classifiers to determine why they made particular predictions. Further work is needed to identify what features of AAE the classifiers are learning to associate with negative classes. Finally, this study has only focused on one dimension of racial bias. Further work is necessary to assess the degree to investigate the extent to which data and models are biased against people belonging to other protected categories.

Acknowledgments

We would like to thank Jonathan Chang, Emily Parker, Ben Rosche, and the four anonymous reviewers for their comments and suggestions. We also thank the authors of the datasets used for making their data available, particularly Su Lin Blodgett, Antigoni Founta, Jennifer Golbeck, and Zeerak Waseem, who diligently responded to our queries.

---

[8]This spelling also exhibits derhotacization, a phonological feature of AAE (Blodgett et al., 2016).

References

Wafa Alorainy, Pete Burnap, Han Liu, Amir Javed, and Matthew L. Williams. 2018. Suspended Accounts: A Source of Tweets with Disgust and Anger Emotions for Augmenting Hate Speech Data Sample. In *2018 International Conference on Machine Learning and Cybernetics (ICMLC)*, pages 581–586, Chengdu. IEEE.

Susan Athey. 2017. Beyond prediction: Using big data for policy problems. *Science*, 355(6324):483–485.

Su Lin Blodgett, Lisa Green, and Brendan O'Connor. 2016. Demographic Dialectal Variation in Social Media: A Case Study of African-American English. In *Proceedings of the 2016 Conference on Empirical Methods in Natural Language Processing*, pages 1119–1130, Austin, Texas. Association for Computational Linguistics.

Su Lin Blodgett and Brendan O'Connor. 2017. Racial disparity in natural language processing: A case study of social media african-american english. In *Fairness, Accountability, and Transparency in Machine Learning (FAT/ML) workshop*.

Tolga Bolukbasi, Kai-Wei Chang, James Y Zou, Venkatesh Saligrama, and Adam T Kalai. 2016. Man is to Computer Programmer as Woman is to Homemaker? Debiasing Word Embeddings. In *30th Conference on Neural Information Processing Systems*, page 9, Barcelona, Spain.

Joy Buolamwini and Timnit Gebru. 2018. Gender Shades: Intersectional Accuracy Disparities in Commercial Gender Classication. In *Proceedings of Machine Learning Research*, volume 81, pages 1–15.

Pete Burnap and Matthew L. Williams. 2015. Cyber hate speech on twitter: An application of machine classification and statistical modeling for policy and decision making. *Policy & Internet*, 7(2):223–242.

Aylin Caliskan, Joanna J. Bryson, and Arvind Narayanan. 2017. Semantics derived automatically from language corpora contain human-like biases. *Science*, 356(6334):183–186.

Thomas Davidson, Dana Warmsley, Michael Macy, and Ingmar Weber. 2017. Automated Hate Speech Detection and the Problem of Offensive Language. In *Proceedings of the 11th International Conference on Web and Social Media (ICWSM)*, pages 512–515, Montreal, Quebec, Canada.

Maria De-Arteaga, Alexey Romanov, Hanna Wallach, Jennifer Chayes, Christian Borgs, Alexandra Chouldechova, Sahin Geyik, Krishnaram Kenthapadi, and Adam Tauman Kalai. 2019. Bias in Bios: A Case Study of Semantic Representation Bias in a High-Stakes Setting. In *Proceedings of the Conference on Fairness, Accountability, and Transparency - FAT* '19*, pages 120–128, Atlanta, GA, USA. ACM Press.

Lucas Dixon, John Li, Jeffrey Sorensen, Nithum Thain, and Lucy Vasserman. 2018. Measuring and Mitigating Unintended Bias in Text Classification. In *Proceedings of the 2018 AAAI/ACM Conference on AI, Ethics, and Society - AIES '18*, pages 67–73, New Orleans, LA, USA. ACM Press.

Nemanja Djuric, Jing Zhou, Robin Morris, Mihajlo Grbovic, Vladan Radosavljevic, and Narayan Bhamidipati. 2015. Hate Speech Detection with Comment Embeddings. In *WWW 2015 Companion*, pages 29–30. ACM Press.

Bradley Efron and Robert Tibshirani. 1986. Bootstrap methods for standard errors, confidence intervals, and other measures of statistical accuracy. *Statistical Science*, 1(1):54–75.

Paula Fortuna and Srgio Nunes. 2018. A Survey on Automatic Detection of Hate Speech in Text. *ACM Computing Surveys*, 51(4):1–30.

Antigoni-Maria Founta, Constantinos Djouvas, Despoina Chatzakou, Ilias Leontiadis, Jeremy Blackburn, Gianluca Stringhini, Athena Vakali, Michael Sirivianos, and Nicolas Kourtellis. 2018. Large Scale Crowdsourcing and Characterization of Twitter Abusive Behavior. In *Proceedings of the Twelfth International AAAI Conference on Web and Social Media*, pages 491–500, Palo Alto, California, USA.

Nikhil Garg, Londa Schiebinger, Dan Jurafsky, and James Zou. 2018. Word embeddings quantify 100 years of gender and ethnic stereotypes. *Proceedings of the National Academy of Sciences*, 115(16):E3635–E3644.

Jennifer Golbeck, Rajesh Kumar Gnanasekaran, Raja Rajan Gunasekaran, Kelly M. Hoffman, Jenny Hottle, Vichita Jienjitlert, Shivika Khare, Ryan Lau, Marianna J. Martindale, Shalmali Naik, Heather L. Nixon, Zahra Ashktorab, Piyush Ramachandran, Kristine M. Rogers, Lisa Rogers, Meghna Sardana Sarin, Gaurav Shahane, Jayanee Thanki, Priyanka Vengataraman, Zijian Wan, Derek Michael Wu, Rashad O. Banjo, Alexandra Berlinger, Siddharth Bhagwan, Cody Buntain, Paul Cheakalos, Alicia A. Geller, and Quint Gergory. 2017. A Large Labeled Corpus for Online Harassment Research. In *Proceedings of the 2017 ACM on Web Science Conference - WebSci '17*, pages 229–233, Troy, New York, USA. ACM Press.

Hila Gonen and Yoav Goldberg. 2019. Lipstick on a Pig: Debiasing Methods Cover up Systematic Gender Biases in Word Embeddings But do not Remove Them. In *NAACL*. ArXiv: 1903.03862.

Gary King, Patrick Lam, and Margaret E. Roberts. 2017. Computer-Assisted Keyword and Document Set Discovery from Unstructured Text. *American Journal of Political Science*, 61(4):971–988.

Svetlana Kiritchenko and Saif M. Mohammad. 2018. Examining gender and race bias in two hundred sentiment analysis systems. In *Proceedings of the 7th*

*Joint Conference on Lexical and Computational Semantics (*SEM)*, pages 42–53, New Orleans, LA, USA. Association for Computational Linguistics.

Irene Kwok and Yuzhou Wang. 2013. Locate the Hate: Detecting Tweets against Blacks. In *Association for the Advancement of Artificial Intelligence*.

Mark Anthony Neal. 2013. NIGGA: The 21st-Century Theoretical Superhero: NIGGA. *Cultural Anthropology*, 28(3):556–563.

Ji Ho Park, Jamin Shin, and Pascale Fung. 2018. Reducing Gender Bias in Abusive Language Detection. In *Proceedings of the 2018 Conference on Empirical Methods in Natural Language Processing*, pages 2799–2804, Brussels, Belgium. ArXiv: 1808.07231.

Anna Schmidt and Michael Wiegand. 2017. A Survey on Hate Speech Detection using Natural Language Processing. In *Proceedings of the Fifth International Workshop on Natural Language Processing for Social Media*, pages 1–10, Valencia, Spain.

Leandro Silva, Mainack Mondal, Denzil Correa, Fabrcio Benevenuto, and Ingmar Weber. 2016. Analyzing the Targets of Hate in Online Social Media. In *Association for the Advancement of Artificial Intelligence*.

Rachael Tatman. 2017. Gender and Dialect Bias in YouTube's Automatic Captions. In *Proceedings of the First ACL Workshop on Ethics in Natural Language Processing*, pages 53–59, Valencia, Spain. Association for Computational Linguistics.

Zeerak Waseem. 2016. Are you a racist or am I seeing things? Annotator influence on hate speech detection on Twitter. In *Proceedings of the 1st Workshop on Natural Language Processing and Computational Social Science*, pages 138–142.

Zeerak Waseem, Thomas Davidson, Dana Warmsley, and Ingmar Weber. 2017. Understanding Abuse: A Typology of Abusive Language Detection Subtasks. In *Proceedings of the 1st Workshop on Abusive Language Online (ACL 2017)*, pages 78–84, Vancouver, Canada.

Zeerak Waseem and Dirk Hovy. 2016. Hateful symbols or hateful people? predictive features for hate speech detection on twitter. In *Proceedings of NAACL-HLT*, pages 88–93.

Zeerak Waseem, James Thorne, and Joachim Bingel. 2018. Bridging the Gaps: Multi Task Learning for Domain Transfer of Hate Speech Detection. In Jennifer Goldbeck, editor, *Online Harassment*, Human-Computer Interaction Series, page 270. Springer, New York, NY.

Michael Wiegand, Josef Ruppenhofer, and Thomas Kleinbauer. 2019. Detection of Abusive Language: the Problem of Biased Datasets. In *Proceedings of NAACL-HLT*, pages 602–608, Minneapolis, Minnesota. Association for Computational Linguistics.

Jieyu Zhao, Tianlu Wang, Mark Yatskar, Vicente Ordonez, and Kai-Wei Chang. 2018. Gender Bias in Coreference Resolution: Evaluation and Debiasing Methods. In *Proceedings of the 2018 Conference of the North American Chapter of the Association for Computational Linguistics: Human Language Technologies, Volume 2 (Short Papers)*, pages 15–20, New Orleans, Louisiana. Association for Computational Linguistics.

Automated Identification of Verbally Abusive Behaviors in Online Discussions

Srećko Joksimović
University of South Australia, Australia
srecko.joksimovic@unisa.edu.au

Ryan S. Baker
University of Pennsylvania, USA
rybaker@upenn.edu

Jaclyn Ocumpaugh
University of Pennsylvania, USA
jlocumpaugh@gmail.com

Juan Miguel L. Andres
University of Pennsylvania, USA
miglimjapandres@gmail.com

Ivan Tot
University of Defence in Belgrade, Serbia
Ivan.tot@va.mod.gov.rs

Elle Yuan Wang
Arizona State University, USA
elle.wang@asu.edu

Shane Dawson
University of South Australia, Australia
shane.dawson@unisa.edu.au

Abstract

Discussion forum participation represents a crucial support for learning and often the only way of supporting social interactions in online settings. However, learner behavior varies considerably in these forums, including positive behaviors such as sharing new ideas or asking thoughtful questions, but also verbally abusive behaviors, which could have disproportionate detrimental effects. To provide means for mitigating potential negative effects on course participation and learning, we developed an automated classifier for identifying communication that show linguistic patterns associated with hostility in online forums. In so doing, we employ several well-established automated text analysis tools and build on common practices for handling highly imbalanced datasets and reducing sensitivity to overfitting. Although still in its infancy, our approach shows promising results (AUC ROC=0.74) towards establishing a robust detector of abusive behaviors. We provide an overview of the classification (linguistic and contextual) features most indicative of online aggression.

1 Introduction

Massive Open Online Courses represent an important part of the educational landscape, offering access to learning at scale for both for-credit and life-long learners (Al-Imarah and Shields, 2019). While there is significant appeal and popularity in MOOC offerings, they bring numerous challenges for designing effective teaching and learning activities at scale (Kovanović et al., 2015). The unprecedented numbers of learners enrolled, and the diversity in learners' motivations and goals are but two factors that add a significant layer of complexity that is seldom experienced in more traditional modes of education (Carlos Alario-Hoyos et al., 2017). A product of the complexity of teaching at scale resides in the lack of student participation in discussion activity (Wise and Cui, 2018; Rosé and Ferschke, 2016). Despite social interactions between peers being a key factor in student learning (Poquet and Dawson, 2016; Joksimović et al., 2016), MOOC discussions often receive limited participation (Wise and Cui, 2018). Numerous studies have shown that participation in discussions is influenced by factors, such as feelings of confusion or isolation, diverse cultural and educational backgrounds, or the lack of ability to navigate when learning in a crowd (Baxter and Haycock, 2014; Poquet et al., 2018). Learners in MOOC settings require the rapid capacity to establish and sustain shared communication practices in order to join a new and often brief-lived online community (Rosé and Ferschke, 2016).

There is thus far relatively limited research on the pragmatics of academic discussions in MOOCs. In one line of work, surveys investigating why students stop posting in MOOC forums

Proceedings of the Third Workshop on Abusive Language Online, pages 36–45
Florence, Italy, August 1, 2019. ©2019 Association for Computational Linguistics

show that many quit because of comments deemed as politeness violations (Mak et al., 2010). Many of these postings involve relatively mild examples of abusive behaviors violations of pragmatic practices around niceness. More extreme violations of politeness conventions in MOOCs have also emerged in the literature, with Comer and her colleagues (Comer et al., 2015) reporting a number of verbally abusive behaviors on the part of students in MOOCs. While such behaviors are relatively infrequent, they can have disproportionate effects on those involved in the course (Mak et al., 2010; Comer et al., 2015).

In this work, we build on prior research on text classification and the analysis of learner generated discourse to build an automated classifier for detecting verbally abusive behaviors in online discussion forums. In so doing, we employ a wide variety of features that range from simple syntactic properties of text (such as unigrams, bigrams, or part-of-speech tags), to more complex linguistic analysis (e.g., text cohesion), in order to identify potentially relevant contextual features. We enhance these detectors through approaches designed to adjust for imbalance in data. The findings from this work bring new insights into the linguistic dimensions that could be indicative of online aggression that can help to mitigate the impacts of hostile and abusive behaviors on other learners.

2 Background Work

2.1 Roots of Negativity in MOOCs

Discourse around negativity in general, and MOOCs in particular, draws on the research on negative emotions in learning and use of abusive language in online learning communities (Comer et al., 2015). Experiencing anxiety, anger or frustration caused by learning activities that are being negatively valued or perceived as aversive, can lead to decreased engagement, motivation, and consequently failure to achieve specific learning outcomes (Pekrun et al., 2002; Rowe, 2017). On the other hand, with the emergence of social media and their use to support development of online learning communities, negativity and abusive online behaviors can potentially have much broader consequences (Salminen et al., 2018). Less extreme manifestations of abusive language in online learning communities could lead towards disengagement from the community (Mak et al., 2010).

In more severe instances, negativity in online communities could lead to cyberbullying and online aggression in general (Holfeld and Grabe, 2012).

Designed to support interactions at scale and facilitated as a fully online learning experience, MOOCs pose multiple challenges to successful participation. For example, success in MOOCs is dependent on learners' motivation, achievement and social emotions, and self-regulatory learning skills (among other factors) (Mak et al., 2010). Therefore, as Rose and Ferschke (2016) posit, it is necessary to create "a supportive environment in which these learners can find community, support, dignity, and respect" (ibid., p664). In that sense, it seems reasonable to build on the approaches to mitigate abusive online behaviors commonly applied in online learning communities, then in more traditional educational settings.

To understand the nature of negativity in MOOCs, we draw on the work by Comer and her colleagues (2015) who discuss three types of negativity in MOOCs: negativity towards i) the course, ii) instructor, and iii) course platform. This multifaceted perspective demonstrates that the main sources of negativity are associated with pedagogy or course design decisions and cannot be easily addressed during course facilitation (Comer et al., 2015). Despite the relatively low proportion of abusive behaviors in MOOCs, Comer and colleagues illustrate the negative impacts they have on instructor presence and the broader levels of participation in discussion forums. Detecting when negativity occurs could provide the opportunity for a more automated or semi-automated approaches to reduce its impact, whether by blocking offensive content or deploying supportive strategies for the individuals impacted (Comer et al., 2015).

In this study we aim to automate the detection of negativity in MOOCs forums. An outcome of this work is to provide a process to enable more efficient responses to abusive online behaviors in MOOC discussion forums. In so doing, we treat negativity as a single construct, rather than differentiating negativity towards the course, platform, or instructor, due to the relative infrequency of negative behaviors. Although we concur that negativity in MOOCs can potentially have multiple facets, our goal in this study is to provide insight into factors that could indicate detrimental and abusive online behaviors in their broadest manifestation even negativity towards the course platform can be upsetting to others (Comer et al., 2015).

2.2 Automated Analysis of Abusive Language

Contemporary literature on affect in MOOC discourse primarily relies on content analysis methods (Joksimović et al., 2018b). To date, this has involved exploring affect and emotions to understand factors that predict persistence and success in MOOCs (Joksimović et al., 2018b). Tucker and colleagues (2014), for example, relied on a word-sentiment lexicon to extract sentiment polarity (i.e., positive, negative, or neutral) and strength (i.e., the magnitude of sentiment) from discussion forum messages. Tucker and colleagues found a strong negative association between the sentiment expressed in forums and average assignment grade. Adamopoluous (2013) opted for a more fine-grained analysis, exploring learners' sentiment towards course instructor, assignments, and course material, utilizing AlchemyAPI. Finally, Yang and colleagues (2015) relied on Linguistic Inquiry and Word Count (LIWC) features, and word categories that depict student affective processes, including positive and negative emotions. to detect confusion within student contributions to the discussion forum.

Although the existing MOOC research recognizes the importance of understanding learners' emotions expressed through interactions in online discussion forums, little has been done to detect negativity and abusive online behaviors. Relevant work exists, however, in efforts to understand online learning communities and social media interactions in general. Several approaches have been developed to detect dimensions of verbal aggression and abusive behavior in social media and online social platforms more broadly (Balci and Salah, 2015; Anzovino et al., 2018). For example, Abozinadah and Jones (2017) used Support Vector Machines (SVM) to detect abusive Twitter accounts. In another example, Anzovino and colleagues (2018), utilized a wide set of linguistic and bag-of-word features to explore the accuracy of various classifiers to identify misogynistic language on Twitter. The best classification accuracy was achieved using an SVM classifier based on unigrams, bigrams, and trigrams.

Additionally, a considerable body of research focuses on detecting verbal aggression in online social games, interactions with virtual partners, or the comments on popular news media (such as CNN.com or Yahoo! News) (Balci and Salah, 2015; Nobata et al., 2016). Relying on wide range of linguistic and contextual features (e.g., learner profile related information), Balci and Ali Salah (2015) used the Bayes Point Machine classification algorithm to identify online profiles that elicit abusive behaviors in social games. Nobata and colleagues (2016), on the other hand, explored the manifestation of abusive language in the comments posted on Yahoo! Finance and News articles. Nobata and colleagues (2016) developed a deep learning approach, utilizing n-grams, linguistic features (e.g., length of tokens, average length of word), syntactic features (e.g., par-of-speech tag of parent), and distributional semantics features.

Our work goes beyond existing approaches to understanding MOOC discourse, trying to detect abusive behaviors that could potentially have detrimental effects on teaching and learning. In so doing, we rely on features commonly identified as being predictive of learners' affective states and emotions in online learning settings. We also utilize algorithms and methods applied in general research on understanding verbal aggression in online learning communities in general.

3 Method

3.1 Data

The dataset for this study was obtained from the Big Data in Education MOOC, delivered from October to December 2013, by Columbia University, taught through the Coursera platform. This course iteration had a total of 45,256 enrolled learners during the course an additional 20,316 joined and accessed the course after its official end date. To successfully complete the course and receive a certificate, learners were required to earn an overall grade average of 70% or above. The overall grade was calculated by averaging the six highest grades extracted out of a total of eight assignments. All assignments were composed of multiple-choice questions and short numerical answers and as such, were available for automatic grading. Discussion participation was not graded. The majority of students only watched videos and did not participate in the assessment tasks. Some 1,380 students completed at least one assignment, while a total of 638 learners successfully completed the course.

Like vast majority of MOOC offerings, the discussion activity consists of a considerably small number of learners (Poquet and Dawson, 2016). For the MOOC under investigation, 747 unique users were engaged in discussion forum (N=747, including teaching staff). In total, the discussion forum contained 4,039 messages, written in English (M=5.41, SD=23.93). Two independent coders coded the dataset, labeling each message as being "negative", if at least one of the negativity types as defined by Comer and colleagues (2015) was found in a message, or "positive/neutral" otherwise. The process was performed through several phases. First 100 messages were analyzed together, to train the researchers and develop the coding scheme. After that, each of the coders independently labeled 200, 300, 400, and 500 messages, until a satisfactory percent agreement (%-agree = 96.6) was reached. The percent agreement was calculated at the end of each stage and all disagreements were discussed and resolved. The remaining messages (from 1,501 to 4,039) were split between the two coders.

Out of these 4,039 messages, 3,917 were positive/neutral, and 122 (3.02%) were coded as negative. From the total number of students who posted to discussion forum, 82 students posted at least one message coded as "negative" (M=1.49, SD=1.09). Nevertheless, only 9 students posted more than two messages coded as negative, showing repeated negativity towards the instructor, course platform, or course content.

3.2 Features

In order to develop a classification system for recognizing negativity in learners' posts in a discussion forum, we utilize several types of features. The extracted features build on those commonly used in the existing work on discourse analysis (Kovanović et al., 2014; Joksimović et al., 2014). Specifically, we rely on basic linguistic features (such as n-grams and part-of-speech tags), features extracted using tools for automated text analysis, and contextual features. The final feature set included 688 features.

3.2.1 Basic Linguistic Features

Our set includes some of the commonly used bag-of-words features, utilized in similar classification problems. Specifically, we extracted *n-gram features* (i.e., unigrams, bigrams, and trigrams),

sequences of words that commonly appear together. Additionally, we extracted *part-of-speech tags* (e.g., noun, verb, adjective) and *syntactic dependency* (i.e., the relation between tokens) features. Although features like n-grams tend to inflate the feature space, these are often used as a baseline feature set, against which other features are compared to evaluate their contribution to the classification accuracy. Due to a limited training set size and unbalanced data, concerns about overfitting led us to use only the top most common 100 n-grams. All the basic features were extracted using Python programming language and the spaCy, open-source library for Natural Language Processing in Python.

3.2.2 Linguistic Facilities

In this study, we utilize three additional tools for advanced text analytics. Specifically, we use Linguistic Inquiry and Word Count (LIWC) to extract counts of different word categories, indicative of various psychological processes, such as social words, cognitive processes, or affect words (Tausczik and Pennebaker, 2010). Previous research demonstrates the potential of LIWC to capture different aspects of students' cognitive engagement during learning. For example, Kovanovic and colleagues (Kovanović et al., 2014), as well as Joksimovic and colleagues (Joksimović et al., 2014), showed that certain LIWC categories, such as the number of question marks or the number of first-person singular pronouns, are among the most important predictors of different phases of cognitive presence. Moreover, dimensions captured by LIWC (e.g., certainty, negations, or causal verbs), have been positively associated with (deactivating) negative emotions, such as boredom, anxiety, or frustration (D'Mello and Graesser, 2012).

We also utilize TAACO, a linguistic tool for automated analysis of text cohesion that provides more than 150 indicators of text coherence linguistic complexity, text readability, and lexical category use (Crossley et al., 2016). Dowell and colleagues (2015), and Joksimovic and colleagues (2018a), established the association between various metrics of text cohesion (e.g., referential or deep cohesion) and multiple social and academic learning outcomes. D'Mello and Graesser (2012), on the other hand, showed the association between cohesion-based metrics and student emotions (e.g.., boredom, engagement, confusion, or frustration) expressed during tutoring.

It seems also reasonable to expect that the negativity in discussion posts would be reflected through various emotional states. Therefore, we also used the IBM Watson Natural Language Understanding API to detect *anger*, *disgust*, *joy*, *fear*, and *sadness*, conveyed in discussion forum messages. Finally, given that research argues for the importance of considering sentiment expressed in discussion forums as being predictive of persistence in MOOCs, we extracted *sentiment polarity* and *sentiment subjectivity*, using TextBlob Python library for natural language processing tasks.

3.2.3 Contextual Features

Drawing on previous research by Kovanovic and colleagues (Kovanović et al., 2014), we further included contextual features into our feature space. As Comer and colleagues (2015) suggest, some of the learners posting negative messages in discussion forums tend to do so consistently. Therefore, for each post we observed whether the previous post by the same student was also negative. Moreover, it seems reasonable to expect that learners would build on the existing discourse, therefore we also observed whether there were negative messages in the same thread, prior to the observed post. Furthermore, we observed whether the posted message is a post or a comment, the start or the end of the thread, and number of votes the observed post received. Finally, for each of the posts we obtained an information whether the message contains positive and negative words, as well as the proportion of words that were positive and the proportion that were negative.

3.3 Model Implementation

We built our classifier using the Python scikit-learn implementation of Support Vector Machines (SVM), one of the most robust classifiers for text analysis (2014). In order to obtain optimal classification results, we performed hyperparameter optimization within the training set with parameters C (0.001, 0.01, 0.1, 1, 10) and *gamma* (0.001, 0.01, 0.1, 1), for each of the four kernels (i.e., "poly", "rbf", "linear", "sigmoid"). We opted for the linear kernel, (C=0.001, *gamma*=0.001) as the settings with linear kernel yielded the best performance.

There are two challenges associated with the dataset that is inherent to the nature of the problem under study. Although the expression of neg-

ative or deactivating emotions is common within learning (Pekrun et al., 2002), verbally abusive behaviors are less common, although still detrimental (Mak et al., 2010; Comer et al., 2015). As indicated in our dataset, a small percentage of messages (3.02%) coded as "negative", resulted in a highly imbalanced dataset, which could have negative effects on the classification results. In addition, participation in discussion forums, including the use of inappropriate or negative behaviors, varies by factors such as student demographics or motivation (Mak et al., 2010). Thus, the tendency to engage in inappropriate behaviors might (and does) vary from one learner to another. That is, only a small subset of students will express negativity in discussion forums.

To address the first problem of the highly imbalanced classes, we employed two strategies. First, the SVM classifier was configured to use balanced class weights. This configuration is used to adjust weights inversely proportional to class frequencies, defining higher weight for the "negative" class in our case. Second, we also implemented a False Positive Rate test into the classification pipeline. The False Positive Rate test controls for the total amount of false detections, which are common in imbalanced datasets with a rare category of interest, as in this study.

Cross-validation is typically used to control for overfitting. Desmarais and Baker (2012), highlight the importance of cross-validating at student level, to estimate goodness for new students rather than for new data from the same students. In our study, we rely on GroupKFold Python implementation of a K-fold iterator with non-overlapping groups (i.e., ensuring that each learner is only represented in a single fold).

4 Results

4.1 Model Training and Evaluation

Table 1 shows the results of our model selection and evaluation. To find the optimal model, we primarily rely on Area Under the Receiver Operating Characteristic Curve (ROC AUC) score, as Cohen's statistics does not yield reliable estimates for highly imbalanced datasets, as it is the case in this study (Jeni et al., 2013). To obtain optimal results, we performed classification including various subsets of the original feature set (Table 1). The highest AUC ROC value with the complete feature set was 0.73 (SD=0.06). The clas-

Feature Set	Total Features	Class. Accuracy	F1 Score	ROC AUC
Baseline (Unigrams)	100	0.86	0.90	0.63
+ Ngrams	300	0.88	0.91	0.60
+ POS	397	0.88	0.91	0.60
+ TAACO	580	0.83	0.88	0.64
+ LIWC	673	0.84	0.89	0.65
+ Sentiment	680	0.84	0.89	0.65
+ Context	**688**	**0.86**	**0.90**	**0.73**
Unigrams + TAACO + LIWC + Sentiment + Context	303	**0.85**	**0.89**	**0.74**

Table 1: Classification results for different SVM configurations, varying the feature set used in predicting abusive language and p-value cutoff point at 0.05 for False Positive Rate test.

sification accuracy for the same set of parameters was .86 (SD=0.02), whereas the F1 score was .90 (SD=0.02).

Table 1 further shows that adding bigrams, trigrams and POS features (including tag and syntactic dependency) resulted in lower AUC ROC values, despite the slight increase in the classification accuracy. The ROC AUC score for the feature set that included Unigrams, TAACO, LIWC, Sentiment, and Contextual features was **0.74** (*SD*=0.06). The classification accuracy for the same set of parameters was .85 (*SD*=0.01), whereas the F1 score was .89 (*SD*=0.01).

4.2 Feature Importance Analysis

Given the size of the feature space (688 features), in the feature importance analysis we focus on the top 40 features used in the data separation task. That is, we observe the top 20 features most predictive of "negative" language and the top 20 features most predictive of "positive/neutral" language in the data set. Figure 2 shows that all groups of features (i.e., basic linguistic, features extracted using automated text analysis tools, and contextual features) are being identified within this subset of important features.

It is noteworthy that *contextual variables* yielded the highest predictive power for negativity (Figure 1). Specifically, `Previous negative thread` at least one of the previous messages in the thread was negative - has been identified as the most important variable in predicting detrimental behaviors. Moreover, whether a message is a post (i.e., reply to a thread) or a comment (i.e., reply to a post), as defined within the Coursera

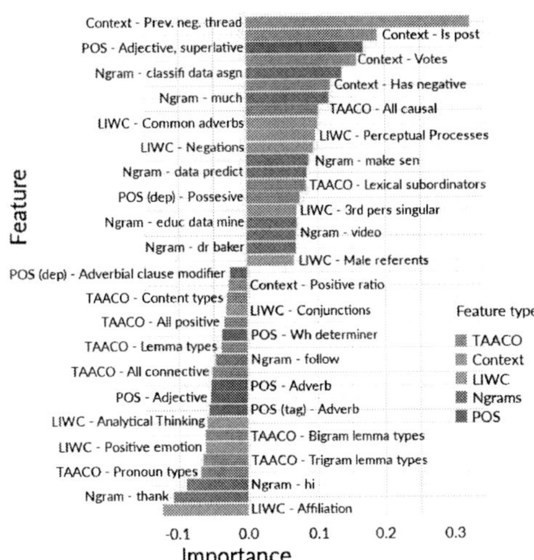

Figure 2: Top 40 features differentiating abusive language from overall positive/neutral language in discussion forum. It should be noted that values higher than 0 indicate features predictive of abusive language.

platform also revealed high predictive power. Finally, the total number of votes and whether message contained negative words were also found to be indicative of messages characteristic of negative behaviors towards the course content and design, course platform or course instructor.

Figure 1 further shows that part-of-speech tags representing `adjective in superlative` (e.g., "most", "worst"), were among the strongest predictors of negativity in online discussions. Other variables labeled as part of the part-of-speech dataset that were highly associated with negative messages are variables indicating the number of possession modifiers in a post (e.g., "... my experiences of the first hour in this class", "WASTE OF MY TIME"). On the other hand, variables indicative of positive/neutral messages were `adjectives`, `wh-determiners` (e.g., "what", "which"), and `adverbial clause modifiers` (e.g., "Confusion is good, just as long as it is addressed").

A considerable number of LIWC features were identified as being highly related to either negative or positive/neutral messages in MOOC discussions (Figure 1). Specifically, words associated with `common adverbs` (e.g., "write", "read", "hope"), `perceptual processes` (e.g., "watched", "said", "showed"), `negations` (e.g., "neither", "don't", "couldn't"), and function words that represent `3rd person singular form` (e.g., "him", "he's", "he"), were associated with messages indicative of abusive behaviors. On the other hand, words indicative of psychological processes representing core drives and needs (i.e., `affiliation` "welcome", "shared"), `positive emotions` (e.g., "helpful", "encourage", "honest"), `analytical thinking`, as well as function words (i.e., `conjunctions` "how", "then", "when"), were highly associated with positive/neutral behaviors (Figure 1).

Likewise, two variables extracted using TAACO linguistic facility were ranked among top 20 features predictive of "negative" messages. Specifically, count of `causal connectives` (e.g., "although", "because") and `lexical subordinates` (e.g., "unless", "whenever") were ranked as important variables in predicting abusive behavior. On the other hand, considerably more TAACO variables were identified as predictive of "positive/neutral" messages. Total number of content types, positive words, lemma types (including bigram and trigram lemmas), connectives, and pronoun types.

Several ngrams were also identified as important variables in differentiating abusive language from "positive/neutral" discourse. In the context of predicting "negative" messages, `classify data assign`, `much`, `make sen`, `data predict`, `educ data mine`, `video`, and `dr baker` emerged as the best predictors of abusive behaviors. Ngrams such as `hi`, `thank`, or `follow`, on the other hand, were associated with "positive/neutral" category of messages.

Observing variable importance with the smaller dataset (excluding part-of-speech, tag, and dependency variables) yielded rather similar results as the complete feature set (Figure 2). Contextual, LIWC, and ngrams (unigrams) still comprise a considerable part of the variables predictive of abusive behavior. Similarly, vide variety of TAACO variables was identified as indicative of "positive/neutral" messages.

5   Discussion and Conclusion

Identifying and mitigating abusive behaviors in the context of MOOCs is important for reducing the detrimental effects of negative language on peers and instructors. In this research, we manually coded all discussion forum messages written in English (N=4,039) from one MOOC, to build an automated classifier for identification of potentially harmful discussion messages. Our re-

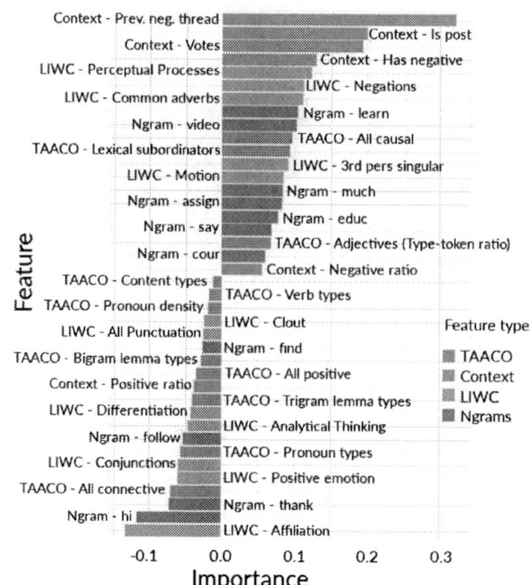

Figure 3: Features differentiating abusive language from overall positive/neutral language in discussion forum, for the model excluding bigram, trigram, and POS (including dependencies) features. It should be noted that values higher than 0 indicate features predictive of abusive language.

sults show that primarily contextual, but also complex linguistic features, such as those extracted using LIWC and TAACO linguistic facilities represent important variables in predicting negativity in MOOCs. As such, our classifier outperforms, by a considerable margin, some of the recent work in identifying hate speech in online communities (Salminen et al., 2018).

Kovanovic and colleagues (2014), argue for the importance of understanding the specific context in which certain messages in discussion forums have been posted. Our analysis on the complete and filtered feature set (without bigram, trigrams, and part-of-speech tag features) further support this finding. Moreover, the most important feature for predicting abusive language in MOOC discussions is a variable that flags whether the thread in which the current message has been posted already contains a "negative" message. This finding directly contributes to the claim made by Mak and colleagues (2010) or others, about the detrimental and likely disproportionate effect abusive language in MOOCs could have on the overall participation. The count of votes, as a contextual variable, also warrants further exploration. Complimenting others or content of others' messages represent one of the indicators identified within the social presence open communication category (Garrison and Akyol, 2013). However, one of the potential implications for future research could be exploration to what extent learners who express abusive behaviors in online communities tend to support each other. That is, to what extend acknowledgment and approval of negative behaviors implies negative connotation for the development of supportive learning environment and consequently learning success.

Our work also supports previous findings on understanding linguistic variables predictive of various dimensions of affect and emotions. For example, D'Mello and Graesser (2012) showed that the high ratio of causal words was positively associated with higher frustration. Whereas, negations were positively and significantly associated with boredom. Similar finding has been observed in our work where total count of all causal words was one of the main predictors of abusive language (Figure 2). Building further on Pekrun's (2002) control-value theory of achievement emotions, it seems that activities learners value negatively and perceive as not being controllable, potentially lead towards the abusive behaviors in online discussions.

It is also noteworthy that variables being identified as important predictors of "positive/neutral" messages, have been found to be associated with higher levels of cognitive engagement. For example, Joksimovic and colleagues [26] showed that the number of conjunctions (LIWC variable) or types of verbs (here captures using TAACO) were some of the variables positively and significantly associated with higher phases of cognitive inquiry, as defined by Garrison and colleagues [34]. This further supports the work by Rowe [13], among others, who showed that surface learners might be more likely to experience negative emotions, suggesting that "surface learners may react negatively to teaching methods which attempt to foster independent learning" (ibid., 299). Such a finding could have significant implications for future research and practice in mitigating abusive behaviors.

Although rather simple syntactic properties of text, such as ngram features, can easily inflate the feature space and result in overfitting, our results show that these variables should not be ignored. In the context of "negative" messages, it is indicative that unigrams, bigrams and trigram that emerged among the most important variables in predict-ing abusive behaviors, are related to specific aspects of the course (Figure 1 and 2). For example, ngrams such as "educ data mine", "video", "data predict", or "dr baker", indicate learners' focus on high level and general aspects of the course, rather than particular content related issues. On the other hand, among the most important variables in predicting positive/neutral messages, unigrams such as "hi" or "thank" emerged. Along with the LIWC variable "affiliation", these represent features indicative of higher levels of social presence [34]. Being recognized as important aspects of open and cohesive communication, as defined by Garrison and colleagues [34], these variables represent important indicators of tendency to establish collaborative and engaging community of learners.

5.1 Limitations

Although the dataset is reasonably large among text classification problems, high data imbalance represents one of the main challenges to this study. Moreover, in this preliminary analysis, we rely on the dataset from a single, technical MOOC (i.e., focused on the topics of big data and statistics). Future work should account for different subject domains and different educational settings (e.g., more formal traditional online courses).

References

Ehab A. Abozinadah and James H. Jones, Jr. 2017. A Statistical Learning Approach to Detect Abusive Twitter Accounts. In *Proceedings of the International Conference on Compute and Data Analysis*, ICCDA '17, pages 6–13. ACM.

Panagiotis Adamopoulos. 2013. What Makes a Great MOOC? An Interdisciplinary Analysis of Student Retention in Online Courses. In *34th International Conference on Information Systems*, United States. Association for Information Systems. The most heavily-cited paper from the ICIS 2013 proceedings (as of August 15th, 2016).

Ahmed A. Al-Imarah and Robin Shields. 2019. MOOCs, Disruptive Innovation and the Future of Gigher Education: A Conceptual analysis. *Innovations in Education and Teaching International*, 56(3):258–269.

M. Anzovino, E. Fersini, and P. Rosso. 2018. Automatic identification and classification of misogynistic language on twitter. *Lecture Notes in Computer Science (including subseries Lecture Notes in Artificial Intelligence and Lecture Notes in Bioinformatics)*, 10859 LNCS:57–64.

Koray Balci and Albert Ali Salah. 2015. Automatic Analysis and Identification of Verbal Aggression and Abusive Behaviors for Online Social Games. *Computers in Human Behavior*, 53:517 – 526.

Jacqueline Baxter and Jo Haycock. 2014. Roles and Student Identities in Online Large Course Forums: Implications for Practice. *The International Review of Research in Open and Distributed Learning*, 15(1).

Carlos Alario-Hoyos, Iria Estévez-Ayres, Mar Pérez-Sanagustín, Carlos Delgado Kloos, and Carmen Fernández-Panadero. 2017. Understanding Learners Motivation and Learning Strategies in MOOCs. *The International Review of Research in Open and Distributed Learning*, 18(3).

Denise Comer, Ryan Baker, and Wang Yuan. 2015. Negativity in Massive Online Open Courses: Impacts on Learning and Teaching and How Instructional Teams May Be Able to Address It. *InSight: A Journal of Scholarly Teaching*, 10:92 – 113.

Scott A Crossley, Kristopher Kyle, and Danielle S McNamara. 2016. The tool for the automatic analysis of text cohesion (TAACO): Automatic assessment of local, global, and text cohesion. *Behavior research methods*, 48(4):1227–1237.

Michel C. Desmarais and Ryan S. J. d. Baker. 2012. A Review of Recent Advances in Learner and Skill Modeling in Intelligent Learning Environments. *User Modeling and User-Adapted Interaction*, 22(1):9–38.

S. K. D'Mello and A. Graesser. 2012. Language and discourse are powerful signals of student emotions during tutoring. *IEEE Transactions on Learning Technologies*, 5(4):304–317.

Nia M Dowell, Oleksandra Skrypnyk, Srećko Joksimović, Arthur C Graesser, Shane Dawson, Dragan Gašević, Thieme A Hennis, Pieter de Vries, and Vitomir Kovanović. 2015. Modeling Learners' Social Centrality and Performance through Language and Discourse. *International Educational Data Mining Society, Paper presented at the 8th International Conference on Educational Data Mining (EDM) (8th, Madrid, Spain, Jun 26-29, 2015)*.

Manuel Fernández-Delgado, Eva Cernadas, Senén Barro, and Dinani Amorim. 2014. Do We Need Hundreds of Classifiers to Solve Real World Classification Problems? *The Journal of Machine Learning Research*, 15(1):3133–3181.

D Randy Garrison and Zehra Akyol. 2013. The Community of Inquiry Theoretical Framework. In *Handbook of distance education*, pages 122–138. Routledge.

Brett Holfeld and Mark Grabe. 2012. Middle School Students' Perceptions of and Responses to Cyber Bullying. *Journal of Educational Computing Research*, 46(4):395–413.

László A Jeni, Jeffrey F Cohn, and Fernando De La Torre. 2013. Facing Imbalanced Data Recommendations for the Use of Performance Metrics. *International Conference on Affective Computing and Intelligent Interaction and workshops : [proceedings]. ACII (Conference)*, 2013:245–251.

Srećko Joksimović, Nia Dowell, Oleksandra Poquet, Vitomir Kovanović, Dragan Gašević, Shane Dawson, and Arthur C. Graesser. 2018a. Exploring Development of Social Capital in a cMOOC Through Language and Discourse. *The Internet and Higher Education*, 36:54 – 64.

Srećko Joksimović, Dragan Gašević, Vitomir Kovanović, Olusola Adesope, and Marek Hatala. 2014. Psychological Characteristics in Cognitive Presence of Communities of Inquiry: A Linguistic Analysis of Online Discussions. *The Internet and Higher Education*, 22:1 – 10.

Srećko Joksimović, Areti Manataki, Dragan Gašević, Shane Dawson, Vitomir Kovanović, and Inés Friss de Kereki. 2016. Translating network position into performance: Importance of centrality in different network configurations. In *Proceedings of the Sixth International Conference on Learning Analytics & Knowledge (LAK'16)*, LAK '16, pages 314–323, New York, NY, USA. ACM.

Srećko Joksimović, Oleksandra Poquet, Vitomir Kovanović, Nia Dowell, Caitlin Mills, Dragan Gašević, Shane Dawson, Arthur C. Graesser, and Christopher Brooks. 2018b. How do we model learning at scale? a systematic review of research on moocs. *Review of Educational Research*, 88(1):43–86.

Vitomir Kovanović, Srećko Joksimović, Dragan Gašević, and Marek Hatala. 2014. Automated cognitive presence detection in online discussion transcripts. In *Proceedings of the Workshops at the LAK 2014 Conference co-located with 4th International Conference on Learning Analytics and Knowledge (LAK'14)*, Indianapolis, IN.

Vitomir Kovanović, Srećko Joksimović, Dragan Gašević, George Siemens, and Marek Hatala. 2015. What public media reveals about MOOCs: A systematic analysis of news reports. *British Journal of Educational Technology*, 46(3):510–527.

Sui Mak, Roy Williams, and Jenny Mackness. 2010. Blogs and forums as communication and learning tools in a MOOC. In *Proceedings of the 7th International Conference on Networked Learning 2010*, pages 275–285. University of Lancaster.

C. Nobata, J. Tetreault, A. Thomas, Y. Mehdad, and Y. Chang. 2016. Abusive language detection in online user content. In *25th International World Wide Web Conference, WWW 2016*, pages 145–153.

Reinhard Pekrun, Thomas Goetz, Wolfram Titz, and Raymond P. Perry. 2002. Academic emotions in students' self-regulated learning and achievement:

A program of qualitative and quantitative research. *Educational Psychologist*, 37(2):91–105.

Oleksandra Poquet and Shane Dawson. 2016. Untangling MOOC learner networks. In *Proceedings of the Sixth International Conference on Learning Analytics & Knowledge*, LAK '16, pages 208–212. ACM.

Oleksandra Poquet, Nia Dowell, Christopher Brooks, and Shane Dawson. 2018. Are MOOC forums changing? In *Proceedings of the 8th International Conference on Learning Analytics and Knowledge*, LAK '18, pages 340–349. ACM. Event-place: Sydney, New South Wales, Australia.

Carolyn Penstein Rosé and Oliver Ferschke. 2016. Technology Support for Discussion Based Learning: From Computer Supported Collaborative Learning to the Future of Massive Open Online Courses. *International Journal of Artificial Intelligence in Education*, 26(2):660–678.

Anna D. Rowe. 2017. *Feelings about feedback: the role of emotions in assessment for learning*, The Enabling power of assessment, pages 159–172. Springer, Springer Nature, United States.

Joni Salminen, Hind Almerekhi, Milica Milenkovi, Soon gyo Jung, Jisun An, Haewoon Kwak, and Bernard Jansen. 2018. Anatomy of Online Hate: Developing a Taxonomy and Machine Learning Models for Identifying and Classifying Hate in Online News Media. In *International AAAI Conference on Web and Social Media*, pages 330–339.

Yla R. Tausczik and James W. Pennebaker. 2010. The Psychological Meaning of Words: LIWC and Computerized Text Analysis Methods. *Journal of Language and Social Psychology*, 29(1):24–54.

Conrad Tucker, Barton K. Pursel, and Anna Divinsky. 2014. Mining Student-Generated Textual Data In MOOCS and Quantifying Their Effects on Student Performance and Learning Outcomes. In *2014 ASEE Annual Conference & Exposition*, Indianapolis, Indiana. ASEE Conferences. Https://peer.asee.org/22840.

Alyssa Friend Wise and Yi Cui. 2018. Unpacking the relationship between discussion forum participation and learning in MOOCs: Content is key. In *Proceedings of the 8th International Conference on Learning Analytics and Knowledge*, LAK '18, pages 330–339. ACM. Event-place: Sydney, New South Wales, Australia.

Diyi Yang, Miaomiao Wen, Iris Howley, Robert Kraut, and Carolyn Rose. 2015. Exploring the effect of confusion in discussion forums of massive open online courses. In *Proceedings of the Second (2015) ACM Conference on Learning @ Scale*, L@S '15, pages 121–130, New York, NY, USA. ACM.

Multi-label Hate Speech and Abusive Language Detection in Indonesian Twitter

Muhammad Okky Ibrohim
Faculty of Computer Science
Universitas Indonesia
Kampus UI, Depok, 16424, Indonesia
okkyibrohim@cs.ui.ac.id

Indra Budi
Faculty of Computer Science
Universitas Indonesia
Kampus UI, Depok, 16424, Indonesia
indra@cs.ui.ac.id

Abstract

Hate speech and abusive language spreading on social media need to be detected automatically to avoid conflicts between citizens. Moreover, hate speech has a target, category, and level that also need to be detected to help the authority in prioritizing which hate speech must be addressed immediately. This research discusses multi-label text classification for abusive language and hate speech detection including detecting the target, category, and level of hate speech in Indonesian Twitter using machine learning approaches with Support Vector Machine (SVM), Naive Bayes (NB), and Random Forest Decision Tree (RFDT) classifier and Binary Relevance (BR), Label Power-set (LP), and Classifier Chains (CC) as the data transformation method. We used several kinds of feature extractions which are term frequency, orthography, and lexicon features. Our experiment results show that in general the RFDT classifier using LP as the transformation method gives the best accuracy with fast computational time.

1 Introduction

Hate speech is a direct or indirect speech toward a person or group containing hatred based on something inherent to that person or group (Komnas HAM, 2015)[1]. Factors that are often used as bases of hatred include ethnicity, religion, disability, gender, and sexual orientation. Hate speech spreading is a very dangerous action which can have some negative effects such as discrimination, social conflict, and even human genocide (Komnas HAM, 2015). One of the most horrific genocides caused by the act of spreading hate speech

was the Tutsi ethnic genocide in Rwanda in 1994 (Stanton, 2009). The cause of the tragedy was hate speech propagated by some groups, claiming that the cause of increasing pressure in politics, economic and social was the Tutsi ethnic.

In everyday life, especially in social media, the hate speech spreading is often accompanied with abusive language (Davidson et al., 2017). Abusive language is an utterance that contains abusive words/phrases that is conveyed to the interlocutor (individuals or groups), both verbally and in writing. Hate speech that contains abusive words/phrases often accelerates the occurrence of social conflict because of the use of the abusive words/phrases that triggers emotions. In Indonesia, abusive words are usually derived from an unpleasant condition such as mental disorder, sexual deviation, physical disability, lack of modernization, a condition where someone does not have etiquette, conditions that is not allowed by religion, and other conditions related to unfortunate circumstances; animals that have a bad characteristic, disgusting, and forbidden in certain religion; astral beings that often interfere with human life; a dirty and bad smell object; a part of the body and an activity that related to sexual activity; and low-class profession that is forbidden by religion (Wijana and Rohmadi., 2010; Ibrohim and Budi, 2018). In general, the use of abusive words aimed to curse someone (spreading hate speech) in Indonesia is divided into three types that are words, phrases, and clauses (Wijana and Rohmadi., 2010). The spread of hate speech that is accompanied with abusive language often accelerates the occurrence of social conflict because of the use of the abusive words/phrases that triggers emotions. Although abusive language are sometimes just being used as jokes (not to offend someone), the use of abusive language in social media still can lead to conflict because of misunderstand-

---

[1]Komisi Nasional Hak Asasi Manusia (Komnas HAM) is an independent institution that functions to carry out studies, research, counseling, monitoring, and mediation of human rights in Indonesia. See https://www.komnasham.go.id/index.php/about/1/tentang-komnas-ham.html

Proceedings of the Third Workshop on Abusive Language Online, pages 46–57
Florence, Italy, August 1, 2019. ©2019 Association for Computational Linguistics

ings among netizens (Yenala et al., 2017). Moreover, children could be exposed to language inappropriate for their age from those abusive language scattered in their social media (Chen et al., 2012).

The hate speech and abusive language on social media must be detected to avoid conflicts between citizens and children learning the hate speech and inappropriate language from the social media they use (Komnas HAM, 2015; Chen et al., 2012). In recent years, many researchers have done research in hate speech detection (Waseem and Hovy, 2016; Alfina et al., 2017, 2018; Putri, 2018; Vigna et al., 2017) and abusive language detection (Turaob and Mitrpanont, 2017; Chen et al., 2012; Nobata et al., 2016; Ibrohim and Budi, 2018; Ibrohim et al., 2018) in various social media genres and languages.

According to (Komnas HAM, 2015), a hate speech has a certain target, category, and level. Hate speeches can belong to a certain category such as ethnicity, religion, race, sexual orientation, etc. that are targeted to a particular individual or group with a certain level of hatred. However, based on our literature study, there has been no research on abusive language and hate speech detection including the detection of hate speech target, category, and level conducted simultaneously. Many research in hate speech detection (Waseem and Hovy, 2016; Alfina et al., 2017, 2018; Putri, 2018) just identifying whether a text is hate speech or not. In 2017, (Vigna et al., 2017) performed research on hate speech level detection. Their research was done to classifying Italian Facebook post and comment into three labels which are *no hate speech*, *weak hate speech*, and *strong hate speech*. However, (Vigna et al., 2017) did not classifying the target and category of hate speech. Similar to research in hate speech detection, many studies in abusive language detection (Turaob and Mitrpanont, 2017; Chen et al., 2012; Nobata et al., 2016) also just identify whether a text is abusive language or not. In 2018, (Ibrohim and Budi, 2018) conducted research on hate speech and abusive language detection. Their research was done to classify Indonesian tweet into three labels that are *no hate speech, abusive but no hate speech*, and *abusive and hate speech*. However, same as other studeis on hate speech and abusive language detection, (Ibrohim and Budi, 2018) did not classify the target and category of hate speech.

Depending on (Hernanto and Jeihan, 2018)[23], detection of the hate speech target, category, and level is important to help authorities prioritize cases of hate speech that must be handled immediately. In this work, we do research on hate speech and abusive language detection in Indonesian Twitter. We chose Twitter as our dataset because Twitter is one of the social media platforms in Indonesia that is often used to spread the hate speech and abusive language (Alfina et al., 2017, 2018; Putri, 2018; Ibrohim and Budi, 2018; Ibrohim et al., 2018). This problem is a multi-label text classification problem, where a tweet can be *no hate speech, no hate speech but abusive, hate speech but no abusive,* and *hate speech and abusive.* Furthermore, hate speech also has a certain target, category, and level.

In doing multi-label hate speech and abusive language detection, we use machine learning approach with several classifiers. The classifiers that we use include Support Vector Machine (SVM), Nave Bayes (NB), and Random Forest Decision Tree (RFDT) using problem transformation methods including Binary Relevance (BR), Label Power-set (LP), and Classifier Chains (CC). Based on several previous works, these three classifiers are algorithms that can produce pretty good performance for hate speech and abusive language detection in Indonesian (Alfina et al., 2017, 2018; Putri, 2018; Ibrohim and Budi, 2018; Ibrohim et al., 2018). We used several kinds of text classification features including term frequency (word n-grams and character n-grams), orthography (exclamation mark, question mark, uppercase, and lowercase), and sentiment lexicon (negative, positive, and abusive). We use accuracy for evaluating our proposed approach (Kafrawy et al., 2015). To validate our experiment results, we use 10-fold cross validation technique (Kohavi, 1995).

In this paper, we built an Indonesian Twitter dataset for abusive language and hate speech detection including detecting the target, category, and level of hate speech. In general, the contributions of this research are:

- Analyzing the target, category, and level of

---

[2]Staff of Direktorat Tindak Pidana Siber Bareskrim Polri

[3]Direktorat Tindak Pidana Siber Badan Reserse Kriminal Kepolisian Negara Republik Indonesia (Bareskrim Polri) is a directorate of the Indonesian national police that charge of fostering and carrying out the function of investigating and investigating cyber crimes in Indonesia. See `https://humas.polri.go.id/category/satker/cyber-crime-bareskrim-polri/`

hate speech to make an annotator guide and gold standard annotation for building Indonesian hate speech and abusive language dataset. Our annotator is arranged based on (Komnas HAM, 2015) and the results of interviews and discussions with the staff of Direktorat Tindak Pidana Siber Bareskrim Polri (Hernanto and Jeihan, 2018) and a linguistic expert (Nurasijah, 2018).

- Building a dataset for abusive language and hate speech detection including detecting the target, category, and level of hate speech in Indonesian Twitter. We provide this research dataset for public[4] so that it can be used by other researchers who are interested in doing future work of this paper.

- Conducting preliminaries experiments on multi-label abusive language and hate speech detection (including hate speech target, category, and level detection) in Indonesian Twitter using machine learning approaches.

This paper is organized as follows. We discuss hate speech target, category, and level in Indonesia in Section 2. Our data collection and annotation process is described in Section 3. Section 4 presenting our experiment results and discussion. Finally, the conclusions and future work of our research are presented in Section 5.

2 Hate Speech Target, Categories, and Level in Indonesia

In this research, we conducted Focus Group Discussion (FGD) with the staff of Direktorat Tindak Pidana Siber Badan Reserse Kriminal Kepolisian Negara Republik Indonesia (Bareskrim Polri), which is the agency responsible for investigating cybercrimes in Indonesia. This is done in order to get a valid definition of hate speech, including the characterization. From the FGD with staff of Bareskrim Polri (Hernanto and Jeihan, 2018), it was obtained that hate speech has a particular target, categories, and level.

Every hate speech is aimed at a particular target. In general, the target of hate speech is divided into two kinds, which are *individual* and *group*. Hate speech with individual target is hate speech that

aimed at someone (an individual person), while hate speech with group target is hate speech that aimed at a particular groups, associations, or communities. These groups, associations, and communities can be in the form of religious groups, races, politics, fan clubs, hobby communities, etc.

Both aimed at individual or group, hate speech has a particular category as the basis of hate. According to FGD results, in general, hate speech categories are as follows:

1. *Religion/creed*, which is hate speech based on a religion (Islam, Christian, Catholic, etc.), religious organization/stream, or a particular creed;

2. *Race/ethnicity*, which is hate speech based on a human race (human groups based on physical characteristics such as face shape, height, skin color, and others) or ethnicity (human groups based on general citizenship or shared cultural traditions in a geographical area);

3. *Physical/disability*, which is hate speech based on physical deficiencies/differences (e.g. shape of face, eye, and other body parts) or disability (e.g. autism, idiot, blind, deaf, etc.), either just cursing someone (or a group) with those words related to physical/disability or those that are truly experienced by those who are the target of the hate speech;

4. *Gender/sexual orientation*, which is hate speech based on gender (male and female), cursing someone (or a group) using words that are degrading to gender (e.g.: gigolo, bitch, etc.), or deviant sexual orientation (e.g.: homosexual, lesbian, etc.);

5. *Other invective/slander*, which is hate speech in the form of swearing/ridicule using crude words/phrases or other slanders/incitement which are not related to the four groups previously explained.

Notice that a hate speech can be categorized in several categories at once except *other invective/slander* category. In other words, a hate speech under category *religion/creed, race/ethnicity, physical/disability,* and *gender/sexual orientation* can not be categorized as *other invective/slander* category, and vice versa.

---

[4]https://github.com/okkyibrohim/id-multi-label-hate-speech-and-abusive-language-detection

Besides having targets and categories, hate speech also has a certain level. Based on the FGD results, we divide hate speech into three levels, which are *weak, moderate,* and *strong.* The explanation for every level of hate speech are as follows:

1. *Weak hate speech,* which is hate speech in the form of swearing/slanders that aimed at individuals without including incitement/provocation to bring open conflict. In Indonesia, hate speech in this form categorized as *weak hate speech* because it is a personal problem. It means, if the target of hate speech does not report to the authorities (feeling ordinary and forgiving people who spread the hate speech towards him) then that hate speech is not too prioritized to be resolved by the authorities.

2. *Moderate hate speech,* which is hate speech in the form of swearing/blasphemy/stereotyping/labeling aimed at groups without including incitement/provocation to bring open conflict. Although it can invite conflict between groups, this kind of hate speech is belonging to moderate hate speech because the conflict that will occur is estimated to be limited to conflict on social media.

3. *Strong hate speech,* which is hate speech in the form of swearing/slanders/blasphemy/stereotyping/labeling aimed at individual or group including incitement/provocation to bring open conflict. This kind of hate speech is belonging to strong hate speech, because it is a hate speech that needs to be prioritized to be resolved soon because it can invite conflicts that are widespread and can lead to conflicts/physical destruction in the real world.

3 Data Collection and Annotation

In this research, we used hate speech and abusive language Twitter dataset from several previous researches consisting of (Alfina et al., 2017, 2018), (Putri, 2018), and (Ibrohim and Budi, 2018). Besides using Twitter dataset from previous researches, we also crawled tweets in order to enrich dataset such that it can include the kinds of writing of hate speech and abusive language that may not yet exist in the data from previous researches. We crawled Twitter data using Twitter Search API[5] which is implemented using Tweepy Library[6]. The queries which we used for crawling Twitter data are words/phrases that often used by netizens when spreading hate speech and abusive language in Indonesian social media, that can be seen in Appendix 1[7]. We crawled the twitter data for about 7 months, from March 20th, 2018 until September 10th, 2018. The purpose of crawling with a long time is to get more tweet writing patterns.

In this research, we used crowdsourcing with a paid mechanism (Sabou et al., 2014) for the annotation process. Since the tweets that we want to annotate has many labels, we decided to conduct two phases of annotation process. This is because annotators who are not linguistic experts should not annotate data with too many labels (Sabou et al., 2014). The first phase annotation process was done to annotate the Twitter data whether tweets are hate speech and abusive language or not, while the second phase annotation process was done to annotate the hate speech target, categories, and level. For tweets from (Alfina et al., 2017, 2018) and (Putri, 2018), tweets were just annotated to determine whether the tweet is an abusive language or not in the first phase annotation process, since the hate speech label is already obtained. Meanwhile, tweets from (Ibrohim and Budi, 2018) can be annotated directly in the second phase since their dataset was annotated for hate speech and abusive labels.

For the annotation process, we built a web based annotation system in order to make it easy for the annotators to annotate data so that it can speed up the annotation process and minimize annotation errors. We conducted an annotator guideline to give the task definition and example for helping the annotators in understanding the annotation task. We also conducted a gold standard annotation for testing whether the annotators already understand the task or not. In this research, we are doing a discussion and consultation with an expert

---

[5]https://developer.twitter.com/en/docs/tweets/search/api-reference/get-search-tweets.html

[6]http://www.tweepy.org/

[7]For complete list of queries, see https://github.com/okkyibrohim/id-multi-label-hate-speech-and-abusive-language-detection

linguistic (Nurasijah, 2018)[8] in order to get a valid annotation guideline and gold standard annotation. Twitter data that used for the gold standard came from previous research (Alfina et al., 2017; Ibrohim and Budi, 2018) and hate speech handbook (Komnas HAM, 2015).

After the annotation system was built and tested well, the next process is the annotator recruitment process. In this research, annotators came from different religious, racial/ethnic, and residential backgrounds. This is done to reduce bias because the annotation of hate speech is quite subjective (Alfina et al., 2017). The selected annotators' criteria are as follows: (a) have the age of 20-30 years old (since most Twitter users in Indonesia came from that age (APJII., 2017)); (b) native in the Indonesian language (Bahasa Indonesia); (c) experienced using Twitter; (d) not members of any political party/organization (this is done to reduce annotation bias, especially when the annotators annotate tweets that are related to politics).

In this research, we use 30 annotators to annotate our dataset from various demographic background. The annotators consist of 14 males and 16 females that have various age (25 annotators aged 20-24 years and 5 annotators aged 25-32 years) and last education background (12 annotators have bachelor degree for last education and 18 annotators have senior high school degree for last education). Furthermore, annotators also come from various jobs, ethnicities, and religions. The kind of annotators' jobs consists of bachelor students (12 annotators), master students (3 annotators), civil servants (1 annotator), honorary employees (1 annotator), teacher/tutor/teaching assistant (5 annotators), and private employees (8 annotators); the annotators' origin ethnic consists of Java (11 annotators), Bali (4 annotators), Tionghoa (4 annotators), Betawi (3 annotators), Batak (2 annotators), and others (6 annotators, came from Melayu, Minang, Sunda, Cirebon, Ambon, Toraja); and the annotator's religion consists of Islam (15 annotators), Christian (5 annotators), Catholic (5 annotators), Hindu (3 annotators), and Buddha (2 annotators).

In the first annotation phase, we collect 16,500 tweets from the crawling process and previous researches (Alfina et al., 2017, 2018; Putri, 2018) to be annotated by those 30 annotators. Every tweet was annotated by 3 annotators and the fi-

---

nal label was decided using 100% agreement technique. From this phase, we get 11,292 (68.44% total tweets that were annotated in the first phase) consisting of 6,187 not hate speech tweets and 5,105 hate speech tweets that have 100% agreement (reliable dataset). According to (McHugh, 2012), this percentage amount of reliable dataset (data can be used for research experiment) shows that the annotation result has a good level of agreement.

Next, in the second annotation phase, we annotated 5,700 hate speech tweets (5,105 tweets from the first phase annotation and 595 tweets from (Ibrohim and Budi, 2018)). In this phase, we use the best three annotators from the first annotation phase to annotate the target, categories, and level of hate speech. The final label in this phase was decided using majority voting. Since we use 3 annotators, each tweet label must have a minimum agreement from two annotators. If there is no agreement among the annotators in giving the label, then the tweet is deleted. From the second phase annotations results, there were 139 tweets that were deleted because there was no agreement in hate speech categories or hate speech level labels. Therefore, we get 5,561 reliable data (97.56% from total tweets that annotated in the second phase) that can be used for the research experiment. According to (McHugh, 2012), this percentage amount of reliable dataset shows that the annotation result has a almost perfect level of agreement.

From these two phase annotation process, we get 13,169 tweets already used for research experiments that consist of 7,608 not hate speech tweets (6,187 tweets from the first phase annotation and 1,421 tweets from (Ibrohim and Budi, 2018)) and 5,561 hate speech tweets. The distribution of abusive language towards not hate speech tweets and hate speech tweets from the collected tweets can be seen in Figure 1. From Figure 1, we can see that not all hate speech is abusive language. On the contrary, an abusive language also not necessarily a hate speech.

From the total 5,561 hate speech tweets we have, most of that hate speech tweets are directed at individuals (3,575 tweets targeted to an individual and 1,986 tweets targeted to a group). Those hate speech tweets consist of several hate speech categories which are 793 tweets related to religion/creed, 566 tweets re-

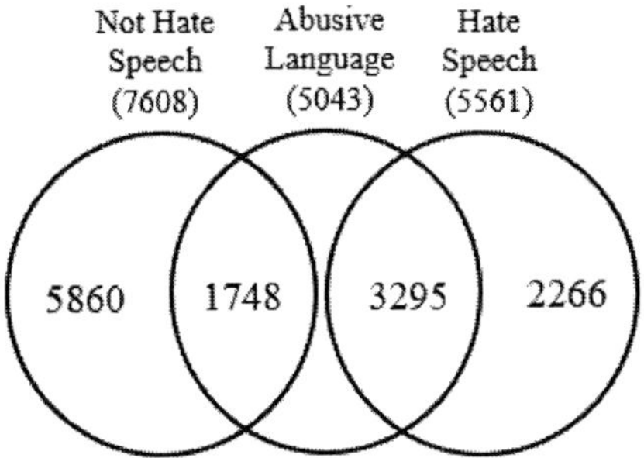

Figure 1: Distribution of abusive language towards not hate speech tweets and hate speech tweets

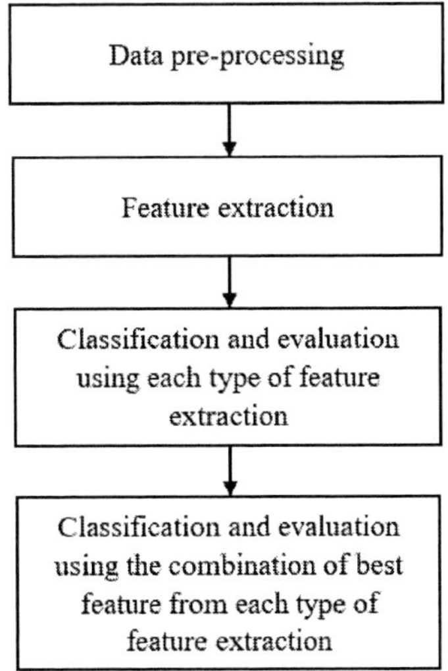

Figure 2: The experiment flowchart

lated to race/ethnicity, 323 tweets related to physical/disability, 306 tweets related to gender/sexual orientation, and 3,740 tweets related to other invective/slander. Notice that the hate speech categories of religion/creed, race/ethnicity, physical/disability, and gender/sexual orientation are multi-label. It means, a tweet of hate speech can be related in several categories. Meanwhile, for the hate speech level labels, our hate speech dataset consists of 3,383 weak hate speech, 1,705 moderate hate speech, and 473 strong hate speech.

4 Experiments and Discussions

We conduct two scenarios for the experiment. The first experiment scenario uses multi-label classification to identify abusive language and hate speech including the target, categories, and level that contained in a tweet. Meanwhile, the second scenario uses multi-label classification to identify abusive language and hate speech that contained in a tweet without identifying the target, categories, and level of hate speech. Both of these scenarios are performed to find out the best classifier, transformation method, and features for each scenario.

In general, both the first scenario and the second scenario have the same flow that can be seen in Figure 2.

First, we do data preprocessing in order to make classification process more efficient and gives better results. We do five processes in data preprocessing consists of case folding, data cleaning, text normalization, stemming, and stop words removal. Case folding was done to make all character in lower case in order to standardize character case. Next, data cleaning was done to remove unnecessary characters such as re-tweet symbol (RT), username, URL, and punctuation. Since we do not use emoticon for feature extraction, we also remove emoticon in data cleaning process. After that, we do text normalization, which is changing non-formal words into formal ones. In this research, we do text normalization simply using dictionary obtained from the combination dictionaries from several previous works (Alfina et al., 2017; Ibrohim and Budi, 2018; Salsabila et al., 2018) and the dictionary that we build based on our dataset. Next, we do stemming to lemmatize words in every tweet. In this paper, stemming was done using Nazief-Adriani Algorithm (Adriani et al., 2007) that implemented using Sastrawi Library[9]. For stop words removal, we used stop word list given by (Tala, 2003).

The next step after data preprocessing is feature extraction. In this research, we used several kinds of feature extractions which are *term frequency, orthography* and *lexicon* features. Term frequency features that we used in our experiments consist of *word n-grams* (unigram, bigrams, trigrams, and the combination of word unigram, bigrams, and trigrams) and *character n-grams* (trigrams, quadgrams, and the combination of character trigrams and quadgrams). For the orthography feature, we used the number of *exclamation mark, question mark, uppercase* and *lowercase*. Meanwhile, for the lexicon features, we used *sentiment lexicon* (negative and positive sentiment) given by (Koto and Rahmaningtyas, 2017) and *abusive lexicon* that we built ourselves compiled from abusive words that used as queries when crawling Twit-

---

[9]https://github.com/har07/PySastrawi

ter data. After the feature extraction process was done, the dataset is ready for classification process.

For the classifier, we used three machine learning classification algorithms which are Naive Bayes (NB), Support Vector Machine (SVM), and Random Forest Decision Tree (RFDT). Based on the previous works (Alfina et al., 2017, 2018; Putri, 2018; Ibrohim and Budi, 2018), those three algorithms can give a pretty good performance in doing hate speech and abusive language detection in Bahasa Indonesia (Indonesian language). Notice that these three classifiers are single label output classifiers. It means, those three classifiers cannot solve multi-label text classification directly. To overcome this problem, we applied data transformation method (Kafrawy et al., 2015) such that the classifiers that we use can solve multi-label text classification problem. We used three data transformation methods that are Binary Relevance (BR), Label Power-set (LP), and Classifier Chains (CC) (Kafrawy et al., 2015). In doing classification, we do classification using each type of feature extraction first. After that, we do classification using the combination of best feature from each type of feature extraction. For the evaluation, we used 10-fold cross-validation technique (Kohavi, 1995) with accuracy as the metric evaluation. Accuracy in this research is calculated using formula as follow (Kafrawy et al., 2015):

$$Accuracy = \left(\frac{1}{D} \sum_{i=1}^{D} \left| \frac{\hat{L}^{(i)} \wedge L^{(i)}}{\hat{L}^{(i)} \vee L^{(i)}} \right| \right) \times 100\%$$
(1)

where D is total document in corpus (dataset), $\hat{L}^{(i)}$ is the prediction result of ith document, and $L^{(i)}$ is the actual label of ith document.

4.1 First Scenario Experiment Result

In this research, the first experiment scenario was done to know the combination of features, classifier, and data transformation method that we used that can give the best accuracy in identifying abusive language and hate speech including the target, categories, and level that was contained in a tweet. To obtain that, we do experiments using every type of feature extractions first. The experiment results for the best type of feature based on average accuracy using all classifiers and data transformation methods for the first scenario is in Table 1.

Based on average accuracy when doing experiments using every type of feature extractions (Table 1), we observe that for the first experiment scenario, the combination of word unigram, bigrams, and trigrams is the best *word n-grams* feature, character quadgrams is the best *character n-grams* feature, question mark is the best *orthography* feature, and negative sentiment is the best *lexicon* feature. However, if viewed individually, RFDT classifier with LP data transformation method when using word unigram feature gives the best performance with 66.12% of accuracy.

After obtaining the best features of each type of features, we do experiments using the combination of best features from each type of features. Based on experiments using the combination of best features from each type of features, we obtain that the combination of best features in this first experiment scenario does not give a significant result on the classification accuracy results. The best performance in experiments using the combination of best features is obtained when using RFDT classifier with LP data transformation method using the combination of character quadgrams, question mark, and negative sentiment just gives 65.73% of accuracy, still cannot exceed the accuracy given by the RFDT classifier with LP data transformation method using word unigram feature that can give 66.12% of accuracy.

Based on classification results and data analysis, we observe that the word unigram features gives the best accuracy may be because they represent the characteristics of each label. In each classification label, there are words that characterize the label. For example, in hate speech label, each tweet that labeled as hate speech contain hate words such as abusive words that demean an individual or group (e.g. *jelek* (ugly), *murahan* (gimrack), etc.), hate words related to politics in Indonesia (e.g. *antek* (henchman), *komunis* (communist), etc.), and

Table 1: Best of each type of feature extraction based on average accuracy for the first scenario

Type of Feature	Best Feature Based on Average Accuracy	Average Accuracy (%)
word n-gram	word unigram + bigram + trigram	59.44
character n-gram	character quadgrams	52.55
ortography	question mark	44.44
lexicon	negative sentiment	44.45

threatening/provoking words (e.g. *bakar* (burn), *bunuh* (kill), etc.). Next, for classifiers analysis, the ensemble method on RFDT relatively can give better accuracy compared to NB and SVM. For data transformation methods, LP can give the best accuracy because each unique label formed from the power-set process will have a correlation between labels so that it can reduce classification error (Kafrawy et al., 2015).

4.2 Second Scenario Experiment Result

The second experiment scenario in this research was done to know the combination of features, classifiers, and data transformation methods that can give the best accuracy in identifying abusive language and hate speech in a tweet without identifying the target, categories, and level of hate speech. Same as the first experiment scenario, we do experiments using every type of feature extractions first. The experiment results for best each type of feature based on average accuracy using all classifier and data transformation method for the second scenario can be seen in Table 2.

Table 2: Best of each type of feature extraction based on average accuracy for the second scenario

Type of Feature	Best Feature Based on Average Accuracy	Average Accuracy (%)
word n-gram	word unigram	73.53
character n-gram	character quadgrams	72.44
ortography	exclamation mark	45.27
lexicon	positive sentiment + abusive lexicon	52.10

Based on average accuracy when doing experiment using every type of feature extractions (Table 2), we obtain that for the second experiment scenario, word unigram feature is the best *word n-grams* feature, character quadgrams is the best *character quadgrams* feature, exclamation mark is the best *orthography* feature, and the combination of positive sentiment and abusive lexicon is the best *lexicon* feature. If viewed individually, RFDT classifier with LP data transformation method when using word unigram feature gives the best performance with 76.16% of accuracy.

After obtaining the best features of each type of features, we do experiment using the combination of best features from each type of feature. Based on the experiment using the combination of best features from each type of features, we obtain that the combination of best features in this second experiment scenario can give slightly better performance compared to when we do not combine the best feature. RFDT classifier with LP data transformation method when using the combination of word unigram, character quadgrams, positive sentiment, and abusive lexicon features can gives the best performance with 77.36% of accuracy.

4.3 Discussions

Based on the first and second experiment scenario results, we obtained that word unigram, RFDT, and LP is the best combination of feature, classifier, and data transformation method for both scenarios. From the second experiment scenario, our approach can reach a good enough performance in doing multi-label text classification to identify abusive language and hate speech without identifying the target, categories, and level of hate speech with 77.36% of accuracy when using RFDT classifier with LP data transformation method and word unigram feature extraction. However, when doing multi-label text classification to identify abusive language and hate speech including its target, categories, and level in the first scenario, the best performance from all our approaches that we use still does not give a good enough performance (only 66.12% of accuracy).

From our error analysis using confusion matrix (Fawcett, 2006) on each classification labels, the most common type of error is false negative. This misclassification is likely due to a large amount of unbalanced data in our dataset. According to (Ganganwar, 2012), unbalanced dataset can give negative results on classification performance because the unbalanced number of dataset between the majority and minority classes tends to make the classification performance on majority class better than classification performance on the minority class, such that it is necessary to balance the dataset. The balancing dataset process can be done by collecting new data and doing the annotation process with a focus on minority labeled data. However, this method needs to consider the data labeling process may be more expensive (Sabou et al., 2014). Some other methods that can be done to balance the dataset are data resampling (Chawla et al., 2002) and data augmentation (Wang and Yang, 2015; Kobayashi, 2018).

Notice that balancing dataset on multi-label problems is a quite difficult process because of the relationship between labels (Giraldo-Forero et al., 2013). To overcome this problem, several techniques can be used, one of which is the hierarchical multi-label classification (Madjarov et al., 2014). In this paper, the multi-label classification problem can be seen as hierarchical multi-label classification problem that can be done by identifying hate speech and abusive language first, and then reclassifying the tweets identified as hate speech to identify the target, categories, and level of hate speech separately. This approach can make the process of dataset balancing easier as classification is done separately for each label type (Feng and Zheng, 2017).

5 Conclusions and Future Works

In this paper, we discussed hate speech and abusive language detection in Indonesian Twitter. We conducted Focus Group Discussion (FGD) with staffs of Direktorat Tindak Pidana Siber Bareskrim Polri as the agency responsible for investigating cyber crimes in Indonesia in order to get a valid definition of hate speech, including the hate speech characterization. The results of the FGD are then poured into annotation guidelines for the purposes of annotating hate speeches. Besides conducted FGD with with staffs of Direktorat Tindak Pidana Siber Bareskrim Polri, we also conducted discussions with an expert linguist in order to make sure that the annotator guidelines we built valid and easy to understand by an annotator who is not a linguistic expert. Moreover, we also built gold standard annotations for testing whether a prospective annotator has read and understood the annotations guide or not. We then built a dataset for abusive language and hate speech identification (including identification of targets, categories, and level hate speech) using annotation guidelines and gold standard annotations that have been made. Our dataset including the annotation guidelines and gold standard annotations are open for public such that other researchers who are interested in doing research in hate speech and abusive language identification in Indonesian social media can use it.

After building the dataset, we did two experiment scenarios. Our experiment results show that word unigram, RFDT, and LP is the best combination of feature, classifier, and data transforma-tion method for all scenarios we did. However, although our approach can reach a good enough performance in doing multi-label classification to identify abusive language and hate speech without identifying the target, categories, and level of hate speech (77.36% of accuracy), all the approaches we used still does not give a good enough performance when doing multi-label classification to identify abusive language and hate speech including identify the target, categories, and level of hate speech (only 66.12% of accuracy).

For future work, we suggest using hierarchical multi-label classification approach (Madjarov et al., 2014) for abusive language and hate speech identification including identify the target, categories, and level of hate speech. Our error analysis shows that a lot of false negative errors is probably caused by the unbalanced dataset (Ganganwar, 2012) such that it is necessary to balance the dataset. This hierarchical multi-label classification approach can make the process of dataset balancing easier because the classification is done separately on each label type (Feng and Zheng, 2017).

Besides doing hierarchical multi-label classification and dataset balancing, another thing that needs to be tried to improve the accuracy of this research is to add a semantic feature, namely *word embedding* (Mikolov et al., 2013) in the feature extraction process. In some text classification experiments in the Indonesian language (Saputri et al., 2018; Jannati et al., 2018), adding *word embedding* features to basic features such as *word n-grams* is shown to improve classification performance because the word embedding feature can recognize word meaning that cannot be captured by features such as frequency term, orthography and lexicon features.

From the FGD results, we obtained that handling hate speech problem in social media is not just about identifying whether a text/document is hate speech or not. There are several other tasks which needs to done to help the authorities in handling hate speech problems such as the identification of buzzers, thread starters, and fake account spreaders of hate speech.

Acknowledgments

The authors acknowledge the PITTA A research grant NKB-0350/UN2.R3.1/HKP.05.00/2019 from Directorate Research and Community Services, Universitas Indonesia.

References

Mirna Adriani, Jelita Asian, Bobby Nazief, S. M.M. Tahaghoghi, and Hugh E. Williams. 2007. Stemming indonesian: A confix-stripping approach. *ACM Transactions on Asian Language Information Processing (TALIP)*, 6(4):1–33.

Ika Alfina, Rio Mulia, Mohamad Ivan Fanany, and Yudo Ekananta. 2017. Hate speech detection in the indonesian language: A dataset and preliminary study. In *International Conference on Advanced Computer Science and Information Systems (ICAC-SIS)*, pages 233–238.

Ika Alfina, Siti Hadiyan Pratiwi, Indra Budi, Rio Mulia, and Yudo Ekanata. 2018. Detecting hate speech against religion in the indonesian language. *Journal of Telecommunication, Electronic and Computer Engineering (JTEC)*.

APJII. 2017. *Infografis Penetrasi dan Pengguna Internet Indonesia Survey 2017*. Pustaka PelajarAsosiasi Penyelenggara Jasa Internet Indonesia, Jakarta.

Nitesh V. Chawla, Kevin W. Bowyer, Lawrence O. Hall, and W. Philip Kegelmeyer. 2002. Smote: Synthetic minority over-sampling technique. *Journal of Artificial Intelligence Research*, 16:321–357.

Ying Chen, Yilu Zhou, Sencun Zhu, and Heng Xu. 2012. Detecting offensive language in social media to protect adolescent online safety. In *Proceedings of the 2012 ASE/IEEE International Conference on Social Computing and 2012 ASE/IEEE International Conference on Privacy, Security, Risk and Trust*, SOCIALCOM-PASSAT '12, pages 71–80, Washington, DC, USA. IEEE Computer Society.

Thomas Davidson, Dana Warmsley, Michael W. Macy, and Ingmar Weber. 2017. Automated hate speech detection and the problem of offensive language. In *International AAAI Conference on Web and Social Media (ICWSM)*, pages 512–515.

T Fawcett. 2006. An introduction to roc analysis. *Pattern Recognition Letters*, 27:861–874.

Fu P. Feng, S. and W. Zheng. 2017. A hierarchical multi-label classification algorithm for gene function prediction. *Algorithms*, 10(4):1–14.

V Ganganwar. 2012. An overview of classification algorithms for imbalanced datasets. *International Journal of Emerging Technology and Advanced Engineering*, 2(4):42–47.

A. F. Giraldo-Forero, J. A. Jaramillo-Garzon, J. F. Ruiz-Munoz, and C. G. Castellanos-Dominguez. 2013. Managing imbalanced data setsin multi-label problems: A case study with the smote algorithm. In *Proceedings of the 18th Iberoamerican Congress on Progress in Pattern Recognition, Image Analysis, Computer Vision, and Applications*, pages 334–342.

Bayu Hernanto and Jeihan. 2018. Personal communication.

Muhammad Okky Ibrohim and Indra Budi. 2018. A dataset and preliminaries study for abusive language detection in indonesian social media. *Procedia Computer Science*, 135:222 – 229.

Muhammad Okky Ibrohim, Erryan Sazany, and Indra Budi. 2018. Identify abusive and offensive language inindonesian twitter using deep learning approach. *Journal of Physics: Conference Series*.

R. Jannati, R. Mahendra, C. W. Wardhana, and M. Adriani. 2018. Stance classification towards political figures on blog writing. In *2018 International Conference on Asian Language Processing (IALP)*, pages 96–101.

Passent El Kafrawy, Amr Mausad, and Heba Esmail. 2015. Article: Experimental comparison of methods for multi-label classification in different application domains. *International Journal of Computer Applications*, 114(19):1–9.

S. Kobayashi. 2018. Contextual augmentation: Data augmentation by words with paradigmatic relations. In *Proceedings of NAACL-HLT 2018*, pages 452–457.

Ron Kohavi. 1995. A study of cross-validation and bootstrap for accuracy estimation and model selection. In *Proceedings of the 14th International Joint Conference on Artificial Intelligence - Volume 2*, IJCAI'95, pages 1137–1143, San Francisco, CA, USA. Morgan Kaufmann Publishers Inc.

Komnas HAM. 2015. *Buku Saku Penanganan Ujaran Kebencian (Hate Speech)*. Komisi Nasional Hak Asasi Manusia, Jakarta.

F. Koto and G. Y. Rahmaningtyas. 2017. Inset lexicon: Evaluation of a word list for indonesian sentiment analysis in microblogs. In *2017 International Conference on Asian Language Processing (IALP)*, pages 391–394.

G. Madjarov, I. Dimitrovski, D. Gjorgjevikj, and S. Dzerosk. 2014. Evaluation of different data-derived label hierarchies in multi-label classification. In *Proceedings of the 3rd International Conference on New Frontiers in Mining Complex Patterns*, pages 19–37.

Mary L. McHugh. 2012. Interrater reliability: the kappa statistic. *Biochemia medica*, 22(3):276–282.

Tomas Mikolov, Ilya Sutskever, Kai Chen, Greg S Corrado, and Jeff Dean. 2013. Distributed representations of words and phrases and their compositionality. In C. J. C. Burges, L. Bottou, M. Welling, Z. Ghahramani, and K. Q. Weinberger, editors, *Advances in Neural Information Processing Systems 26*, pages 3111–3119. Curran Associates, Inc.

C. Nobata, J. Tetreault, A. Thomas, Y. Mehdad, and Y Chang. 2016. Abusive language detection in online user content. In *International World Wide Web Conference Committee (IW3C2)*, pages 145–153.

Muzainah Nurasijah. 2018. Personal communication.

Tansa Trisna Astono Putri. 2018. Analisis dan deteksi hate speech pada sosial twitter berbahasa indonesia. Master's thesis, Faculty of Computer Science, Universitas Indonesia.

Marta Sabou, Kalina Bontcheva, Leon Derczynski, and Arno Scharl. 2014. Corpus annotation through crowdsourcing: Towards best practice guidelines. In *Proceedings of the Ninth International Conference on Language Resources and Evaluation (LREC-2014)*. European Language Resources Association (ELRA).

Nikmatun Aliyah Salsabila, Yosef Ardhito Winatmoko, and Ali Akbar Septiandri. 2018. Colloquial indonesian lexicon. In *2018 International Conference on Asian Language Processing (IALP)*, pages 236–239.

M. S. Saputri, R. Mahendra, and M. Adriani. 2018. Emotion classification on indonesian twitter dataset. In *2018 International Conference on Asian Language Processing (IALP)*, pages 90–95.

Gregory H. Stanton. 2009. The rwandan genocide: Why early warning failed. *Journal of African Conflicts and Peace Studies*, 1(2):6–25.

F. Z. Tala. 2003. A study of stemming effects on information retrieval in bahasa indonesia. Master's thesis, Universiteti van Amsterdam The Netherlands.

S. Turaob and J.L Mitrpanont. 2017. Automatic discovery of abusive thai language. In *International Conference on Asia-Pacific Digital Libraries*, pages 267–278.

Fabio Del Vigna, Andrea Cimino, Felice Dell'Orletta, Marinella Petrocchi, and Maurizio Esconi. 2017. Hate me, hate me not: Hate speech detection on facebook. In *Proceedings of the First Italian Conference on Cybersecurity (ITASEC17)*, pages 86–95.

W. Y. Wang and D. Yang. 2015. Thats so annoying!!!: A lexical and frame-semantic embedding based data augmentation approach to automatic categorization of annoying behaviors using #petpeeve tweets. In *EMNLP*, pages 2557–2563.

Zeerak Waseem and Dirk Hovy. 2016. Hateful symbols or hateful people? predictive features for hate speech detection on twitter. In *Proceedings of the NAACL Student Research Workshop*, pages 88–93, San Diego, California. Association for Computational Linguistics.

I Dewa Putu Wijana and Muhammad Rohmadi. 2010. *Sosiolinguistik: Kajian, Teori, dan Analisis*. Pustaka Pelajar, Yogyakarta.

Harish Yenala, Ashish Jhanwar, Manoj K. Chinnakotla, and Jay Goyal. 2017. Deep learning for detecting inappropriate content in text. In *International Journal of Data Science and Analytics*.

Appendix 1: Example of query used for crawling Twitter data

Query	Description	Citation
keparat	Abusive word (other)	(Wijana and Rohmadi., 2010)
anjing	Abusive word (other)	(Wijana and Rohmadi., 2010)
asu	Abusive word (other), other form of *anjing*	(Ibrohim and Budi, 2018)
banci	Abusive word related to gender/sexual orientation	(Wijana and Rohmadi., 2010)
bangsat	Abusive word (other)	(Wijana and Rohmadi., 2010)
bencong	Abusive word related to gender/sexual orientation, another form of *banci*	(Wijana and Rohmadi., 2010)
jancuk	Abusive word related to gender/sexual orientation	(Wijana and Rohmadi., 2010)
budek	Abusive word related to physical/disability	(Wijana and Rohmadi., 2010)
burik	Abusive word related to physical/disability	(Wijana and Rohmadi., 2010)
cocot	Abusive word (other)	(Ibrohim and Budi, 2018)
ngewe	Abusive word related to gender/sexual orientation	(Ibrohim and Budi, 2018)
kafir	Abusive word related to religion/creed	(Wijana and Rohmadi., 2010)
kapir	Abusive word related to religion/creed, another form of *kafir*	(Ibrohim and Budi, 2018)
sinting	Abusive word related to physical/disability	(Wijana and Rohmadi., 2010)
antek	Word related to hate speech issue in politics	(Hernanto and Jeihan, 2018)
asing	Word related to hate speech issue in politics	(Hernanto and Jeihan, 2018)
aseng	Word related to hate speech issue in politics, another form of *asing*	(Hernanto and Jeihan, 2018)
ateis	Abusive word related to religion/creed	(Wijana and Rohmadi., 2010)
sitip	Abusive word related to race/ethnicity	(Wijana and Rohmadi., 2010)
autis	Abusive word related to physical/disability	(Wijana and Rohmadi., 2010)
picek	Abusive word related to physical/disability	(Ibrohim and Budi, 2018)
ayam kampus	Abusive phrase related to gender/sexual orientation	(Ibrohim and Budi, 2018)
bani kotak	Phrase related to hate speech issue in politics	(Hernanto and Jeihan, 2018)
cebong	Word related to hate speech issue in politics	(Hernanto and Jeihan, 2018)
cina	Word related to hate speech issue in politics and race/ethnicity	(Hernanto and Jeihan, 2018)
china	Word related to hate speech issue in politics and race/ethnicity, other form of cina	(Hernanto and Jeihan, 2018)
hindu	Word related to hate speech issue in religion/creed	(Hernanto and Jeihan, 2018)
katolik	Word related to hate speech issue in religion/creed	(Hernanto and Jeihan, 2018)
katholik	Word related to hate speech issue in religion/creed, another form of *katolik*	(Hernanto and Jeihan, 2018)
komunis	Word related to hate speech issue in politics and race/ethnicity	(Hernanto and Jeihan, 2018)
kristen	Word related to hate speech issue in religion/creed	(Hernanto and Jeihan, 2018)
onta	Word related to hate speech issue in politics	(Hernanto and Jeihan, 2018)
pasukan nasi	Phrase related to hate speech issue in politics	(Hernanto and Jeihan, 2018)
tionghoa	Word related to hate speech issue in politics and race/ethnicity	(Hernanto and Jeihan, 2018)

The Discourse of Online Content Moderation: Investigating Polarized User Responses to Changes in Reddit's Quarantine Policy

Qinlan Shen
Carnegie Mellon University
`qinlans@cs.cmu.edu`

Carolyn P. Rosé
Carnegie Mellon University
`cprose@cs.cmu.edu`

Abstract

Recent concerns over abusive behavior on their platforms have pressured social media companies to strengthen their content moderation policies. However, user opinions on these policies have been relatively understudied. In this paper, we present an analysis of user responses to a September 27, 2018 announcement about the quarantine policy on Reddit as a case study of to what extent the discourse on content moderation is polarized by users' ideological viewpoint. We introduce a novel partitioning approach for characterizing user polarization based on their distribution of participation across interest subreddits. We then use automated techniques for capturing framing to examine how users with different viewpoints discuss moderation issues, finding that right-leaning users invoked censorship while left-leaning users highlighted inconsistencies on how content policies are applied. Overall, we argue for a more nuanced approach to moderation by highlighting the intersection of behavior and ideology in considering how abusive language is defined and regulated.

1 Introduction

In response to the rising surge of abusive behavior online, large social media platforms, such as Facebook, Twitter, and Youtube have been pressured to strengthen their stances against offensive content and increase their transparency in how content policies are enforced. Facebook, for example, first released its community standards publicly in April 2018 and has made efforts to ban white nationalist and separatist content (Stack, 2018), while Twitter announced a new policy against "dehumanizing speech" in September 2018 (Matsakis, 2018).

Nevertheless, the problem of how to define what behaviors are abusive and how these behaviors should be handled remains a challenge. One major issue in terms of defining a content policy for a major platform is that defining what abusive behavior is requires consideration of both behavior *and* ideology – political ideology is inextricably tied with abusive language on major platforms where sensitive discussion can occur. For example, Reddit (Statt, 2018) and Twitter (Newton, 2019) have faced recent backlash for allowing racist content to remain on their platforms over concerns of bias against right-leaning viewpoints. Prior research (Shen et al., 2018; Jiang et al., 2019) has also demonstrated that ideology can be used as a tool to challenge moderation decisions.

In this paper, we argue that ideology is inextricably tied to how abusive language is defined and regulated in real-world applications in social media. To demonstrate the role of political ideology in the problem of defining abusive language, we present the first NLP study of polarized user responses towards policy. We examine how users frame their arguments in supporting or opposing stronger moderation policies to draw insight into ideologically-related user concerns over their impact. As a case study, we focus on users' responses towards changes to the quarantine policy on Reddit.[1] Reddit provides an interesting site of study into content moderation issues due to a culture of debate over whether free speech is a principal tenet of the platform (Robertson, 2015). Here, we focus on a specific policy change to provide an in-depth analysis of the polarized stances users take.

The rest of the paper is organized as follows. First, we give an overview of related work and describe the recent Reddit quarantine policy update. Next, we present a general topic analysis of discussion surrounding the quarantine policy. We then describe how we operationalized polarization by characterizing users based on their participation across subreddits, then examine how different

---

[1] `https://www.reddit.com/r/announcements/comments/9jf8nh/`

Proceedings of the Third Workshop on Abusive Language Online, pages 58–69
Florence, Italy, August 1, 2019. ©2019 Association for Computational Linguistics

users frame issues within topics. Finally, we discuss the implications and limitations of our work.

2   Related Work

One of the primary roles of moderation in online spacesis the regulation of anti-social behaviors (Kiesler et al., 2012), such as spamming, cyberbullying, and hate speech. The design and best practices for moderating abusive content on large social media platforms, however, is a fundamentally challenging issue (Gillespie, 2018), due to the tension between providing a space for open and meaningful interaction and determining what behaviors are acceptable and how unacceptable behaviors should be handled. While social media companies, as private organizations, can legally curate content on their platforms (Robertson, 2015), cracking down on content can lead to tension with users, who may view it as setting a precedent for banning behaviors or even political ideologies in the future. Previous research Shen et al. (2018); Jiang et al. (2019), has demonstrated that tensions and backlash can arise in communities if participants perceive moderation decisions as biased against minority viewpoints, even if decisions seem "fair" after accounting for behavior.

Previous research on the effect of moderation policies has focused primarily on the effect of moderation on directly affected users. For example, Chandrasekharan et al. (2017) investigated the impact of the 2015 Reddit hateful content ban on users who participated on the banned subreddits, while Chang and Danescu-Niculescu-Mizil (2019) examined the participation trajectories of users blocked by community moderators on Wikipedia. User opinions on moderation policies, however, remains relatively understudied from a large-scale quantitative perspective, though previous work has drawn insights from structured interviews and surveys with users. Jhaver et al. (2018) interviewed both users who used blocklists on Twitter and users who have been blocked on their insights about harassment and blocking. Myers West (2018) surveyed participants on OnlineCensorship.org about their experiences with content moderation to gather insights into folk theories about how moderation policies work.

Most closely related to our work, which focuses on ideologically motivated user viewpoints, Jhaver et al. (2017) used a mixed-methods approach to investigate how users on r/KotakuInAction, a sub-reddit associated with the Gamergate movement, view free expression, harassment, and censorship within their own community. Rather than focusing on users who share certain views within a particular subreddit, however, we focus on users who responded to a Reddit-wide moderation policy change. This allows us to examine how users who have participated across a wide range of subreddits present their opinions, with the goal of understanding what elements of the debate between moderation and censorship are polarized.

3   Reddit Quarantine Policy Announcement

On September 27, 2018, Reddit announced changes to their quarantine policy in response to growing concerns over the visibility of offensive content on their platform. The quarantine feature allows site administrators to hide "communities that, while not prohibited, average redditors may nevertheless find highly offensive or upsetting"[2] from being searched, recommended, or monetized. While the quarantine function was initially announced in August 2015 as part of a broader initiative to address offensive content, the September announcement specifically focused on expanding use of the quarantine function. The two major aspects of the announcement were 1) a quarantine wave of 20+ communities of interest or *subreddits* and 2) the introduction of an appeals process for moderators of quarantined subreddits.

The announcement was posted in the r/announcements subreddit, which allows users to respond to major Reddit-internal policy changes. To investigate the discourse surrounding the announcement, we collected comments that were posted in response to the r/announcements over the course of one month using the Pushshift API.[3] After filtering out 6 comments that were deleted by users or removed by moderators, as we no longer had access to the original comment texts, we then identified 13 well-known meta-bots[4] among the remaining users. Both comments by and responses to these meta-bots were removed,

---

[2]`https://www.reddithelp.com/`
`en/categories/rules-reporting/`
`account-and-community-restrictions/`
`quarantined-subreddits`

[3]`https://pushshift.io/api-parameters/`

[4]CommonMisspellingBot, WikiTextBot, Link-Help-Bot, YTubeInfoBot, HelperBot_, LimbRetrieval-Bot, BigLebowskiBot, FatFingerHelperBot, RemindMeBot, imguralbumbot, opinionated-bot, societybot, svenska_subbar

Topic	Top Words
T0: Accessibility of Quarantined Content (13.6%)	quarantine, reddit, subs, subreddit, content, community, view, find, offensive, list, users, mobile, quarantining, site, access
T1: Heated Outbursts (11.7%)	shit, fuck, lol, racist, ca [CringeAnarchy], literally, stop, td [the_Donald], stupid, show, love, dude, alt, call, thread, leftist
T2: Content in r/The_Donald (11.2%)	t_d, ban, post, subreddit, the_donald, propaganda, admins, rules, russian, subs, users, violence, racism, page, link
T3: Conservative vs. Liberal Politics [U.S.] (10.1%)	trump, politics, left, time, wing, posts, evidence, comments, day, stuff, donald, top, ago, hard, conservative
T4: Censorship of Political Views/Debate (9.8%)	people, bad, censorship, agree, make, wrong, political, point, opinions, disagree, thought, fact, ideas, understand, discussion, feel
T5: Moderation/Free Speech on Social Media (9.2%)	reddit, speech, free, hate, hitler, site, heil, internet, platform, thing, censorship, website, private, open, freedom
T6: Far-Right/Far-Left Ideologies (9.0%)	white, nazi, anti, people, genocide, holocaust, support, great, fascist, jews, communism, capitalism, country, claim, socialism
T7: Personal Experience (7.1%)	people, things, talking, thing, time, men, matter, person, real, years, talk, life, made, lot, world
T8: Laws/Government-level Policies (6.2%)	people, society, violence, person, power, words, point, world, rights, groups, political, majority, control, argue, definition, part
T9: Miscellaneous (12.0%)	good, make, ca, yeah, read, back, man, money, question, side, wo, big, end, full, care

Table 1: Identified topics, proportion in our dataset, and top 15 associated words. Topic names were assigned after examining both the top words and the top comments associated with each topic.

as they are usually formulaic and unrelated to the content of our analyses (e.g. "Good bot", complaints about bot responses), leaving us with a final announcement dataset containing 9,836 posts from 3,640 users.

4 Topical Analysis

Topic choice has been commonly used in NLP (Tsur et al., 2015; Field et al., 2018; Demszky et al., 2019) as a proxy for *agenda-setting*, the strategic highlighting of what aspects of a subject are worth discussing (McCombs, 2002). Here, we first describe our preliminary topic analysis for discovering the range of topics discussed.

4.1 Models

We used Latent Dirichlet Allocation (LDA) (Blei et al., 2003) to construct our topics. While Structural Topic Models (STM) (Roberts et al., 2013) are popular for social science analyses for enabling document metadata to act as topic covariates, STM consistently performed worse than LDA on our data, both in topical coherence measures and human interpretability.[5]

For the LDA models, we considered each comment to be a document. Comments were tokenized using SpaCy (Honnibal and Montani, 2017) and stopwords and punctuation-only tokens were removed. We trained models with 5, 10, 15, 20, 25, 30, 40, and 50 topics. We selected the model with 10 topics for further analysis for having the highest CV coherence, which has been shown to more closely correlate with human ratings of interpretability (Röder et al., 2015) than semantic coherence (Mimno et al., 2011). When analyzing and interpreting the topics discovered, we examined both the highest weighted words and example comments associated with each topic.

4.2 Results

Table 1 presents the topics discovered by the model. The most prevalent topic (**T0**) in the discussion thread focuses on accessibility to quarantined subreddits. This is unsurprising, as this

---

[5]A potential challenge for STM for our data is the lack of global consistency in our metadata. Comments in Reddit

threads are organized in broad semi-topical hierarchical trees and threads can contain thousands of comments (Weninger, 2014). As a result, user participation on a single thread can be scattered and upvoted comments in one subthread may substantially overlap in content with downvoted comments in another. Thus, the simpler LDA model, with fewer global priors on the structure and content of the data, may have better generalization.

topic directly addresses the short-term impact of the quarantine wave, such as the ability to search for and list quarantined subreddits, access to quarantined content on the mobile app, and whether quarantined content will generate ad revenue. The proportion of **T0** across comments, however, is relatively low (13.6%), compared to discussion centered around the broader implications of quarantining. For example, **T3:** Conservative vs. Liberal Politics and **T6:** Far-Right/Far-Left Ideologies center around broader ideologies associated with controversial content, while **T4:** Censorship of Political Views/Debate, **T5:** Moderation/Free Speech on Social Media Platforms, and **T8:** Laws/Government-Level Policies discuss the legal implications of online content moderation.

One notable topic in our model was **T2:** Content in r/The_Donald. Despite not being one of the subreddits quarantined during the quarantine wave, much of the discussion surrounding the announcement centered around The_Donald, due to its prominent reputation for controversial behavior. We can see evidence of discussion about controversial behavior on The_Donald, as many of the highly weighted words in the discussion of The_Donald are words describing negative behaviors that have been associated with the subreddit in past research, such as propaganda/fake news (Kang, 2016), promotion of violence and racism (Squirrell, 2017), and visibility manipulation and mobilization through bots (Carman et al., 2018; Flores-Saviaga et al., 2018). The_Donald is often considered an "elephant in the room" with regards to content moderation on Reddit, as the subreddit remains one of the most visible and active subreddits on the site despite its controversial reputation.

A somewhat surprising omission from the topics discovered was discussion around the new appeals process for quarantined subreddits. While the bulk of the text in the original post of the thread centered around the introduction of the appeals process, only 0.13% of the posts explicitly used the words "appeal" and "appeals" in reference to the appeals policy. The addition of an appeals process is relatively uncontroversial for increasing the transparency of quarantines and primarily affects moderators of quarantined subreddits. This suggests that what *is* driving discussion within the thread are the more controversial issues that may have a personal, ideological impact on users. As a result, we expect that users with differing view-

points may highlight different aspects within the general topics discussed here.

5 Characterizing User Participation on Reddit

In order to better understand how different users highlight or *frame* particular aspects within each topic (Entman, 2007; Nguyen et al., 2013; Card et al., 2016), we first want to characterize the types of users who participated in the r/announcements discussion. Because subreddits on Reddit represent interest-based subcommunities, previous work has used participation across subreddits as a signal of user interests or viewpoint (Olson and Neal, 2015; Chandrasekharan et al., 2017). We follow in the lines of this work by characterizing users using their participation in subreddits prior to the announcement. In this section, we describe a graph-partitioning approach for characterizing common interests across subreddits.

5.1 Constructing the Interest Graph

For each user who participated in the r/announcements quarantine thread, we collect all submissions and comments posted by the user in the month preceding the quarantine policy update (August 27 - September 26). We then counted how many times each user posted in each subreddit. In order to ensure that users both showed sustained interest in a subreddit and to limit the number of users who participate in subreddits to challenge the widely held view of a subreddit, we consider a user to be interested in a subreddit if they have posted at least 3 times[6] in the preceding month with a positive score.

To capture similarities between the subreddits users participate in, we then cluster them by performing graph partitioning over a subreddit interest graph (Olson and Neal, 2015). We construct a subreddit interest graph by drawing an undirected edge e_{ij} between two subreddit nodes i and j if the same user participates in both subreddits. A_{ij}, the weight of e_{ij}, is set equal to the number of users in common between i and j. We reduce the number of edges in the graph by setting a global edge threshold $A_{ij} >= 5$.[7]

---

[6]The threshold was determined based on the distribution of user-subreddit participation pairs across users who participated in the r/announcements thread.

[7]While we can threshold the edges of a graph using a significance-based backbone extraction algorithm, our subreddit graph is based only on the users from the

Category	Central Subreddits	Accuracy	Cohen's κ
C0: Tech/Sports	technology, Games, pcmasterrace, nba, PS4,	56.25	68.31
C1: Internet Compilation	WTF, WhitePeopleTwitter, trashy, BlackPeopleTwitter, mildlyinfuriating	84.38	75.13
C2: Right-Leaning	CringeAnarchy, unpopularopinion, the_Donald, Libertarian, TumblrInAction	78.13	66.14
C3: Memes	greentext, starterpacks, dankmemes, PrequelMemes, MemeEconomy	50.00	27.64
C4: Left-Leaning	TopMindsOfReddit, SubredditDrama, ChapoTrapHouse, The_Mueller, FuckTheAltRight	81.25	52.71

Table 2: Identified subreddit categories, central subreddits, averaged annotator performance and agreement on intrusion task.

5.2 Louvain Community Detection

We use the Louvain community detection algorithm (Blondel et al., 2008) to define a partition over the constructed subreddit interest graph. The objective of the Louvain algorithm is to maximize the *modularity* of a partition, which measures the density of links within vs. between communities. The Louvain modularity Q is defined as

$$Q = \frac{1}{2m} \sum_{i,j} \left[A_{ij} - \frac{k_i k_j}{2m} \right] \delta(c_i, c_j) \qquad (1)$$

where $k_i = \sum_j A_{ij}$ is the sum of the weights of edges attached to node i, $\delta(c_i, c_j) = 1$ if nodes i and j belong to the same community, 0 otherwise, and $m = \frac{1}{2} \sum_{i,j} A_{ij}$. Because ΔQ from moving node i from one community to another is easy to compute, the algorithm finds the best partition through a simple two-stage process:

1. Assign each node to its own community

2. Repeat until convergence

   (a) Iterate through nodes i, moving i into the community that gives the highest increase in modularity, until convergence.

   (b) Construct new graph where nodes are communities and edge weights between communities are equal to sum of edge weights between lower-level nodes.

We use a resolution factor (Lambiotte et al., 2008) of 1.0 and select the highest modularity partition of the dendrogram for our subreddit categories. The resulting 5 categories are shown in Table 2.

r/announcements thread. As a result, a significance-based method of thresholding edges can give uneven results based on how many users were sampled from each subreddit.

5.3 Evaluation

To ensure that the 5 discovered subreddit categories gave us high-quality and coherent notions of user interests, we run a human evaluation of the discovered categories using a subreddit intrusion task, analogous to word intrusion tasks used for evaluating topic model interpretability (Chang et al., 2009). The subreddit intrusion task was presented to two native English speaker annotators who used Reddit on a daily basis to ensure familiarity with the types of user interests on Reddit. Given a set of four subreddits belonging to one of the categories, and an "intruder" subreddit from another category, annotators were asked to identify the intruder. Annotators were provided with the description and 5 highly-ranked thread titles for each subreddit for additional context in determining the intruder. For each category, all the other categories were selected as an intruder instance 4 times, giving us 16 sets per category. After completing the intrusion task, the annotators discussed their decision-making process during the intrusion task and assigned labels to the five discovered subreddit categories.

Results for the intrusion task for each category are included in Table 2. For all the subreddit categories except **C3: Memes**, the annotators achieved moderate-to-high agreement and performed significantly better than a random baseline. The category of **C3: Memes** is more abstract compared to the other categories and contains many subreddits that are not easily identifiable by name and description alone. Nevertheless, the annotators were able to reach an agreement on the interests covered by **C3** in discussion after the intrusion task.

From these discovered subreddit categories, for each user, we calculate their distribution of participation across the five categories and an additional category for unidentified subreddits. One limitation of considering user viewpoints based on these categories, however, is that only **C2:** Right-Leaning and **C4:** Left-Leaning are directly related to political viewpoint. Rather, these five categories more closely represent shared sets of interests or personas users can engage in. While this limits what we can say in terms of polarization across the traditional definitions of left-leaning vs. right-leaning political ideologies, we argue that considering user participation in these interest categories is more representative of how users on Reddit engage in politics across the site.

6   Analyzing Polarized Viewpoints Towards the Quarantine Policy

In the previous sections, we first identified the general topics discussed within the r/announcements thread about the quarantine policy. We then characterized users who participated in the r/announcements thread based on their distribution of participation across different subreddits in the month preceding the announcement. In this section, we examine the relationship between a user's ideological views and how they strategically highlight particular aspects of each topic. Rather than using a static left vs. right framework for operationalizing user viewpoint, we examine how users highlight different aspects as they move along the left-right spectrum. We then analyze the relationship between users' polarization and their framing within the topics identified in Section 3 in an unsupervised manner.

6.1   User Polarization

While we can label users strictly as left vs. right based on whether they spend more of their time on left-leaning and right-leaning subreddits in their participation distribution, we can get a more nuanced view of the differences between left-leaning and right-leaning users by additionally considering how polarized users are along the left-right spectrum. Rather than using a simple majority-based assignment, we introduce a polarization margin hyperparameter β that controls for how skewed a user must be towards one side to be considered a left-leaning or right-leaning user. For a given β, we can assign the class of each user u_i

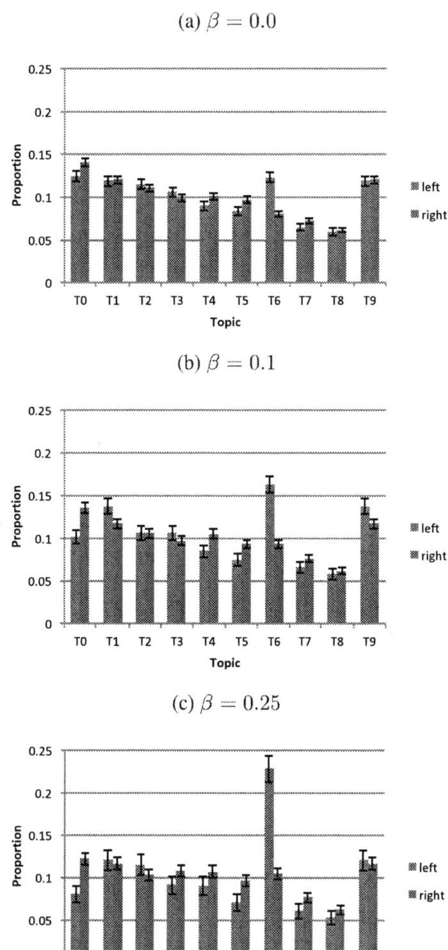

Figure 1: Topic prevalence across left and right-leaning users at different levels of polarization, with 95% confidence intervals.

based on their participation distribution p:

$$C_\beta(u_i) = \begin{cases} \text{left,} & \text{if } p_l(u_i) - p_r(u_i) > \beta \\ \text{right,} & \text{if } p_r(u_i) - p_l(u_i) > \beta \\ \text{neutral,} & \text{otherwise} \end{cases} \tag{2}$$

$\beta = 0$ is equal to the majority case. For our remaining analyses on agenda-setting and framing, we compare results for $\beta = \{0, 0.1, 0.25\}$.

6.2   Polarized Agenda-Setting

Figure 1 shows the prevalence of each topic across left-leaning and right-leaning users at differing values of β. We found that right-leaning users were significantly more likely to invoke **T0:** Accessibility of Quarantined Content, **T4:** Censorship of Political Views/Debate, and **T5**: Moderation/Free Speech on Social Media for all values of β. The high prevalence **T0** is unsurprising, as the majority of the newly quarantined subreddits (listed in the Supplementary Material) were associated with conservative views and users. Thus, accessibility to the newly quarantined subreddits would be a concern for many right-leaning users. The increased prevalence of topics **T4** and **T5**, which are focused on the relationship between content moderation online spaces and censorship, suggests that right-leaning users may be challenging the ability or approach of Reddit administrators to expand the quarantine policy as a form of censorship. Finally, the higher prevalence of **T7**: Personal Experience topic, which is focused on users' personal participation on the quarantined or other controversial subreddits, suggests that to some extent, right-leaning users are leaning into their participation on controversial subreddits in their responses towards the announcement.

Across all values of β, left-leaning users use **T6**: Far-Right/Far-Left Ideologies significantly more than right-leaning users. This difference increases as the polarization margin β increases. This suggests that left-leaning users were likely to invoke the controversial behaviors associated with the extremism, particularly the far-right. Interestingly, while extremist ideology is more likely to be invoked by left-leaning users, there was no significant difference in prevalence between left-leaning and right-leaning users for discussion of US politics (**T3**: Conservative vs. Liberal Politics).

Overall, we note that while the relative prevalence of topics for left-leaning and right-leaning users generally remained the same at different values of β, the major differences between left-leaning and right-leaning users became larger as we increase the polarity margin.

6.3 Within-Topic Framing

We expect users who have different positions to highlight different aspects of each topic. To separate out the salient words within each topic t for left-leaning and right-leaning users, for each word w, we use the z-score of the log-odds ratio with a Dirichlet prior (Monroe et al., 2008) as a salience score, $\delta_w^{r(t)-l(t)}$:

$$\delta_w^{c(t)} = \log \frac{y_w^{c(t)} + \alpha_w^t}{n^{c(t)} + \alpha_0^t - (y_w^{c(t)} + \alpha_w^t)} \tag{3}$$

$$\delta_w^{r(t)-l(t)} = \delta_w^{r(t)} - \delta_w^{l(t)} \tag{4}$$

$$\sigma\big(\delta_w^{r(t)-l(t)}\big) = \frac{1}{y_w^{r(t)} + \alpha_w^t} + \frac{1}{y_w^{l(t)} + \alpha_w^t} \tag{5}$$

$$z\big(\delta_w^{r(t)-l(t)}\big) = \frac{\delta_w^{r(t)-l(t)}}{\sqrt{\sigma\big(\delta_w^{r(t)-l(t)}\big)}} \tag{6}$$

where $n^{c(t)}$ is the number of words in corpus c, $y_w^{c(t)}$ is the count of word w in corpus $c(t)$, $l(t)$ and $r(t)$ are the left-leaning and right-leaning corpora for topic t, and α_0^t and α_w^t are corpus and word priors from a background corpus. We set the Dirichlet prior by using the posts from "neutral" users as a background corpus, with the size and count of words in the background corpus as the corpus and word priors respectively.. We extend the salience score to bigrams and trigrams and sampled posts containing the top 50 salient terms for each topic and faction to analyze framing strategies at different levels of polarization.

First, we found that, across topics, right-leaning users framed the issues surrounding content moderation in terms of censorship and suppression, while left-leaning users tended to frame issues in terms of consistency. For example, in **T4**: Censorship of Political Views/Debate, right-leaning users consistently used terms such as "silencing", "echo chamber", and "censorship" in reference to impact of the announcement, directly accusing the quarantine policy of being used to silence political viewpoints. This supports our hypothesis from Section 5.2 that right-leaning users invoked **T4** to criticize the quarantine policy as a form of censorship. On the other hand, when left-leaning users invoked **T4**, they used terms such as "picking and choosing", "bad faith" in reference to uneven and insufficient application of the policy. Left-leaning users also often compared the quarantine feature to "bans" in **T4**, arguing that many subreddits quarantined under the announcement shared similarities with subreddits that were banned in the past.

We see similar patterns in **T5**: Moderation/Free Speech on Social Media, though many of the salient terms used are specific to internet platforms. Right-leaning users emphasize the ideal of a free and open internet, using terms such as "open platforms" and invoking the name of "Aaron Swartz", the late Reddit co-founder known for his anti-censorship views. Left-leaning users, on the other hand, consistently highlighted that private organizations like Reddit ("private company", "privately owned") had the right to remove or hide content in violation of their policies.

One of the more salient framing strategies related to consistency by left-leaning users is the comparison of quarantines with Reddit's handling of pornographic content, primarily in **T0: Accessibility of Quarantined Content** and **T8: Laws/Government-level Policies**. While opinions about how to handle porn on Reddit are mixed, porn is commonly used as an analogue for many of the consistency issues involved with quarantining subreddits with abusive language. For example, some users argue that the intent and functionality of quarantining should be similar to the not-safe-for-work (NSFW) filtering system already in place for pornographic subreddits, which does not explicitly block a subreddit from being searched or shown in r/all. Others compare the liability of hosting pornography vs. other forms of offensive content, such as violence or hate speech.

We also found that across factions, users tried to highlight controversial, even violent, behavior by users on the opposite side. In Section 5.2, while we suggested that left-leaning users invoked **T6: Far-Right/Far-Left Ideologies** to highlight controversial behaviors in far-right subreddits, **T6** is also associated with talk surrounding the quarantine of r/FULLCOMMUNISM, described as a "self-aware socialist satire sub". Thus, invocation of **T6** may also be reflective of their personal investment in participating in a quarantined subreddit. We see, however, that discussions about "socialism" and "communism" are highly salient for right-leaning users, who commonly accused subreddits associated with these ideologies of supporting dictatorships and inciting violence. Similarly, for left-leaning users, "nazi", "ethnic", "fascist", and "genocide" are highly salient in **T6**, which were used to argue that many right-leaning subreddits, quarantined or not, expressed racist views, supported fascism, and denied genocides.

The framing strategy of highlighting controversial behavior from the opposing viewpoint was also apparent in **T2: Content in r/The_Donald**. While the most salient terms for right-leaning users focused on the how The_Donald governs itself ("admins", "moderators", "users", "rules"), left-leaning users explicitly emphasized that the_Donald has content encouraging violence ("kill", "doxxing", "encouraged", "attacking", "spread"). One of the most common associations between The_Donald and incitement of violence cited by left-leaning users was the case of u/Seattle4Truth, a The_Donald user, who murdered his own father (Neiwert, 2017).

Like with our analysis of topic choice, the specific strategies on each side remained generally consistent at the different levels of polarity.

7 Discussion

From our analysis, we find that right-leaning users tend to frame the issues surrounding content moderation in terms of censorship of political viewpoints, while left-leaning users highlight the issues surrounding consistency in how moderation is applied, especially in regards to unmoderated offensive content. On the surface, these findings seem to reflect stereotypes about how freedom of expression is viewed by liberals and conservatives offline in the debate over campus free speech (Friedman, 2019). However, we argue that the emphasis on censorship vs. consistency is not entirely reflective of stereotypical, surface-level differences between conservative and liberal viewpoints on the tension between moderation and free speech. Both left-leaning and right-leaning users, for example, used statements decrying both hate speech and censorship and highlighted concerns with how the Reddit quarantine policy was implemented. Instead, we argue that these strategies are employed as a defense of a user's legitimate participation on Reddit. While previous work has examined the use of free speech discourse as a defense against ego or expressive threat (White et al., 2017), further exploration is needed into why the specific strategies of censorship vs. consistency are applied in the context of online discussion.

As an example for needing more nuance in understanding how opinions on policy are used strategically in argumentation, one common framing strategy we see across both sides is the association of opposing viewpoints with the incitement or encouragement of violence. The question of whether something incites or encourages violence is important, as the encouragement and incitement of violence is explicitly prohibited by

Reddit's content policy.[8] While "encouraging and inciting violence" provides a more concrete frame of judgment than broader definitions of offensive language, there still is ambiguity in terms of how administrators should respond to content that violates Reddit policy, especially on the level of broader communities. At the level of subreddits, it is unclear to what extent a community has to demonstrate violent behavior before the administrators take action to quarantine or ban a subreddit. Many users[9] argue that this ambiguity allows for the Reddit administration to protect popular but controversial subreddits like The_Donald.

7.1 Limitations and Future Work

Our work in this paper is focused on polarized responses to a specific content moderation policy change on Reddit. While we perform an in-depth analysis of the issues raised by the quarantine policy change, our findings may be specific to the context surrounding this particular event, such as the majority of subreddits quarantined in conjunction with the announcement being right-leaning. A longitudinal analysis, where we examine responses to announcements affecting content moderation on Reddit over time may give us a more general view of how users on Reddit talk about free speech and how the discourse of free speech on Reddit has evolved in response to major events. As of June 2019, there have not been other major notifications regarding moderation policy changes in the r/announcements subreddit since the quarantine policy changes. Nevertheless, finding textual signals of user opinions for other moderation-related events, like the progression and eventual banning of quarantined subreddits (e.g. CringeAnarchy, watchpeopledie), remains an interesting area of study.

While we introduced the polarization margin as a method for capturing differences beyond a static left vs. right ideological assignment over users, we found very few differences between users in the same class at different levels of polarization. One limitation of our approach, however, is that we still rely on a hard left-right distinction at the different values of polarization margin β. Relaxing the assumption that users must be assigned to a class for our topic choice and salience analyses and instead

using the raw distribution of participation across all subreddit categories may give us better insight into the range of users' framing strategies across a wider, more nuanced range viewpoints.

7.2 Ethical Considerations

The investigation of the discourse surrounding the Reddit quarantine policy requires us to handle sensitive information related to users' political leanings. To limit the impact of this study on users' privacy and participation on Reddit (Fiesler and Proferes, 2018), usernames were only used to collect user activity outside of the r/announcements thread. After data collection, all usernames were anonymized by replacement with a random numeric id. Additionally, this study focuses on the relationship between discussion about moderation and polarization in aggregate. Though individual researchers viewed example posts, these posts were not matched with individual users by either username or id. Finally, while the full anonymized data from the r/announcements thread is publicly available[10], we only release the user distribution across subreddit categories to prevent the user tracking across subreddits.

8 Conclusion

In this paper, we used techniques for examining agenda-setting and framing to investigate how users discuss their opinions on an update to Reddit's quarantine policy. We presented a novel approach for operationalizing user polarization for our framing analyses, finding that as a whole, right-leaning users tended to invoke censorship while left-leaning users tended to invoke consistency in how policies are applied. While this seems to reflect stereotypes about how freedom of expression is viewed by conservatives and liberals, we argue for a more nuanced view of formalizing differences in how users frame their opinions about policy. Overall, this work builds towards understanding the relationship between ideology and policy with regards to offensive language.

Acknowledgments

This research was supported in part by NSF Grant DGE1745016 and the K&L Gates Presidential Scholarship Fund. We thank Michael Miller Yoder, Daniel Clothiaux, and the anonymous reviewers for their helpful comments and feedback.

---

[8] `https://www.redditinc.com/policies/content-policy`

[9] See r/AgainstHateSubreddits, which tracks behaviors across subreddits that violate Reddit's content policy.

[10] `https://github.com/qinlans/alw3_data`

References

David M Blei, Andrew Y Ng, and Michael I Jordan. 2003. Latent dirichlet allocation. *Journal of Machine Learning Research (JMLR)*.

Vincent D Blondel, Jean-Loup Guillaume, Renaud Lambiotte, and Etienne Lefebvre. 2008. Fast unfolding of communities in large networks. *Journal of Statistical Mechanics: Theory and Experiment*.

Dallas Card, Justin Gross, Amber Boydstun, and Noah A Smith. 2016. Analyzing framing through the casts of characters in the news. In *Proceedings of the Conference on Empirical Methods in Natural Language Processing (EMNLP)*.

Mark Carman, Mark Koerber, Jiuyong Li, Kim-Kwang Raymond Choo, and Helen Ashman. 2018. Manipulating Visibility of Political and Apolitical Threads on Reddit via Score Boosting. In *Proceedings of the IEEE International Conference On Trust, Security And Privacy In Computing And Communications*.

Eshwar Chandrasekharan, Umashanthi Pavalanathan, Anirudh Srinivasan, Adam Glynn, Jacob Eisenstein, and Eric Gilbert. 2017. You can't stay here: The efficacy of Reddit's 2015 ban examined through hate speech. *Proceedings of ACM Conference on Computer-Supported Cooperative Work and Social Computing (CSCW)*.

Jonathan Chang, Sean Gerrish, Chong Wang, Jordan L Boyd-Graber, and David M Blei. 2009. Reading tea leaves: How humans interpret topic models. In *Advances in Neural Information Processing Systems (NIPS)*.

Jonathan P Chang and Cristian Danescu-Niculescu-Mizil. 2019. Trajectories of Blocked Community Members: Redemption, Recidivism and Departure. *arXiv preprint arXiv:1902.08628*.

Dorottya Demszky, Nikhil Garg, Rob Voigt, James Zou, Matthew Gentzkow, Jesse Shapiro, and Dan Jurafsky. 2019. Analyzing Polarization in Social Media: Method and Application to Tweets on 21 Mass Shootings. *Proceedings of the North American Chapter of the Association for Computational Linguistics (NAACL)*.

Robert M Entman. 2007. Framing bias: Media in the distribution of power. *Journal of communication*.

Anjalie Field, Doron Kliger, Shuly Wintner, Jennifer Pan, Dan Jurafsky, and Yulia Tsvetkov. 2018. Framing and Agenda-setting in Russian News: a Computational Analysis of Intricate Political Strategies. *Proceedings of the Conference on Empirical Methods in Natural Language Processing (EMNLP)*.

Casey Fiesler and Nicholas Proferes. 2018. "Participant" Perceptions of Twitter Research Ethics. *Social Media + Society*.

Claudia I. Flores-Saviaga, Brian C. Keegan, and Saiph Savage. 2018. Mobilizing the Trump train: Understanding collective action in a political trolling community. In *Proceedings of the International AAAI Conference on Web and Social Media (ICWSM)*.

Jonathan Friedman. 2019. Chasm in the Classroom: Campus Free Speech in a Divided America. Technical report, PEN America.

Tarleton Gillespie. 2018. *Custodians of the Internet: Platforms, content moderation, and the hidden decisions that shape social media*. Yale University Press.

Matthew Honnibal and Ines Montani. 2017. spaCy 2: Natural language understanding with Bloom embeddings, convolutional neural networks and incremental parsing. *To appear*.

Shagun Jhaver, Larry Chan, and Amy Bruckman. 2017. The view from the other side: The border between controversial speech and harassment on kotaku in action. *arXiv preprint arXiv:1712.05851*.

Shagun Jhaver, Sucheta Ghoshal, Amy Bruckman, and Eric Gilbert. 2018. Online harassment and content moderation: The case of blocklists. *ACM Transactions on Computer-Human Interaction (TOCHI)*.

Shan Jiang, Ronald E Robertson, and Christo Wilson. 2019. Bias Misperceived: The Role of Partisanship and Misinformation in YouTube Comment Moderation.

Cecilia Kang. 2016. Fake news onslaught targets pizzeria as nest of child-trafficking. *The New York Times*. *https://www.nytimes.com/2016/11/21/technology/fact-check-this-pizzeria-is-not-a-child-trafficking-site.html. Accessed.*

Sara Kiesler, Robert Kraut, Paul Resnick, and Aniket Kittur. 2012. Regulating behavior in online communities. *Building Successful Online Communities: Evidence-Based Social Design*.

Renaud Lambiotte, J-C Delvenne, and Mauricio Barahona. 2008. Laplacian dynamics and multiscale modular structure in networks. *arXiv preprint arXiv:0812.1770*.

Louise Matsakis. 2018. Twitter releases new policy on "dehumanizing speech". *Wired*. *https://www.wired.com/story/twitter-dehumanizing-speech-policy/. Accessed.*

Maxwell McCombs. 2002. The agenda-setting role of the mass media in the shaping of public opinion. In *Proceedings of the 2002 Conference of Mass Media Economics*.

David Mimno, Hanna M. Wallach, Edmund Talley, Miriam Leenders, and Andrew McCallum. 2011. Optimizing semantic coherence in topic models. In *Proceedings of the Conference on Empirical Methods in Natural Language Processing (EMNLP)*.

Burt L Monroe, Michael P Colaresi, and Kevin M Quinn. 2008. Fightin'words: Lexical feature selection and evaluation for identifying the content of political conflict. *Political Analysis*.

Sarah Myers West. 2018. Censored, suspended, shadowbanned: User interpretations of content moderation on social media platforms. *New Media & Society*.

David Neiwert. 2017. Alt-righter 'Seattle4Truth' charged with killing father over conspiracy theories. *Southern Poverty Law Center.* *https://www.splcenter.org/hatewatch/2017/10/23/alt-righter-seattle4truth-charged-killing-father-over-conspiracy-theories. Accessed.*

Casey Newton. 2019. Why Twitter has been slow to ban white nationalists. *The Verge.* *https://www.theverge.com/interface/2019/4/26/18516997/why-doesnt-twitter-ban-nazis-white-nationalism. Accessed.*

Viet-An Nguyen, Jordan L Ying, and Philip Resnik. 2013. Lexical and hierarchical topic regression. In *Advances in Neural Information Processing Systems (NIPS)*, pages 1106–1114.

Randal S Olson and Zachary P Neal. 2015. Navigating the massive world of Reddit: Using backbone networks to map user interests in social media. *PeerJ Computer Science*.

Margaret E Roberts, Brandon M Stewart, Dustin Tingley, Edoardo M Airoldi, et al. 2013. The structural topic model and applied social science. In *Advances in Neural Information Processing Systems (NIPS) Workshop on Topic Models: Computation, Application, and Evaluation*.

Adi Robertson. 2015. Was Reddit always about free speech? Yes, and no. *The Verge.* *https://www.theverge.com/2015/7/15/8964995/reddit-free-speech-history. Accessed.*

Michael Röder, Andreas Both, and Alexander Hinneburg. 2015. Exploring the space of topic coherence measures. In *Proceedings of the ACM International Conference on Web Search and Data Mining (WSDM)*.

Qinlan Shen, Michael Miller Yoder, Yohan Jo, and Carolyn P Rosé. 2018. Perceptions of Censorship and Moderation Bias in Political Debate Forums. In *Proceedings of the International AAAI Conference on Web and Social Media (ICWSM)*.

Tim Squirrell. 2017. Linguistic data analysis of 3 billion Reddit comments shows the alt-right is getting stronger. *Quartz. https://qz. com/1056319/what-is-the-alt-righta-linguistic-data-analysis-of-3-billion-reddit-comments-shows-a-disparate-group-thatis-quickly-uniting/. Accessed.*

Liam Stack. 2018. Facebook Announces New Policy to Ban White Nationalist Content". *The New York Times.* *https://www.nytimes.com/2019/03/27/business/facebook-white-nationalist-supremacist.html. Accessed.*

Nick Statt. 2018. Reddit CEO says racism is permitted on the platform, and users are up in arms. *The Verge.* *https://www.theverge.com/2018/4/11/17226416/reddit-ceo-steve-huffman-racism-racist-slurs-are-okay. Accessed.*

Oren Tsur, Dan Calacci, and David Lazer. 2015. A frame of mind: Using statistical models for detection of framing and agenda setting campaigns. In *Proceedings of the Annual Meeting of the Association for Computational Linguistics (ACL)*.

Tim Weninger. 2014. An exploration of submissions and discussions in social news: Mining collective intelligence of Reddit. *Social Network Analysis and Mining*.

Il White, H Mark, and Christian S Crandall. 2017. Freedom of racist speech: Ego and expressive threats. *Journal of Personality and Social Psychology*.

A   Quarantined Subreddits

Here, we list the subreddits included in the quarantine wave associated with the announcement, with their status as of May 3rd, 2019. All these following subreddits were quarantined on September 27-28th, though some have been banned or privatized by their moderators in the meantime:

- **Quarantined:**   theredpill, Ice_Poseidon, FULLCOMMUNISM, Braincels, 911truth, WhiteBeauty, fragilejewishredditor, White-Nationalism, GentilesUnited, ZOG, AmericanJewishPower, CringeChaos, Northwest-Front, BritishJewishPower, mayo_town, Ice_Poseidon2

- **Banned:**   watchpeopledie, CringeAnarchy, hearpeopledie, SubOfPeace, White_Pride, GoyimDefenseForce

- **Privatized:**   BlackPillCentral, AgainstGay-Marriage

Pay "Attention" to Your Context when Classifying Abusive Language

Tuhin Chakrabarty[†] **Kilol Gupta**[†] **Smaranda Muresan**[†‡]

[†]Department of Computer Science, Columbia University

[‡] Data Science Institute, Columbia University

{tc2896, kilol.gupta, smara}@columbia.edu

Abstract

The goal of any social media platform is to facilitate healthy and meaningful interactions among its users. But more often than not, it has been found that it becomes an avenue for wanton attacks. We propose an experimental study that has three aims: 1) to provide us with a deeper understanding of current datasets that focus on different types of abusive language, which are sometimes overlapping (racism, sexism, hate speech, offensive language and personal attacks); 2) to investigate what type of attention mechanism (contextual vs. self-attention) is better for abusive language detection using deep learning architectures; and 3) to investigate whether stacked architectures provide an advantage over simple architectures for this task.

1 Introduction

Any social interaction whether in online forums, comment sections or micro-blogging platforms such as Twitter often involves an exchange of ideas or beliefs. Unfortunately, we often see that users resort to verbal abuse to win an argument or overshadow someone's opinion.

Natural Language Processing (NLP) could aid in the process of detecting and flagging abusive language and thus signaling abusive behaviour online. This is a particularly challenging task due to the noisiness of user-generated text and the diverse types of abusive language ranging from racism, sexism, and hate speech to harassment and personal attacks (Zeerak et al., 2017; Waseem and Hovy, 2016; Golbeck et al., 2017; Davidson et al., 2017; Djuric et al., 2015; Badjatiya et al., 2017; Park and Fung, 2017; Pavlopoulos et al., 2017). Zeerak et al. (2017) point out that different types of abusive language can be reduced to two primary factors:

1.	Obama is kinder to **islam** than any other future western leader is likely to be
2.	you can not even imagine how i think because i cannot imagine how anyone would take such a vile religion as **islam**

Table 1: Tweets where the word "islam" is used in two separate contexts: the top tweet is labeled as None while the bottom as Racism (Waseem and Hovy, 2016).

- Is the language directed towards a specific individual or entity or is it directed towards a generalized group?

- Is the abusive content explicit or implicit?

Table 1 shows two examples of tweets from the first large-scale Twitter abusive language detection dataset, where the second tweet expresses racism, while the first one does not (Waseem and Hovy, 2016). The usage of words in a particular context is important in determining the author's intended meaning. For example, the contexts of the word "islam" in the two tweets in Table 1 are different (a non-racist vs. a racist use of the word, respectively). Traditional bag-of-words models or simple deep learning models often cannot distinguish and handle such differences. This motivates us to explore deep learning models that use *contextual attention* for detecting abusive language and compare their performance against models with self-attention.

We make the following contributions:

- Conduct an empirical study to deepen our understanding of current datasets that focus on different types of abusive language, which are sometimes overlapping (racism, sexism, hate speech, offensive language and personal attacks). Show that our stacked Bidirectional Long Short Term Memory architecture with contextual attention is comparable to or out-

Proceedings of the Third Workshop on Abusive Language Online, pages 70–79
Florence, Italy, August 1, 2019. ©2019 Association for Computational Linguistics

performs state of the art approaches on all the existing datasets.

- Investigate what type of attention mechanism in deep learning architectures (contextual attention vs. self-attention) is better for abusive language detection. We show that contextual attention models outperform self-attention models on most cases (datasets and architectures), and present a thorough error analysis showing how contextual attention works better than self-attention particularly when it comes to modeling implicit abusive content.

- Investigate whether stacked architectures are better than simple architectures for abusive language detection when using Biderectional Long Short Term Memory (Bi-LSTM) networks. We show that stacked architectures are better than simple architectures on all datasets. In addition, we discuss the importance of pre-trained word embeddings for deep learning models. We make the code and all the experimental setups available in `https://github.com/tuhinjubcse/ALW3-ACL2019`.

2   Related Work

Work on abusive language detection has focused on specific types. Waseem and Hovy (2016) present a dataset of 16k tweets annotated as belonging to SEXISM, RACISM or NONE class and provide a feature engineered machine learning approach to classify tweets in the three classes. Davidson et al. (2017) uses a similar handcrafted feature engineered model to identify OFFENSIVE LANGUAGE and distinguish it from HATE SPEECH. Wulczyn et al. (2017) have contributed a Wikipedia Attacks dataset consisting of 115k English wiki talk page comments labeled as PERSONAL ATTACKS or NONE, while Golbeck et al. (2017) introduced a dataset labeled as HARASSMENT or NON-HARASSMENT. We present the first empirical investigation across all these existing datasets.

In recent years, deep learning models have been proposed for detecting different types of abusive language (Djuric et al., 2015; Badjatiya et al., 2017; Park and Fung, 2017). Djuric et al. (2015) propose an approach that learns low-dimensional, distributed representations of user comments in or-

der to detect expressions of hate speech. Badjatiya et al. (2017) experiment with multiple deep learning architectures for the task of hate speech detection on Twitter using the same data set as Waseem and Hovy (2016) and report best F1-scores using Long Short Term Memory Networks (LSTM) and Gradient Boosting. Park and Fung (2017) use a Hybrid Convolution Neural Network (CNN) with the intuition that character level input would counter the purposely or mistakenly misspelled words and made-up vocabularies. Finally, Pavlopoulos et al. (2017) exploit deep learning methods with attention for abuse detection, where they use a self-attention model to detect abuse in news portals and Wikipedia. In this paper, we present an empirical study that investigates what type of attention mechanism (contextual vs. self-attention) is better for this task and whether stacked architectures are better than simple architectures. Yang et al. (2016) introduced a hierarchical *contextual attention* in a GRU architecture for document classification. The attention in this hierarchical model is both at the word and sentence level. For our study we use contextual attention only at word level because our Twitter datasets contains mostly single sentence tweets. Unlike Yang et al. (2016), we use a stacked Bidirectional Long-Short Term Memory (Bi-LSTM) network, and show that it is superior to using a single Bi-LSTM network.

3   Types of Abusive Language and Datasets

Abusive language can be of different types, and previous literature and datasets have focused on some of these types. Before introducing the existing datasets we use in our study, we provide the definitions for the types of abusive language used in existing work and examples for each type (Table 2):

- **Racism**: a belief that race is the primary determinant of human traits and capacities and that racial differences produce an inherent superiority of a particular race.

- **Sexism**: prejudice or discrimination based on sex; especially: discrimination against women.

- **Hate Speech**: is a language that is used to expresses hatred towards a targeted group or

Type	Example
Racism	The only reason the overall numbers increase is because Muslims breed like rats, just like their prophet told them to do. #Islam
Sexism	Don't ever let women drive, they'll break your arm!
Hate Speech	#westvirginia is full of white trash
Offensive Lang	I probably wouldnt mind school as much if we didnt have to deal with bitch ass teachers.
Harassment	yes ! whites who do not want to be a minority and will not accept being blended out of existence need to be shot ! #whitegenocide.
Personal Attack	what to do with elitist assholes who do not allow anybody else to edit certain pages? people such as alkivar? We must get rid of elitism, Wikipedia is a democracy for the contribution of ideas.

Table 2: Examples of different types of abusive language.

is intended to be derogatory, to humiliate, or to insult the members of the group (Davidson et al., 2017).

- **Offensive Language**: is a kind of abuse that causes someone to feel hurt, angry, or upset. It is usually rude or insulting and often very unpleasant.

- **Harassment**: is a type of abuse that is constructed with the identity of sincerely wishing to be part of the group in question, including professing, or conveying pseudosincere intentions, but its real intention(s) is/are to cause disruption and/or to trigger or exacerbate conflict for the purposes of amusement (Golbeck et al., 2017).

- **Personal Attack**: is a type of abuse that usually involves insulting or belittling one's opponent to invalidate his or her argument, but can also involve pointing out factual but ostensible character flaws or actions which are irrelevant to the opponent's argument.

We experiment with four benchmark datasets currently used in the related work on abusive language detection. Three of them are from Twitter (Table 3) and the fourth one from Wikipedia (Table 4), and together they showcase all the above mentioned types of abusive language.

- **D1** (Waseem and Hovy, 2016) — This is the first large-scale dataset for abusive tweet detection. Each of the $15,844$ tweets in the dataset is classified into three classes: RACISM, SEXISM, and NONE. Waseem and Hovy (2016) bootstrapped the corpus collection by performing an initial manual search of common slurs.

- **D2** (Davidson et al., 2017) — This dataset contains a total of $25,112$ tweets, each classified into one of the three classes: HATE SPEECH, OFFENSIVE LANGUAGE, and NEITHER. Davidson et al. (2017) began with a hate speech lexicon containing words and phrases identified by internet users as hate speech, compiled by Hatebase.org. They crawled 85.4 million using words from these lexicons before taking a random sample of 25k tweets manually coded by CrowdFlower (CF) workers.

- **D3** (Golbeck et al., 2017) — This dataset consists of $20,362$ tweets, with binary classes: HARASSMENT, and NON-HARASSMENT. Golbeck et al. (2017) (2017) settled on the following list of search terms ("#whitegenocide", "#fuckniggers", "#WhitePower", "#WhiteLivesMatter", "you fucking nigger", "fucking muslim", "fucking faggot", "religion of hate", "the jews", "feminist"). Though it produced a higher rate of tweets from alt-right / white nationalist tweeters, they were willing to accept a corpus that was not necessarily representative of all harassing content in order to achieve higher density.

- **D4** (Wulczyn et al., 2017) — The Wikipedia attacks dataset contains approximately 115K English Wikipedia talk page comments with binary classes: PERSONAL ATTACK, and NONE. Wulczyn et al. (2017) used a corpus that contains 63M comments from discussions relating to user pages and articles dating from 2004-2015. In order to get reliable estimates of whether a comment is a personal attack, each comment was labeled by at least 10 different Crowdflower annotators.

Table 3 shows the class-wise distribution for the three Twitter datasets **D1**, **D2** and **D3**, respectively. Table 4 refers to the class distribution of

	Class-wise Tweets			Total
D1	**Racism**	**Sexism**	**None**	15844
	1924	3058	10862	
D2	**Offensive**	**Hate**	**None**	25112
	19326	1428	4288	
D3	**Harass**		**N-harass**	20362
		5235	15127	

Table 3: Statistics of the Twitter datasets (**D1, D2, D3**).

D4	**None**	**Personal Attack**	**Total**
Train	61,447	8,079	69,526
Dev	20,405	2,755	23,160
Test	20,442	2,756	23,178

Table 4: Statistics of the Wikipedia dataset (**D4**).

Wikipedia comments labeled as PERSONAL AT-TACKS or NONE (our **D4** dataset) divided among train, dev and test splits.

4   Methods

Long Short Term Memory Networks (LSTMs) (Hochreiter and Schmidhuber, 1997) are one of the most used deep learning architectures for different NLP tasks because of their ability to capture long-distance dependencies. For our task, we use Bidirectional LSTMs because of their inherent capability of capturing information both from the past and the future states.

Graves et al. (2013) show that LSTMs can benefit from stacking multiple recurrent hidden layers on top of each other. Thus, we choose to compare the simple Bi-LSTM architecture with a stacked Bi-LSTM architecture.

Attention mechanisms for deep learning models, including LSTMs serve two benefits: they often result in better performance in terms of metrics, and they provide insights into which words contribute to the classification decision which can be of value in applications and (error) analysis. There are several types of attention mechanisms. The key difference between *contextual attention* introduced by Yang et al. (2016) and self-attention is that it uses a word level context vector u_c that is randomly initialized and jointly learned during the training process (equation (2) vs. equation (3)).

$$u_i = tanh(W_h.h_i + b_h) \qquad (1)$$

$$a_i^{contextual} = \frac{exp(u_i^T \mathbf{u_c})}{\sum_{j=1}^{T} exp(u_j^T \mathbf{u_c})} \qquad (2)$$

$$a_i^{self} = \frac{exp(u_i^T)}{\sum_{j=1}^{T} exp(u_j^T)} \qquad (3)$$

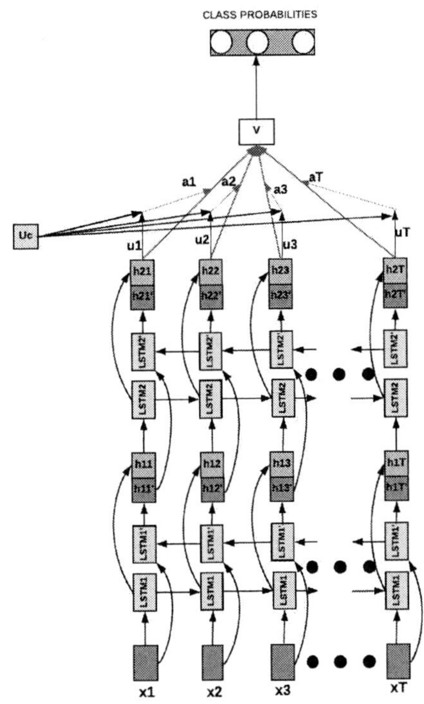

Figure 1: Architecture for Stacked BiLSTM + Word Level Contextual Attention. Figure is inspired by (Yang et al., 2016)

In this paper, we compare the effect of contextual attention as compared to self attention on both simple Bi-LSTMs and stacked Bi-LSTMs. Figure 1 shows the high-level architecture of our stacked Bi-LSTM model with contextual attention. The Bi-LSTM output h_i of each word x_i is fed through a Multi Layer Perceptron to get u_i as its hidden representation. u_c is our word level context vector that is a randomly initialized parameter of the neural network and is learned as we train our network. Once u_i is obtained we calculate the importance of the word as the similarity of u_i with u_c and get a normalized importance weight a_i through a softmax function. The context vector can be treated as a global importance measure of the words in the text. It takes into account which word to attend to based on how that word has been used in different contexts while training on the entire training set. The attention mechanism assigns a weight to each word annotation that is obtained from the Bi-LSTM layer. We compute the fixed representation **V** of the whole message as a weighted sum of all the word annotations, which is then fed to a final fully-connected Softmax layer to obtain the class probabilities.

4.1 Implementation Details

We pre-process the text using `Ekphrasis`[1] — a text processing tool built specially for social media platforms such as Twitter.

For the Twitter datasets we experimented with word vectors that are initialized with pre-trained Twitter-specific embeddings (Baziotis et al., 2017), as well as ELMo embeddings (Peters et al., 2018), which are deep contextualized word representations modeling both complex characteristics of word use (e.g., syntax and semantics), and usage across various linguistic contexts.

For the Wikipedia Attacks dataset we relied on both fastText embeddings (Bojanowski et al., 2017) and ELMo embeddings. Out of vocabulary issues in pre-trained word embeddings are a major limitation for sentence representations. To solve this, we use fastText embeddings (Bojanowski et al., 2017), which rely on subword information. Also, these embeddings were trained on Wikipedia.

The embedding dimension of the words in our model for pre-trained Twitter embeddings and fastText embedding is set to 300, while for ELMo its set to 1024. We use a dropout rate of 0.25 and train the network using a learning rate of 0.001 for 10 epochs.

The results are reported by averaging over 10-fold cross-validation for datasets **D1** and **D3** and 5-fold cross-validation for **D2**. These protocols are consistent with all previously published results on the datasets. We report weighted-F1 scores for all the datasets to minimize the effect of class imbalance. For **D4** we train for 10 epochs and perform early stopping on a validation set. In order to be consistent with previous results we also report AUC scores for **D4** when comparing with state-of-the-art.

5 Results and Error Analysis

Our experimental study looks at several issues: the effect of contextual attention compared to self-attention; the stacked Bi-LSTM architecture compared to the simple Bi-LSTM architecture; the effect of pre-trained word embeddings; the effect of cross-datasets training/testing; and comparison of

---

[1] https://github.com/cbaziotis/ekphrasis

	Bi-LSTM + Self Attention	Bi-LSTM + Context Attention	Stacked Bi-LSTM + Self Attention	Stacked Bi-LSTM + Context Attention
D1	83.34	83.24	83.69	**84.25**
D2	89.27	89.83	89.95	**91.10**
D3	69.18	70.01	70.57	**72.75**
D4	94.22	94.87	95.11	**95.48**

Table 5: Weighted F1 scores on all datasets for all models.

the best model against state-of-the-art results on each dataset.

Contextual vs. Self-Attention. Table 5 show all our models: simple Bi-LSTMs with self and contextual attention (column 2 and 3) as well as stacked Bi-LSTM models with self and contextual attention (column 4 and 5). We can see that contextual attention models outperform the self-attention models for both simple and stacked architectures on all datasets except on D1 for simple BiLSTM (i.e., columns 5 vs. 4, and 3 vs. 2; results are statistically significant with $p \leq .001$ using Chi Squared Test). For datset D1 and D2, we have several classes of abusive language (RACISM, SEXISM for **D1**; and HATE SPEECH and OFFENSIVE LANGUAGE in **D2**). Thus, we wanted to see the performance of the contextual vs self-attention on these finer grained classes (Tables 7 and 8). Table 7 shows that the contextual attention models have significant improvement over the models with self-attention when it comes to identifying RACISM and SEXISM. For the **D2** dataset we see that the most affected class is HATE SPEECH, the primary reason for this being that the percentage of data labeled as hate-speech is really small (5.6%). Even then the contextual attention models perform better than the ones using self-attention as shown in Table 8.

One of the main questions is **Why contextual attention is better than self attention?** What is there in the structure of context attention that leads to performance improvements over self attention? As discussed in Section 4, the context vector can be treated as global importance measure of words in text because it takes into account which word to attend to based on how that word has been used in different contexts while training on the entire training set. To highlight this behavior, in Table 6 we show several tweets from our data sets along with their true label. These tweets were predicted correctly by the context attention but incorrectly

	TWEET	TRUE LABEL	POTENTIAL EXPLANATION FOR PREDICTION
D1	Turkey and Egypt used to be mostly Christian and the muslims have mostly exterminated them	Racism	There are no jews in Saudi or many of the gulf states because the muslims exterminated them Jews used to live on 40% of the Arabian peninsula. muslims have virtually exterminated them
D1	Science was moving forward in India and Persia before islam , islam only slowed it down	Racism	People were making scientific discoveries , including algebra , before islam And notice that the Persian culture was more advanced and advancing and discovering before islam
D1	I don't think women can make tough military decisions. notice hilary's face during the bin laden raid	Sexism	i am not trying to be sexist but i do not think women should announce football games call me sexist but i do not think women should be allowed to grow beards
D2	Sonnen is a faggot	HateSpeech	Kanye West is a faggot Joshua is a faggot . just suspend him on those grounds

Table 6: Examples correctly classified by : Context Attention (CA) but mis-classified by Self Attention (SA)

	RACISM	SEXISM
Stacked Bi-LSTM + Context Attention	**79**	75
Stacked Bi-LSTM + Self Attention	74	73
Single Bi-LSTM + Context Attention	76	75
Single Bi-LSTM + Self Attention	73	73

Table 7: F1 scores of RACISM and SEXISM on **D1** on one of the test splits

	HS	OL	NONE
Stacked Bi-LSTM + Context Attention	**40**	95	90
Stacked Bi-LSTM + Self Attention	35	95	88
Single Bi-LSTM + Context Attention	38	95	88
Single Bi-LSTM + Self Attention	34	95	86

Table 8: F1 scores of OFFENSIVE LANGUAGE (OL) and HATE SPEECH (HS) and NONE on **D2** on one of the test splits.

DataSet	ELMo (Wiki)	Glove_Twitter
D1	83.10	**84.25**
D2	88.44	**91.10**
D3	68.78	**72.75**

Table 9: Weighted F1 scores comparing pre-trained embeddings on the Twitter datasets.

by Self attention. The first three tweets were predicted as NONE by the self attention model while the last tweet was labeled as OFFENSIVE LANGUAGE. The "potential explanation for prediction" column shows tweets from the training data that have the same gold label and that are similar to the tweets in the test set shown in column 2, suggesting that the context attention indeed encapsulates the information by looking at examples globally through the training data, unlike self attention which only focuses on words for that particular tweet while trying to classify it.

Stacked vs Simple Bi-LSTM. Table 5 shows that the stacked Bi-LSTM models outperformed the simple Bi-LSTM models, when using the same type of attention mechanism on all datasets (columns 5 vs. 3 and 4 vs. 2; results are statistically significant, with $p \leq .001$ using Chi Squared Test). When looking at Table 7 and 8, we notice that the stacked Bi-LSTM models do better than the simple Bi-LSTMs when using the same type of attention, only for the RACISM class and the HATE SPEECH class. The best performing model is the stacked Bi-LSTM with contextual attention.

Effect of pre-trained embeddings. The models presented above in Table 5 used Twitter-specific pre-trained embeddings for datasets **D1**, **D2** and **D3** and fasText embeddings trained on Wikipedia for **D4** (i.e., pre-trained embeddings from the same genre as the datasets). To compare the effect of pre-trained embeddings, we chose to compare our best model (Stacked Bi-LSTM with contextual attention) with the same model but trained using ELMo embeddings on the Twitter datasets. ELMo embeddings have been shown to outperform other types of embeddings on a variety of NLP tasks (Peters et al., 2018). The currently released ELMo embeddings are trained on news crawl data and Wikipedia and not on Twitter, which allows us to test the effect of pre-trained embeddings (genre,

Training Dataset	Weighted F1
D1+D2	64.50
D3	**72.75**

Table 10: Cross-datasets training (same CV test splits of D3)

method of training) on the performance of the deep network architectures. Table 9 shows that using the ELMo pre-trained embeddings instead of Twitter pre-trained embeddings lead to a statistically significant decrease in performance on all the Twitter datasets, with the biggest drop on **D2** and **D3**, which are the datasets on hate speech and harassment.

Cross datasets training/testing. The definition of the category HARASSMENT in the **D3** dataset states that it refers to language that is deeply racist, misogynistic or homophobic, bigoted, involved threats or hate speech. Given that the datasets D1 and D2 contain the categories RACISM, SEXISM and HATE SPEECH and are also from Twitter, we wanted to conduct a study where we train on **D1** and **D2** and test on **D3**. We considered data labelled as RACISM, SEXISM and HATE SPEECH as HARASSMENT and NONE as NON-HARASSMENT. This led to consistent class balance across train and test. The cross validation setting used for individual experiments on D3 was maintained here as well. Table 10 demonstrates that cross dataset training leads to worse performance when it comes to abusive language detection, showing that each dataset has its own particularities on defining and collecting the data.

Comparison with State-of-the-Art. We compare our best model (stacked Bi-LSTM with contextual attention) with various state-of-the-art models developed for each of the datasets we considered. For the Twitter datasets we compared against (1) an n-gram model with various linguistic features (Waseem and Hovy, 2016), (2) another model with hand-crafted features including n-grams, POS tags (Davidson et al., 2017); (3) a hybrid CNN model (Park and Fung, 2017), and (4) an LSTM model with an additional classifier using Gradient Boosting trees with LSTM embeddings as features (Badjatiya et al., 2017). Table 11 shows the weighted-F1 obtained by the models on the three Twitter datasets (**D1, D2, D3**). Note that none of the existing approaches show results on all the datasets. Thus, we report results using their

	D1	**D2**	**D3**
Majority Baseline	56.0	66.0	63.0
(Waseem and Hovy, 2016)	73.8†	82.3	63.0
(Davidson et al., 2017)	78.0	90.0†	63.8
(Park and Fung, 2017)	82.7†	88.0	68.6
(Badjatiya et al., 2017)	**93.1**†	NA	NA
(Badjatiya et al., 2017)_OurRep	81	88.0	67.4
Our Model	84.2	**91.1**	**72.7**

Table 11: Comparison of our best model with state-of-the-art models on the three Twitter datasets. †Results as reported in the respective papers.

METHOD	DEV	TEST
Majority Baseline	51.23	50.40
Our best model	97.39	97.44
(Wulczyn et al., 2017)	96.59	96.71
(Pavlopoulos et al., 2017)	**97.46**	**97.68**

Table 12: Comparisons with state-of-the-art models on **D4** DEV and TEST.

publicly available implementations on the remaining datasets, and highlight for which datasets they report results in their work.

Most abusive language datasets are highly imbalanced and thus we also report the scores for the majority baseline in Table 11 and Table 12. For D1, D3, D4 we predict everything as the majority class (Non-Abusive) and for D2 everything as offensive language. We see our best model beats the majority baseline by a huge margin. Our model obtains significantly better results ($p \leq .001$ using Chi Squared Test) than all the existing models on the datasets **D2** and **D3**. Notably, the improvements over the previous best performing models on these datasets are 1 F1 point and 2 F1 points respectively. On dataset **D1**, our model is outperformed by (Badjatiya et al., 2017), who mentioned that using Gradient Boosting Trees with LSTM embeddings boosted their model's performance by 12 points in weighted-F1. Unfortunately, while trying to replicate their results on dataset **D1**, we found no improvement from their simple LSTM model (the authors did not released the Gradient Boosting Trees with LSTM embeddigs implementation so we reimplemented that ourselves; weighted-F1 score of 81). Thus, for this model where we could not replicate the results on the original dataset, we report both the original results on that dataset and our re-implementation results on all datasets.

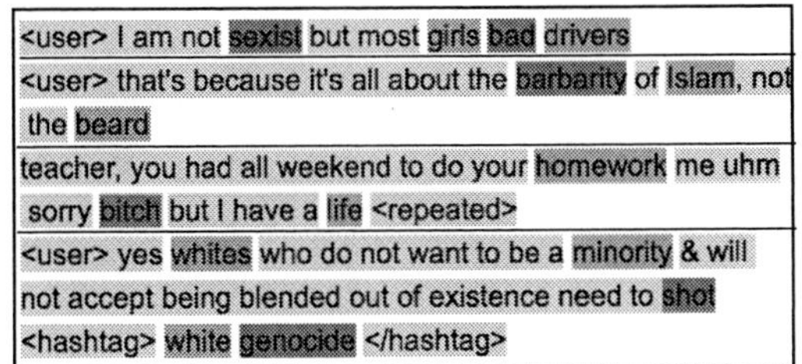

Figure 2: Attention heat map visualization demonstrating the focus on abusive-language signaling words in various tweets.

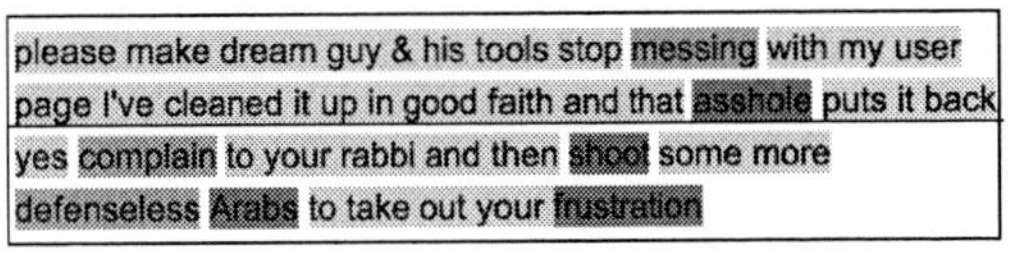

For the **D4** dataset which is Wikipedia, we compared our best model (stacked Bi-LSTM with contextual attention) with the existing models on this dataset. Wulczyn et al. (2017) use a Multilayer Perceptron over char n-grams as features and reported results only on the Dev set. We use their online implementation to report results on the test set. Pavlopoulos et al. (2017) use a deeper self attention mechanism and report results both on the Dev and Test sets. Both approaches report results using AUC. Table 12 shows that our model outperforms (Wulczyn et al., 2017) and is comparable to (Pavlopoulos et al., 2017).

6 Visualizing the Contextual Attention Weights

The contextual attention mechanism enables our model to focus on the relevant parts of the text (e.g., tweet) while performing the prediction task. As shown in Figure 2 and 3 our model learns to focus on relevant keywords that govern the abusive nature of a text. The color intensity here denotes the relative weight assigned to words. In figure 2, we see four tweets where the first tweet is labeled as SEXISM and the second tweet is labeled as RACISM from the **D1** dataset (Waseem and Hovy, 2016). The third tweet is a tweet from the **D2** dataset (Davidson et al., 2017) labeled as OFFENSIVE LANGUAGE and correctly identified by our model. The last tweet is from the **D3** dataset (Golbeck et al., 2017) labeled as HARASSMENT and correctly identified by our model. Figure 3 shows two such comments from the Wikipedia attacks dataset (**D4**), which were classified correctly by our model.

Moreover, it it encouraging to see that the contextual attention assigns higher weight to potentially abusive words when used with an abusive meaning. For example, refer to the two tweets

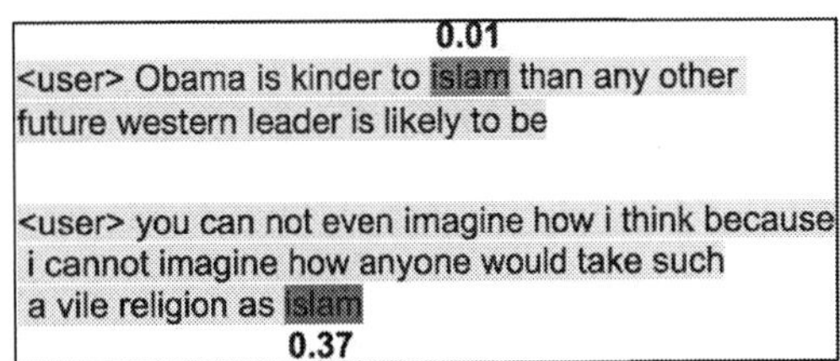

Figure 3: Attention heat map visualization demonstrating the focus on abusive words in Wikipedia Personal Attacks dataset.

Figure 4: Attention weights learned by our model for the same word "islam" on two tweets.

in figure 4. The first tweet belongs to the NONE class while the second tweet belongs to RACISM class. The word "islam" may appear in the realm of racism as well as in any normal conversation. We find that our model successfully identifies the two distinct contextual usages of the word "islam" in the two tweets, as demonstrated by a much higher attention weight in the second case and a relatively smaller one in the first case.

7 Conclusion

Abusive language detection on the web is challenging for two reasons: (1) the inherent nature of noise in online discussions and (2) the contextual use of words that convey abuse only in certain contexts. We presented an extensive empirical study on several existing datasets that reflect different but possibly overlapping types of abusive language. We show that contextual attention is better than self-attention for deep learning models and using a stacked architecture outperforms a simple architecture (our basic architecture being a Bi-LSTM). We also show that using pre-trained embeddings from the same genre as the datasets is more important than better models for training the embeddings. Our best performing model, the stacked Bi-LSTM model with contextual attention is comparable to or outperforms state-of-the-art models on all the datasets. We also conduct a cross-dataset training/testing experiment that highlights the particularities of various datasets when it comes to the collection and labeling of abusive language. We present an error analysis of the results and a visualization of the contextual attention weights — an important step towards better interpretation of any deep learning models.

While we notice that the visualization of attention weights is indicative of the classifier decision for multiple examples based on our context-attention model, some recent work has claimed that attention is not explanation (Jain and Wallace, 2019). As a future step, we would like to conduct experiments to measure the correlation between the highest attention weights chosen by models and humans (Ghosh et al., 2017) to further strengthen the interpretability of the attention-based models.

References

Pinkesh Badjatiya, Shashank Gupta, Manish Gupta, and Vasudeva Varma. 2017. Deep learning for hate speech detection in tweets. In *Proceedings of the 26th International Conference on World Wide Web Companion*, pages 759–760. International World Wide Web Conferences Steering Committee.

Christos Baziotis, Nikos Pelekis, and Christos Doulkeridis. 2017. Datastories at semeval-2017 task 4: Deep lstm with attention for message-level and topic-based sentiment analysis. In *Proceedings of the 11th International Workshop on Semantic Evaluation (SemEval-2017)*, pages 747–754. Association for Computational Linguistics.

Piotr Bojanowski, Edouard Grave, Armand Joulin, and Tomas Mikolov. 2017. Enriching word vectors with subword information. *Transactions of the Association for Computational Linguistics*, 5:135–146.

Thomas Davidson, Dana Warmsley, Michael Macy, and Ingmar Weber. 2017. Automated hate speech detection and the problem of offensive language. In *(ICWSM 2017)*, pages 3952–3958. Proceedings of the Eleventh International AAAI Conference on Web and Social Media.

Nemanja Djuric, Jing Zhou, Robin Morris, Mihajlo Grbovic, Vladan Radosavljevic, and Narayan Bhamidipati. 2015. Hate speech detection with comment embeddings. In *Proceedings of the 24th international conference on world wide web*, pages 29–30. ACM.

Debanjan Ghosh, Alexander Richard Fabbri, and Smaranda Muresan. 2017. The role of conversation context for sarcasm detection in online interactions. In *Proceedings of the 18th Annual SIGdial Meeting on Discourse and Dialogue*, pages 186–196, Saarbrücken, Germany. Association for Computational Linguistics.

Jennifer Golbeck, Zahra Ashktorab, Rashad O Banjo, Alexandra Berlinger, Siddharth Bhagwan, Cody Buntain, Alicia A Cheakalos, Paul Geller, Quint Gergory, Rajesh Kumar Gnanasekaran, Raja Rajan Gunasekaran, Kelly M Hoffman, Jenny Hottle, Vichita Jienjitlert, Shivika Khare, Ryan Lau, Marianna Martindale, J Shalmali Naik, Heather L Nixon, Piyush Ramachandran, Kristine M Rogers, Lisa Rogers, Meghna Sardana Sarin, Jayanee Shahane, Gaurav Thanki, Priyanka Vengataraman, Zijian Wan, and Derek Michael Wu. 2017. A large human-labeled corpus for online harassment research. In *ACM*, pages 229–233. Proceedings of the 2017 ACM on Web Science Conference.

Alex Graves, Abdel-rahman Mohamed, and Geoffrey Hinton. 2013. Speech recognition with deep recurrent neural networks. *International Conference on Acoustics, Speech, and Signal Processing*.

Sepp Hochreiter and Jurgen Schmidhuber. 1997. Long short-term memory. In *Neural computation, 791*, pages 1735–1780.

Sarthak Jain and Byron C. Wallace. 2019. Attention is not explanation. In *https://arxiv.org/abs/1902.10186*.

Ji Ho Park and Pascale Fung. 2017. One-step and two-step classification for abusive language detection on twitter.

John Pavlopoulos, Prodromos Malakasiotis, and Ion Androutsopoulos. 2017. Deeper attention to abusive user content moderation. In *Proceedings of the 2017 Conference on Empirical Methods in Natural Language Processing*.

Matthew E. Peters, Mark Neumann, Mohit Iyyer, Matt Gardner, Christopher Clark, Kenton Lee, and Luke Zettlemoyer. 2018. Deep contextualized word representations. In *Proc. of NAACL*.

Zeerak Waseem and Dirk Hovy. 2016. Hateful symbols or hateful people? predictive features for hate speech detection on twitter. In *Proceedings of the NAACL student research workshop*, pages 88–93.

Ellery Wulczyn, Nithum Thain, and Lucas Dixon. 2017. Ex machina: Personal attacks seen at scale. In *Proceedings of the 26th International Conference on World Wide Web*, pages 1391–1399. International World Wide Web Conferences Steering Committee.

Zichao Yang, Diyi Yang, Chris Dyer, Xiaodong He, Alex Smola, and Eduard Hovy. 2016. Hierarchical attention networks for document classification. In *Proceedings of the 2016 Conference of the North American Chapter of the Association for Computational Linguistics: Human Language Technologies*, pages 1480–1489. Association for Computational Linguistics.

Waseem Zeerak, Thomas Davidson, Dana Warmsley, and Ingmar Weber. 2017. Understanding abuse:a typology of abusive language detection subtasks. In

Proceedings of the First Workshop on Abusive Language Online, pages 78–84.

Challenges and frontiers in abusive content detection

Bertie Vidgen
The Alan Turing Institute,
London, United Kingdom
bvidgen@turing.ac.uk

Dong Nguyen
The Alan Turing Institute,
London, United Kingdom
dnguyen@turing.ac.uk

Rebekah Tromble
The Alan Turing Institute,
London, United Kingdom
rtromble@turing.ac.uk

Alex Harris
The Alan Turing Institute,
London, United Kingdom
aharris@turing.ac.uk

Scott Hale
The Alan Turing Institute,
London, United Kingdom
shale@turing.ac.uk

Helen Margetts
The Alan Turing Institute,
London, United Kingdom
hmargetts@turing.ac.uk

Abstract

Online abusive content detection is an inherently difficult task. It has received considerable attention from academia, particularly within the computational linguistics community, and performance appears to have improved as the field has matured. However, considerable challenges and unaddressed frontiers remain, spanning technical, social and ethical dimensions. These issues constrain the performance, efficiency and generalizability of abusive content detection systems. In this article we delineate and clarify the main challenges and frontiers in the field, critically evaluate their implications and discuss solutions. We also highlight ways in which social scientific insights can advance research.

1   Introduction

Developing robust systems to detect abuse is a crucial part of online content moderation and plays a fundamental role in creating an open, safe and accessible Internet. It is of growing interest to both host platforms and regulators, in light of recent public pressure (HM Government, 2019). Detection systems are also important for social scientific analyses, such as understanding the temporal and geographic dynamics of abuse.

Advances in machine learning and NLP have led to marked improvements in abusive content detection systems' performance (Fortuna & Nunes, 2018; Schmidt & Wiegand, 2017). For instance, in 2018 Pitsilis et al. trained a classification system on Waseem and Hovy's 16,000 tweet dataset and achieved an F-Score of 0.932, compared against Waseem and Hovy's original 0.739; a 20-point increase (Pitsilis, Ramampiaro, & Langseth, 2018; Waseem & Hovy, 2016). Key innovations include the use of deep learning and ensemble architectures, using contextual word embeddings, applying dependency parsing, and the inclusion of user-level variables within models (Badjatiya, Gupta, Gupta, & Varma, 2017; Zhang et al., 2018). Researchers have also addressed numerous tasks beyond binary abusive content classification, including identifying the target of abuse and its strength as well as automatically moderating content (Burnap & Williams, 2016; Davidson, Warmsley, Macy, & Weber, 2017; Santos, Melnyk, & Padhi, 2018). However, considerable challenges and unaddressed frontiers remain, spanning technical, social and ethical dimensions. These issues constrain abusive content detection research, limiting its impact on the development of real-world detection systems.

We offer critical insights into the challenges and frontiers facing the use of computational methods to detect abusive content. We differ from most previous research by taking an interdisciplinary approach, routed in both the computational and social sciences. Broadly, we advocate that social science should be used in a complementary way to advance research in this field. We also highlight the lack of support given to researchers and provide guidelines for working with abusive content.

The paper is structured as follows. First, we outline three reasons why, from a research perspective, abusive content detection poses such a challenge (Section 2). Second, we identify challenges facing

Proceedings of the Third Workshop on Abusive Language Online, pages 80–93
Florence, Italy, August 1, 2019. ©2019 Association for Computational Linguistics

the abusive content detection research community (Section 3). Third, we identify research frontiers; un- and under- addressed areas which would benefit from further investigation (Section 4).

2 Research Challenges

2.1 Categorizing abusive content

The categorization of abusive content refers to the criteria, and process, by which content is identified as abusive and, secondly, what *type* of abusive content it is identified as. This is a social and theoretical task: there is no objectively 'correct' definition or single set of pre-established criteria which can be applied. The determination of whether something is abusive is also irreducible to legal definitions as these are usually minimalistic (HM Government, 2019). Similarly, using the host platforms' guidelines is often inappropriate as they are typically reactive and vague. More generally, academia should not just accept how platforms frame and define issues as this might be influenced by their commercial interests.

Clarity in sub-tasks. Detecting abusive content generically is an important aspiration for the field. However, it is very difficult because abusive content is so varied. Research which purports to address the generic task of detecting abuse is typically actually addressing something much more specific. This can often be discerned from the datasets, which may contain systematic biases towards certain types and targets of abuse. For instance, the dataset by Davidson et al. is used widely for tasks described generically as abusive content detection yet it is highly skewed towards racism and sexism (Davidson et al., 2017).

Sartori's work in political science on the 'ladder of abstraction' can be used to understand this issue (Sartori, 1970). He argues that all concepts can be defined and described with varying degrees of abstraction. For instance, 'democracy' can be defined very broadly in relation to how 'the people' is represented or very narrowly as a set of specific institutions and procedures. The degree of abstraction should be chosen by considering the goals and nature of the research – otherwise we risk 'swim[ming] in a sea of empirical and theoretical messiness.' (Sartori, 1970, p. 1053)

Abusive content detection research is currently marked by too much of what Sartori labels 'high' and 'low' level abstraction. Some researchers use highly abstract terms to describe tasks, such as detection of 'abuse' or 'flagged' content. These terms are not very informative, and it is difficult to know exactly what sub-task is being addressed. For instance, flagged content may be abusive but is likely to also include other forms of non-abusive (albeit prohibited) content. On the other side, some research uses very narrow terms which are at an overly 'low' level of abstraction. For instance, 'hate' denotes a specific aggressive and emotional behavior, excluding other varieties of abuse, such as dismissal, insult, mistrust and belittling.

Addressing an appropriate level of abstraction is important for creating useable detection systems. It requires that subtasks are clearly disambiguated and labelled. This is a much-discussed but still unresolved problem in existing research (Waseem, Davidson, Warmsley, & Weber, 2017). Waseem et al. suggest that one of the main differences between subtasks is whether content is 'directed towards a specific entity or is directed towards a generalized group' (Waseem et al., 2017). This distinction has been widely adopted (Zampieri et al., 2019). We propose that subtasks are further disambiguated into three types of directed abuse:

Individual-directed abuse. Abuse directed against an individual. This may involve tagging the individual (e.g. '@Username you are a f*cking id*ot) or just referring to them (e.g. 'I think Tom W. is a tw*t') These two varieties can be called 'tagged individual-directed' and 'referenced individual-directed' respectively. Most research in this area falls under cyberbullying (Sugandhi, Pande, Chawla, Agrawal, & Bhagat, 2016) although there are notable exceptions (Wulczyn, Thain, & Dixon, 2017).

Identity-directed abuse. Abuse directed against an identity, such as a social group, demographic or affiliation (e.g. 'I hate Conservatives' or 'Ban Muslims') (Silva, Mondal, Correa, Benevenuto, & Weber, 2016). This can be hard to separate from individual-directed abuse as, in some cases, individuals receive abuse *because* of their identity. This might be reasonably obvious (e.g. 'You stupid b*tch', indicating misogyny) but in other cases it is hard to discern as the content alone does not reveal prejudice. Establishing when abuse is truly individual-directed compared with identity-directed needs to be investigated further, especially given evidence that some identities receive more individual-directed abuse (Gorrell, Greenwood, Roberts, Maynard, & Bontcheva, 2018).

Concept-directed abuse: abuse which is directed against a concept or entity, such as a belief system, country or ideology, e.g. 'Capitalism sucks *ss.'. Concept-directed abuse may not be considered a form of abuse in all cases as it can be very similar to simply expressing criticism of something. We include it here because there are deep links between hatred of a concept and hatred of those who embody that concept. For instance, there are cross-overs between anti-Islamic and anti-Muslim abuse, whereby abuse of the concept (Islam) is used as a proxy for abusing the associated identity (Muslims) (Allen, 2011). At the same time, we caution against automatically moderating concept-directed abuse as this could have concerning implications for freedom of expression.

This typology can be integrated with other dimensions of abuse to create additional subtasks. One consideration is who the system detects abuse for; that is, who actually receives abuse (Salminen et al., 2018). Within identity-directed abuse, this can be separated into different identities and affiliations (e.g. Muslims or the Republican party). Within individual-directed abuse, this includes different roles (such as content producers vs. moderators) and social relations (such as friends vs. strangers). Either one or several recipients of abuse can be studied within any model. Specifying the recipient not only makes tasks tractable, but also helps build social scientific and policy-relevant knowledge.

A further consideration is how abuse is articulated, which can include hatefulness, aggression, insults, derogation, untruths, stereotypes, accusations and undermining comments. Detecting different articulations of abuse within a single system involves multi-label or multi-class modelling and can be computationally difficult. However, it also leads to more nuanced outcomes. A key distinction is whether abuse is explicit or implicit (Waseem et al., 2017; Zampieri et al., 2019). Other articulations of abuse can also be addressed. For instance, Anzovino et al. develop a system that not only

detects misogyny but also whether it consists of stereotypes, discrediting, objectification, harassment, dominance, derailing or threats of violence (Anzovino, Fersini, & Rosso, 2018).

Drawing these points together, we propose that researchers consider at least three dimensions of abusive content. They can be incorporated in various ways to produce different tasks.

1. What the abuse is directed against
2. Who receives the abuse
3. How the abuse is articulated

Clarity in terminology. Clarifying terminology will help delineate the scope and goals of research and enable better communication and collaboration. Some of the main problems are (1) researchers use terms which are not well-defined, (2) different concepts and terms are used across the field for similar work, and (3) the terms which are used are theoretically problematic. Specifically, three aspects of existing terminology have considerable social scientific limitations.

The intention of the speaker. Abusive content is often defined in reference to, and focuses on, the speakers' intentions. In particular, it is central in the notion of 'hate', which suggests a specific orientation of the speaker. For instance, Pitsilis et al. describe hate as 'all published text that is used to express hatred towards some particular group with the intention to humiliate its members' (Pitsilis et al., 2018). Elsewhere, Kumar et al. distinguish 'overt' from 'covert' hate (Kumar, Ojha, Malmasi, & Zampieri, 2018). The implication of 'covert' is that speakers are behaving surreptitiously to hide their abusive intentions. However, the intention of speakers is difficult to discern using socially-generated data and may not directly correspond with their actions (Crawford & Gillespie, 2016; Margetts, John, Hale, & Yasseri, 2015). The way in which meaning is 'encoded' in online contexts cannot be easily ascertained, particularly given the anonymity of many users and the role of 'context collapse'. (Marwick & boyd, 2010). The true audience which speakers address may be different from the ones that they imagine they are addressing (Ibid.). As such, little should be assumed about speakers' intentions, and it can be considered an unsuitable basis for definitions of abuse.

The effect of abuse. Many definitions pre-empt the effects of abusive language. For instance, Lee et al. describe abusive language as 'any type of insult, vulgarity, or profanity that debases the target; it also can be anything that causes aggravation' (Lee, Yoon, & Jung, 2018). Similarly, in Wulczyn et al.'s dataset of over 100,000 Wikipedia comments, 'toxicity' is defined in relation to how likely it is to make individuals leave a discussion (Wulczyn et al., 2017). These definitions are not only very subjective but they also risk conflating distinct types of abuse: first, content which expresses abuse and, second, content which has an abusive effect. These two aspects often coincide, but not always, as shown in sociological studies of prejudice. In relation to Islamophobia, Allen distinguishes between 'Islamophobia-as-process' and 'Islamophobia-as-product', whereby the first refers to actions which can be considered Islamophobic (intrinsically) and the second to outcomes which can be considered Islamophobic (extrinsically) (Allen, 2011). This distinction should also be used to understand abusive content: language which does not express an inherently abusive viewpoint but is experienced as abusive is very different and, as such, should be addressed separately, to language which is intrinsically abusive.

The sensibilities of the audience. Online audiences are hugely varied and attempts to discern their sensibilities are fundamentally flawed: inevitably, some proportion of the audience will be mischaracterized. This is reflected by research into inter-annotator agreement, whereby annotators often vary considerably in what they consider to be hateful or abusive, even with training and guidance (Salminen & Almerekhi, 2018). Binns et al. show that male and female annotators have different perceptions of what is considered toxic (Binns, Veale, Van Kleek, & Shadbolt, 2017). Assumptions about the sensibilities of the audience are entailed by the widely-used term 'offensiveness' (Davidson et al., 2017), which is intrinsically subject-oriented: it begs the question, *offensive for whom?* What is considered offensive by one audience, or in one context, might not be offensive elsewhere. As such, we advocate avoiding definitions of abuse which make strong assumptions about the audience without in-depth empirical analysis.

2.2 Recognizing abusive content

We identify five linguistic difficulties which increase the challenge of detecting abusive content. They have all been associated with classification errors in previous work. However, they are not always discussed and handled systematically, and their impact is hard to assess as they are often discussed qualitatively rather than measured.

Humor, irony and sarcasm. Supposedly humorous, ironic or sarcastic abusive content is often viewed as a source of classification error (Nobata, Thomas, Mehdad, Chang, & Tetreault, 2016; van Aken, Risch, Krestel, & Löser, 2018). However, drawing on critical studies of prejudice and hate, we propose that such content is still abusive (Weaver, 2010). There are three reason for this. First, these rhetorical devices have been shown to serve as ways of hiding, spreading and legitimating genuine abuse (Ji Hoon Park, Gabbadon, & Chernin, 2006). Second, individuals who view such content may be unaware of who the author is and the broader context, and as such not recognize that it is humorous – as discussed above, intentions are hard to discern online. A supposedly ironic comment which is intended to lampoon abuse may be indistinguishable from genuine abuse (LaMarre, Landreville, & Beam, 2009). Third, purportedly ironic, satirical and humorous abusive content usually relies on a kernel of prejudice: the lynchpin of the rhetorical strategy is that the audience recognizes, and perhaps implicitly accepts, the negative tropes and ideas associated with the targeted group (Ma, 2014). Thus, whilst humor, irony and sarcasm are often seen as being non-abusive, we recommend that they are re-evaluated.

Spelling variations. Spelling variations are ubiquitous, especially in social media (Eisenstein, 2013). Examples of spelling variation include the elongation of words (e.g., 'oh' to 'ohh') and use of alternatives (e.g., 'kewl' instead of 'cool'). Spelling variation is often socially significant, reflecting expressions of identity and culture (Sabba, 2009). At the same time, some variations reflect semantically near-identical content (e.g. 'whaaaaa?' and 'whaaa?'). Spelling variations are also sometimes used adversarially to obfuscate and avoid detection (e.g. by using unusual punctuation or additional spaces) (Eger et al., 2019; Gröndahl, Pajola, Juuti, Conti, & Asokan, 2018). In most contexts, it is hard to identify why spelling varies.

Spelling variations increase the likelihood of errors as they create many 'out of vocabulary' terms which have to be handled (Serrà et al., 2017). Text normalization has been proposed as a solution, however this risks losing meaningful social information (Eisenstein, 2013). Using larger and more diverse datasets will only partly mitigate this problem as no dataset will ever account for all variations, and language use changes over time. A more promising way of addressing this is to model language at the character or subword level (Devlin, Chang, Lee, & Toutanova, 2018; Mehdad & Tetreault, 2016). More empirical research into why particular spelling variations occur would also be useful.

Polysemy. This is when a word with a single spelling has multiple meanings. Which meaning is elicited depends on the context. Magu and Luo describe how 'euphemistic' code words, such as 'Skype' or 'Bing', are used to derogate particular groups (Magu, Joshi, & Luo, 2017). Similarly, Palmer et al. describe how adjectival nominalization (e.g. changing 'Mexicans' to 'the Mexicans') can transform otherwise neutral terms into derogations (Palmer, Robinson, & Phillips, 2017). Polysemy is a particular challenge with abusive content as many users avoid obvious and overt forms of hate (which are likely to be automatically removed by platforms) and instead express hate more subtly (Daniels, 2013). Word representations which explicitly take into account context are one way of overcoming this issue (Devlin et al., 2018).

Long range dependencies. Much existing research is focused on short posts, such as Tweets (Schmidt & Wiegand, 2017). However, socially generated content can cross over multiple sentences and paragraphs. Abuse may also only be captured through conversational dynamics, such as multi-user threads (Raisi & Huang, 2016). This has been well-addressed within studies of cyberbullying, but is also highly relevant for the field of abusive content detection more widely (Van Hee et al., 2018). Creation of more varied datasets will help to address this problem, such as using data taken from Reddit or Wikipedia.

Language change. The syntax, grammar, and lexicons of language change over time, often in unexpected and uneven ways. This is particularly true with informal forms of 'everyday' language, which proliferate in most online spaces (Eisenstein, O'Connor, Smith, & Xing, 2014). One implication is that the performance of systems trained on older datasets degrades over time as they cannot account for new linguistic traits. Using multiple temporally separated datasets to evaluate systems will help to address this, as well as further research into the impact of time on language.

2.3 Accounting for context

Meaning is inherently ambiguous, depending upon the subjective outlook of both speaker and audience, as well as the specific situation and power dynamics (Benesch, 2012). These factors have long been given insufficient attention in the study of online abuse, which has mostly focused on just the content alone. This has clear limitations. For instance, in most cases, the term "N***a" has an almost opposite meaning if uttered by a white compared to a black person.

Some recent work has started to explicitly account for context by including user-level variables in classification systems. Unsvåg and Gambäck evaluate a system on three datasets and find that, compared with a baseline using logistic regression with n-grams, inclusion of individual-level features, such as gender, social network, profile metadata and geolocation, improves performance (Unsvåg & Gambäck, 2018). Other studies report similar results, using both local and global social network features, noticeably through incorporating the node2vec algorithm (Papegnies, Labatut, Dufour, & Linarès, 2017; Raisi & Huang, 2017). The use of network representations is supported by social science research which shows evidence of homophily online; it is likely that abusive users are connected to other abusive users (Caiani & Wagemann, 2009; Tien, Eisenberg, Cherng, & Porter, 2019). We propose that anonymity should also be explicitly modelled in future work as it has disinhibiting effects (Amichai-hamburger & McKenna, 2006) and is empirically associated with users posting abuse (Hine et al., 2017).

The inclusion of user-level features helps to drive improvements in classification performance and should be welcomed as an important step towards more nuanced and contextually-aware models. That said, we offer four warnings. First, it may make temporal or network analysis difficult as the classification of users' content is based on these features, creating clear risk of confounding. Second, it may lead to new types of unfairness and bias whereby the content of certain network topologies or certain nodes are more likely to be detected as hateful – which may, in turn, be related to meaningful social characteristics, such as gender or age. Third, these systems are largely trained on a snapshot of data and do not explicitly take into account temporality. It is unclear how much data is required for them to be trained. Fourth, models may be biased by the training data. Wiegand et al. show that if most abusive content in a dataset comes from only a few users then including user-level information risks overfitting: the classifier just picks up on those authors' linguistic traits (Wiegand, Ruppenhofer, & Kleinbauer, 2019).

Context goes beyond just the identity of the speaker. It also includes the social environment in which they operate, which in most cases comprises both the platform and the specific group or community, such as the subreddit or Facebook page. Existing research can be leveraged to address this: Qian et al. report a model which identifies the origins of posts from 40 far right hate groups on Twitter (Qian, ElSherief, Belding, & Wang, 2018) Chandrasekharan et al similarly build a model that identifies whether content is from 9 different communities on niche social media platforms (Chandrasekharan, Samory, Srinivasan, & Gilbert, 2017). This is promising research which should be integrated into the detection of online abuse, thereby accounting explicitly for the social environment in which content is shared. To more fully address the role of context we also need more empirical analysis of which aspects most greatly impact perceptions of abuse.

3 Community Challenges

Abusive content detection is a relatively new field of study; in only 2016, Waseem and Hovy wrote 'NLP research on hate speech has been very limited' (Waseem & Hovy, 2016). Since then it has expanded propitiously. Noticeably, a recent shared task had over 800 teams enter of which 115 reported results (Zampieri et al., 2019). The creation of a research community is fundamental for advancing knowledge by enabling collaboration and resource sharing. However, the abusive content detection community currently faces several challenges which potentially constrain the development of new and more efficient methods.

3.1 Creating and sharing datasets

Creating appropriate datasets for training hate detection systems is a crucial but time-consuming task (Golbeck et al., 2017). Currently available datasets have several limitations.

Degradation. With many datasets, including those from Twitter, content cannot be shared directly but, instead, IDs are shared and the dataset recreated each time. This can lead to considerable degradations in the quality of datasets over time. For instance, Founta et al. shared a dataset of 80,000 tweets but soon after this was reduced to 70,000 (Founta et al., 2018; Lee et al., 2018). This not only decreases the quantity of data, reducing variety, but also the class distribution changes. This makes it difficult to compare performance of different models on even one dataset. To address this issue, we encourage more collaborations with online platforms to make datasets available. A successful example of this is Twitter's release of the IRA disinformation dataset (Twitter, 2018).

Annotation. Annotation is a notoriously difficult task, reflected in the low levels of inter-annotator agreement reported by most publications, particularly on more complex multi-class tasks (Sanguinetti, Poletto, Bosco, Patti, & Stranisci, 2018). Noticeably, van Aken suggests that Davidson et al.'s widely used hate and offensive language dataset has up to 10% of its data mislabeled (van Aken et al., 2018). Few publications provide details of their annotation process or annotation guidelines. Providing such information is the norm in social scientific research and is viewed as an integral part of verifying others' findings and robustness (Bucy & Holbert, 2013). In line with the recommendations of Sabou et al., we advocate that annotation guidelines and processes are shared where possible (Sabou, Bontcheva, Derczynski, & Scharl, 2014) and that the field also works to develop best practices.

Dataset variety. The quality, size and class balance of datasets varies considerably. Understanding the decisions behind dataset creation is crucial for identifying the biases and limitations of systems trained on them. When creating datasets, researchers need to weigh up ensuring there are sufficient instances of abuse (by biased sampling through e.g. using abusive keywords) with making sure the variety of non-abusive content is great enough for the system to be applied in 'the wild' and avoid overfitting. Wiegand et al. measure the impact of biased sampling on several widely used datasets (Wiegand et al., 2019). They find it can lead to confounding whereby non-abusive terms serve as signals for identifying abuse as they are highly correlated – but such signals are unlikely to exist in the real world. To enable greater research transparency, sampling methods should always be reported in accessible dataset documentation.

At present, the main goal of biased sampling is to increase the incidence of abusive content. We propose that this should be adjusted to focus on dataset *variety*. Datasets could be curated to include linguistically difficult instances, as well as 'edge cases': content which is non-abusive but very similar to abuse. Three examples are:

1. *Non-abusive profanities.* Most detection systems use the existence of profanities (also known as 'obscenities') as an input feature. However, profanities are not inherently abusive and can be used to express other emotions.
2. *Abusive reporting.* Content which reports/comments on the abuse of others or aims to challenge/counter such abuse.
3. *Same topic but non-abusive.* Content which is on the same topic as the abusive content but is non-abusive. For instance, if the classification system detects xenophobia, then a suitable edge case is non-abusive content about foreigners.

3.2   Research ethics

The ethics of social scientific and socially-relevant computational research has received considerable scrutiny in recent times (Buchanan, 2017). Most abusive content detection systems are presented as neutral classifiers which merely aim to achieve a well-defined task. However, it is difficult to separate the descriptive from normative aspects of any social system. Academic research can be used to not only monitor and capture social behaviors but also influence and manipulate them (Ruppert, Law, & Savage, 2013). As such, given the sensitivity of this area, ethics should be at the forefront of all research.

Impact on users. Individuals and groups suffer considerably from online abuse, and there is evidence that online abuse is linked with offline attacks (Müller & Schwarz, 2017). Political science research also suggests that any form of extremist behavior, such as online hate, could fuel social antagonisms and even reprisals (Eatwell, 2006). As such, the ethical case for moderating online content is strong. However, at present, research is unevenly distributed, with far more attention paid to abuse in English as well as abuse directed against certain targets, such as racism and sexism rather than anti-Semitism, transphobia or anti-disability prejudice. This is partly due to how research is organized. For example, much research has focused on detecting abuse in Hindi-English – primarily because of a shared competition with a publicly available dataset (Kumar, Reganti, Bhatia, & Maheshwari, 2018). The uneven nature of existing research has unintended harmful consequences as certain targets of abuse receive more focus and as such are better protected. Researchers should aim to diversify the types and targets of abuse which are studied, where possible.

Impact on researchers. Researching online abuse inevitably involves viewing and thinking about abusive content, often for prolonged periods. This can inflict considerable emotional harm on researchers, particularly through vicarious trauma. Social and mental health support is necessary to protect the wellbeing of researchers and to ensure that research is sustainable in the long-term. In our online appendix, we provide a checklist of actions to help reduce the harmful impacts of viewing, annotating and researching abusive content.[1]

Researchers conducting work around sensitive topics are increasingly at risk of receiving online abuse themselves, which can range from spreading false information to 'doxing' (where identifying features, such as a home address, are published online) and 'swatting' (where a false threat is reported to the police). Researchers should not have to compromise on the type of research that

---

[1] https://github.com/bvidgen/Challenges-and-frontiers-in-abusive-content-detection

they conduct for fear of victimization. The abuse suffered by researchers may also reflect other prejudices, whereby women and minorities are targeted more often. We encourage that best practices are shared between institutions so that individuals can work within the safest and most supportive environments possible. We also recommend that Marwick et al.'s existing guidelines for dealing with harassment are used (Marwick, Blackwell, & Lo, 2016).

4   Research frontiers

4.1   Multimedia content

Most abusive content detection research focuses on text. Little research considers other forms of content, such as images, audio, memes, GIFs, and videos – all of which can be used to spread hate. One noticeable exception is research by Zannettou et al. who create a system for detecting hateful memes by mining hateful Internet forums (Zannettou, Caulfield, Blackburn, & Cristofaro, 2018). The lack of research into non text-based abuse is a severe restriction given the multimedia nature of behavior on social media. It also means that the true recall rate for abusive content detection is potentially orders of magnitude lower than what is reported.

Multimedia content poses both technical and social challenges. Technical challenges relate to the fact that different tools are needed, such as optical character recognition (OCR), image recognition and audio translation. Social challenges relate to the fact that abuse can be expressed in different ways with multimedia. For instance, in Memes, the whole is often more than the sum of its parts: a non-abusive image and non-abusive text can be used which when combined express an abusive message. Figure 1 shows an example of such a meme. It consists of a non-hateful image (Muslims in prayer) and non-hateful text ('Australia, America, England, woken up yet?'). If the image or text were changed (e.g. to a cup of coffee or the phrase 'united in prayer'), then the meme would not be Islamophobic. This kind of abuse only emerges through the text and image combination, and as such is qualitatively different to text which is abusive on its own.

Figure 1, Islamophobic Meme

4.2   Implementation

Fairness. Fairness is a growing concern within abusive content detection. Recent research has shown that systems often perform better for content aimed against certain targets, such as women rather than men (Badjatiya, Gupta, & Varma, 2019; Ji Ho Park, Shin, & Fung, 2018). This feeds into broader research which shows that computational methods can encode and reinforce social biases – even when they are meant to ameliorate them (Garg, Schiebinger, Jurafsky, & Zou, 2017). Metrics have been developed to evaluate bias which enable post-hoc quantification of the extent of these issues (Zhang et al., 2018). However, it would be particularly valuable if detection systems were automatically debiased at the point of creation, for instance by adjusting model parameters given relevant demographic variables, as suggested by Dixon et al. (Dixon, Li, Sorensen, Thain, & Vasserman, 2018). This is important for not only measuring but also removing bias.

A social scientific challenge in this space is that, at present, only biases which are socially 'recognized' can be identified, measured and thus accounted for within models (Fraser, 1997). Potentially, there are other social biases which have not yet received considerable attention but still effect social outcomes and warrant debiasing. For instance, recognition of transphobia has increased considerably over the last ten years, despite previously not being recognized in some parts of society as an important issue (Hines et al., 2018). A related area of bias that needs further investigation is how systems perform at detecting abuse produced by different types of actors, such as those in particular linguistic communities. For instance, systems may have far more false positives when detecting abuse *from* certain types of users, whose content is thus mislabeled and may be incorrectly censored.

Explainability. Closely linked to the notion of fairness is explainability. Abuse detection systems should be explainable to those whose content has been classified and they should avoid becoming 'black boxes'. This is particularly important given the contentious nature of online content moderation and its intersection with issues of censorship, free speech and privacy. One challenge here is that 'explainability' is itself a contested term and what it entails is not well stipulated (Lipton, 2016). Some have also criticized the idea of building secondary post-hoc explanative models as they can be misleading and unreliable. Rudin argues that a better approach is to 'design models that are inherently interpretable' (Rudin, 2018, p. 1). This would also be beneficial from a research perspective, reflecting the scientific process. If we can understand and explain what aspects of a system drive the classifications, then we are more likely to make advances and correct errors. As such, we encourage researchers to develop interpretable models. Nonetheless, given the utility of even hard-to-explain models, such as those using deep learning, post-hoc explanations should also be used where appropriate.

Efficiency. Few publications focus specifically on the challenge of implementing abusive content detection systems at scale and in a timely manner, although there are exceptions (Robinson, Zhang, & Tepper, 2018; Yao, Chelmis, & Zois, 2018). Ensuring that systems can be implemented efficiently is crucial if the research community is to meaningfully impact wider society.

4.3 Cross domain applications

Ensuring that abusive content detection systems can be applied across different domains is one of the most difficult but also important frontiers in existing research. Thus far, efforts to address this has been unsuccessful. Burnap and Williams train systems on one type of hate speech (e.g. racism) and apply them to another (e.g. sexism) and find that performance drops considerably (Burnap & Williams, 2016). Karan and Šnajder use a simple methodology to show the huge differences in performance when applying classifiers on different datasets without domain-specific tuning (Karan & Šnajder, 2018). Noticeably, in the EVALITA hate speech detection shared task, participants were asked to (1) train and test a system on Twitter data, (2) on Facebook data and (3) to train on Twitter and test on Facebook (and vice versa). Even the best performing teams reported their systems scored around 10 to 15 F1 points fewer on the cross-domain task. Part of the challenge is that domains vary across many characteristics, including: type of platforms, linguistic practices and dialects of users, how content is created, length of content, social context and the subtask (see above). Accounting for all these sources of variation is a considerable task.

Potential solutions are available to address this issue, such as transfer learning. Initial studies show this can help improve performance by leveraging existing datasets when there is little training data available (Agrawal & Awekar, 2018; Karan & Šnajder, 2018). However, a key challenge in transfer learning is that systems may develop 'bad' learning habits and as such newly created transfer-based models could be more simplistic and unfair (Pan & Fellow, 2009). Thus, whilst transfer learning is a promising avenue for future research, the implications need to be fully investigated.

5 Conclusion

Abusive content detection is a pressing social challenge for which computational methods can have a hugely positive impact. The field has matured considerably and in recent times there have been many advances, particularly in the development of technically sophisticated methods. However, several critical challenges are unsolved, including both those which are longstanding (such as the lack of dataset sharing) and those which have only recently received attention (such as classification biases). There are also many unaddressed frontiers of research. In this paper we have summarized and critically discussed these issues and proposed and discussed possible solutions. We have also demonstrated the utility of social scientific insights for clarifying issues.

Acknowledgements

We thank the anonymous reviewers. Thanks to Ohad Kammar for discussing the Memes example.

Agrawal, S., & Awekar, A. (2018). Deep learning for detecting cyberbullying across multiple social media platforms. In *ECIR: Advances in Information Retrieval* (pp. 141–153). https://doi.org/10.1007/978-3-319-76941-7_11

Allen, C. (2011). *Islamophobia*. Surrey: Ashgate.

Amichai-hamburger, Y., & McKenna, K. (2006). The Contact Hypothesis Reconsidered: Interacting via the Internet. *Journal of Computer-Mediated Communication, 11*(1), 825–843. https://doi.org/10.1111/j.1083-6101.2006.00037.x

Anzovino, M., Fersini, E., & Rosso, P. (2018). Automatic identification and classification of misogynistic language on Twitter. In *NLDB* (pp. 57–64). https://doi.org/10.1007/978-3-319-91947-8_6

Badjatiya, P., Gupta, M., & Varma, V. (2019). Stereotypical Bias Removal for Hate Speech Detection Task using Knowledge-based Generalizations. In *World Wide Web* (pp. 49–59).

Badjatiya, P., Gupta, S., Gupta, M., & Varma, V. (2017). Deep Learning for Hate Speech Detection in Tweets. In *World Wide Web* (pp. 759–760). https://doi.org/10.1145/3041021.3054223

Benesch, S. (2012). *Dangerous Speech: A Proposal to Prevent Group Violence*. New York.

Binns, R., Veale, M., Van Kleek, M., & Shadbolt, N. (2017). Like trainer, like bot? Inheritance of bias in algorithmic content moderation. In *Lecture Notes in Computer Science* (pp. 1–12). https://doi.org/10.1007/978-3-319-67256-4_32

Buchanan, E. (2017). Considering the ethics of big data research: A case of Twitter and ISIS / ISIL. *PLoS ONE, 12*(12), 1–6.

Bucy, E., & Holbert, L. (2013). *Sourcebook for political communication research*. London: Routledge.

Burnap, P., & Williams, M. (2016). Us and Them: Identifying Cyber Hate on Twitter across Multiple Protected Characteristics.

EPJ Data Science, 5(1), 1–15. https://doi.org/10.1140/epjds/s13688-016-0072-6

Caiani, M., & Wagemann, C. (2009). Online networks of the Italian and German Extreme Right. *Information, Communication & Society*, 66–109. https://doi.org/10.1080/13691180802158482

Chandrasekharan, E., Samory, M., Srinivasan, A., & Gilbert, E. (2017). The Bag of Communities. In *CHI* (pp. 3175–3187). https://doi.org/10.1145/3025453.3026018

Crawford, K., & Gillespie, T. (2016). What is a flag for? Social media reporting tools and the vocabulary of complaint. *New Media and Society, 18*(3), 410–428. https://doi.org/10.1177/1461444814543163

Daniels, J. (2013). Race and racism in Internet Studies: A review and critique. *New Media and Society, 15*(5), 695–719. https://doi.org/10.1177/1461444812462849

Davidson, T., Warmsley, D., Macy, M., & Weber, I. (2017). Automated Hate Speech Detection and the Problem of Offensive Language. In *ICWSM* (pp. 1–4).

Devlin, J., Chang, M.-W., Lee, K., & Toutanova, K. (2018). BERT: Pre-training of Deep Bidirectional Transformers for Language Understanding. *ArXiv:1810.04805v2*, 1–16. Retrieved from http://arxiv.org/abs/1810.04805

Dixon, L., Li, J., Sorensen, J., Thain, N., & Vasserman, L. (2018). Measuring and Mitigating Unintended Bias in Text Classification. In *AAAI/ACM Conference on AI, Ethics, and Society* (pp. 67–73). https://doi.org/10.1145/3278721.3278729

Eatwell, R. (2006). Community Cohesion and Cumulative Extremism in Contemporary Britain. *Political Quarterly, 77*(2), 204–216. https://doi.org/10.1111/j.1467-923X.2006.00763.x

Eger, S., Şahin, G. G., Rücklé, A., Lee, J.-U., Schulz, C., Mesgar, M., … Gurevych, I. (2019). Text Processing Like Humans Do: Visually Attacking and Shielding NLP Systems. *ArXiv:1903.11508v1*, 1–14.

Eisenstein, J. (2013). What to do about bad language on the Internet. *NAACL HLT,*

359–369.

Eisenstein, J., O'Connor, B., Smith, N., & Xing, E. (2014). Diffusion of lexical change in social media. *PLoS ONE, 9*(11), 1–13. https://doi.org/10.1371/journal.pone.011311 4

Fortuna, P., & Nunes, S. (2018). A Survey on Automatic Detection of Hate Speech in Text. *ACM Computing Surveys, 51*(4), 1–30. https://doi.org/10.1145/3232676

Founta, A., Djouvas, C., Chatzakou, D., Leontiadis, I., Blackburn, J., Stringhini, G., … Kourtellis, N. (2018). Large Scale Crowdsourcing and Characterization of Twitter Abusive Behavior. In *ICWSM* (pp. 1–11).

Fraser, N. (1997). *Justice Interruptus: Critical Reflections on the "Postsocialist" Condition*. London: Routledge.

Garg, N., Schiebinger, L., Jurafsky, D., & Zou, J. (2017). Word Embeddings Quantify 100 Years of Gender and Ethnic Stereotypes. *PNAS, 115*(16), 3635–3644. https://doi.org/10.1073/pnas.1720347115

Golbeck, J., Geller, A. A., Thanki, J., Naik, S., Hoffman, K. M., Wu, D. M., … Jienjitlert, V. (2017). A Large Labeled Corpus for Online Harassment Research. In *WebSci* (pp. 229–233). https://doi.org/10.1145/3091478.3091509

Gorrell, G., Greenwood, M., Roberts, I., Maynard, D., & Bontcheva, K. (2018). Twits, Twats and Twaddle: Trends in Online Abuse towards UK Politicians. In *ICWSM* (pp. 600–603).

Gröndahl, T., Pajola, L., Juuti, M., Conti, M., & Asokan, N. (2018). All You Need is "Love": Evading Hate-speech Detection. *ArXiv:1808.09115v2*, 1–11.

Hine, G. E., Onaolapo, J., De Cristofaro, E., Kourtellis, N., Leontiadis, I., Samaras, R., … Blackburn, J. (2017). Kek, Cucks, and God Emperor Trump: A Measurement Study of 4chan's Politically Incorrect Forum and Its Effects on the Web. In *ICWSM* (pp. 92–101).

Hines, S., Davy, Z., Monro, S., Motmans, J., Santos, A. C., & Van Der Ros, J. (2018). Introduction to the themed issue: Trans* policy, practice and lived experience within a European context. *Critical Social Policy, 38*(1), 5–12. https://doi.org/10.1177/0261018317732879

HM Government. (2019). *Online Harms White Paper*. London: Department of Digital, Culture, Media and Society.

Karan, M., & Šnajder, J. (2018). Cross-Domain Detection of Abusive Language Online. In *2nd Workshop on Abusive Language Online* (pp. 132–137). Retrieved from http://takelab.fer.hr/alfeda

Kumar, R., Ojha, A. K., Malmasi, S., & Zampieri, M. (2018). Benchmarking Aggression Identification in Social Media. In *1st Workshop on Abusive Language Online* (pp. 1–11).

Kumar, R., Reganti, A., Bhatia, A., & Maheshwari, T. (2018). Aggression-annotated Corpus of Hindi-English Code-mixed Data. In *LREC* (pp. 1–7). Retrieved from http://arxiv.org/abs/1803.09402

LaMarre, H., Landreville, K., & Beam, M. (2009). The irony of satire: Political ideology and the motivation to see what you want to see in The Colbert Report. *International Journal of Press/Politics, 14*(2), 212–231. https://doi.org/10.1177/1940161208330904

Lee, Y., Yoon, S., & Jung, K. (2018). Comparative Studies of Detecting Abusive Language on Twitter. In *2nd Workshop on Abusive Language Online* (pp. 101–106).

Lipton, Z. (2016). The Mythos of Model Interpretability. In *ICML Workshop on Human Interpretability in Machine Learning* (pp. 1–9). New York.

Ma, C. (2014). *What are you laughing at? A social semiotic analysis of ironic racial stereotypes in Chappelle's Show*. London.

Magu, R., Joshi, K., & Luo, J. (2017). Detecting the Hate Code on Social Media. In *ICWSM* (pp. 608–611). https://doi.org/10.1016/j.vetimm.2017.02.003

Margetts, H., John, P., Hale, S., & Yasseri, T. (2015). *Political Turbluence: How Social Media Shape Collective Action*. New Jersey: Princeton University Press.

Marwick, A., Blackwell, L., & Lo, K. (2016). *Best practices for conducting risky research and protecting yourself from online harassment*. New York: Data & Society.

Marwick, A., & Boyd, D. (2010). I tweet honestly, I tweet passionately: Twitter users, context collapse, and the imagined audience. *New Media and Society, 13*(1), 114–133. https://doi.org/10.1177/1461444810365313

Mehdad, Y., & Tetreault, J. (2016). Do Characters Abuse More Than Words? In *SIGDAL* (pp. 299–303). https://doi.org/10.18653/v1/w16-3638

Müller, K., & Schwarz, C. (2017). Fanning the Flames of Hate: Social Media and Hate Crime. *CAGE Working Paper Series*, 1–82. https://doi.org/10.2139/ssrn.3082972

Nobata, C., Thomas, A., Mehdad, Y., Chang, Y., & Tetreault, J. (2016). Abusive Language Detection in Online User Content. In *World Wide Web* (pp. 145–153). https://doi.org/10.1145/2872427.2883062

Palmer, A., Robinson, M., & Phillips, K. (2017). Illegal is not a Noun: Linguistic Form for Detection of Pejorative Nominalizations. In *1st Workshop on Abusive Language Online* (pp. 91–100). https://doi.org/10.18653/v1/w17-3014

Pan, S. J., & Fellow, Q. Y. (2009). A Survey on Transfer Learning. *IEEE Transactions on Knowledge and Data Engineering*, 1–15.

Papegnies, E., Labatut, V., Dufour, R., & Linarès, G. (2017). Graph-based features for automatic online abuse detection. In *SLSP* (pp. 70–81). https://doi.org/10.1007/978-3-319-68456-7_6

Park, Ji Ho, Shin, J., & Fung, P. (2018). Reducing Gender Bias in Abusive Language Detection. In *EMNLP* (pp. 2799–2804).

Park, Ji Hoon, Gabbadon, N. G., & Chernin, A. R. (2006). Naturalizing racial differences through comedy: Asian, black, and white views on racial stereotypes in rush hour 2. *Journal of Communication, 56*(1), 157–177. https://doi.org/10.1111/j.1460-2466.2006.00008.x

Pitsilis, G. K., Ramampiaro, H., & Langseth, H. (2018). Detecting Offensive Language in Tweets Using Deep Learning. *ArXiv:1801.04433v1*, 1–17.

Qian, J., ElSherief, M., Belding, E., & Wang, W. Y. (2018). Hierarchical CVAE for Fine-Grained Hate Speech Classification. In *EMNLP* (pp. 3550–3559). https://doi.org/arXiv:1809.00088v1

Raisi, E., & Huang, B. (2016). Cyberbullying Identification Using Participant-Vocabulary Consistency. In *ICML Workshop on #Data4Good* (pp. 46–50). Retrieved from http://arxiv.org/abs/1606.08084

Raisi, E., & Huang, B. (2017). Cyberbullying Detection with Weakly Supervised Machine Learning. In *ASONAM* (pp. 1–8). https://doi.org/10.1145/3110025.3110049

Robinson, D., Zhang, Z., & Tepper, J. (2018). Hate speech detection on Twitter: Feature engineering v.s. feature selection. *ESWC*, 46–49. https://doi.org/10.1007/978-3-319-98192-5_9

Rudin, C. (2018). Please Stop Explaining Black Box Models for High Stakes Decisions. In *NIPS* (pp. 1–15). Retrieved from http://arxiv.org/abs/1811.10154

Ruppert, E., Law, J., & Savage, M. (2013). Reassembling Social Science Methods: The Challenge of Digital Devices. *Theory, Culture & Society, 30*(4), 22–46. https://doi.org/10.1177/0263276413484941

Sabba, M. (2009). Spelling as a social practice. In J. Maybin & J. Swann (Eds.), *Routledge Companion to English Language Studies* (pp. 243–257). London: Routledge.

Sabou, M., Bontcheva, K., Derczynski, L., & Scharl, A. (2014). Corpus Annotation through Crowdsourcing: Towards Best Practice Guidelines. *LREC*, 859–866.

Salminen, J., & Almerekhi, H. (2018). Online Hate Interpretation Varies by Country, But More by Individual. In *SNAMS* (pp. 1–7). https://doi.org/10.1109/SNAMS.2018.8554954

Salminen, J., Almerekhi, H., Milenković, M., Jung, S.-G. G., An, J., Kwak, H., & Jansen, B. (2018). Anatomy of Online Hate: Developing a Taxonomy and Machine Learning Models. In *ICWSM* (pp. 330–339).

https://doi.org/10.1109/SNAMS.2018.8554954

Sanguinetti, M., Poletto, F., Bosco, C., Patti, V., & Stranisci, M. (2018). An Italian Twitter Corpus of Hate Speech against Immigrants. In *LREC* (pp. 2798–2805). https://doi.org/10.1561/1500000001

Santos, C. N. dos, Melnyk, I., & Padhi, I. (2018). Fighting Offensive Language on Social Media with Unsupervised Text Style Transfer. In *Meeting for ACL* (pp. 189–194). Retrieved from http://arxiv.org/abs/1805.07685

Sartori, G. (1970). Concept misinformation in comparative politics. *American Political Science Review, 64*(4), 1033–1053. https://doi.org/10.2307/1958356

Schmidt, A., & Wiegand, M. (2017). A Survey on Hate Speech Detection using Natural Language Processing. In *International Workshop on NLP for Social Media* (pp. 1–10). Valencia, Spain. https://doi.org/10.18653/v1/w17-1101

Serrà, J., Leontiadis, I., Spathis, D., Stringhini, G., Blackburn, J., & Vakali, A. (2017). Class-based Prediction Errors to Detect Hate Speech with Out-of-vocabulary Words. In *1st Workshop on Abusive Language Online* (pp. 36–40). Vancouver, Canada. https://doi.org/10.18653/v1/w17-3005

Silva, L., Mondal, M., Correa, D., Benevenuto, F., & Weber, I. (2016). Analyzing the Targets of Hate in Online Social Media. In *IWCSM* (pp. 687–690).

Sugandhi, R., Pande, A., Chawla, S., Agrawal, A., & Bhagat, H. (2016). Methods for detection of cyberbullying: a survey. In *International Conference on Intelligent Systems Design and Applications* (pp. 173–177). https://doi.org/10.1109/ISDA.2015.7489220

Tien, J. H., Eisenberg, M. C., Cherng, S. T., & Porter, M. A. (2019). *Online reactions to the 2017 'Unite the Right' rally in Charlottesville: Measuring polarization in Twitter networks using media followership.*

Twitter. (2018). Enabling further research of information operations on Twitter. Retrieved May 30, 2019, from https://blog.twitter.com/en_us/topics/company/2018/enabling-further-research-of-information-operations-on-twitter.html

Unsvåg, E., & Gambäck, B. (2018). The Effects of User Features on Twitter Hate Speech Detection. In *2nd Workshop on Abusive Language Online* (pp. 75–85). Retrieved from http://aclweb.org/anthology/W18-5110

van Aken, B., Risch, J., Krestel, R., & Löser, A. (2018). Challenges for Toxic Comment Classification: An In-Depth Error Analysis. In *2nd Workshop on Abusive Language Online* (pp. 33–42).

Van Hee, C., Lefever, E., De Pauw, G., Daelemans, W., Hoste, V., Jacobs, G., … Verhoeven, B. (2018). Automatic detection of cyberbullying in social media text. *PLoS ONE, 13*(10), 1–21. https://doi.org/10.1371/journal.pone.0203794

Waseem, Z., Davidson, T., Warmsley, D., & Weber, I. (2017). Understanding Abuse: A Typology of Abusive Language Detection Subtasks. In *1st Workshop on Abusive Language Online* (pp. 78–84). https://doi.org/10.1080/17421770903114687

Waseem, Z., & Hovy, D. (2016). Hateful Symbols or Hateful People? Predictive Features for Hate Speech Detection on Twitter. In *NAACL-HLT* (pp. 88–93). https://doi.org/10.18653/v1/n16-2013

Weaver, S. (2010). Developing a rhetorical analysis of racist humour: examining anti-black jokes on the Internet. *Social Semiotics, 20*(5), 537–555. https://doi.org/10.1080/10350330.2010.513188

Wiegand, M., Ruppenhofer, J., & Kleinbauer, T. (2019). Detection of Abusive Language: the Problem of Biased Datasets. In *NAACL-HLT* (pp. 602–608).

Wulczyn, E., Thain, N., & Dixon, L. (2017). Ex Machina: Personal Attacks Seen at Scale. In *World Wide Web* (pp. 1391–1399). Perth, Australia. https://doi.org/10.1039/C5CC05843K

Yao, M., Chelmis, C., & Zois, D. S. (2018). Cyberbullying detection on Instagram with optimal online feature selection. In

ASONAM (pp. 401–408).
https://doi.org/10.1109/ASONAM.2018.85
08329

Zampieri, M., Malmasi, S., Nakov, P.,
Rosenthal, S., Farra, N., & Kumar, R.
(2019). SemEval-2019 Task 6: Identifying
and Categorizing Offensive Language in
Social Media (OffensEval).
ArXiv:1903.08983v3, 1–12.

Zannettou, S., Caulfield, T., Blackburn, J., &
Cristofaro, E. De. (2018). On the Origins of
Memes by Means of Fringe Web
Communities. In *18th ACM Internet
Measurement Conference* (pp. 1–23).

Zhang, Z., Robinson, D., Tepper, J., Gangemi,
A., Navigli, R., Vidal, M. E., … Alam, M.
(2018). Detecting hate speech on Twitter
using a convolution-GRU based deep
neural network. In *ESWC* (pp. 745–760).
https://doi.org/10.1007/978-3-319-93417-
4_48

A Hierarchically-Labeled Portuguese Hate Speech Dataset

Paula Fortuna[1,3]**, João Rocha da Silva**[1,2]**,**
Juan Soler-Company[3]**, Leo Wanner**[3,4]**, Sérgio Nunes**[1,2]

[1]INESC TEC, [2]FEUP, University of Porto
Rua Dr. Roberto Frias, s/n 4200-465 Porto, Portugal
[3]NLP Group, ETIC, Pompeu Fabra University, Barcelona, Spain
[4]Catalan Institute for Research and Advanced Studies (ICREA), Barcelona, Spain
`paula.fortuna@fe.up.pt, joaorosilva@gmail.com`
`juan.soler@upf.edu, leo.wanner@upf.edu, sergio.nunes@fe.up.pt`

Abstract

Over the past years, the amount of online offensive speech has been growing steadily. To successfully cope with it, machine learning is applied. However, ML-based techniques require sufficiently large annotated datasets. In the last years, different datasets were published, mainly for English. In this paper, we present a new dataset for Portuguese, which has not been in focus so far. The dataset is composed of 5,668 tweets. For its annotation, we defined two different schemes used by annotators with different levels of expertise. First, non-experts annotated the tweets with binary labels ('hate' vs. 'no-hate'). Then, expert annotators classified the tweets following a fine-grained hierarchical multiple label scheme with 81 hate speech categories in total. The inter-annotator agreement varied from category to category, which reflects the insight that some types of hate speech are more subtle than others and that their detection depends on personal perception. The hierarchical annotation scheme is the main contribution of the presented work, as it facilitates the identification of different types of hate speech and their intersections. To demonstrate the usefulness of our dataset, we carried a baseline classification experiment with pre-trained word embeddings and LSTM on the binary classified data, with a state-of-the-art outcome.

1 Introduction

The Internet is the source of an immense variety of knowledge repositories (Wikipedia, Wordnet, etc.) and applications (YouTube, Reddit, Twitter, etc.) that everybody can access and take advantage of; it is also **the** communication forum of our time and the most important instrument to ensure freedom of speech. It allows us to freely state and disseminate our view on any private or public matter to vast audiences. But unfortunately it also opens the door to manipulation of masses and defamation of specific individuals or groups of people. One of these observed negative phenomena is the propagation of hate speech. Hate speech leads to a negative self-image and social exclusion of the targeted individuals, groups or populations, and incites violence against them. A clear example of the extreme harm that can be caused by hate speech is the 1994 Rwandan genocide; see Schabas (2000) for a detailed analysis. The detection of online hate speech is thus a pressing problem that calls for solutions. Over the last decade, a considerable number of supervised machine learning-based works tackled the problem. Most of them focused on English (Waseem and Hovy, 2016; Davidson et al., 2017; Nobata et al., 2016; Jigsaw, 2018), see also the overview by Schmidt and Wiegand (2017). As a result, also many more annotated datasets, which are the precondition for the use of supervised machine learning, are available for English (e.g., Waseem and Hovy (2016); Davidson et al. (2017); Nobata et al. (2016); Jigsaw (2018)) than for other languages. However, hate speech is not a phenomenon that is observed only in English discourse; it is notorious in online media in other languages as well; cf., e.g., Spanish (Fersini et al., 2018), Italian (Poletto et al., 2017; Sanguinetti et al., 2018), or German (Ross et al., 2016).

In this work, we aim to contribute to the field of hate speech detection. Our contribution is twofold: (i) diversification of the research on hate speech by provision of a new dataset of hate speech in another language than English, namely Portuguese; (ii) introduction of a novel fine-grained hate speech typology that improves on the common state-of-the-art used typologies, which tend to disregard the existence of subtypes of hate speech and either consider hate speech recognition as a binary classification task, or take into account only a few classes, such as 'racism'

Proceedings of the Third Workshop on Abusive Language Online, pages 94–104
Florence, Italy, August 1, 2019. ©2019 Association for Computational Linguistics

and 'sexism' (Waseem and Hovy, 2016) – despite the fact that such broad distinctions unduly overgeneralize. For instance, by classifying discrimination against both black people and refugees simply as 'racism', we ignore that in this case, different characteristics with a different motivation are targeted (also reflected in a different language style). In particular, we compile and annotate a new dataset composed of 5,668 tweets in Portuguese, which is one of the most commonly-used languages online (Fox, 2013). Two types of annotations are carried out. For the first, non-expert annotators classify the messages in a binary fashion ('hate' vs. 'no-hate'). For the second, we build a multilabel hate speech hierarchical annotation schema with 81 hate categories in total[1]. To demonstrate the usefulness of our dataset, we carried a baseline classification experiment with pretrained word embeddings and LSTM on the binary classified data, with a state-of-the-art outcome.

The remainder of the paper is structured as follows: Section 2 reviews the literature. Section 3 describes our crawling procedure. In Section 4, we present the two annotation schemas we work with: the binary and the hierarchical schema. Section 5 discusses a baseline hate speech experiment that we carried out to validate our new dataset. Section 6 presents some ethical considerations of this work. In Section 7, finally, the conclusions of our work are presented.

2 Related Work

2.1 Hate Speech Concepts

Fortuna and Nunes (2018) analyze and compare several aggression-related concepts. As a result of their analysis, they present the following definition of *hate speech*:

> "Hate speech is language that attacks or diminishes, that incites violence or hate against groups, based on specific characteristics such as physical appearance, religion, descent, national or ethnic origin, sexual orientation, gender identity or other, and it can occur with different linguistic styles, even in subtle forms or when humour is used."

We adopted this definition in our work. Our work has also been inspired by the taxonomy provided by Salminen et al. (2018), which includes 29 hate categories characterized in terms of hateful language, target, and sub-target types. To create

their taxonomy, Salminen et al. followed an iterative and qualitative procedure called "open coding" (Glaser and Strauss, 2017).

There are obvious similarities between Salminen et al.'s approach and ours. However, there are also some significant differences. The first difference concerns the underlying definition of hate. While they use the very generic definition "hateful comments toward a specific group or target", the definition we adopt is more specific (cf. above). This leads to differences in the taxonomy. For instance, they introduce 'hate against media' and 'hate against religion', which is hate against abstract entities and not considered by us. Additionally, they merge in the same hate speech taxonomy the targets of hate and the type of discourse. In our case, we focus on the targets of hate speech only.

2.2 Dataset Annotation

Several hate speech datasets are publicly available, e.g., for English (Waseem and Hovy, 2016; Davidson et al., 2017; Nobata et al., 2016; Jigsaw, 2018), Spanish (Fersini et al., 2018), Italian (Poletto et al., 2017; Sanguinetti et al., 2018), German (Ross et al., 2016), Hindi (Kumar et al., 2018), and Portuguese (de Pelle and Moreira, 2017). In this section, we analyze the data collection strategy, the annotation method and the dataset properties of three representative hate speech datasets: the Hate speech, Racism and Sexism dataset by Waseem and Hovy (2016), the Offensive Language Dataset by Davidson et al. (2017), and the Portuguese News Comments dataset by de Pelle and Moreira (2017). We have chosen the first two because they are the most widely used datasets for English hate speech automatic classification. They show how Twitter can be used to retrieve information and how to conduct the manual classification relying on both expert and non-expert annotators. The third is another annotated and published dataset for Portuguese, which is rather different from ours.

Hate speech, Racism and Sexism Dataset. This dataset[2] (Waseem and Hovy, 2016) contains 16,914 tweets in English, which were classified by two annotators using the classes "Racism", "Sexism" and "Neither". Regarding the tweet collection, an initial manual search was conducted on Twitter to collect common slurs and terms related to religious, sexual, gender, and ethnic minorities.

---

[1] https://github.com/paulafortuna/Portuguese-Hate-Speech-Dataset

[2] https://github.com/ZeerakW/hatespeech

The authors identified frequently occurring terms in tweets that contain hate speech and used those terms to retrieve more messages. The messages were then annotated by the main researcher, together with a gender studies student; in total, 3,383 tweets as sexist, 1,972 as racist, and 11,559 as neither sexist nor racist. The inter-annotator agreement had a Cohen's Kappa of 0.84. The authors of the study concluded that the use of n-grams provides good results in the task of automatic hate speech detection, and adding demographic information leads to little improvement in the performance of the classification model.

Offensive Language Dataset. Davidson et al. (2017) annotated a dataset[3] with 14,510 tweets in English, using the classes "Hate", "Offensive" and "Neither". Regarding the collection of the messages, they started with an English hate speech lexicon compiled by Hatebase.org, searching for tweets that contained terms from this lexicon. The outcome was a collection of tweets written by 33,458 Twitter users. The collected tweets were completed by further follow-up tweets of these users, which resulted in a corpus of 85.4 million tweets. Finally, from this corpus, a random sample of 25,000 tweets containing terms from the lexicon has been extracted and manually annotated by CrowdFlower workers. Three or more workers from CrowdFlower annotated each message. The majority voting was used to assign a label to each tweet. Tweets that did not have a majority class were discarded. This resulted in a sample of 24,802 labeled tweets. The inter-annotator agreement score provided by CrowdFlower was 92%. However, a total percentage of only 5% of tweets were labeled as hate speech by the majority of the workers.

Portuguese News Comments Dataset. de Pelle and Moreira (2017) collected a dataset[4] with 1,250 random comments from the Globo news site on politics and sports news. Each comment was annotated by three annotators, who were asked to indicate whether it contained 'racism', 'sexism', 'homophobia', 'xenophobia', 'religious intolerance', or 'cursing'. 'Cursing' was the most frequent label, while the other labels had few instances in the corpus. Regarding the annotator

agreement, the value was 0.71.

In comparison to this work, the dataset that we have compiled provides more data and is not restricted to specific topics. Additionally, our annotation focuses only on hate speech, instead of general offensive content. We also use and provide a complete labeling schema.

Compared to the previous two datasets, our second annotation schema is considerably more fine-grained. As we will see below, our annotation procedure with the fine-grained schema is similar to that of Waseem and Hovy (2016).

2.3 Classification methods

Different studies conclude that deep learning approaches outperform classical machine learning algorithms in the task of hate speech detection; see, e.g., Mehdad and Tetreault (2016); Park and Fung (2017); Del Vigna et al. (2017); Pitsilis et al. (2018); Founta et al. (2018); Gambäck and Sikdar (2017). For instance, Badjatiya et al. (2017) compare the use of different types of neural networks (CNN, LSTM) and deep learning libraries such as FastText with the use of classical machine learning techniques and experiment with different types of word embeddings. The setup that achieved the best performance consists of the combination of deep techniques with standard ML classifiers, and more precisely, of embeddings learned by an LSTM model, combined with gradient boosted decision trees. We will follow a similar methodology for classification.

3 Message Collection

Our overall approach to message collection is outlined in Figure 1. In what follows, we introduce in detail the individual steps.

Use of Keywords and Profiles. We used Twitter's search API for keywords and profiles because both can be complementary as message sources. With the first, we access a wider range of tweets from different profiles, but we restrict the search to specific words or expressions that indicate hate. With the second, we obtain more spontaneous discourse, but from a more restricted number of users:

- **Hate-related keywords:** We used Twitter's API search feature to look for keywords and hashtags related to hate speech, such as *fufas*, *sapatão* 'dyke' or *#LugarDeMulherENaCozinha* '#womensPlaceIsInTheKitchen'.

---

[3]https://github.com/t-davidson/hate-speech-and-offensive-language

[4]https://github.com/rogersdepelle/OffComBR

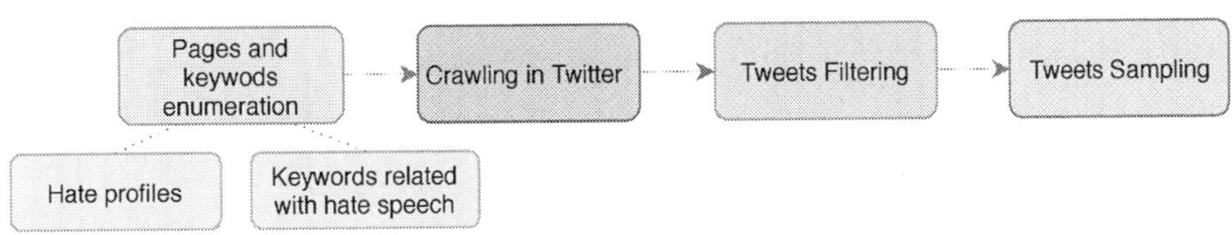

Figure 1: Method for message collection.

- **Hate-related profiles:** Using the profile search API, we query with words like *ódio* 'hate', *discurso de ódio* 'hate speech' and *ofensivo* 'offensive' in order to find accounts that post hateful messages. In Portuguese, there are social media users whose profile is built specifically for sharing hateful content against certain minorities. We collect the messages from those accounts with the expectation to find hate speech messages. This search also allowed us to find counter hate profiles. Those also use the same words in their description. It seemed adequate to keep these profiles because they reproduce hate speech messages from other users.

We looked at 29 specific profiles and used 19 keywords and ten hashtags in a total for 58 search instances.[5] The goal has been to be exhaustive and cover different types of discrimination, based on religion, gender, sexual orientation, ethnicity, and migration. We compiled this collection of search instances because there was no specific hate speech lexicon available for Portuguese, e.g., Hatebase contains generic hate (Hatebase, 2019).

Crawling. We used R to crawl content with respect to both keywords and profiles content on the 8th and 9th of March of 2017. A total of 42,930 messages were collected.

Tweet Filtering. We kept tweets categorized by Twitter as written in Portuguese. We eliminated repetitions and retweets from already collected messages to avoid duplication and removed HTML tags and messages with less than three words.

Tweet Sampling. The procedure previously described resulted in 33,890 tweets. We noticed that the search instances returned several tweets from different magnitudes (e.g., some profiles had only around 30 messages while others had more than

3,000). We decided then to use a maximum of 200 tweets per search instance in order to keep a more diverse source of tweets.

Final Dataset. Our final dataset contains 5,668 tweets, containing content from 1,156 different users. The majority of the tweets (more than 95%) are from January, February, and March of 2017.

4 Annotation of Hate Speech

In what follows, we present the annotation procedures for binary hate speech and hierarchical hate speech annotation.

4.1 Binary annotation

Three annotators classified every message. 18 Portuguese native speakers (Information Science student volunteers) were given annotation guidelines to perform the task (cf. Appendix A.1). All of them received an equivalent number of messages. The annotation was binary and the annotators had to label each message as 'hate speech' or 'not hate speech'.

To check the agreement between the three classifications of every message, we used Fleiss's Kappa (Fleiss, 1971). We observed a low agreement with a value of $K = 0.17$. We think that this low value is the result of relying exclusively on non-expert annotators for classifying hate speech. For instance, in Waseem and Hovy (2016), the two annotators were the author of the study plus a gender studies student. On the other hand, the two other studies mentioned in Section 2 (de Pelle and Moreira, 2017; Davidson et al., 2017), are more generic in that they do not focus exclusively on hate speech (as we do), but rather consider offensive speech in general, which includes insults that are more explicit and easier to recognize, while hate speech is subtler and more difficult to identify.

For our final annotation, we applied the majority vote, which resulted in a dataset in which 31.5% of the messages are annotated as 'hate speech'.

---

[5]We use the term "search instance" to refer to profiles, keywords or hashtags used for the Twitter search.

4.2 Hierarchical annotation

When studying hate speech, it is possible to distinguish between different categories of it, like 'racism', 'sexism', or 'homophobia'. A more fine-grained view can be useful in hate speech classification because each category has a specific vocabulary and ways to be expressed, such that creating a language model for each category may be helpful to improve the automatic detection of hate speech (Warner and Hirschberg, 2012).

Another phenomenon we can observe when analyzing different categories of hate speech is their *intersectionality*. This concept appeared as an answer to the historical exclusion of black women from early women's rights movements often concerned with the struggles of white women alone. Intersectionality brings attention to the experiences of people who are subjected to multiple forms of discrimination within a society (e.g., being woman and black) (Collins, 2015). Waseem (2016) introduce a hate speech labeling scheme that follows an intersectional approach. In addition to 'racism', 'sexism', and 'neither', they use the label "both" arguing that the intersection of multiple oppression categories can differ from the forms of oppression it consists of (Crenshaw, 2018).

To better take into account different hate speech categories from an intersectional perspective, we approach the definition of the hate speech annotation schema in terms of a hierarchical structure of classes.

4.2.1 Hate speech and hierarchical classification

In hierarchical classification, there is a structure defining the hierarchy between the categories of the problem (Dumais and Chen, 2000). This is opposed to flat classification, where categories are treated in isolation. Several structures can be used to represent a hierarchy of classes. One of them is a *Rooted Directed Acyclic Graph* (rooted DAG), where each class corresponds to a node and can have more than one parent. Another property of this graph is that documents can be assigned to terminal categories and to non-terminal node categories alike (Hao et al., 2007). In the specific case of hate speech classification, we propose to use a rooted DAG in order to be able to cover hate speech subtypes and their intersections, as exemplified in Figure 2. The graph of classes has the following properties:

- The 'hate speech' class corresponds to the root of the graph.

- If hate speech can be divided into several types of hate, several nodes descend from the root node. This gives rise to the second level of classes (Table 1) according to the targets of the hate (e.g., 'racism', 'homophobia', and 'sexism').

- This second level of nodes can also be divided into subgroups of targets. For instance, racist messages can be targeted against black people, Chinese people, Latinos, etc.

- The division of classes can continue until we do not find more distinct groups, resulting in a terminal node.

- The lower nodes of the graph inherit the classes from the upper nodes, up to the root.

- The lower nodes of the graph can have one or more parents. In the second case, this gives rise to a class that intersects the parent classes.

- Instances are classified according to a multi-label approach and can belong to classes assigned to both terminal and/or non-terminal nodes.

Class	Definition
Sexism	Hate speech based on gender. Includes hate speech against woman.
Body	Hate speech based on body, such as fat, thin, tall or short people.
Origin	Hate speech based on the place of origin.
Homophobia	Hate speech based on sexual orientation.
Racism	Hate speech based on ethnicity.
Ideology	Hate speech based on a person's ideas, such as feminist or left wing ideology.
Religion	Hate speech based on religion.
Health	Hate speech based on health conditions, such as against disabled people.
Other-Lifestyle	Hate speech based on life habits, such as vegetarianism.

Table 1: Direct subtypes of the 'hate speech' type.

This annotation schema has several advantages compared to standard binary or disjoint flat classification. Firstly, it models in a better way the relationships between different subtypes of hate speech. Additionally, it preserves rare classes, while signaling them as part of more generic

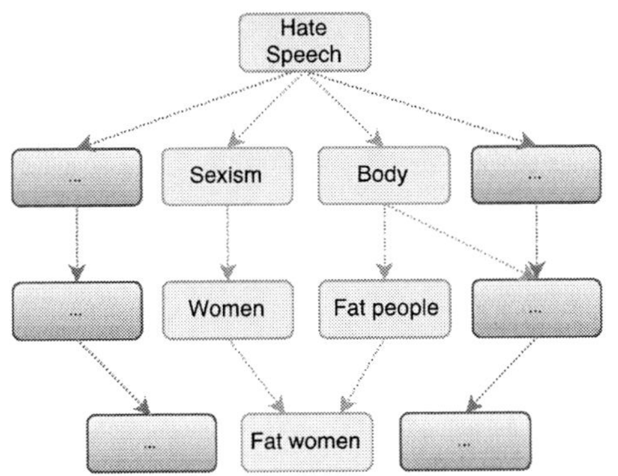

Figure 2: Part of the rooted directed acyclic graph used for hate speech classification.

classes. For instance, with this classification, we can use a message to build a model for predicting sexism even if the message was cataloged as 'hate against fat women'. Finally, with this approach, it is possible to study each subtype of hate speech individually or in relation to others, depending on the goal of the study.

In the next subsection, we outline the hierarchical annotation procedure conducted with the dataset described in Section 3, which complements the non-expert annotation.

4.2.2 Building the hierarchy of hate speech

Similarly to Salminen et al. (2018), we use for the annotation a data-driven approach based on an open coding methodology. This means that we iteratively protocol the different classes as they appear in the dataset while we read and classify the data. The classification hierarchy is then built by creating and reorganizing categories until all available data was analyzed. For this annotation, we applied an intersectional approach by enumerating all the possible groups cited in our dataset, no matter their frequency (e.g., 'feminist men' appears only once).

Based on all instances of the dataset, the hierarchy of classes was built by one researcher working in the area of automatic detection of hate speech, with training in social psychology. Then, the same researcher classified all the dataset messages using the hierarchical class structure.

4.2.3 Agreement between annotators

For verifying the validity of this annotation procedure, a second annotator classified 500 messages. Then, we used Cohens Kappa (Gamer et al., 2012) for checking the agreement between both. We

observed K = 0.72. We also consider the agreement of the annotators by type of hate speech. We ranked the classes by the best agreement and removed the classes with only one instance for any of the annotators. We found diverse values in the different categories (Table 2), which points out that some specific types of hate speech can be more difficult to classify than others.

Classes	K	Annotator 1	Annotator 2
Lesbians	0.879	59	53
Health	0.856	3	4
Homofobia	0.823	69	61
Disabled people	0.799	2	3
Refugees	0.763	13	13
Migrants	0.751	15	14
Sexism	0.669	134	104
Trans women	0.662	6	9
Men	0.657	12	15
Women	0.642	109	75
Fat women	0.637	30	16
Body	0.637	32	17
Fat people	0.637	32	17
Ideology	0.609	14	15
Feminists	0.581	13	14
Hate speech	0.569	245	213
Racism	0.501	18	13
Religion	0.493	5	11
Black people	0.435	11	7
Origin	0.329	3	3
Islamists	0.329	2	10
Gays	0.300	4	9
Ugly women	0.276	24	4

Table 2: Annotator agreement by class, with the number of messages annotated by each annotator.

4.3 Hierarchical dataset

After the annotation phase, we obtain a multi-labeled dataset with 22% of hate speech instances. The resulting hierarchy, the node depth (ND) and class frequencies (Freq) are presented in Table 3. As expected, the classes corresponding to nodes with a higher depth tend to have a smaller frequency. Note that our schema also identifies categories that are less commonly mentioned in hate speech classification experiments, among them, e.g., 'fat people', 'fat women', 'ugly people', 'ugly women', 'men', 'feminists', 'people with left-wing ideology'. Some of them (such as, e.g., 'men') may look neutral at the first glance, but, in reality, they group messages whose vocabulary and language style reflect negative expectations towards the corresponding collective (in the case of men those expectations reflect toxic masculinity norms).

Class	ND	Parent nodes	Freq	Class	ND	Parent nodes	Freq
Hate speech	0	-	1228	Ageing	1	Hate speech	4
Sexism	1	Hate speech	672	Angolans	3	Africans	4
Women	2	Sexism	544	Nordestines	3	Rural people, Brazilians	4
Homophobia	1	Hate speech	322	Chinese	3	Asians	3
Homossexuals	2	Homophobia	288	Homeless	2	Other/Lifestyle	3
Lesbians	3	Homossexuals, Woman	248	Arabic	2	Origin	2
Body	1	Hate speech	164	Bissexuals	2	Homophobia	2
Fat people	2	Body	160	Blond women	2	Women, Body	2
Fat women	3	Women, Fat people	153	East europeans	2	Origin	2
Ugly people	2	Body	131	Jews	2	Religion	2
Ugly women	3	Women, Ugly people	130	Jornalists	2	Other/Lifestyle	2
Racism	1	Hate speech	94	Old people	2	Ageing	2
Ideology	1	Hate speech	92	Thin people	2	Body	2
Migrants	1	Hate speech	82	Thin women	3	Women, Thin people	2
Men	2	Sexism	70	Vegetarians	2	Other/Lifestyle	2
Refugees	2	Migrants	70	White people	2	Racism	2
Feminists	2	Ideology, Sexism	65	Young people	2	Ageing	2
Gays	3	Homossexuals	56	Agnostic	2	Ideology	1
Black people	2	Racism	52	Argentines	3	Latins	1
Religion	1	Hate speech	30	Autists	2	Health	1
Left wing ideology	2	Ideology	26	Brazilian women	3	Women, South Americans	1
Origin	1	Hate speech	26	Egyptians	3	Arabic	1
Trans women	3	Women, Transexuals	26	Football players women	2	Women, Other/Lifestyle	1
OtherLifestyle	1	Hate speech	20	Gamers	2	Other/Lifestyle	1
Islamists	2	Religion	17	Homeless women	3	Women, Homeless	1
Immigrants	2	Migrants	15	Indigenous	2	Racism	1
Transexuals	2	Sexism	14	Iranians	3	Arabic	1
Muslims	2	Religion	11	Japaneses	3	Asians	1
Black Women	3	Women, Black people	8	Men Feminists	3	Feminists, Men	1
Criminals	2	Other/Lifestyle	8	Mexicans	3	Latins	1
Latins	2	Racism, Origin	7	Muslim women	3	Muslims, Women	1
Health	1	Hate speech	6	Old women	3	Women, Old people	1
Rural people	2	Origin	6	Polyamorous	2	Other/Lifestyle	1
Travestis	3	Women	6	Poor people	2	Other/Lifestyle	1
Aborting women	3	Women	5	Russians	3	East europeans	1
Asians	2	Racism, Origin	5	Sertanejos	3	Rural people, Brazilians	1
Brazilians	3	South Americans	5	Street artists	2	Other/Lifestyle	1
Disabled people	2	Health	5	Ucranians	3	East europeans	1
South Americans	2	Origin	5	Venezuelans	3	Latins	1
Africans	2	Origin	4				

Table 3: Hate subclasses (Class) and respective parent categories (Parent nodes) sorted by frequency (Freq). Information of the node depth is also provided (ND).

5 Binary classification experiment

In order to obtain a first indicator of the usefulness of our dataset, we carry out a preliminary binary classification experiment.

5.1 Methodology

To perform the experiment, we use 10-fold cross-validation (Chollet, 2017), combined with holdout validation, in which one part of the data is used for cross-validation and parameter tuning with grid search and the other part of unseen data is then used for testing.

As already Badjatiya et al. (2017), we provide our source code [6]. We use Python 3.6, Keras (Chollet et al., 2015), Gensim (Řehůřek and Sojka, 2010) and Scikit-learn (Pedregosa et al., 2011) as main libraries. The following subsections describe how we implement each step performed by our system.

Text pre-processing As far as text pre-processing is concerned, we remove stop words using Gensim, and punctuation using the default string library and transform all tokens in the tweets to lower case.

Feature extraction: Regarding the features in our experiment, we use pre-trained Glove word embeddings with 300 dimensions for Portuguese (Hartmann et al., 2017). Methods provided by Keras are then used to map each token in the input to an embedding.

Classification: For classification, we use a deep learning model, namely LSTMs, in an architecture as already proposed by Badjatiya et al. (2017). The architecture contains an embedding Layer with the weights from the word embeddings extraction procedure, an additional LSTM layer with 50 dimensions, and dropouts at the end of both layers. As loss function, we used binary cross-entropy and for optimization Adam, 10 epochs and 128 for batch size. With this model, we classify data into binary classes, and we save the last layer

---

[6] https://github.com/paulafortuna/SemEval_2019_public

before the classification to extract 50 dimensions as input to the xgBoost algorithm,[7] which is a gradient boosting implementation from the Python library (Chen and Guestrin, 2016).

For xgBoost, the default parameter setting has been used, except for 'eta' and 'gamma'. In this case, we conducted a grid search combining several values of both (eta: 0, 0.3, 1; and gamma: 0.1, 1, 10) in order to obtain the optimal eta and gamma settings. Figure 3 shows a graphical representation of our model.

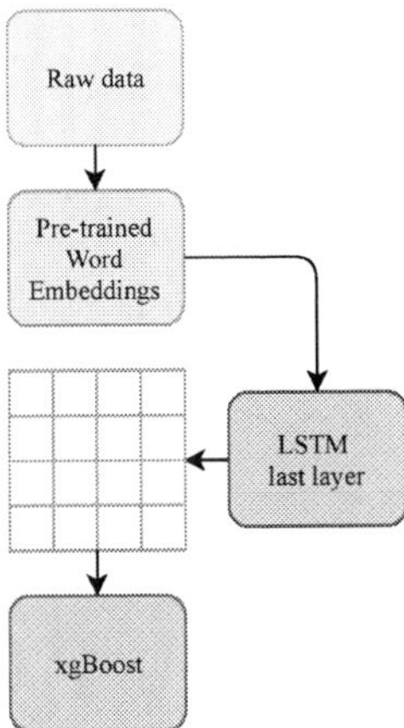

Figure 3: Classification method used as baseline for binary hate speech classification with the Portuguese dataset.

5.2 Results

In this section, we present the results of our classification experiment for classification of hate speech in Portuguese. Table 4 shows the baseline results of the LSTM-based model on our new dataset. We provide the cross validation and test set F1 scores and also the number of instances we used in each of these (N). The results show a state-of-the-art outcome. We can thus assume that even if annotated merely in terms of basic binary ('hate' vs. 'not hate speech') labels, our dataset already constitutes a valid hate speech resource.

6   Ethical considerations

Regarding the ethical aspects of this study, we took into consideration the privacy of the authors of the collected messages. However, we acknowledge the limitations of our sampling procedure when studying online hate speech. The data was

---

⁷We also experimented with higher dimensionality, but this did not improve the performance of the classifier.

	Hate speech dataset (PT)
CV f1-score	0.78
training data (N)	5099
test set f1-score	0.72
testing data (N)	567

Table 4: Results of Portuguese hate speech classification with the new dataset presented in this paper for binary classification. We provide the micro-averaged F1 scores and also the number of instances used in each of the datasets (N).

anonymized by omitting the tweet id. As a consequence, it is possible to reach the original tweet and user only by a search for the exact text of the tweet. To also prevent this, we make our dataset available in GitHub only for research purposes under the condition that no such a search is performed. A disclaimer is attached, stating that any attempt to violate the privacy of Twitter users is against the established usage conditions, and that the authors of this paper cannot be made liable for this violation.

As far as the quality of the data collection is concerned, sampling bias may have been introduced. Firstly, because Twitter API was used and this provides only a subset of the all posted data in the platform. Secondly, we use a set of keywords and crawl profiles based on our decision criteria, as explained in Section 3. However, we do not aim to have a representative sample of online hate speech on Twitter. We consider that for building a dataset with examples of hate speech, our method is adequate, and that we could find diverse hate speech instances belonging to 80 different classes.

7   Conclusions and Future Work

In this work, we built a Portuguese dataset for research in hate speech detection.

To gather our data, we crawled Twitter for messages and manually annotated them using guidelines. Firstly, we developed a method for binary classification using the classification of three annotators per message as ground truth. With this dataset, we conducted a baseline classification experiment using pre-trained word embeddings and LSTM, achieving very competitive performance.

Furthermore, we provided a hate speech hierarchical labeling schema that integrates the complexity of hate speech subtypes and their intersections. This allowed us to find out that distinct types of hate speech present different agreement levels between annotators. Therefore, future guidelines for annotation may benefit from specifying the particularities of the different subtypes of hate speech.

As far as future work is concerned, in the context of the annotation procedure, the agreement between annotators can still be improved. We think that the subjectivity of the task makes the learning process challenging and more specific training is necessary for the annotators. Additionally, based on our experiment, we suggest that future data collection procedures should assure sampling of different subtypes of hate to improve the identification of less common subtypes.

Finally, in future explorations of this dataset, we will experiment with multilabel classification of hate speech to identify not only whether a message contains hate, but also the targeted groups.

Acknowledgments

This work was partially funded by the Google DNI project Stop PropagHate. Soler-Company and Wanner have been supported by the European Commission under the contract numbers H2020–7000024-RIA and H2020-786731-RIA. We would like to thank the anonymous reviewers for their insightful comments and to the annotators for their contribution to this work.

References

Pinkesh Badjatiya, Shashank Gupta, Manish Gupta, and Vasudeva Varma. 2017. Deep learning for hate speech detection in tweets. In *Proceedings of the 26th International Conference on World Wide Web Companion*, pages 759–760. International World Wide Web Conferences Steering Committee.

Tianqi Chen and Carlos Guestrin. 2016. XGBoost: A scalable tree boosting system. In *Proceedings of the 22nd ACM SIGKDD International Conference on Knowledge Discovery and Data Mining*, KDD '16, pages 785–794, New York, NY, USA. ACM.

François Chollet et al. 2015. Keras. `https://keras.io`, accessed last time in February 2019.

Francois Chollet. 2017. *Deep learning with python*. Manning Publications Co.

Patricia Hill Collins. 2015. Intersectionality's definitional dilemmas. *Annual Review of Sociology*, 41:1–20.

Kimberle Crenshaw. 2018. Demarginalizing the intersection of race and sex: A black feminist critique of antidiscrimination doctrine, feminist theory, and antiracist politics [1989]. In *Feminist legal theory*, pages 57–80. Routledge.

Thomas Davidson, Dana Warmsley, Michael Macy, and Ingmar Weber. 2017. Automated Hate Speech Detection and the Problem of Offensive Language. In *Proceedings of ICWSM*.

Fabio Del Vigna, Andrea Cimino, Felice Dell?Orletta, Marinella Petrocchi, and Maurizio Tesconi. 2017. Hate me, hate me not: Hate speech detection on facebook. In *Proceedings of the First Italian Conference on Cybersecurity*, pages 86–95.

Susan Dumais and Hao Chen. 2000. Hierarchical classification of web content. In *Proceedings of the 23rd annual international ACM SIGIR conference on Research and development in information retrieval*, pages 256–263. ACM.

Elisabetta Fersini, Paolo Rosso, and Maria Anzovino. 2018. Overview of the task on automatic misogyny identification at ibereval 2018.

Joseph L Fleiss. 1971. Measuring nominal scale agreement among many raters. *Psychological bulletin*, 76(5):378.

Paula Fortuna and Sérgio Nunes. 2018. A survey on automatic detection of hate speech in text. *ACM Computing Surveys (CSUR)*, 51(4):85.

Antigoni-Maria Founta, Despoina Chatzakou, Nicolas Kourtellis, Jeremy Blackburn, Athena Vakali, and Ilias Leontiadis. 2018. A unified deep learning architecture for abuse detection. *arXiv preprint arXiv:1802.00385*.

Zoe Fox. 2013. Top 10 most popular languages on twitter. Available in `http://mashable.com/2013/12/17/twitter-popular-languages/`, accessed last time in May 2017.

Björn Gambäck and Utpal Kumar Sikdar. 2017. Using Convolutional Neural Networks to Classify Hate-speech. In *Proceedings of the First Workshop on Abusive Language Online*, pages 85–90.

Matthias Gamer, Jim Lemon, Maintainer Matthias Gamer, A Robinson, and W Kendall's. 2012. Package ?irr? *Various coefficients of interrater reliability and agreement*.

Barney G Glaser and Anselm L Strauss. 2017. *Discovery of grounded theory: Strategies for qualitative research*. Routledge.

Pei-Yi Hao, Jung-Hsien Chiang, and Yi-Kun Tu. 2007. Hierarchically svm classification based on support vector clustering method and its application to document categorization. *Expert Systems with applications*, 33(3):627–635.

Nathan Hartmann, Erick Fonseca, Christopher Shulby, Marcos Treviso, Jéssica Silva, and Sandra Aluísio. 2017. Portuguese word embeddings: Evaluating on word analogies and natural language tasks. In

Proceedings of the 11th Brazilian Symposium in Information and Human Language Technology, pages 122–131, Uberlândia, Brazil. Sociedade Brasileira de Computação.

Hatebase. 2019. Hatebase. Available in `https://www.hatebase.org/`, accessed last time in February 2019.

Jigsaw. 2018. Toxic comment classification challenge identify and classify toxic online comments. Available in `https://www.kaggle.com/c/jigsaw-toxic-comment-classification-challenge`, accessed last time in 23 May 2018.

Ritesh Kumar, Atul Kr. Ojha, Shervin Malmasi, and Marcos Zampieri. 2018. Benchmarking Aggression Identification in Social Media. In *Proceedings of the First Workshop on Trolling, Aggression and Cyberbulling (TRAC)*, Santa Fe, USA.

Yashar Mehdad and Joel Tetreault. 2016. Do characters abuse more than words? In *Proceedings of the SIGdial 2016 Conference: The 17th Annual Meeting of the Special Interest Group on Discourse and Dialogue*, pages 299–303.

Chikashi Nobata, Joel Tetreault, Achint Thomas, Yashar Mehdad, and Yi Chang. 2016. Abusive language detection in online user content. In *Proceedings of the 25th International Conference on World Wide Web*, pages 145–153. International World Wide Web Conferences Steering Committee.

Ji Ho Park and Pascale Fung. 2017. One-step and Two-step Classification for Abusive Language Detection on Twitter. In *Proceedings of the First Workshop on Abusive Language Online*.

F. Pedregosa, G. Varoquaux, A. Gramfort, V. Michel, B. Thirion, O. Grisel, M. Blondel, P. Prettenhofer, R. Weiss, V. Dubourg, J. Vanderplas, A. Passos, D. Cournapeau, M. Brucher, M. Perrot, and E. Duchesnay. 2011. Scikit-learn: Machine learning in Python. *Journal of Machine Learning Research*, 12:2825–2830.

Rogers Prates de Pelle and Viviane P Moreira. 2017. Offensive comments in the brazilian web: a dataset and baseline results. In *6º Brazilian Workshop on Social Network Analysis and Mining (BraSNAM 2017)*, volume 6. SBC.

Georgios K Pitsilis, Heri Ramampiaro, and Helge Langseth. 2018. Detecting offensive language in tweets using deep learning. *arXiv preprint arXiv:1801.04433*.

Fabio Poletto, Marco Stranisci, Manuela Sanguinetti, Viviana Patti, and Cristina Bosco. 2017. Hate speech annotation: Analysis of an italian Twitter corpus. In *Ceur Workshop Proceedings*, volume 2006, pages 1–6. CEUR-WS.

Radim Řehůřek and Petr Sojka. 2010. Software Framework for Topic Modelling with Large Corpora. In *Proceedings of the LREC 2010 Workshop on New Challenges for NLP Frameworks*, pages 45–50, Valletta, Malta. ELRA. `http://is.muni.cz/publication/884893/en`.

Björn Ross, Michael Rist, Guillermo Carbonell, Ben Cabrera, Nils Kurowsky, and Michael Wojatzki. 2016. Measuring the Reliability of Hate Speech Annotations: The Case of the European Refugee Crisis. In *Proceedings of NLP4CMC III: 3rd Workshop on Natural Language Processing for Computer-Mediated Communication*, pages 6–9.

Joni Salminen, Hind Almerekhi, Milica Milenković, Soon-gyo Jung, Jisun An, Haewoon Kwak, and Bernard J Jansen. 2018. Anatomy of online hate: developing a taxonomy and machine learning models for identifying and classifying hate in online news media. In *Twelfth International AAAI Conference on Web and Social Media*.

Manuela Sanguinetti, Fabio Poletto, Cristina Bosco, Viviana Patti, and Marco Stranisci. 2018. An italian Twitter corpus of hate speech against immigrants. In *Proceedings of LREC*.

William A Schabas. 2000. Hate speech in rwanda: The road to genocide. *McGill Law Journal*, 46:141.

Anna Schmidt and Michael Wiegand. 2017. A survey on hate speech detection using natural language processing. *SocialNLP 2017*, page 1.

William Warner and Julia Hirschberg. 2012. Detecting hate speech on the world wide web. In *Proceedings of the Second Workshop on Language in Social Media*, pages 19–26. Association for Computational Linguistics.

Zeerak Waseem. 2016. Are you a racist or am i seeing things? annotator influence on hate speech detection on Twitter. In *Proceedings of the 1st Workshop on Natural Language Processing and Computational Social Science*, pages 138–142.

Zeerak Waseem and Dirk Hovy. 2016. Hateful symbols or hateful people? predictive features for hate speech detection on twitter. In *Proceedings of NAACL-HLT*, pages 88–93.

A Appendices

A.1 Non-expert annotators guidelines translated to English

Analyse the tweets from the first set and evaluate if according* to your opinion, these tweets contain hate speech.

For every tweet, mark manually with 1 or 0 if you think the tweet contains or not hate, respectively, accordingly with Table 5.

Tweet	HS	A
Black people should go back to their land!!	1	A
Meat and black beans are delicious!	0	A
Muslim people are terrorists!	1	A

Table 5: Hate speech (HS) annotation examples with respective annotator (A) in English.

A System to Monitor Cyberbullying based on Message Classification and Social Network Analysis

Stefano Menini[‡], Giovanni Moretti[‡], Michele Corazza[†]
Elena Cabrio[†], Sara Tonelli[‡], Serena Villata[†]
[‡]Fondazione Bruno Kessler, Trento, Italy
[†]Université Côte d'Azur, CNRS, Inria, I3S, France
{menini,moretti,satonelli}@fbk.eu
{michele.corazza}@inria.fr
{elena.cabrio,serena.villata}@unice.fr

Abstract

Social media platforms like Twitter and Instagram face a surge in cyberbullying phenomena against young users and need to develop scalable computational methods to limit the negative consequences of this kind of abuse. Despite the number of approaches recently proposed in the Natural Language Processing (NLP) research area for detecting different forms of abusive language, the issue of identifying cyberbullying phenomena at scale is still an unsolved problem. This is because of the need to couple abusive language detection on textual message with network analysis, so that repeated attacks against the same person can be identified. In this paper, we present a system to monitor cyberbullying phenomena by combining message classification and social network analysis. We evaluate the classification module on a data set built on Instagram messages, and we describe the cyberbullying monitoring user interface.

1 Introduction

The presence on social networks like Twitter, Facebook and Instagram is of main importance for teenagers, but this may also lead to undesirable and harmful situations. We refer to these forms of harassment as *cyberbullying*, i.e., 'an aggressive, intentional act carried out by a group or an individual, using electronic forms of contact, repeatedly and over time against a victim who cannot easily defend him or herself' (Smith et al., 2008). In online social media, each episode of online activity aimed at offending, menacing, harassing or stalking another person can be classified as a cyberbullying phenomenon. This is connected even with concrete public health issues, since recent studies show that victims are more likely to suffer from psycho-social difficulties and affective disorders (Tokunaga, 2010).

Given its societal impact, the implementation of cyberbullying detection systems, combining abusive language detection and social network analysis, has attracted a lot of attention in the last years (Tomkins et al., 2018; Hosseinmardi et al., 2015a; Ptaszynski et al., 2015; Dinakar et al., 2012). However, the adoption of such systems in real life is not straightforward and their use in a black box scenario is not desirable, given the negative effects misleading analyses could have on potential abusers and victims. A more transparent approach should be adopted, in which cyberbullying identification should be mediated by human judgment.

In this paper, we present a system for the monitoring of cyberbullying phenomena on social media. The system aims at supporting supervising persons (e.g., educators) at identifying potential cases of cyberbullying through an intuitive, easy-to-use interface. This displays both the outcome of a hate speech detection system and the network in which the messages are exchanged. Supervising persons can therefore monitor the escalation of hateful online exchanges and decide whether to intervene or not, similar to the workflow introduced in Michal et al. (2010). We evaluate the NLP classifier on a set of manually annotated data from Instagram, and detail the network extraction algorithm starting from 10 Manchester high schools. However, this is only one possible use case of the system, which can be employed over different kinds of data.

2 Network Extraction

Since cyberbullying is by definition a repeated attack towards a specific victim by one or more bullies, we include in the monitoring system an algorithm to identify local communities in social networks and isolate the messages exchanged only

Proceedings of the Third Workshop on Abusive Language Online, pages 105–110
Florence, Italy, August 1, 2019. ©2019 Association for Computational Linguistics

within such communities. In this demo, we focus on high-schools, but the approach can be extended to other communities of interest. Our case study concerns the network of Manchester high-school students, and we choose to focus on Instagram, since it is widely used by teenagers of that age.

Reconstructing local communities on Instagram is a challenging task. Indeed, differently from how other social networks operate (e.g., Facebook), Instagram does not provide a page for institutions such as High Schools, that therefore need to be inferred. To overcome this issue, and to identify local communities of students, we proceed in two steps that can be summarised as follow:

- *Expansion stage.* We start from few users that are very likely to be part of the local high school community, and we use them to identify an increasing number of other possible members expanding our network coverage.

- *Pruning stage.* We identify, within the large network, smaller communities of users and we isolate the ones composed by students. For these, we retrieve the exchanged messages in a given period of time (in our case, the ongoing school year), which will be used to identify abusive messages.

2.1 Expansion Stage

In this stage, we aim to build an inclusive network of people related to local high schools. Since schools do not have an Instagram account, we decide to exploit the geo-tagging of pictures. We manually define a list of 10 high schools from Manchester, and we search for all the photos associated with one of these locations by matching the geo-tagged addresses.

Given that anyone can tag a photo with the address of a school, this stage involves not only actual students, but also their teachers, parents, friends, alumni and so on. The reason to adopt this inclusive approach is that not every student is directly associated with his/her school on Instagram (i.e., by sharing pictures in or of the school), therefore we need to exploit also their contacts with other people directly related to the schools. We restrict our analysis to pictures taken from September 2018 on to focus on the current school year and obtain a network including actual students rather than alumni.

With this approach, we identify a first layer of 756 users, corresponding to the authors of the pho-

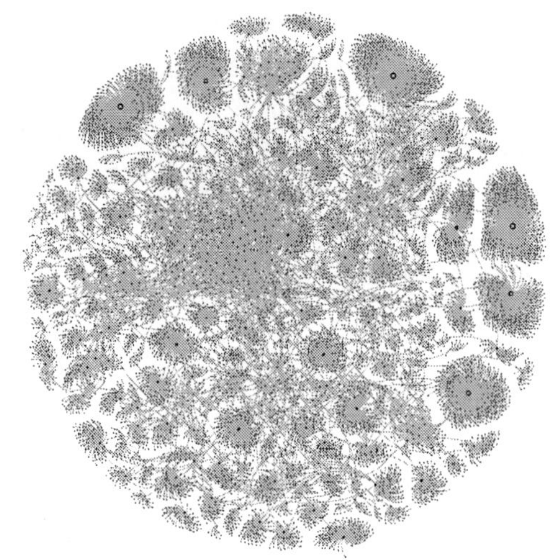

Figure 1: Network obtained starting from 10 Manchester schools and expanding +2 layers

tos tagged in one of the 10 schools. Starting from these users, we expand our network with a broader second layer of users related to the first ones. We assume that users writing messages to each other are likely to be somehow related, therefore we include in the network all users exchanging comments with the first layer of users in the most recent posts. In this step, we do not consider the connections given by *likes*, since they are prone to introduce noise in the network. With this step we obtain a second layer of 17,810 users that we consider related to the previous ones as they interact with each other in the comments. Using the same strategy, we further expand the network with a third layer of users commenting the contents posted by users in the second layer. It is interesting to notice that in the first layer of users, i.e. the ones directly related to the schools, the groups of users associated with each school are well separated. As soon as we increase the size of the network with additional layers, user groups start to connect to each other through common "friends".

We stop the expansion at a depth of three layers since additional layers would exponentially increase the number of users. At the end of the expansion stage, we gather a list of 544,371 unique users obtained from an exchange of 1,539,292 messages. The resulting network (Figure 1) is generated by representing each user as a node, while the exchanged messages correspond to edges. Each edge between two users is weighted according to the number of messages between the two.

2.2 Pruning Stage

After generating a large network of users starting from the list of schools, the following step consists in pruning the network from *unnecessary nodes* by identifying within the network *smaller communities* of high school students and teenagers. These communities define the scenario in which we want to monitor the possible presence of cyberbullying. To identify local communities, we proceed incrementally dividing the network into smaller portions. For this task, we apply the modularity function in Gephi (Blondel et al., 2008), a hierarchical decomposition algorithm that iteratively optimizes modularity for small communities, aggregating then nodes of the same community to build a new network.

Then, we remove the groups of people falling out of the scope of our investigation by automatically looking for geographical or professional cues in the user biographies. For example, we remove nodes that contain the term *blogger* or *photographer* in the bio, and all the nodes that are only connected to them in the network. This step is done automatically, but we manually check the nodes that have the highest centrality in the network before removing them, so as to ensure that we do not prune nodes of interest for our use case.

We then run again the modularity function to identify communities among the remaining nodes. Finally, we apply another pruning step by looking for other specific cues in the user bios that may identify our young demographic of interest. In this case, we define regular expressions to match the *age*, *year of birth* or *school attended*, reducing the network to a core of 892 nodes (users) and 2,435 edges, with a total of 14,565 messages (Figure 2).

3 Classification of abusive language

To classify the messages exchanged in the network extracted in the previous step as containing or not abusive language, we use a modular neural architecture for binary classification in Keras (Chollet et al., 2015), which uses a single feedforward hidden layer of 100 neurons, with a ReLu activation and a single output with a sigmoid activation. The loss used to train the model is binary cross-entropy. We choose this particular architecture because it proved to be rather effective and robust: we used it to participate in two shared tasks for hate speech detection, one for Italian (Corazza et al., 2018a) and one for German (Corazza et al.,

Figure 2: Manchester network after pruning

2018b), obtaining competitive results w.r.t. state-of-the-art systems.

The architecture is built upon a recurrent layer, namely a Long Short-Term Memory (LSTM) whose goal is to learn an encoding derived from word embeddings, obtained as the output of the recurrent layer at the last timestep. We use English Fasttext embeddings[1] trained on Common Crawl with a size of 300. Concerning hyperparameters, our model uses no dropout and no batch normalization on the outputs of the hidden layer. Instead, a dropout on the recurrent units of the recurrent layers is used (Gal and Ghahramani, 2016) with value 0.2. We select a batch size of 32 for training and a size of 200 for the output (and hidden states) of the recurrent layers. Such hyperparameters and features have been selected from a system configuration that performed consistently well on the above mentioned shared tasks for hate speech detection, both on Facebook and on Twitter data.

4 Experimental setting and evaluation

Although our use case focuses on Instagram messages, we could not find available datasets from this social network with annotated comments. The widely used dataset used by (Hosseinmardi et al., 2015b) has indeed annotations at thread level.

We therefore train our classification algorithm using the dataset described in (Waseem and Hovy, 2016), containing 16k English tweets manually

---

[1]`https://fasttext.cc/docs/en/english-vectors.html`

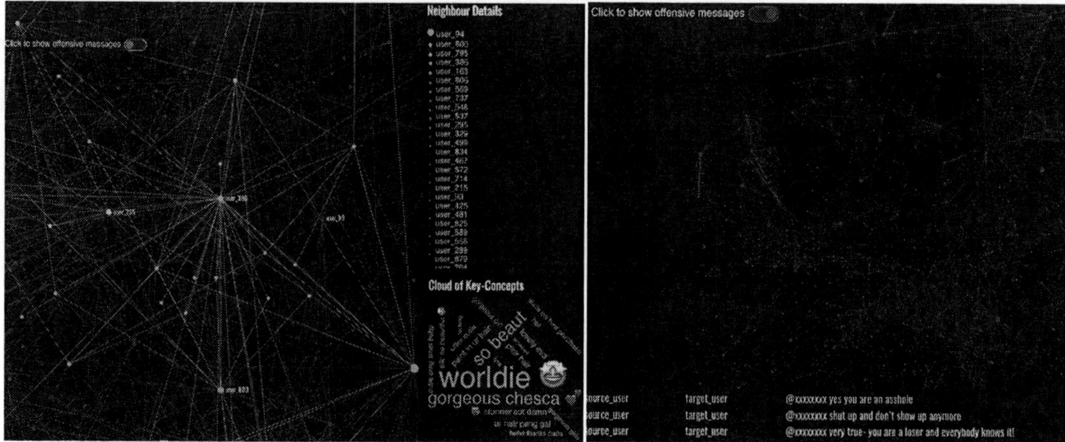

Figure 3: Interface view for network exploration	Figure 4: Interface view for hate speech monitoring

annotated for hate speech. More precisely, 1,924 are annotated as containing racism, 3,082 as containing sexism, while 10,884 tweets are annotated as not containing offensive language. We merge the sexist and racist tweets in a single class, so that 5,006 tweets are considered as positive instances of hate speech. As a test set, we manually annotate 900 Instagram comments, randomly extracted from the Manchester network, labeling them as hate speech or not. Overall, the test set contains 787 non-offensive and 113 offensive messages.

We preprocess both data sets, given that hashtags, user mentions, links to external media and emojis are common in social media interactions. To normalize the text as much as possible while retaining all relevant semantic information, we first replace URLs with the word "url" and "@" user mentions with "username" by using regular expressions. We also use the Ekphrasis tool (Baziotis et al., 2017) to split hashtags into sequences of words, when possible.

The system obtained on the test set a micro-averaged F1 of 0.823. We then run the classifier on all messages extracted for the Manchester network, and make the output available through the platform interface.

5   Interface

The system[2] relies on a relational database and a tomcat application server. The interface is based on existing javascript libraries such as C3.js (`https://c3js.org`) and Sigma.js (`http:`

---

[2]A video of the demo is available at `https://dh.fbk.eu/sites/dh.fbk.eu/files/creepdemo_1.m4v`

`//sigmajs.org`).

The platform can be used with two settings: in the first one (Figure 3), the Manchester network is displayed, with colors denoting different sub-communities characterised by dense connections. By clicking on a node, the platform displays the cloud of key-concepts automatically extracted from the conversations between the given user and her connections using the KD tool (Moretti et al., 2015). This view is useful to understand the size and the density of the network and to browse through the topics present in the threads. In the second setting (Figure 4), which can be activated by clicking on "Show offensive messages", the communities are all colored in grey, while the system highlights in red the messages classified as offensive by the system described in Section 3. By clicking on red edges it is possible to view the content of the messages classified as offensive, enabling also to check the quality of the classifier. This second view is meant to support educators and stakeholders in monitoring cyberbullying without focusing on single users, but rather keeping an eye on the whole network and zooming in only when hateful exchanges, flagged in red, are escalating.

6   Discussion

The current system has been designed to support the work of educators in schools, although it is not meant to be open to everyone but only to specific personnel. For example, in Italy there must be one responsible teacher to counter cyberbullying in every school, and access to the system could be given only to that specific person. For the same reason, the system does not show the actual usernames but only placeholders, and the possibility to de-anonymise the network of users could be activated only after cyberbullying phenomena have been identified, and only for the users involved in such cases. Indeed, we want to avoid the use of this kind of platforms for the continuous surveillance of students, and prevent a malicious use of the monitoring platform.

The system relies on public user profiles, and does not have access to content that users want to keep private. This limits the number of cyberbullying cases and hate messages in our use case, where detected abusive language concerns less than 1% of the messages, while a previous study on students' simulated WhatsApp chats around controversial topics reports that 41% of the collected tokens were offensive or abusive (Sprugnoli et al., 2018). This limitation is particularly relevant when dealing with Instagram, but the workflow presented in this paper can be potentially applied to other social networks and chat applications. Another limitation of working with Instagram is the fact that the monitoring cannot happen in real time. In fact, the steps to extract and prune the network require some processing time and cannot be performed on the fly, especially in case of large user networks. We estimate that the time needed to download the data, extract the network, retrieve and classify the messages and upload them in the visualisation tool would be around one week.

7 Conclusion

In this paper, we presented a platform to monitor cyberbullying phenomena that relies on two components: an algorithm to automatically detect online communities starting from geo-referenced online pictures, and a hate speech classifier. Both components have been combined in a single platform that, through two different views, allows educators to visualise the network of interest and to detect in which sub-communities hate speech is escalating. Although the evaluation has been carried out only on English, the system supports also Italian, and will be showcased in both languages. In the future, we plan to improve the classifier performance by extending the Twitter training set with more annotated data from Instagram. We will also experiment with cross-lingual strategies to train the classifier on English datasets and

use it on other languages.

Acknowledgments

Part of this work was funded by the CREEP project (http://creep-project.eu/), a Digital Wellbeing Activity supported by EIT Digital in 2018 and 2019. This research was also supported by the HATEMETER project (http://hatemeter.eu/) within the EU Rights, Equality and Citizenship Programme 2014-2020.

References

Christos Baziotis, Nikos Pelekis, and Christos Doulkeridis. 2017. DataStories at SemEval-2017 Task 4: Deep LSTM with Attention for Message-level and Topic-based Sentiment Analysis. In *Proceedings of the 11th International Workshop on Semantic Evaluation (SemEval-2017)*, pages 747–754, Vancouver, Canada. Association for Computational Linguistics.

Vincent D Blondel, Jean-Loup Guillaume, Renaud Lambiotte, and Etienne Lefebvre. 2008. Fast unfolding of communities in large networks. *Journal of statistical mechanics: theory and experiment*, 2008(10):P10008.

François Chollet et al. 2015. Keras. https://github.com/fchollet/keras.

Michele Corazza, Stefano Menini, Pinar Arslan, Rachele Sprugnoli, Elena Cabrio, Sara Tonelli, and Serena Villata. 2018a. Comparing Different Supervised Approaches to Hate Speech Detection. In *Proceedings of the Sixth Evaluation Campaign of Natural Language Processing and Speech Tools for Italian. Final Workshop (EVALITA 2018) co-located with the Fifth Italian Conference on Computational Linguistics (CLiC-it 2018), Turin, Italy, December 12-13, 2018.*, volume 2263 of *CEUR Workshop Proceedings*.

Michele Corazza, Stefano Menini, Pinar Arslan, Rachele Sprugnoli, Elena Cabrio, Sara Tonelli, and Serena Villata. 2018b. Inriafbk at germeval 2018: Identifying offensive tweets using recurrent neural networks. In *GermEval 2018 Workshop*.

Karthik Dinakar, Birago Jones, Catherine Havasi, Henry Lieberman, and Rosalind W. Picard. 2012. Common Sense Reasoning for Detection, Prevention, and Mitigation of Cyberbullying. *TiiS*, 2(3):18:1–18:30.

Yarin Gal and Zoubin Ghahramani. 2016. A theoretically grounded application of dropout in recurrent neural networks. In *Advances in Neural Information Processing Systems 29: Annual Conference on Neural Information Processing Systems 2016, December 5-10, 2016, Barcelona, Spain*, pages 1019–1027.

Homa Hosseinmardi, Sabrina Arredondo Mattson, Rahat Ibn Rafiq, Richard Han, Qin Lv, and Shivakant Mishra. 2015a. Analyzing labeled cyberbullying incidents on the instagram social network. In *Social Informatics - 7th International Conference, SocInfo 2015, Beijing, China, December 9-12, 2015, Proceedings*, pages 49–66.

Homa Hosseinmardi, Sabrina Arredondo Mattson, Rahat Ibn Rafiq, Richard O. Han, Qin Lv, and Shivakant Mishra. 2015b. Prediction of Cyberbullying Incidents on the Instagram Social Network. *CoRR*, abs/1503.03909.

Ptaszynski Michal, Dybala Pawel, Matsuba Tatsuaki, Masui Fumito, Rzepka Rafal, Araki Kenji, and Momouchi Yoshio. 2010. In the service of online order: Tackling cyber-bullying with machine learning and affect analysis. *International Journal of Computational Linguistics Research*, 1(3):135–154.

Giovanni Moretti, Rachele Sprugnoli, and Sara Tonelli. 2015. Digging in the Dirt: Extracting Keyphrases from Texts with KD. In *Proceedings of the Second Italian Conference on Computational Linguistics*.

Michal Ptaszynski, Fumito Masui, Yasutomo Kimura, Rafal Rzepka, and Kenji Araki. 2015. Automatic extraction of harmful sentence patterns with application in cyberbullying detection. In *Human Language Technology. Challenges for Computer Science and Linguistics - 7th Language and Technology Conference, LTC 2015, Poznań, Poland, November 27-29, 2015, Revised Selected Papers*, pages 349–362.

Peter K. Smith, Jess Mahdavi, Manuel Carvalho, Sonja Fisher, Shanette Russell, and Neil Tippett. 2008. Cyberbullying: its nature and impact in secondary school pupils. *Journal of Child Psychology and Psychiatry*, 49(4):376–385.

Rachele Sprugnoli, Stefano Menini, Sara Tonelli, Filippo Oncini, and Enrico Piras. 2018. Creating a whatsapp dataset to study pre-teen cyberbullying. In *Proceedings of the 2nd Workshop on Abusive Language Online (ALW2)*, pages 51–59. Association for Computational Linguistics.

Robert S. Tokunaga. 2010. Following you home from school: A critical review and synthesis of research on cyberbullying victimization. *Computers in Human Behavior*, 26(3):277 – 287.

Sabina Tomkins, Lise Getoor, Yunfei Chen, and Yi Zhang. 2018. A socio-linguistic model for cyberbullying detection. In *IEEE/ACM 2018 International Conference on Advances in Social Networks Analysis and Mining, ASONAM 2018, Barcelona, Spain, August 28-31, 2018*, pages 53–60.

Zeerak Waseem and Dirk Hovy. 2016. Hateful Symbols or Hateful People? Predictive Features for Hate Speech Detection on Twitter. In *SRW@HLT-NAACL*.

L-HSAB: A Levantine Twitter Dataset for Hate Speech and Abusive Language

Hala Mulki[*§], **Hatem Haddad**[†§], **Chedi Bechikh Ali**[**] and **Halima Alshabani**[***]

[*]Department of Computer Engineering, Konya Technical University, Turkey
[†]RIADI Laboratory, National School of Computer Sciences, University of Manouba, Tunisia
[**]LISI Laboratory, INSAT, Carthage University, Tunisia
[***]Department of Computer Engineering, Kırıkkale University, Turkey
[§]iCompass Consulting, Tunisia
halamulki@selcuk.edu.tr, haddad.Hatem@gmail.com
chedi.bechikh@gmail.com, halima.alshabani@gmail.com

Abstract

Hate speech and abusive language have become a common phenomenon on Arabic social media. Automatic hate speech and abusive detection systems can facilitate the prohibition of toxic textual contents. The complexity, informality and ambiguity of the Arabic dialects hindered the provision of the needed resources for Arabic abusive/hate speech detection research. In this paper, we introduce the first publicly-available Levantine Hate Speech and Abusive (L-HSAB) Twitter dataset with the objective to be a benchmark dataset for automatic detection of online Levantine toxic contents. We, further, provide a detailed review of the data collection steps and how we design the annotation guidelines such that a reliable dataset annotation is guaranteed. This has been later emphasized through the comprehensive evaluation of the annotations as the annotation agreement metrics of Cohen's Kappa (k) and Krippendorff's alpha (α) indicated the consistency of the annotations.

1 Introduction

With the freedom of expression privilege granted to social media users, it became easy to spread abusive/hate propaganda against individuals or groups. Beyond the psychological harm, such toxic online contents can lead to actual hate crimes (Matsuda, 2018). This provoked the need for automatic detection of hate speech (HS) and abusive contents shared across social media platforms.

In (Nockleby, 2000), hate speech (HS) is formally defined as *"any communication that disparages a person or a group on the basis of some characteristic such as race, color, ethnicity, gender, sexual orientation, nationality, religion, or other characteristic"*. HS detection can be conducted as a subtask of the abusive language detection (Waseem et al., 2017); yet, HS detection remains challenging since it requires to consider the correlation between the abusive language and the potential groups that are usually targeted by HS as per the definition of (Nockleby, 2000). Further challenges could be met when HS detection is investigated with complex, rich and ambiguous languages such as the Arabic language which combines different informal language variants known as dialects.

Compared to the increasing studies of abusive/HS detection in Indo-European languages, similar research for Arabic dialects is still very limited. This is due to the lack of the publicly-available resources needed for abusive/HS detection in Arabic social media texts. Building such resources involves several difficulties in terms of data collection and annotation, especially for underrepresented dialects such as Syrian, Lebanese, Palestinian and Jordanian dialects which are all combined within the Levantine dialect.

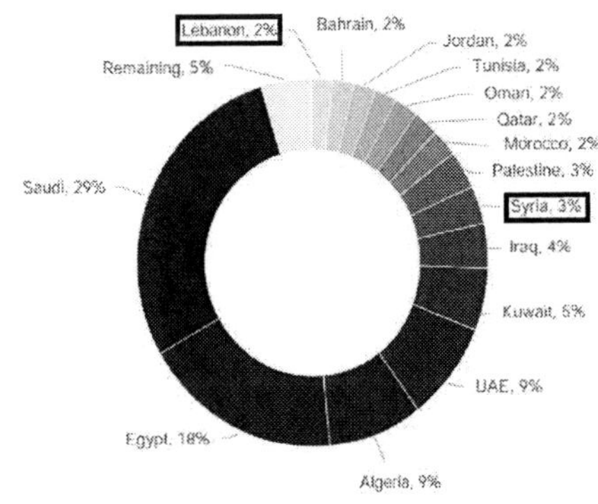

Figure 1: Twitter usage in the Arab region, 2017

Although Levantine is not among the top-ranking Arabic dialects used on Twitter (Salem) (see Figure 1), the volatile political/social atmosphere in Levantine-speaking countries, have been always associated with intensive debates; a considerable part of which took place on Twitter. With

Proceedings of the Third Workshop on Abusive Language Online, pages 111–118
Florence, Italy, August 1, 2019. ©2019 Association for Computational Linguistics

Study	Type	Platform	Size	Language
(Alakrota et al., 2018)	offensive	Youtube	16K	Egyptian, Iraqi and Libyan
(Mubarak et al., 2017)	obscene, offensive, and clean	Twitter	1.1K and 32K	MSA/DA
(Albadi et al., 2018)	religious hate, not hate	Twitter	6.6K	Arabic
(Al-Ajlan and Ykhlef, 2018)	bullying, nonbullying	Twitter	20K	Arabic

Table 1: Arabic Hate/Abusive Speech Presented Datasets

multiple opposite parties being involved in such debates, the relevant tweets tend to contain abusive and HS content. Thus, we believe that providing a Levantine abusive/HS dataset would support the research of automatic detection of abusive/HS in underrepresented Arabic dialects.

In this study, we introduce the first **L**evantine **H**ate **S**peech and **AB**usive (**L-HSAB**) Twitter dataset. Our dataset combines 5,846 tweets labeled as Hate, Abusive or Normal[1]. With the objective of providing a reliable, high quality benchmark dataset, and unlike the previous studies whose proposed Arabic corpora lack the needed annotation evaluation, we provide a comprehensive quantitative evaluation for L-HSAB. This was done through using agreement without chance correction and Inter-annotator agreement (IAA) reliability measures. In addition, our dataset was examined as a benchmark abusive/HS dataset by subjecting it to supervised machine learning experiments conducted by SVM and NB classifiers.

2   Dialectal Arabic Hate/Abusive Speech

As seeking to propose a new dialectal Arabic dataset for abusive and HS, we opted to review the Arabic abusive and HS datasets proposed in the State-Of-The-Art focusing on their characteristics in terms of: source, the tackled toxic categories, size, annotation strategy, metrics, the used machine learning models, etc. According to (Al-Hassan and Al-Dossari, 2019), the toxic online content on social media can be classified into: Abusive, Obscene, Offensive, Violent, Adult content, Terrorism and Religious hate speech. Table 1 lists a summary of the proposed abusive/HS datasets while a detailed review of these datasets is provided below.

In (Alakrota et al., 2018), the authors investigated the offensive language detection in Youtube comments. A dataset of 16K Egyptian, Iraqi and Libyan comments was created. Three annotators from Egypt, Iraq and Libya were asked to annotate

the comments as: offensive, inoffensive and neutral. The annotation evaluation measurements for the Egyptian and Lybian annotators were 71% and 69.8% for inter-annotator agreement and Kappa metric, respectively. With Support Vector Machines (SVM) algorithm applied for classification, the best achieved F-measure was 82%.

(Mubarak et al., 2017) proposed two datasets: a Twitter datasets of 1,100 dialectal tweets and a 32K inappropriate comments dataset collected from a popular Arabic news site. To support the offensive content detection, the authors relied on on common patterns used in offensive and rude communications to construct a list of obscene words and hashtags. Three Egyptian annotators annotated the data as obscene, offensive, and clean. With only obscene instances considered, the average inter-annotator agreement was 85% for the Twitter dataset and 87% for the comments dataset.

The religious HS detection was investigated in (Albadi et al., 2018) where a multi-dialectal Arabic dataset of 6.6K tweets was introduced. The annotation task was assigned to 234 different annotators; each of which was provided with an identification of the religious groups targeted by HS such as Muslims, Jews, Christians, Sunnis, Shia and so forth. Out of the resulting annotated corpus, three Arabic lexicons were constructed using chi-square, Pointwise Mutual Information (PMI) and Bi-Normal Separation (BNS) scoring methods. Each lexicon combined the terms commonly used in religious discussions accompanied with scores representing their polarity and strength. As an annotation evaluation, the authors indicated that the inter-rater agreement regarding differentiating religious HS tweets from non-religious ones was 81% while this value decreased to 55% when it comes to specify which religious groups were targeted by the religious HS. The proposed corpus was further examined as a reference dataset using three classification models: Lexicon-based, SVM and GRU-based RNN. The results revealed that the GRU-based RNN model with pre-trained

---

[1]will be made publicly available on github.

word embedding was the best-performing model where it achieved an F-measure of 77%.

Another type of HS was tackled by (Al-Ajlan and Ykhlef, 2018) where the authors presented a Twitter dataset for bullying detection. A dataset of 20K multi-dialectal Arabic tweets was collected and annotated manually with bullying and non-bullying labels. In their study, neither inter-rater agreement measures nor classification performances were provided.

3 L-HSAB Dataset

L-HSAB can be described as a political dataset since the majority of tweets was collected from the timelines of politicians, social/political activists and TV anchors. In the following subsections, we provide a qualitative overview of the proposed dataset, while a detailed quantitative analysis is presented in Section 5.

3.1 Data Collection and Processing

The proposed dataset was constructed out of Levantine tweets harvested using Twitter API[2]. We collected the tweets based on multiple queries formulated from the potential entities that are usually targeted by abusive/hate speech such as "اللاجئين" (*refugees*), "البنات" (*females*), "العرب" (*Arabs*), "الدروز" (*Druze*), etc. In addition, some user timelines (verified or having more than 100k followers) which belong to certain politicians, social/political activists and TV anchors, were adopted as data resources, since their tweets and tweets' replies are rich of the abusive/hate content. Aiming to maximize the size of the abusive/HS tweets, relevant to hot debates and major events, we scraped tweets posted within the time period: March 2018- February 2019.

Initially, we retrieved 57,058 tweets; to cope with goal of the paper which is to provide a Levantine dataset, we manually reduced the non-Levantine tweets. In addition, we filtered out the non-Arabic, non-textual, promoted and duplicated instances. Thus, we ended up with 6,000 tweets, written in the Levantine dialect (Syrian and Lebanese).

In order to prepare the collected tweets for annotation, they were normalized through eliminating Twitter-inherited symbols such as Rt, @ and #, Emoji icons, digits, in addition to non-Arabic characters found in URLs and user mentions.

[2]http://www.tweepy.org

3.2 Annotation Guidelines

The annotation task requires labeling the tweets of L-HSAB dataset as Hate, Abusive or Normal. Based on the definition of hate and abusive speech stated in the introduction, differentiating HS from abusive is quite difficult and is usually prone to personal biases; which, in turn, yields low inter-rater agreement scores (Waseem et al., 2017; Schmidt and Wiegand, 2017). However, since HS tends to attack specific groups of people, we believe that, defining the potential groups to be targeted by HS, within the scope of the domain, time period and the context of the collected dataset, can resolve the ambiguity between HS and abusive resulting in better inter-rater agreement scores. Hence, we designed the annotation guidelines such that all the annotators would have the same perspective about HS. Our annotation instructions defined the 3 label categories as:

- Normal tweets are those instances which have no offensive, aggressive, insulting and profanity content.

- Abusive tweets are those instances which combine offensive, aggressive, insulting or profanity content.

- Hate tweets are those instances that: (a) contain an abusive language, (b) dedicate the offensive, insulting, aggressive speech towards a specific person or a group of people and (c) demean or dehumanize that person or that group of people based on their descriptive identity (race, gender, religion, disability, skin color, belief).

Table 2 lists the relevant examples to each class.

Label	Example
Normal	أحلى شي دولة طفرانة بدّا تشلّح شعب مفلس The nicest thing is that a government in an abject poverty loots its own bankrupt people
Abusive	انت كعب صرمايتي القديمه اطهر من نيعك I consider the bottom of my old nasty shoes more clean than your own mouth
Hate	أصلن خلفة البنات بتجيب العار To have a girl kid brings disgrace

Table 2: Tweet examples of the annotation labels

3.3 Annotation Process

The annotation task was assigned to three annotators, one male and two females. All of them are Levantine native speakers and at a higher educational level (Postdoc/PhD).

Besides the previous annotation guidelines, and based on the domain and context of the proposed dataset, we had the annotators aware of the ethnic origin, religion, and the geographic region represented by each political party. Moreover, we provided them with the nicknames usually used to refer to certain political parties, minorities and ethnic/religion groups. For example, "تيار المستقبل" (*Future Movement Party*), which represents the Sunnis ethnic group, is usually called by its nickname "تيار المستهبل" (*Dumb Party*) in hate speech contexts. More examples are shown in Table 3. Having all the annotation rules setup, we

Nickname	Entity	Ethnic/Religion
تيار المستهبل	تيار المستقبل	السنة (*Sunnis*)
العونية	تيار الوطني الحر	الموارنة (*Maronites*)
عرب الشمال		السوريين (*Syrians*)
سكان الضاحية		الشيعة (*Shia*)
أهل الجبل		الدروز (*Druze*)

Table 3: A sample of the entities targeted by HS

asked the three annotators to label the 6,000 tweets as Normal, Abusive or Hate. For the whole dataset, we received a total of 18,000 judgments. By exploring the annotations, we faced three cases:

1. Unanimous agreement: the three annotators annotated a tweet with the same label. This was encountered in 4,222 tweets.

2. Majority agreement: two out of three annotators agreed on a label of a tweet. This was encountered in 1,624 tweets.

3. Conflicts: each annotator annotated a tweet differently. They were found in 154 tweets.

Annotation Case	# Tweets
Unanimous agreement	4,222
Majority agreement (2 out of 3)	1,624
Conflicts	154

Table 4: Summary of annotation statistics

After excluding the tweets that have 3 different judgments, the final version of L-HSAB composed of 5,846 tweets. A summary of the annotation statistics is presented in Table 4.

4 Annotation Results

With the annotation process accomplished, we decided the final label of each tweet in the dataset considering the annotation cases in Section 3.3. For tweets falling under the first annotation case, the final labels were directly deduced, while for those falling under the second annotation case, we selected the label that has been agreed upon by two annotators out of three. Consequently, we got 3,650 normal tweets, 1,728 abusive and 468 hate tweets. A detailed review of the statistics of L-HSAB final version is provided in Table 5 where Avg-S-L denotes the average length of tweets in the dataset, calculated based on the number of words in each tweet.

	Normal	Abusive	Hate
# Tweets	3,650	1,728	468
Avg-S-L	9	7	10
Word Count	31,598	11,938	4,380
Vocabulary	14,064	7,059	2,971
Ratio	62.43%	29.55 %	8.00 %

Table 5: Tweets distribution across 3 classes

Hate	Dist.	Abusive	Dist.
كلب (*dog*)	1%	هوا (*sh*t*)	1.58%
كلاب (*dogs*)	0.98%	كول (*swallow*)	1.52%
لبنان (*Lebanon*)	0.55%	كلب (*dog*)	0.97%
قطر (*Qatar*)	0.55%	حمار (*donkey*)	0.59%
سوري (*Syrian*)	0.39%	خراس (*chup*)	0.52%
العرب (*Arabs*)	0.39%	يلعن (*damn*)	0.45%
شعب (*people*)	0.37%	لبنان (*Lebanon*)	0.39%
ولاك (*jerk*)	0.37%	بشار (*Bashar*)	0.37%
حزب (*party*)	0.34%	واطي (*mean*)	0.36%
معراب (*a region*)	0.30%	صرمایة (*shoe*)	0.30%

Table 6: Distribution of ten most frequent terms

As seeking to identify the words commonly used within hate and abusive speech contexts, we investigated the lexical distribution of the dataset words across both hate and abusive classes. Therefore, we subjected L-HSAB to further normalization, where we removed stopwords based on a manually built Levantine stopwords list. Later, we constructed a visualization map for the most frequent occurring words/terms under each of Hate and Abusive categories (Figure 2 and Figure 3). The ten most frequent words and their frequencies in each class are reviewed in Table 6, where Dist. denotes the word's distribution in a specific class.

Figure 2: Most frequent terms in hate tweets

Figure 3: Most frequent terms in abusive tweets

As it can be seen from Table 6, Figure 2 and Figure 3, both Hate and abusive classes have many terms in common. These terms are not only limited to the offensive/insulting words but also combine entity names representing ethnic groups. This on one hand, explains the difficulty faced by annotators while recognizing HS tweets. On the other hand, it justifies our annotation guidelines for hate tweets identification, where we stressed that the joint existence of abusive language and an entity cannot indicate a HS, unless the abusive language is targeting that entity.

In order to evaluate how distinctive are the vocabulary of our dataset with respect to each class category, we conducted word-class correlation calculations. First, we calculated the Pointwise Mutual Information (PMI) for each word towards its relevant category such that, for a word w and a class c, PMI is calculated as in equation 1:

$$PMI_c(w) = log(P_c(w)/P_c) \quad (1)$$

Where $P_c(w)$ represents the appearance of the word w in the tweets of the class c, while P_c refers to the number of tweets of the class c.

$$HtS(w) = PMI(w, hate) - PMI(w, normal) \quad (2)$$

$$AbS(w) = PMI(w, abusive) - PMI(w, normal) \quad (3)$$

Then, to decide whether the words under the hate/abusive classes are discriminating, their correlation with the Normal class should be identified as well (de Gibert et al., 2018). This is done by assigning a hate score (HtS) and an abusive score (AbS) for each of the most/least words under Hate and Aabusive classes. Both scores indicate the difference of the PMI value of a word w under a hate/abusive category and its PMI value with the Normal category. The formula to calculate HtS and AbS is given in equations 2 and 3.

Most hate	HtS	Least hate	HtS
كلاب (*dogs*)	5.85	الوزير (*minister*)	-2.30
و لاك (*jerk*)	4.86	حق (*right*)	-2.23
كلب (*dog*)	4.77	معالي (*highness*)	-2.07
معراب (*a region*)	3.96	شكرا (*thanks*)	-1.58
سوري (*Syrian*)	2.15	العهد (*promise*)	-1.09
العرب (*Arabs*)	1.39	وطن (*homeland*)	-1.00
حزب (*party*)	1.36	العربية (*Arabic*)	-1.00
شعب (*people*)	1.17	الإعلام (*media*)	-0.96
قطر (*Qatar*)	0.42	حكومة (*government*)	-0.31
لبنان (*Lebanon*)	-0.06	كبير (*big*)	-0.28

Table 7: HtS score for most/least hateful words

Table 7 and Table 8 list the HtS and AbS scores calculated for the 10 most and least words under hate/abusive category against the normal category.

Most abusive	AbS	Least abusive	AbS
حمار (*donkey*)	4.25	فخامة (*excellency*)	-1.37
يلعن (*damn*)	3.99	الجمهورية (*republic*)	-1.27
كول (*swallow*)	3.82	نعيم (*bless*)	-1.27
واطي (*mean*)	3.76	مبروك (*congrats*)	-1.20
كلب (*dog*)	3.65	خير (*good*)	-1.20
هوا (*sh*t*)	3.63	حليف (*ally*)	-0.86
خراس (*chup*)	3.43	قصة (*story*)	-0.46
صرماية (*shoe*)	2.89	طبيعي (*natural*)	-0.64
بشار (*Bashar*)	0.79	يحتاج (*need*)	-0.55
لبنان (*Lebanon*)	-1.49	المنطقة (*region*)	-0.50

Table 8: AbS score for most/least abusive words

It could be observed from Table 7 and Table 8 that HtS and AbS scores for the most hateful and abusive words are positive indicating that they appear significantly under Hate and Abusive categories. In contrast, HtS and AbS scores for the least hate/abusive words are negative which emphasizes their appearance within Normal tweets more than hate/abusive ones. On the other hand, given the specificity of the HS, used in our dataset, it is common to involve named entities such as location, person or a party name while disgracing, dehumanizing certain entities; this justifies why the country name "لبنان" (*Lebanon*) has a negative HtS and AbS scores as this word can be among the most hateful/abusive words, yet, it is naturally used in Normal tweets.

5 Annotation Evaluation

We conducted the annotation evaluation following the study of (Artstein and Poesio, 2008). Observed agreement A_0, All categories are equally likely (S) and Cohen's kappa as agreement without chance correction measures, were adopted for evaluation. For agreement with chance correction, we used Krippendorff's α.

5.1 Agreement Without Chance Correction

Observed agreement A_0 is the simplest measure of agreement between annotators. It is defined as the proportion of the agreed annotations out of the total number of annotations (Artstein and Poesio, 2008). For our annotations, A_0 is 81.5%; while Pairwise Percent Agreement Measure (PRAM) values between each pair of the three annotators are 78.43%, 87.24% and 78.77% (Table 9). However, observed agreement and Pairwise Percent Agreements are criticized for their inability to account for chance agreement (McHugh, 2012). Therefore, to take into account the chance agreement described in (Artstein and Poesio, 2008), we considered that all the categories are equally likely and computed the S coefficient which measures if the random annotations follow a uniform distribution in the different categories, in our case: three (3) categories. With S value deduced as high as 72.3%, it could be said that for an agreement constant observation, the coefficient S is not sensitive to the elements distribution across the categories.

Annotators	PRAM	Cohen's K
1 & 2	78.43%	0.599
1 & 3	87.24%	0.758
2 & 3	78.77%	0.594

Table 9: PRAM and pairwise Cohen's K results

Cohen's kappa (Cohen's K) (Cohen, 1960) is another metric that also considers the chance agreement. It represents a correlation coefficient ranged from -1 to +1, where 0 refers to the amount of agreement that can be expected from random chance, while 1 represents the perfect agreement between the annotators. As it can be seen from Table 9, the agreement values between annotators 1 & 2 and 2 & 3 are moderate while the agreement between annotators 1 & 3 is substantial.

It is noted that, A_0, S and Cohen's K values obtained based on the annotations of our dataset, are high and show a little bias. Nevertheless, they put, on the same level, very heterogeneous categories: two minority but significant which are Abusive and Hate categories, and a non-significant majority which is the Normal category as the categories were found highly unbalanced (Table 5). Here, we can observe that, despite the strong agreement on the prevailing category, the coefficients seem to be very sensitive to disagreements over the minority categories. Thus, to ensure that the calculated coefficients for the three categories, reflect a significant agreement on the two minority categories: Abusive and Hate, we used a weighted coefficient (Inter-annotator agreement) which gives more importance to certain disagreements rather than treating all disagreements equally, as it is the case in A_0, S and Cohen's K (Artstein and Poesio, 2008).

5.2 Inter-Annotator Agreement (IAA)

According to (Artstein and Poesio, 2008), weighted coefficients can give more importance to certain disagreements. IAA measures can estimate the annotation reliability to a certain extent, on the assigned category. The kind of extent is determined by the method chosen to measure the agreement. For annotation reliability, the agreement coefficient Krippendorff's α has been used in the vast majority of the studies. Krippendorff's α is based on the assumption that expected agreement is calculated by looking at the overall distribution of judgments regardless of the annotator who produced these judgments. Based on Krippendorff's α value, the annotation is considered: (a) Good: for any data annotation with an agreement in the interval [0.8, 1], (b) Tentative: for any data annotation with an agreement in the interval [0.67, 0.8] or (c) Discarded: for any data annotation with an agreement below 0.67. For L-HSAB dataset, the obtained Krippendorff's α was 76.5% which indicates the agreement on the minority categories without considering the majority category.

5.3 Discussion

The agreement measures with/without chance correlation show a clear agreement about the categories Normal and Abusive. Indeed, our detailed study of the annotation results revealed that the three annotators identified abusive tweets in the same way while conflicts were encountered in tweets having an ironic content. On the other hand, more disagreement is observed when it comes to the Hate category and it is mainly related to the annotator's background knowledge, their personal taste and personal assumptions. In addition, the conflicts are not related to the annotator's gender; since, although annotator 1 & 3 are from different genders, they achieved the highest Pairwise Percent Agreement and Pairwise Cohen's K results. Finally, based on the deduced value of Krippendorff's α which is 76.5%, we can conclude that L-HSAB is a reliable HS and abusive dataset.

6 Classification Performance

L-HSAB dataset was used for the abusive/HS detection task within two experiments:

1. Binary classification: tweets are classified into Abusive or Normal. This requires merging the Hate class with the Abusive one.

2. Multi-class classification: tweets are classified into Abusive, Hate or Normal.

We filtered out the Levantine stopwords, then split the dataset into a training and a test set as it is shown in Table 10, where Classes denotes the number of classification classes.

Classes	Training			Test		
	Abusive	Normal	Hate	Abusive	Normal	Hate
2	1,708	2,968	-	488	682	-
3	1,369	2,968	339	359	682	129
Total		4,676			1,170	

Table 10: Training and Test sets of L-HSAB

We employed two supervised classifiers: SVM (Chang and Lin, 2011) and NB from NLTK (Bird et al., 2009). Both classifiers were trained with several n-gram schemes: unigrams, unigrams+bigrams and unigrams+bigrams+trigrams. Term frequency (TF) weighting was employed to reduce the features size according to two predefined frequency thresholds: 2 and 3. Among several runs with various n-gram schemes and TF val-

ues, we selected the best results to be listed in Table 11, where the classification algorithm, Precision, Recall, F-measure and Accuracy are referred to as Alg., P., R., F1 and Acc., respectively.

Classes	Alg.	P.(%)	R.(%)	F1(%)	Acc.(%)
2	NB	**90.5**	**89.0**	**89.6**	**90.3**
	SVM	84.7	81.1	82.0	83.2
3	NB	**86.3**	**70.8**	**74.4**	**88.4**
	SVM	74.0	64.2	66.8	78.6

Table 11: Classification results over L-HSAB

As it can be observed in Table 11, NB classifier performed better than SVM in both classification experiments. This is due to the fact that NB from NLTK is implemented as a multinomial NB decision rule together with binary-valued features (Bird et al., 2009). This explains its effectiveness while dealing with our feature vectors that were formulated from binary values denoting the presence/absence of n-gram schemes.

7 Conclusion

In this paper, we introduced L-HSAB, the first publicly available Levantine dataset for HS and abusive Language. The proposed dataset was aimed to be a benchmark dataset for automatic detection of online Levantine toxic contents. To build L-HSAB, we crawled Twitter for tweets while 3 annotators manually labeled the tweets following a set of rules. The dataset combined 5,846 tweets with 3 categories: Normal, Abusive and Hate. High values were achieved in agreement without chance correction and inter-annotator agreement which indicates the reliability of annotations. However, the agreement between annotators remains an issue when it comes to identify HS. This is because HS annotation does not only rely on rules, but it is also related to the annotators' background knowledge, their personal tastes and assumptions. L-HSAB was subjected to machine learning-based classification experiments conducted using NB and SVM classifiers. The results indicated the outperformance of NB over SVM in both binary and multi-class classification experiments. A natural future step would involve building publicly-available HS and abusive datasets for other underrepresented Arabic dialects such as Tunisian and Gulf.

References

Monirah A. Al-Ajlan and Mourad Ykhlef. 2018. Optimized twitter cyberbullying detection based on deep learning. In *Proceedings of the 21st Saudi Computer Society National Computer Conference (NCC)*, pages 52–56.

Areej Al-Hassan and Hmood Al-Dossari. 2019. Detection of hate speech in social networks: A survey on multilingual corpus. *Computer Science & Information Technology (CS & IT)*, 9(2):83–100.

Azalden Alakrota, Liam Murray, and Nikola S.Nikolov. 2018. Dataset construction for the detection of anti-social behaviour in online communication in arabic. *Procedia Computer Science*, 142:174–181.

Nuha Albadi, Maram Kurdi, and Shivakant Mishra. 2018. Are they our brothers? analysis and detection of religious hate speech in the arabic twittersphere. In *Proceedings of IEEE/ACM International Conference on Advances in Social Networks Analysis and Mining (ASONAM)*, pages 69–76.

Ron Artstein and Massimo Poesio. 2008. Inter-coder agreement for computational linguistics. *Computational Linguistics*, 34(4):555–596.

Steven Bird, Ewan Klein, and Edward Loper. 2009. *Natural language processing with Python: analyzing text with the natural language toolkit.* " O'Reilly Media, Inc.".

Chih-Chung Chang and Chih-Jen Lin. 2011. Libsvm: A library for support vector machines. *ACM transactions on intelligent systems and technology (TIST)*, 2(3):27.

Jacob Cohen. 1960. A coefficient of agreement for nominal scales. *Educational and Psychological Measurement*, 1(20):37–46.

Ona de Gibert, Naiara Perez, Aitor García-Pablos, and Montse Cuadros. 2018. Hate speech dataset from a white supremacy forum. In *Proceedings of the 2nd Workshop on Abusive Language Online*, pages 11–20.

Mari J Matsuda. 2018. Public response to racist speech: Considering the victim's story. In *Words that wound*, pages 17–51. Routledge.

Mary L McHugh. 2012. Interrater reliability: the kappa statistic. *Biochemia medica: Biochemia medica*, 22(3):276–282.

Hamdy Mubarak, Kareem Darwish, and Walid Magdy. 2017. Abusive language detection on arabic social media. In *Proceedings of the First Workshop on Abusive Language Online*, pages 52–56.

John T. Nockleby. 2000. *Hate Speech*, volume 1. Encyclopedia of the American Constitution (2nd ed., edited by Leonard W. Levy, Kenneth L. Karst et al. New York: Macmillan, New York: Macmillan.

Fadi Salem. Social media and the internet of things towards data-driven policymaking in the arab world: potential, limits and concerns.

Anna Schmidt and Michael Wiegand. 2017. A survey on hate speech detection using natural language processing. In *Proceedings of the Fifth International Workshop on Natural Language Processing for Social Media*, pages 1–10.

Zeerak Waseem, Thomas Davidson, Dana Warmsley, and Ingmar Weber. 2017. Understanding abuse: A typology of abusive language detection subtasks. In *Proceedings of the First Workshop on Abusive Language Online*, pages 78–84.

At the Lower End of Language—
Exploring the Vulgar and Obscene Side of German

Elisabeth Eder   **Ulrike Krieg-Holz**

Institut für Germanistik

Alpen-Adria-Universität Klagenfurt, Klagenfurt, Austria

{elisabeth.eder | ulrike.krieg-holz}@aau.at

Udo Hahn

Jena University Language & Information Engineering (JULIE) Lab

Friedrich-Schiller-Universität Jena, Jena, Germany

udo.hahn@uni-jena.de

Abstract

In this paper, we describe a workflow for the data-driven acquisition and semantic scaling of a lexicon that covers lexical items from the lower end of the German language register— terms typically considered as rough, vulgar or obscene. Since the fine semantic representation of grades of obscenity can only inadequately be captured at the categorical level (e.g., obscene *vs.* non-obscene, or rough *vs.* vulgar), our main contribution lies in applying best-worst scaling, a rating methodology that has already been shown to be useful for emotional language, to capture the relative strength of obscenity of lexical items. We describe the empirical foundations for bootstrapping such a low-end lexicon for German by starting from manually supplied lexicographic categorizations of a small seed set of rough and vulgar lexical items and automatically enlarging this set by means of distributional semantics. We then determine the degrees of obscenity for the full set of all acquired lexical items by letting crowdworkers comparatively assess their pejorative grade using best-worst scaling. This semi-automatically enriched lexicon already comprises 3,300 lexical items and incorporates 33,000 vulgarity ratings. Using it as a seed lexicon for fully automatic lexical acquisition, we were able to raise its coverage up to slightly more than 11,000 entries.

1 Introduction

With the rapid diffusion of social media in our daily lives, we currently experience (and many of us foster) a fundamental change of social communication habits. A main feature of this new era is an unprecedented degree of public exposure and visibility of individuals via (very) large and intentionally open networks of "friends" or "followers." Blogs, chat rooms and online fora constitute even looser connected social networks with lots of personally weakly acquainted or even unknown interlocutors engaged in digital discourses. Unfortunately, the chance for malicious interactions is promoted by the sheer mass of players in these networks and easy ways of hiding real individual identities via nick names or technically slightly more advanced means of camouflage, such as fake Web identities, including non-benevolent software agents and chatbots (McIntire et al., 2010).

These promiscuous communication groups face a high risk of anti-social behavior by aggressive, ruthless or entirely hostile actors (Dadvar et al., 2014; Wester et al., 2016; Li et al., 2017b; Talukder and Carbunar, 2018). The phenomena encountered range from (political, religious, ethnic, sexual) harassment, flaming, cybertrolling, and cyberbullying to extremely evaluative (derogatory, hurtful, rough, rude, offensive, abusive, vulgar, taboo, obscene) language use (for a typological clarification attempt, cf. Waseem et al. (2017)).

NLP research has recently directed its attention towards these unwarranted effects of social media activities and targets the automatic recognition of toxic language for the purpose of alerting and warning (Huang et al., 2018), filtering and blocking (Yoon et al., 2010; Ghauth and Sukhur, 2015; Chernyak, 2017; Wu et al., 2018), or reformulating suspicious contents of this type by non-obtrusive paraphrases (Su et al., 2017; Nogueira dos Santos et al., 2018).

Yet, how can we distinguish sloppy colloquial language we all use here and there from explicitly abusive and inacceptable wording, the topic we focus on in this paper, i.e., the kind of linguistic behavior typically socially banned from civilized discourse?

Proceedings of the Third Workshop on Abusive Language Online, pages 119–128

Florence, Italy, August 1, 2019. ©2019 Association for Computational Linguistics

The standard way to deal with this challenge is to define category systems (binary ones, such as obscene *vs.* non-obscene, or staged ones, as illustrated by pejorative *vs.* rough *vs.* vulgar) and letting people decide on the assignment of lexical items to these discrete categories. Once such categorical features are available, these lexical resources can be exploited for analytic purposes. Traditionally, these decisions were made by few lexicographers but this approach suffers from subjectivity and lack of flexibility, since this lexicon of improper words is rapidly growing due to the productiveness of language and thus changing almost every day.

Alternatively, a larger number of crowdworkers can be hired to provide such category assignments which increases the level of objectivity (on the basis of inter-worker consensus) and currency (campaigns can be run without delay, on demand, with low budgets). Yet, crowdsourced assessments, as with lexicographers' judgments, inherently suffer from the problems of permeable and soft category boundaries—what is rough for one person may be vulgar for another and *vice versa*.

We challenge the established view that the representation of obscenity of language is a discrete categorical classification problem—no matter which category system is chosen—but rather assume that it is a matter of differential degree. Accordingly, we describe the empirical foundations for bootstrapping and scaling such a lexicon from the low end of stylistic conventions on *degrees of obscenity*. We start from expert-level lexicographic categorizations of a small set of pejorative/rough/vulgar lexical items, enlarge this set by distributional semantics methods and, then, determine the degree of obscenity of the items assembled this way by letting crowdworkers make individual assessments relative to the semantic poles "neutral" and "vulgar" using a best-worst scaling approach (Kiritchenko and Mohammad, 2016, 2017).

The resulting lexicon targeting that lower end of German language comprises already 3,300 lexical items, incorporates 33,000 human ratings, and serves as a seed lexicon for fully automatically acquiring and scoring new lexical items from the same register. After several iterations, we finally come up with VULGER, a lexicon of VULgar GERman, totalling slightly more than 11,000 entries.

2 Related Work

Lexicons covering offensive language are almost only available for the English language. Perhaps the earliest collection of such lexical items (including phrases and multi-word expressions) is due to Razavi et al. (2010) who manually assembled approximately 2,700 dictionary entries. More recent work on an alternative verb-centered lexicon (size is not specified) with a focus on hate speech is reported by Gitari et al. (2015). The currently largest and most up to date English lexicon of abusive words is provided by Wiegand et al. (2018a) who manually and automatically collected around 8,500 lexical items.[1]

Languages other than English are incorporated in HURTLEX[2] (Bassignana et al., 2018) which forms a multilingual lexical resource of words that hurt for 53 languages, among them Italian, Spanish, English and German. This lexicon grew out of a manual selection of roughly 1,000 Italian hate words originally organized around 17 categories, with particular focus on derogatory words. It was further semi-automatically extended with complementary borrowings from the Italian MULTI-WORDNET[3] and BABELNET.[4] HURTLEX also excels with additional linguistic information (parts of speech, lexicographic definitions) for its lemmas. The lexicon integration step yields roughly 1,160 multilingual lexical items (with the help of the BABELNET API).

Manual curation (for the Italian portion) included a categorization step for each lemma sense into one of three categories: 'Not Offensive'–'Neutral'–'Offensive'. In a subsequent step, the 'Neutral' category was split into 'Not Literally Pejorative' (insult by means of a semantic shift, e.g. metaphorically) and 'Negative Connotation' (not necessarily a direct derogatory use but used in a derogatory way). 2-expert agreements plunged from 87.6% for the 3-category decisions to 61% for the extended 5-category decisions. Clearly, an indicator that such categorical decisions are hard to make even for competent native speakers.

As far as canonical German lexical resources are concerned, their coverage at the low end of lan-

---

[1]https://github.com/uds-lsv/
lexicon-of-abusive-words
[2]http://hatespeech.di.unito.it/
resources.html
[3]http://multiwordnet.fbk.eu/english/
home.php
[4]https://babelnet.org/

guage is, not surprisingly, more than incomplete. In effect, GERMANET V13.0,[5] for instance, covers only 1,774 lexical items from our seed lexicon (3,300 lexical items, in total). Yet, this ratio is even higher than for other lexical resources such as HATEBASE,[6] a repository which covers 95 languages (with 2,691 hate terms), yet only enumerates 95 manually provided German hate speech entries at all.

In conclusion, the compilation of lexicons for offensive, abusive or hate language typically consists of two steps. First, already available lexical resources covering such pejorative lexical items are identified and bundled in a seed lexicon. Next, this seed is incrementally enlarged—using additional lexical resources (such as WORD-NETs, WIKTIONARY, or BABELNET), or employing some sort of machine learning process (Wiegand et al., 2018a). Yet, the semantic core of such lexicons are (manual or automatic) categorical assignments of either bi-polar (e.g., 'Offensive' *vs.* 'Non-Offensive') or multi-polar categories (e.g., 'Colloquial' *vs.* 'Rough' *vs.* 'Obscene').

As an alternative to this scheme, our work focuses on substituting discrete categorical decisions by continuous grading of the above distinctions based on Best-Worst Scaling (Louviere et al., 2015). We thus target a research desideratum already described by Schmidt and Wiegand (2017, p.3-4) in the following way: *"Despite their general effectiveness, relatively little is known about the creation process and the theoretical concepts that underlie the lexical resources that have been specially compiled for hate speech detection."*

3   (Tentatively) Characterizing Vulgar Language

In our study, we not only consider hate speech and abusive terms, but take a much broader perspective on the topic of offensive language and its lexicalizations. Still, this goal is very hard to characterize by distinctive criteria since many lexical-semantic dimensions seem to be involved and strongly interact.

Vulgar language, as we conceive it, is predominantly signalled by an overly lowered language register, the taboo layer, with disgusting and obscene lexicalizations generally banned from any type of civilized discourse. Primarily (yet not only), it addresses the lexical fields of sexuality (sexual organs and activities, in particular), as well as body orifices or other specific body parts (e.g., *"Fresse"* (*"puss"*) as a negative denotation for *"Gesicht/Mund"* (*"face/mouth"*)) and scatologic expressions. One often also observes meaning transfers from animals with culture-dependent negative connotations to humans (e.g., *"Ratte"* (*"rat"*)). Pejorative words with marked negative connotation also play a significant role here (e.g., *"abkratzen"* (*"croak"*)). Especially religious, ethnic and political orientations, the primary targets of hate speech, gain a strong vulgar status when they are combined with (animal-related) swearwords such as *"Schwein"* (*"pig"*).

We are aware of the preliminary status of this characterization of vulgar language, but consider our work as a starting point for clarifying its nature and systematicity in more depth.

4   Lexicon Acquisition Method

Since a broad-coverage lexicon of obscene German (ranging on an interval from neutral to vulgar) is missing, we decided on a weakly supervised approach to lexicon acquisition based on bootstrapping. It consists of the following steps (the over-all workflow is fundamentally inspired by the work of Wiegand et al. (2018a), yet complements it by a hitherto unexplored methodology to scale the degree of obscenity of lexical items based on best-worst scaling):

1. **Language Resources**: Select a *seed lexicon* (possibly combining numerous relevant resources) which contains a collection of lexical items already tagged as rough and vulgar. Typically, this step reuses manually pre-categorized lexical items (work typically due to experienced lexicographers). Further, this lexical collection can be enhanced by exploiting large-scale *corpora*—these can either be already annotated for (some degree of) vulgarity or lack any annotation of this kind at all—or representational derivatives therefrom, such as (word) embeddings.

2. **Human Assessment**: Refine the seed lexicon by complementary human assessments of obscenity/vulgarity on the basis of *crowdsourcing* using differential *best-worst scaling*.

[5] http://www.sfs.uni-tuebingen.de/
GermaNet/
[6] https://hatebase.org

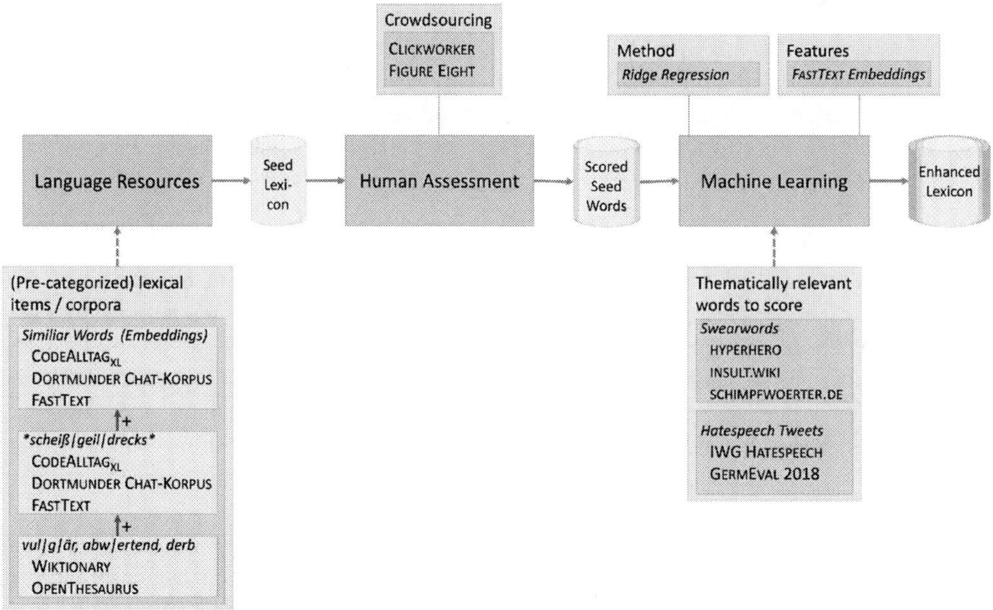

Figure 1: Generic language-independent workflow for lexicon acquisition (in blue) and its instantiation for German (in green); solid blue arrows indicate control flow, data flow is represented by dashed blue arrows, green arrows and '+' stand for lexical data harvesting (with RegEx-style expressions for matching search terms), thin blue lines link particular choices to realizations (implementations) of the blue main components of VULGER's acquisition system

3. **Machine Learning**: Use the resulting lexicon scored on a continuous neutrality-vulgarity scale as training data for automatically identifying and scoring new, thematically relevant lexical items, ideally from corpora containing a high amount of words regarding the property of interest (rough and vulgar wording).

The first step of this workflow (illustrated in Fig. 1), consisting of the assembly of relevant lexical material from scratch, will be described in Section 5. The second one, adding human assessments for that lexical material, is dealt with in Section 6, while the third step, automatic lexicon enhancement, is described in Section 7.

5 Building the Seed Lexicon

From the German slice of WIKTIONARY,[7] we extracted all words marked as vulgar, rough and pejorative.[8] Additionally, we gathered entries tagged with corresponding categories[9] from the German

OPENTHESAURUS.[10] As the focus of our corpus lies on single words[11] from a vulgar vocabulary, we excluded phrases from this processing step.

The list resulting from this first step contained some entries used as affixes in morphologically productive word formation, such as *"*geil"*, *"scheiß*"*, *"Scheiß*"* and *"Drecks*"*, the latter ones denoting variants of *"shit"* and *"dirt"*. We cancelled these rudimentary entries from the list because there is no way to get meaningful judgments for them in isolation due to the many possible combinations yielding highly diverse degrees of vulgarity.

In order to account for these terms in a reasonable way we extended our list by harvesting rough and vulgar word forms concatenated with the affixes mentioned above from the CODE ALLTAG$_{S+d}$ email corpus[12] (Krieg-Holz et al., 2016), the DORTMUNDER CHAT KORPUS (Beißwenger, 2013)[12] and from entries in

---

[7] https://de.wiktionary.org

[8] The exact terms and corresponding abbreviations are: 'vulgär', 'vulg.', 'vul.', 'derb' and 'abwertend', 'abw.'.

[9] 'vulg.', 'derb', 'abwertend'

[10] https://www.openthesaurus.de

[11] The vast potential of the German language for productive noun composition within single compounds makes this decision less restrictive than it seems; cf., e.g., the English phrase form *"son of a bitch"* and its German single compound equivalent *"Hurensohn"*.

[12] We only took words with a minimum frequency of 3.

FASTTEXT (Grave et al., 2018) word embeddings, the latter being based on COMMON CRAWL and WIKIPEDIA.

Yet, we not only incorporated plain text corpora or computationally derived lexical items (exploiting the FASTTEXT embeddings) into our study, but also included word embeddings as a representation format based on the distributional semantics hypothesis and computationally derived from corpora (see also Tulkens et al. (2016); Wiegand et al. (2018a). Utilizing the word embeddings from the corpora mentioned above and the GENSIM module (Řehůřek and Sojka, 2010) we further generated, using the lexical seeds from the previous round, *similar words*, i.e., close semantic neighbors of these seed words by iteratively minimizing the threshold for similarity, until we found too much noise was returned (a common procedure, cf. also Tulkens et al. (2016)). We manually edited the resulting list in regard to inflected forms, misspellings and case sensitivity, but we intentionally kept the 'lexical noise', i.e., presumably neutral words. Since we planned to annotate the lexical items identified this way by crowdsourcing in a later phase, these neutral words also help counterbalance the impact of rough and vulgar expressions during assessments. In total, based on this procedure we gathered a seed lexicon with 3,300 entries.

6 Enriching the Seed Lexicon: Scaling Degrees of Vulgarity

We chose to annotate our seed words with Best-Worst-Scaling (BWS), because it delivers high-quality annotations with only a relatively small number of annotation steps. BWS is an extension of the method of paired comparison to multiple choices, originally developed by Louviere et al. (2015) and introduced into NLP for emotion scaling by Kiritchenko and Mohammad (2016, 2017). For BWS, annotators are presented with n items at a time (an n-tuple, where $n > 1$, and typically $n = 4$). They then have to decide which item from the n-tuple under scrutiny is the *best* (highest in terms of the property of interest) and which is the *worst* (lowest in terms of the property of interest).

In our case, judges had to select the *most neutral* and the *most vulgar* terms per given n-tuple. We used the BWS tool[13] from Kiritchenko and

Mohammad (2016, 2017) to generate $2N$ decision alternatives (N denotes the size of our seed lexicon) and thus came up with 6,600 4-tuples to be assessed. Tuples were produced randomly under the premise that each term has to occur only once in eight different tuples and each tuple is unique.

For the annotation process proper, we used the crowdsourcing platforms FIGURE EIGHT[14] and CLICKWORKER,[15] where each n-tuple was assessed by five annotators. In order to get real-valued scores from the BWS annotations we applied COUNTS ANALYSIS (Orme, 2009)[16] and thus got scores between $+1$ (most neutral) and -1 (most vulgar). Scores were calculated by subtracting the percentage of times the term was chosen as worst from the percentage of times the term was chosen as best. We computed the split-half reliability[16] like Kiritchenko and Mohammad (2017) by randomly splitting the annotations of a tuple into two halves, calculating scores independently for these halves and measuring the correlation between the resulting two sets of scores. We got an average Pearson correlation of 0.9102 $(+/-0.0022)$ over 100 trials.

7 Automatic Lexicon Extension

7.1 Regression Models

In order to further extend the lexicon in a purely automatic way and also inspired by studies on automatic word emotion induction (especially by Li et al. (2017a) and Buechel and Hahn (2018)) we employed regression models to predict scores for input words. The seed words served as training and testing data for a linear regression and a ridge regression model (linear regression with L_2 regularization during training).[17] As features for the words we used their respective word embeddings (this, obviously, excludes lexical items from further consideration for which no embeddings exist).

We experimented with different word embeddings. We built 100-dimensional word embeddings from CODE ALLTAG$_{XL}$ (Krieg-Holz et al., 2016) using WORD2VEC (Mikolov et al., 2013) for all words occurring at least 3 times in CODE ALLTAG$_{XL}$. Furthermore, we employed WORD2VEC word embeddings from Reimers

---

[13]http://www.saifmohammad.com/WebPages/BestWorst.html

[14]https://www.figure-eight.com

[15]https://www.clickworker.de

[16]Again we used the scripts from Kiritchenko and Mohammad (2016, 2017).

[17]For both we used the scikit-learn.org implementation using the default parameters.

et al. (2014) with a minimum word frequency of 5 and 100 dimensions (UKP), 300-dimensional FASTTEXT word embeddings from SPINNING-BYTES (Cieliebak et al., 2017) trained on German tweets (TWITTER) and, finally, FASTTEXT word embeddings (Grave et al., 2018) based on COMMON CRAWL and WIKIPEDIA (FASTTEXT). We also tried to utilize embeddings generated from the German TWITTER HATESPEECH corpora from Ross et al. (2016) and Wiegand et al. (2018b) under the assumption that they might contain a large number of rough and vulgar words. But due to their small size and their nevertheless high proportion of out-of-vocabulary words we had to exclude both of these resources from further consideration.

Table 1 shows that the ridge regression model performs equally or slightly better compared to the linear regression model. Regarding the input features the FASTTEXT token embeddings performed best (see Table 2).

Embeddings	LinReg	RidgeReg	p
CODE ALLTAG$_{XL}$	0.574	0.575	0.004
UKP	0.682	0.682	0.121
TWITTER	0.735	0.735	0.073
FASTTEXT	0.766	0.779	0.001

Table 1: Averaged Pearson correlation (10-fold cross validation) and p-value (two-sided t-test) for Linear Regression (LinReg) and Ridge Regression (Ridge-Reg)

Embeddings	Pearson r	p
CODE ALLTAG$_{XL}$	0.575	< 0.001
UKP	0.682	< 0.001
TWITTER	0.735	< 0.001
FASTTEXT	0.779	—

Table 2: Averaged Pearson correlation (10-fold cross validation) for different embeddings with Ridge Regression, with significance difference to best performing embeddings (p-value from two-sided t-test)

7.2 Applying Regression Models to Enhance the Lexicon

We used the best method (ridge regression and FASTTEXT embeddings) to extend our lexicon with three German swearword lists.[18] There is an overlap between swearwords and vulgar lexicalizations, but not every swearword has strong vulgar status,[19] e.g., *"Schwein" ("pig")*, a subtle distinction which our scaling approach accounts for (cf. also the remarks made in Section 3).

We trained a ridge regression model on the seed words (cf. Sections 5 and 6), i.e., the respective word embeddings and the scores. This model was then applied to the input swearwords (from the three sources mentioned above), which do not occur in the seed lexicon already, and predicted the neutrality/vulgarity scores of the remaining entries on the basis of their word embeddings provided that an embedding for the respective word was found in the FASTTEXT embeddings.[20] We excluded out-of-vocabulary words in order to avoid getting too much noise in terms of wrongly scored lexical items in our lexicon. Further we thus dropped really rare words. With the words already contained in our seed lexicon and words not present as embeddings removed, we assembled 2,046 additional entries following this approach.

Assuming that corpora for hate speech detection include a higher amount of vulgar and rough words, we also made use of such datasets. There exist two publicly available German-language text corpora annotated for hate speech from which we extracted lexical material. The first of them, IWG HATESPEECH, originating from Ross et al. (2016), contains about 500 tweets which were annotated by two judges using a binary categorization scheme ("hate speech": Yes or No) and a 6-point Likert scale ranging from "not offensive" to "very offensive".[21] The second corpus collected by Wiegand et al. (2018b) contains more than 8,500 tweets and was compiled for GERMEVAL 2018, a challenge task addressing the recognition and classification of offensive German language.[22] The latter corpus was coarsely annotated with binary 'Offense' and 'Other' categories, but it also comes with a 4-way classification schema where besides the non-offensive 'Other' class 'Offense' was subdivided in three ways: 'Profanity' (no intent to insult someone, yet the lexical choice is negatively marked, with swearwords such as sca-

---

[18]These lists were retrieved from `http://www.hyperhero.com/de/insults.htm`, `http://www.insult.wiki/wiki/Schimpfwort-Liste` and `https://www.schimpfwoerter.de`

[19]Also not every vulgar word is a swearword.

[20]We also checked for different spellings regarding case sensitivity.

[21]The corpus is available at `https://github.com/UCSM-DUE/IWG_hatespeech_public`

[22]The corpus is available at `https://projects.cai.fbi.h-da.de/iggsa/`

tologic *"Scheiße" (shit)*), 'Insult' (clear intent to offend someone) and 'Abuse' (an even stronger form of 'Insult', i.e., an abusive utterance that degrades a target person/group by ascribing a social identity to a person/group that is judged negatively by a (perceived) majority of society).

From these two corpora we extracted words from all tweets marked as 'Offense' = 'YES' by one of the annotators and further removed stop words, hashtags and words with non-alphabetic characters excluding hyphens or a word length smaller than 4. We also tried to lemmatize the words[23] and normalize spellings in regard to case sensitivity, but admittedly inserted some noise into our input words, i.e., some inflected forms and other forms of semantic duplication could not be normalized. After excluding words already present in the seed lexicon or in the German swearwords lists we applied the same procedure as used for the swearwords and obtained another 5,700 new scored lexical entries.

Due to the lack of better resources we tried to measure the reliability of the resulting scores in a preliminary way by calculating the correlation between the probability of a word being in an offensive post and its score. We got a Pearson correlation coefficient of only -0.35, probably also caused by many words occurring just once, but the correlation may also be inherently weak. In future work, we plan to evaluate the automatically determined extension of our seed word lexicon by feeding the lexical items back into another crowdsourcing round and determining the correlation between the human assessment and the automatically derived scoring values.

The final version of VULGER, a lexicon with VULgarity ratings of GERman words, enhanced with swearwords and words from the two hate speech corpora in the end comprises 11,046 entries (see Table 3).

Resource	# Lexical Items
Seed Words	3,300
German Swearwords	2,046
Twitter Hate Speech Corpora	5,700
Total	11,046

Table 3: Decomposition of contributions from various language resources for VULGER, the current version of the lexicon of VULgar GERman

---

[23]We used SPACY: https://spacy.io/

8 Conclusion

In this paper, we are concerned with the lexical segment at the lower stylistic end of each natural language often referred to as rough, vulgar and obscene. This register typically covers very explicit and rude linguistic expressions (taboo words). Standard lexical repositories have mostly neglected lots of these expressions on purpose although a pressing need can now be derived for such an extension, e.g., for the purpose of identifying and neutralizing or blocking offensive and humiliating utterances in social media.

Our workflow for building such a lower-end lexicon is based on three steps: assembling already existing lexicons (or fragments therefrom) for this stylistic subvariety of language, assigning degrees of vulgarity for each lexical item included, and using this seed for continuous automatic enhancement by weakly supervised machine learning procedures.

As far as the representation of the semantics of these lexical items are concerned, we propose a continuous grading system to substitute overly simplistic discrete categorical schemata which have been prevailing so far. Still, the claim that such a fine-grained representation is helpful at all must also be demonstrated by experiments in the future. In any case, we plan to use and iteratively extend our newly developed lexicon on text corpora with similar biases into pejorative languages (including scores for obscenity). However, merely (automatically) extending a specialized lexicon might not necessarily prove beneficial as evidenced by the results of Tulkens et al. (2016) that showed no performance boost for a system using such an extended dictionary, at least for detecting Dutch racist language.

In order to by-pass the sparse data problem, methods like transfer learning might also be appropriate here (Sahlgren et al., 2018). Still, the validity of these new items and their scores have to be experimentally validated, e.g., by feeding newly found lexical material back to annotators and compare their judgments with automatically predicted ones.

We are also aware of the fact that purely lexically driven approaches to account for obscene, offensive or vulgar language may not be sufficient to solve the recognition problem completely and that a broader discourse context has to be taken into account, as well as the linguistic conventions in different communities (Owsley Sood et al., 2012). Still, a lexicon of significant size and quality might form the backbone for machines sensitive to rude and vulgar language.

References

Elisa Bassignana, Valerio Basile, and Viviana Patti. 2018. HURTLEX: a multilingual lexicon of words to hurt. In *CLiC-it 2018 — Proceedings of the 5th Italian Conference on Computational Linguistics. Torino, Italy, December 10-12, 2018*, number 2253 in CEUR Workshop Proceedings, page #49.

Michael Beißwenger. 2013. Das Dortmunder Chat-Korpus. *Zeitschrift für germanistische Linguistik*, 41(1):161–164.

Sven Buechel and Udo Hahn. 2018. Word emotion induction for multiple languages as a deep multi-task learning problem. In *NAACL-HLT 2018 — Proceedings of the 2018 Conference of the North American Chapter of the Association for Computational Linguistics: Human Language Technologies. New Orleans, Louisiana, USA, June 1-6, 2018*, volume 1: Long Papers, pages 1907–1918, Stroudsburg/PA. Association for Computational Linguistics (ACL).

Ekaterina Chernyak. 2017. Comparison of string similarity measures for obscenity filtering. In *BSNLP 2017 — Proceedings of the 6th Workshop on Balto-Slavic Natural Language Processing @ EACL 2017. Valencia, Spain, April 4, 2017*, pages 97–101, Stroudsburg/PA. Association for Computational Linguistics (ACL).

Mark Cieliebak, Jan Deriu, Dominic Egger, and Fatih Uzdilli. 2017. A Twitter corpus and benchmark resources for German sentiment analysis. In *SocialNLP 2017 — Proceedings of the 5th International Workshop on Natural Language Processing for Social Media of the AFNLP SIG SocialNLP @ EACL 2017. Valencia, Spain, April 3, 2017*, pages 45–51, Stroudsburg/PA. Association for Computational Linguistics (ACL).

Maral Dadvar, Dolf Trieschnigg, and Franciska M. G. De Jong. 2014. Experts and machines against bullies: a hybrid approach to detect cyberbullies. In *Advances in Artificial Intelligence. Canadian AI 2014 — Proceedings of the 27th Canadian Conference on Artificial Intelligence. Montréal, Québec, Canada, May 6-9, 2014*, number 8436 in Lecture Notes in Articificial Intelligence (LNAI), pages 275–281, Cham, Switzerland. Springer International Publishing.

Khairil Imran Ghauth and Muhammad Shurazi Sukhur. 2015. Text censoring system for filtering malicious content using approximate string matching and Bayesian filtering. In *Computational Intelligence in Information Systems. INNS-CIIS 2014 — Proceedings of the 4th INNS Symposia Series on Computational Intelligence in Information Systems. Bandar Seri Begawan, Brunei, November 2014*, number 331 in Advances in Intelligent Systems and Computing Book Series (AISC), pages 149–158, Cham, Switzerland. Springer International Publishing.

Njagi Dennis Gitari, Zhang Zuping, Hanyurwimfura Damien, and Jun Long. 2015. A lexicon-based approach for hate speech detection. *International Journal of Multimedia and Ubiquitous Engineering*, 10(4):215–230.

Edouard Grave, Piotr Bojanowski, Prakhar Gupta, Armand Joulin, and Tomáš Mikolov. 2018. Learning word vectors for 157 languages. In *LREC 2018 — Proceedings of the 11th International Conference on Language Resources and Evaluation. Miyazaki, Japan, May 7-12, 2018*, pages 3483–3487, Paris. European Language Resources Association (ELRA).

Qianjia Huang, Jianhong Zhang, Diana Z. Inkpen, and David Van Bruwaene. 2018. Cyberbullying intervention interface based on convolutional neural networks. In *TRAC 2018 — Proceedings of the 1st Workshop on Trolling, Aggression and Cyberbullying @ COLING 2018. Santa Fe, New Mexico, USA, 25 August, 2018*, pages 42–51, Stroudsburg/PA. Association for Computational Linguistics (ACL).

Svetlana Kiritchenko and Saif M. Mohammad. 2016. Capturing reliable fine-grained sentiment associations by crowdsourcing and best-worst scaling. In *NAACL-HLT 2016 — Proceedings of the 2016 Conference of the North American Chapter of the Association for Computational Linguistics: Human Language Technologies. San Diego, California, USA, June 12-17, 2016*, pages 811–817, Stroudsburg/PA. Association for Computational Linguistics (ACL).

Svetlana Kiritchenko and Saif M. Mohammad. 2017. Best-worst scaling more reliable than rating scales: a case study on sentiment intensity annotation. In *ACL 2017 — Proceedings of the 55th Annual Meeting of the Association for Computational Linguistics. Vancouver, British Columbia, Canada, July 30 - August 4, 2017*, volume 2: Short Papers, pages 465–470, Stroudsburg/PA. Association for Computational Linguistics (ACL).

Ulrike Krieg-Holz, Christian Schuschnig, Franz Matthies, Benjamin Redling, and Udo Hahn. 2016. CODE ALLTAG: A German-language e-mail corpus. In *LREC 2016 — Proceedings of the 10th International Conference on Language Resources and Evaluation. Portorož, Slovenia, 23-28 May 2016*, pages 2543–2550, Paris. European Language Resources Association (ELRA-ELDA).

Minglei Li, Qin Lu, Yunfei Long, and Lin Gui. 2017a. Inferring affective meanings of words from word embedding. *IEEE Transactions on Affective Computing*, 8(4):443–456.

Tai Ching Li, Joobin Gharibshah, Evangelos E. Papalexakis, and Michalis Faloutsos. 2017b. TROLLSPOT: detecting misbehavior in commenting platforms. In *ASONAM 2017 — Proceedings of the 2017 IEEE/ACM International Conference on Advances in Social Networks Analysis and Mining 2017. Sydney, Australia, July 31 - August 03, 2017*, pages 171–175, New York/NY. Association for Computing Machinery (ACM).

Jordan J. Louviere, Terry N. Flynn, and A. A. J. Marley. 2015. *Best-Worst Scaling: Theory, Methods and Applications.* Cambridge University Press, Cambridge, U.K.

John P. McIntire, Lindsey K. McIntire, and Paul R. Havig. 2010. Methods for chatbot detection in distributed text-based communications. In *CTS 2010 — Proceedings of the 2010 International Symposium on Collaborative Technologies and Systems. Chicago, Illinois, USA, 17-21 May 2010*, pages 463–472. IEEE.

Tomáš Mikolov, Ilya Sutskever, Kai Chen, Gregory S. Corrado, and Jeffrey Dean. 2013. Distributed representations of words and phrases and their compositionality. In *Advances in Neural Information Processing Systems 26 — NIPS 2013. Proceedings of the 27th Annual Conference on Neural Information Processing Systems. Lake Tahoe, Nevada, USA, December 5-10, 2013*, pages 3111–3119, Red Hook/NY. Curran Associates, Inc.

Bryan Orme. 2009. Maxdiff analysis: simple counting, individual-level logit, and HB. *Sawtooth Software, Inc.*

Sara Owsley Sood, Judd Antin, and Elizabeth F. Churchill. 2012. Profanity use in online communities. In *CHI 2012 — Proceedings of the 30th ACM SIGCHI Conference on Human Factors in Computing Systems. Austin, Texas, USA, May 5-10, 2012*, pages 1481–1490, New York/NY. Association for Computing Machinery (ACM).

Amir Hossein Razavi, Diana Z. Inkpen, Sasha Uritsky, and Stan Matwin. 2010. Offensive language detection using multi-level classification. In *Advances in Artificial Intelligence. Canadian AI 2010 — Proceedings of the 23rd Canadian Conference on Artificial Intelligence. Ottawa, Ontario, Canada, May 31 - June 2, 2010*, number 6085 in Lecture Notes in Computer Science (LNCS), pages 16–27, Berlin, Heidelberg. Springer-Verlag.

Radim Řehůřek and Petr Sojka. 2010. Software framework for topic modelling with large corpora. In *Proceedings of the Workshop on New Challenges for NLP Frameworks @ LREC 2010. La Valletta, Malta, May 22, 2010*, pages 45–50, Paris. European Language Resources Association (ELRA).

Nils Reimers, Judith Eckle-Kohler, Carsten Schnober, Jungi Kim, and Iryna Gurevych. 2014. GERMEVAL2014: nested named entity recognition with neural networks. In *KONVENS 2014 — Proceedings of the Workshops of the 12th Edition of the KONVENS Conference: GermEval. Hildesheim, Germany, October 8-10, 2014*, pages 117–120, Hildesheim, Germany. Universitätsverlag Hildesheim.

Björn Ross, Michael Rist, Guillermo Carbonell, Benjamin Cabrera, Nils Kurowsky, and Michael Wojatzki. 2016. Measuring the reliability of hate speech annotations: the case of the European refugee crisis. In *NLP4CMC III — Proceedings of the 3rd Workshop on Natural Language Processing for Computer-Mediated Communication. Bochum, Germany, 22 September 2016*, number 17 in Bochumer Linguistische Arbeitsberichte (BLA), pages 6–9.

Magnus Sahlgren, Tim Isbister, and Fredrik Olsson. 2018. Learning representations for detecting abusive language. In *ALW 2 — Proceedings of the 2nd Workshop on Abusive Language Online @ EMNLP 2018. Brussels, Belgium, October 31, 2018*, pages 115—123, Stroudsburg/PA. Association for Computational Linguistics (ACL).

Cícero Nogueira dos Santos, Igor Melnyk, and Inkit Padhi. 2018. Fighting offensive language on social media with unsupervised text style transfer. In *ACL 2018 — Proceedings of the 56th Annual Meeting of the Association for Computational Linguistics. Melbourne, Victoria, Australia, July 15-20, 2018*, volume 2: Short Papers, pages 189–194, Stroudsburg/PA. Association for Computational Linguistics (ACL).

Anna Schmidt and Michael Wiegand. 2017. A survey on hate speech detection using natural language processing. In *SocialNLP 2017 — Proceedings of the 5th International Workshop on Natural Language Processing for Social Media of the AFNLP SIG SocialNLP @ EACL 2017. Valencia, Spain, April 3, 2017*, pages 1–10. Association for Computational Linguistics (ACL).

Hui-Po Su, Zhen-Jie Huang, Hao-Tsung Chang, and Chuan-Jie Lin. 2017. Rephrasing profanity in Chinese text. In *ALW 1 — Proceedings of the 1st Workshop on Abusive Language Online @ ACL 2017. Vancouver, British Columbia, Canada, August 4, 2017*, pages 18–24, Stroudsburg/PA. Association for Computational Linguistics (ACL).

Sajedul Talukder and Bogdan Carbunar. 2018. ABUSNIFF : automatic detection and defenses against abusive FACEBOOK friends. In *ICWSM 2018 — Proceedings of the 12th International AAAI Conference on Web and Social Media. Stanford, California, USA, June 25-28, 2018*, pages 385–394, Palo Alto/CA. AAAI Press.

Stéphan Tulkens, Lisa Hilte, Elise Lodewyckx, Ben Verhoeven, and Walter Daelemans. 2016. A dictionary-based approach to racism detection in

Dutch social media. In *TA-COS 2016 — Proceedings of the Workshop on Text Analytics for Cybersecurity and Online Safety @ LREC 2016. Portorož, Slovenia, 23 May 2016*, pages 11–17.

Zeerak Waseem, Thomas Davidson, Dana Warmsley, and Ingmar Weber. 2017. Understanding abuse: a typology of abusive language detection subtasks. In *ALW 1 — Proceedings of the 1st Workshop on Abusive Language Online @ ACL 2017. Vancouver, British Columbia, Canada, August 4, 2017*, pages 78–84, Stroudsburg/PA. Association for Computational Linguistics (ACL).

Aksel Wester, Lilja Øvrelid, Erik Velldal, and Hugo Lewi Hammer. 2016. Threat detection in online discussions. In *WASSA 2016 — Proceedings of the 7th Workshop on Computational Approaches to Subjectivity, Sentiment and Social Media Analysis @ NAACL-HLT 2016. San Diego, California, USA, June 16, 2016*, pages 66–71, Stroudsburg/PA. Association for Computational Linguistics (ACL).

Michael Wiegand, Josef Ruppenhofer, Anna Schmidt, and Clayton Greenberg. 2018a. Inducing a lexicon of abusive words: a feature-based approach. In *NAACL-HLT 2018 — Proceedings of the 2018 Conference of the North American Chapter of the Association for Computational Linguistics: Human Language Technologies. New Orleans, Louisiana, USA, June 1-6, 2018*, volume 1: Long Papers, pages 1046–1056, Stroudsburg/PA. Association for Computational Linguistics (ACL).

Michael Wiegand, Melanie Siegel, and Josef Ruppenhofer. 2018b. Overview of the GERMEVAL 2018 Shared Task on the Identification of Offensive Language. In *Proceedings of the GERMEVAL 2018 Workshop @ KONVENS 2018. Vienna, Austria, September 21, 2018*, pages 1–10.

Zhelun Wu, Nishant Kambhatla, and Anoop Sarkar. 2018. Decipherment for adversarial offensive language detection. In *ALW 2 — Proceedings of the 2nd Workshop on Abusive Language Online @ EMNLP 2018. Brussels, Belgium, October 31, 2018*, pages 149–159, Stroudsburg/PA. Association for Computational Linguistics (ACL).

Taijin Yoon, Sun-Young Park, and Hwan-Gue Cho. 2010. A smart filtering system for newly coined profanities by using approximate string alignment. In *CIT 2010 — Proceedings of the IEEE 10th International Conference on Computer and Information Technology. Bradford, UK, 29 June - 1 July 2010*, pages 643–650. IEEE.

Preemptive Toxic Language Detection in Wikipedia Comments Using Thread-Level Context

Mladen Karan and Jan Šnajder
Faculty of Electrical Engineering and Computing
Unska 3, Zagreb
{mladen.karan, jan.snajder}@fer.hr

Abstract

We address the task of automatically detecting toxic content in user generated texts. We focus on exploring the potential for preemptive moderation, i.e., predicting whether a particular conversation thread will, in the future, incite a toxic comment. Moreover, we perform preliminary investigation of whether a model that jointly considers all comments in a conversation thread outperforms a model that considers only individual comments. Using an existing dataset of conversations among Wikipedia contributors as a starting point, we compile a new large-scale dataset for this task consisting of labeled comments and comments from their conversation threads.

1 Introduction

Due to the ever-growing amount of user generated content online, manual moderation of such content is becoming increasingly difficult to scale up. On the other hand, the relative anonymity and lack of personal contact between participants of web conversations lowers inhibitions and increases the risk of toxic behavior, making adequate moderation increasingly important. Consequently, automated detection of toxic language in user generated content is an increasingly important area of research. While automated classification models are unlikely to ever fully replace human moderators, they can make their task easier by suggesting which content to prioritize for moderation.

The typical way to approach this problem is via supervised machine learning, where an input to a model is a user-generated text, and the output is a classification decision (toxic or non-toxic) or a numerical toxicity score. In this paper, we explore two possible extensions of this approach: *preemptive classification* and *thread-level models*.

While practically very useful, standard models are only applicable in a post-hoc scenario, i.e., to detect a toxic comment after if has already been posted. An alternate approach would be to have models detect situations that are likely to lead to toxic comments. If successful, such models would enable moderators to preemptively focus on potentially problematic discussion threads and then either intervene and guide the discussion away from conflict or respond in near real-time after the toxic comment is posted. Large-scale implementation of such near real-time moderation might be unnecessary and require too many moderators. However, for limited parts of discussions that are known to pertain to specially vulnerable social groups, this might be a feasible approach. Our first research question is whether such preemptive toxic comment detection is viable.

The second research question pertains to the benefits of including thread-level information when detecting toxic comments. Namely, most existing models consider every comment in isolation, therefore ignoring the context provided by the other comments in the discussion. For post-hoc models, while useful, this additional information may not be crucial, as the main indicators of toxicity are most present in the text of the comment being classified rather than in the rest of the thread. In the preemptive scenario, however, the model has access only to comments that appeared before a toxic one. We hypothesize that considering the entire thread of comments might be of greater importance in this case.

The contribution of this paper is threefold. First, using a large data set of conversations among Wikipedia contributors, we compile and make publicly available a new dataset with complete discussion threads and with semi-automatically generated toxicity labels. Secondly, we explore the viability of models for the preemptive toxic detection task. Third, we investigate the potential benefits of including thread-level information into models.

129

Proceedings of the Third Workshop on Abusive Language Online, pages 129–134
Florence, Italy, August 1, 2019. ©2019 Association for Computational Linguistics

2   Related Work

Many varieties of toxic language have been considered in NLP research, including sexism, racism (Waseem and Hovy, 2016a; Waseem, 2016), toxicity (Kolhatkar et al., 2018), hatefulness (Gao and Huang, 2017a), aggression (Kumar et al., 2018), attack (Wulczyn et al., 2017a), obscenity, threats, and insults. Waseem et al. (2017) proposed a systematic typology of toxic language.

Post-hoc detection of toxic text has been tackled by traditional machine learning approaches, such as logistic regression (Waseem and Hovy, 2016b; Davidson et al., 2017; Wulczyn et al., 2017b), and support vector machines (SVM) (Xu et al., 2012; Schofield and Davidson, 2017). However, the best performance is most often attained by deep learning approaches, such as convolutional neural networks (CNN) (Gambäck and Sikdar, 2017; Potapova and Gordeev, 2016; Pavlopoulos et al., 2017) and variants of recurrent neural networks (RNN) (Pavlopoulos et al., 2017; Gao and Huang, 2017b; Pitsilis et al., 2018; Zhang et al., 2018b). In our experiments we focus mainly on deep learning-based models.

All the above-mentioned approaches deal with the post-hoc scenario. Other work we are aware of that explores the preemptive scenario is that of Zhang et al. (2018a). There, the task is to predict – given an initial courteous exchange of two user comments – whether the third comment will be toxic. The authors create a manually labeled data set and perform an extensive study on which pragmatic and rhetorical devices are indicative of conversation toxicity. Moreover, there is the work of (Liu et al., 2018), where a logistic regression classifier with a rich feature set (including thread level features) is evaluated on a data set of manually labeled 30000 Instagram comments. In contrast, the data set produced in our work is much bigger, but has only silver labels.

In our work we consider the use of thread-level information for toxic comment detection. Within the scope of this work we limit ourselves to simple mechanisms for including this information into deep learning models. Recently, deep learning models have been proposed that leverage graph structures, such as TreeLSTM (Tai et al., 2015) and GraphSAGE (Hamilton et al., 2017), which might be useful for modeling thread-level structure in our task. We leave the investigation of this possibility for future work.

3   Dataset

At the time of writing we were not aware of the data set from (Liu et al., 2018). At first we considered using the dataset from (Zhang et al., 2018a), but found it rather small (~1200 examples) for deep learning approaches. Furthermore, this dataset was constructed using a very carefully designed methodology for a specific experiment – detecting whether a toxic comment will appear given a courteous initial exchange of two comments. We are interested in a more general case, where conversation threads might be longer and not necessarily start in a courteous manner. Moreover, we aimed at a setting which would better reflect the realistic working conditions in which our models would be used and allow us to measure their practical impact. Consequently, we decided to create a new dataset from the data collected by Hua et al. (2018). It contains the entire conversational history of comments on Wikipedia modeled as a graph of actions. The possible actions are *Creation, Addition, Modification, Deletion*, and *Restoration*. Automatically derived toxicity scores are also provided for each example.

We apply the following steps to this dataset:

Step 1. Filter the data to remove all threads with less than 2 different participants. This leaves ~8.7M threads.

Step 2. Apply all *Modification* actions, to update the comments to their most recent version.

Step 3. Flag comments that were deleted. A comment is considered deleted if there is a *Deletion* action on it, without a subsequent *Restoration* action that would undo the effect.

Step 4. Split the threads into the train (70%), dev (15%), and test (15%) sets. The split is done across time: the test set contains the most recent threads, while the train set contains the least recent.

Step 5. Semi-automatically label the examples for toxicity. An example is considered toxic if its toxicity or severe toxicity scores are above 0.64 or 0.92, respectively. [1] and it was deleted by a person who is not the comment author. This heuristic takes into account two signals: (1) the fact that a toxic classifier has high confidence for a comment and (2) the fact the comment was deleted.

---

[1] The same thresholds as those used by Hua et al. (2018) tuned to give equal error rate on a dataset of Wikipedia comments manually labeled for toxicity. The thresholds yield 86% precision and 84% recall on the tuning data. The thresholds differ as the number of severely toxic comments in the tuning data was much smaller than the number of toxic comments.

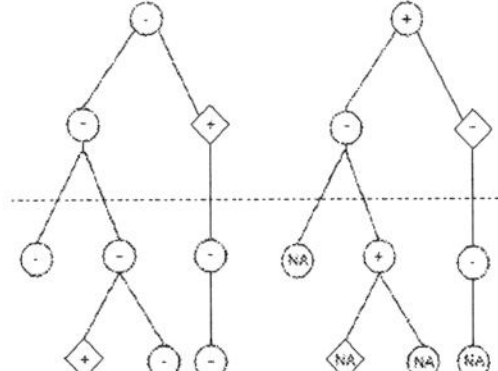

Figure 1: An illustration of examples generated for the post-hoc (left tree) and preemptive (right tree) case. Diamond shaped nodes represent toxic comments while round nodes represent non-toxic comments. Positive examples for the classifier are denoted by + and negative ones by –. Examples denoted by NA are not considered by the classifier: these are the leaf nodes in the preemptive scenario. The filtering from Step 7 has the effect of ignoring all examples with an insufficient number of preceding comments, e.g., for $L_{min} = 2$ all comments above the dotted line would be ignored in the *rich-context* setting.

Considering only deleted examples as toxic would yield noisy labels, as comments are often deleted for reasons other than being toxic. Manual inspection of the silver-labeled dataset reveals that the combination of the toxicity classifier and observed deletion is effective in identifying some of the toxic comments. However, this approach fails to identify those toxic comments which were not deleted or those for which the toxicity classifier failed. The former issue is not problematic, as it was shown by Hua et al. (2018) that toxic comments on Wikipedia get deleted by the community very quickly. Thus toxic comments that are not deleted are quite rare. The latter issue, however, represents a limitation of our work. Our results apply only to those types of toxic language that are detectable by current post-hoc models. Extending this data set to account for more complex types of toxic language would require considerable annotation effort and we leave it as a possibility for future work.

Step 6. Generate examples from each thread in the train/dev/test set for the (1) preemptive scenario and (2) post-hoc scenario as shown in Figure 1. For the post-hoc scenario, examples are generated from all comments in the tree. Positive examples are those comments that are labeled as toxic, while all other comments are negative examples. In the preemptive scenario, examples are generated from all comments that are not leaves of the tree. Positive examples are those comments that have a toxic child and no toxic ancestors, while all other comments are negative examples. The number of pre-

Setting	Scenario	train	dev	test
real-context	post-hoc	357K	47K	35K
real-context	preemptive	226K	32K	25K
rich-context	post-hoc	119K	21K	15K
rich-context	preemptive	53K	11K	8K

Table 1: Statistics of the generated data set variants.

ceding comments available for each comment in this data can vary from 0 to over 100 (median is 2). Consequently, to differentiate from the setting in the next step, we will refer to this setting as the *real-context setting*.

Step 7. While the previous setting is more realistic, in order to better assess their full potential, we wished to evaluate the thread level models in a setting where the context provided by preceding comments is always available. To this end, we filter the examples from the previous step such that only those are left that have at least $L_{min} = 2$ comments on the path to the root.[2] We will refer to the datasets obtained in this step as being in the *rich-context setting*.

As the label distribution of the examples obtained in this way is extremely skewed (positive examples account for 0.5 to 1 percent of the data, depending on the setting and scenario), we undersample the negative class. For completeness, we also retain the non-undersampled versions of the dev and test sets for some of the experiments.

Lastly, to additionally evaluate the quality of the silver labels we manually labeled 100 examples from the balanced version of the data set. We found that on these examples the silver labels have 0.51 precision and 1.00 recall. This yields 0.67 F1 measure and is somewhat lower than the expected 0.85 obtained for this classifier in (Hua et al., 2018). The difference indicates that the thresholds from (Hua et al., 2018) obtained on non-deleted comments from Wikipedia may not perform equally well on deleted comments. To address this and increase the quality of the labels, more deleted comments should be manually labeled and thresholds retuned using, e.g., the same error rate method of (Wulczyn et al., 2017a).

Some statistics of the finally generated data set are given in Table 1, and some examples in Table 2. We make the dataset and the code for generating it available.[3]

---

[2]Following the choice of (Zhang et al., 2018a).
[3]`http://takelab.fer.hr/data/pretox`

Text	Toxic
Go fuck yourself. Anways.	+
Lazy Bast*rd	+
Superman is a total loser batman would win	+
Sick of this article and the shitty writing	+
When did it become an inherently evil thing to be concerned for human welfare?	–
Please elaborate; this is fascinating.	–

Table 2: Examples of comments from the dataset.

Setting	Scenario	train	dev	test
real-context	post-hoc	357K	47K	35K
real-context	preemptive	226K	32K	25K
rich-context	post-hoc	119K	21K	15K
rich-context	preemptive	53K	11K	8K

Table 3: Statistics of the generated data set variants.

4 Models

We implement several baseline models to get some preliminary results on this data.

Our simplest model is a linear support vector machine (SVM) on TF-IDF weighted unigrams and bigrams. We include the most frequent 10k n-grams into the model, and tune the C hyperparameter on the dev data. This model ignores thread context, even when it is available.

For the deep learning models we use an neural network based encoder to derive a vector representation for each comment in our data. We denote this encoder as enc_{com}. For models that ignore preceding comments, the output of this encoder is fed directly to linear and softmax layers and produces a classification decision for each comment. Thus, the output of our model for a comment c, which is a sequence of word embeddings, could be written as:

$$y_c = softmax(\mathbf{W}^T enc_{com}(\mathbf{c}))$$

For models that take preceding comments into account, the input is not a single comment but a sequence of comments, $\mathbf{t} = (\mathbf{c_1}, \ldots, \mathbf{c_n})$, which includes the comment to classify, $\mathbf{c_n}$, and all of its ancestors, $(\mathbf{c_1}, \ldots, \mathbf{c_{n-1}})$. We first apply enc_{com} to each individual $\mathbf{c_i}$, obtaining comment representations $\mathbf{r_i} = enc_{com}(\mathbf{c_i})$. We then feed the sequence $\mathbf{s} = (\mathbf{r_1}, \ldots, \mathbf{r_n})$ as features into another encoder, which we denote by enc_{thr}. The output of the model for the given input is similar as before:

$$y_t = softmax(\mathbf{W}^T enc_{thr}(\mathbf{s}))$$

For implementing the encoder, we performed preliminary experiments with convolutional neural networks (CNN) (Krizhevsky et al., 2012), long short-term memory networks (LSTM) (Hochreiter and Schmidhuber, 1997), and gated recurrent units (GRU) (Cho et al., 2014), tuning hyperparameters on the development data. We found that, on the development data for this task, GRU and LSTM perform similarly and slightly better than CNN. We also found that bidirectional recurrent models perform slightly better than standard ones. To represent the words we use the freely available 50-dimensional GloVE embeddings (Pennington et al., 2014) trained on 6 billion tokens. Preliminary experiments also reveal models perform better when the embeddings are also updated during training. For our final experiments we use two BiLSTM models with a cell/hidden-state size of 50 to implement enc_{com} and enc_{thr}. We use Adam (Kingma and Ba, 2015) to train the models with a learning rate of 0.001, minibatch size of 128, and early stopping using the dev set. We denote the variants of the model that are thread-agnostic and thread-aware as BiLSTM and BiLSTM-context, respectively. All models are implemented in PyTorch (Paszke et al., 2017) and the code is available online.[4]

5 Results

The results are given in Table 4. Each column represents one dataset variant. All differences within the same variant are statistically significant at p<0.05 (tested used bootstrap resampling).

While differences across different dataset variants are not directly comparable, there is a tendency for models to perform much better in the post-hoc scenario than in the preemptive scenario, which is expected. Preemptive models are, however, able manually labeled to beat the random baseline and achieve scores that are numerically similar to those of Zhang et al. (2018a) on their data.

The BiLSTM-context model performs similarly or worse than the BiLSTM model in all cases except the preemptive real case where context does help, but both LSTM-based models are outperformed by a simple SVM. This indicates that the additional information provided by the thread context is, in this case, not very useful for determining the correct class. Manual inspection of the data set confirms that humans could determine the toxicity of most comments without referring to the thread for additional context.This intuition is invalid in

---

[4]http://takelab.fer.hr/data/pretox

	Preemptive		Post-hoc	
Model	Real	Rich	Real	Rich
Random	.500	.500	.500	.500
SVM	**.601**	.578	.883	.893
BiLSTM	.558	**.620**	.901	**.902**
BiLSTM-context	.586	.602	**.904**	.900

Table 4: Results in various settings and scenarios. Random is the expected performance of choosing a random class with uniform probability across the classes. The numbers are F1-scores on perfectly balanced test data.

cases when the thread context for preemptive detection already contains a toxic comment. A presence of a toxic comment in a thread is a good indicator of a situation where more toxicity will follow. Thus considering the entire thread leads to better performance in such cases. This, however, is not true *preemptive* detection, as toxicity already occurred earlier in thread. Consequently, we filtered out such cases from the data by requiring comments that are positive examples for the preemptive case to have no toxic ancestors (as described in Chapter 3). It is however worth mentioning that, for this reason, our preliminary experiments which omit this filtering step indeed showed more noticeable benefits of having the thread available in the preemptive case.

We also note that the unbalanced nature of this data has a very negative effect on performance in a practical setting. For example, even after tuning the classification threshold to maximize F1 on unbalanced dev data, the F1-score for the best post-hoc model on the unbalanced test is still below 0.5. Thus, more work is required to make models for this task that are applicable in a real-world setting.

6 Conclusion

We compiled a large semi-automatically labeled dataset for studying preemptive toxic language detection in Wikipedia conversations. We explored two types of deep learning models for this task: those that only consider a single comment and those that take into account the context by considering preceding comments in a conversation. In our experiments, the context-sensitive models did not significantly outperform context-agnostic ones. While all preemptive models would beat a random baseline, their performance is still too low for practical applications.

There are numerous possibilities for future work. One is to employ more sophisticated graph-based deep learning methods such as GraphSAGE (Hamilton et al., 2017). Another direction would be exploring ways to better address the class unbalance typical for this task. Yet another possibility would be to enrich the input features with information available about the user who is commenting, e.g., whether they had toxic comments in the past, or their personality profile derived from text using models such as that of Gjurković and Šnajder (2018). Finally, combining deep learning with discourse and pragmatic features, such as those of Zhang et al. (2018a), might be a good next step to improve the models in the preemptive setting.

References

Kyunghyun Cho, Bart van Merrienboer, Caglar Gulcehre, Dzmitry Bahdanau, Fethi Bougares, Holger Schwenk, and Yoshua Bengio. 2014. Learning phrase representations using rnn encoder–decoder for statistical machine translation. In *Proceedings of the 2014 Conference on Empirical Methods in Natural Language Processing (EMNLP)*, pages 1724–1734.

Thomas Davidson, Dana Warmsley, Michael Macy, and Ingmar Weber. 2017. Automated Hate Speech Detection and the Problem of Offensive Language. In *Proceedings of ICWSM*.

Björn Gambäck and Utpal Kumar Sikdar. 2017. Using Convolutional Neural Networks to Classify Hatespeech. In *Proceedings of the First Workshop on Abusive Language Online*, pages 85–90.

Lei Gao and Ruihong Huang. 2017a. Detecting online hate speech using context aware models. In *Proceedings of Recent Advances in Natural Language Processing (RANLP)*, pages 260–266, Varna, Bulgaria.

Lei Gao and Ruihong Huang. 2017b. Detecting online hate speech using context aware models. *arXiv preprint arXiv:1710.07395*.

Matej Gjurković and Jan Šnajder. 2018. Reddit: A gold mine for personality prediction. In *Proceedings of the Second Workshop on Computational Modeling of Peoples Opinions, Personality, and Emotions in Social Media*, pages 87–97.

Will Hamilton, Zhitao Ying, and Jure Leskovec. 2017. Inductive representation learning on large graphs. In *Advances in Neural Information Processing Systems*, pages 1024–1034.

Sepp Hochreiter and Jürgen Schmidhuber. 1997. Long short-term memory. *Neural computation*, 9(8):1735–1780.

Yiqing Hua, Cristian Danescu-Niculescu-Mizil, Dario Taraborelli, Nithum Thain, Jeffery Sorensen, and Lucas Dixon. 2018. Wikiconv: A corpus of the complete conversational history of a large online collaborative community. In *Proceedings of the 2018 Conference on Empirical Methods in Natural Language Processing*, pages 2818–2823. Association for Computational Linguistics.

Diederik P Kingma and Jimmy Ba. 2015. Adam: A method for stochastic optimization. pages 1–13.

Varada Kolhatkar, Hanhan Wu, Luca Cavasso, Emilie Francis, Kavan Shukla, and Maite Taboada. 2018. The sfu opinion and comments corpus: A corpus for the analysis of online news comments.

Alex Krizhevsky, Ilya Sutskever, and Geoffrey E Hinton. 2012. Imagenet classification with deep convolutional neural networks. In *Advances in neural information processing systems*, pages 1097–1105.

Ritesh Kumar, Aishwarya N. Reganti, Akshit Bhatia, and Tushar Maheshwari. 2018. Aggression-annotated Corpus of Hindi-English Code-mixed Data. In *Proceedings of the 11th Language Resources and Evaluation Conference (LREC)*, pages 1425–1431, Miyazaki, Japan.

Ping Liu, Joshua Guberman, Libby Hemphill, and Aron Culotta. 2018. Forecasting the presence and intensity of hostility on instagram using linguistic and social features. In *Twelfth International AAAI Conference on Web and Social Media*.

Adam Paszke, Sam Gross, Soumith Chintala, Gregory Chanan, Edward Yang, Zachary DeVito, Zeming Lin, Alban Desmaison, Luca Antiga, and Adam Lerer. 2017. Automatic differentiation in pytorch. In *NIPS-W*.

John Pavlopoulos, Prodromos Malakasiotis, and Ion Androutsopoulos. 2017. Deep learning for user comment moderation. In *Proceedings of the First Workshop on Abusive Language Online*, pages 25–35.

Jeffrey Pennington, Richard Socher, and Christopher D. Manning. 2014. Glove: Global vectors for word representation. In *Empirical Methods in Natural Language Processing (EMNLP)*, pages 1532–1543.

Georgios K Pitsilis, Heri Ramampiaro, and Helge Langseth. 2018. Detecting offensive language in tweets using deep learning. *arXiv preprint arXiv:1801.04433*.

Rodmonga Potapova and Denis Gordeev. 2016. Detecting state of aggression in sentences using cnn. *arXiv preprint arXiv:1604.06650*.

Alexandra Schofield and Thomas Davidson. 2017. Identifying Hate Speech in Social Media. *XRDS: Crossroads, The ACM Magazine for Students*, 24(2):56–59.

Kai Sheng Tai, Richard Socher, and Christopher D Manning. 2015. Improved semantic representations from tree-structured long short-term memory networks. In *Proceedings of the 53rd Annual Meeting of the Association for Computational Linguistics and the 7th International Joint Conference on Natural Language Processing (Volume 1: Long Papers)*, volume 1, pages 1556–1566.

Zeerak Waseem. 2016. Are you a racist or am i seeing things? annotator influence on hate speech detection on twitter. In *Proceedings of the first workshop on NLP and computational social science*, pages 138–142, Austin, Texas.

Zeerak Waseem, Thomas Davidson, Dana Warmsley, and Ingmar Weber. 2017. Understanding Abuse: A Typology of Abusive Language Detection Subtasks. In *Proceedings of the First Workshop on Abusive Langauge Online*.

Zeerak Waseem and Dirk Hovy. 2016a. Hateful symbols or hateful people? predictive features for hate speech detection on twitter. In *Proceedings of the NAACL student research workshop*, pages 88–93, San Diego, California.

Zeerak Waseem and Dirk Hovy. 2016b. Hateful symbols or hateful people? predictive features for hate speech detection on twitter. In *Proceedings of the NAACL student research workshop*, pages 88–93.

Ellery Wulczyn, Nithum Thain, and Lucas Dixon. 2017a. Ex machina: Personal attacks seen at scale. In *Proceedings of the 26th International Conference on World Wide Web*, pages 1391–1399. International World Wide Web Conferences Steering Committee.

Ellery Wulczyn, Nithum Thain, and Lucas Dixon. 2017b. Ex machina: Personal attacks seen at scale. In *Proceedings of the 26th International Conference on World Wide Web*, pages 1391–1399. International World Wide Web Conferences Steering Committee.

Jun-Ming Xu, Kwang-Sung Jun, Xiaojin Zhu, and Amy Bellmore. 2012. Learning from bullying traces in social media. In *Proceedings of the 2012 conference of the North American chapter of the association for computational linguistics: Human language technologies*, pages 656–666. Association for Computational Linguistics.

Justine Zhang, Jonathan Chang, Cristian Danescu-Niculescu-Mizil, Lucas Dixon, Yiqing Hua, Dario Taraborelli, and Nithum Thain. 2018a. Conversations gone awry: Detecting early signs of conversational failure. In *Proceedings of the 56th Annual Meeting of the Association for Computational Linguistics (Volume 1: Long Papers)*, volume 1, pages 1350–1361.

Ziqi Zhang, David Robinson, and Jonathan Tepper. 2018b. Detecting Hate Speech on Twitter Using a Convolution-GRU Based Deep Neural Network. In *Lecture Notes in Computer Science*. Springer Verlag.

Neural Word Decomposition Models for Abusive Language Detection

Sravan Babu Bodapati   Spandana Gella   Yaser Al-Onaizan
Amazon AI, USA
{sravanb, sgella, onaizan}@amazon.com

Abstract

User generated text on social media often suffers from a lot of undesired characteristics including hatespeech, abusive language, insults etc. that are targeted to attack or abuse a specific group of people. Often such text is written differently compared to traditional text such as news involving either explicit mention of abusive words, obfuscated words and typological errors or implicit abuse i.e., indicating or targeting negative stereotypes. Thus, processing this text poses several robustness challenges when we apply natural language processing techniques developed for traditional text. For example, using word or token based models to process such text can treat two spelling variants of a word as two different words. Following recent work, we analyze how character, subword and byte pair encoding (BPE) models can be aid some of the challenges posed by user generated text. In our work, we analyze the effectiveness of each of the above techniques, compare and contrast various word decomposition techniques when used in combination with others. We experiment with finetuning large pretrained language models, and demonstrate their robustness to domain shift by studying Wikipedia attack, toxicity and Twitter hatespeech datasets.

1 Introduction

In recent years, with the growing popularity of social media applications, there has been an exponential increase in the amount of user-generated text including microblog posts, status updates and comments posted on the web. The power of communicating freely with large number of users has resulted in not only sharing news and exchanging content but has also led to a problem of large number of harmful, offensive and aggressive interactions online (Duggan, 2017). Previous work on identifying abusive language has tackled this problem by training computational methods that are capable of automatically recognizing offensive content for text on MySpace (Yin et al., 2009), Twitter (Waseem and Hovy, 2016; Davidson et al., 2017), Wikipedia comments (Wulczyn et al., 2017) and Facebook posts (Vigna et al., 2017; Kumar et al., 2018).

Most of these models are based on features extracted from words or word n-grams or the recurrent neural networks that operate on word embeddings (Pavlopoulos et al., 2017; Badjatiya et al., 2017) with few exceptions of models that utilize character n-grams that can model noisy text and out-of-vocabulary words (Waseem and Hovy, 2016; Nobata et al., 2016; Wulczyn et al., 2017). However, these models are not very effective at modeling obfuscated words such as *w0m3n, nlgg3r* which are prominent in user generated text that are intended at evading hate speech detection (Mishra et al., 2018). In this work, we aim to address this by investigating word, subword and character-based models for abusive language detection.

Recent advances in unsupervised pre-training of language models have led to strong improvements on various general natural language processing and understanding tasks such as question answering, sentiment and natural language inference (Peters et al., 2018; Devlin et al., 2018). However, it is unclear how such models trained on standard text would transfer information when fine-tuned on noisy user generated text. In additional to studying word, subword and character-based model performances on abusive language detection we also combine these with pre-trained embeddings and fine-tuning these pre-trained language models and understand their efficiency and robustness in identifying abusive text.

Specifically, in this work, we address the effectiveness of character-based models, subword or Byte Pair Encoding (BPE) based models and word

Proceedings of the Third Workshop on Abusive Language Online, pages 135–145
Florence, Italy, August 1, 2019. ©2019 Association for Computational Linguistics

features based models along with pre-trained word embeddings and fine tuning pretrained language models for detecting abusive language in text. Precisely we make following contributions:

- We compare the effectiveness of end-to-end character based models, with word + character embedding models, byte pair encoding and subword models, to show which of the techniques perform better than pure word based models.

- We demonstrate how fine-tuning large pre-trained language models, the latest breakthrough in NLP, enhance state of the art on few of the abusive language datasets, and show that the domain shift isn't considerable when applied to abusive language datasets.

- We also examine how preprocessing documents with byte pair encoding model pretrained on a large corpus, boost the performance of several word embedding based models massively.

2   Related Work

Identifying abusive context on the web is one of the widely studied topics on social media text. This problem has been studied for Hate Speech detection (Kwok and Wang, 2013; Waseem and Hovy, 2016; Waseem, 2016; Ross et al., 2016; Saleem et al., 2017; Warner and Hirschberg, 2012), Harassment (Yin et al., 2009; Cheng et al., 2015), Cyberbullying (Willard, 2007; Tokunaga, 2010; Schrock and Boyd, 2011), Abusive language detection (Sahlgren et al., 2018; Nobata et al., 2016), aggression identification (Kumar et al., 2018; Aroyehun and Gelbukh, 2018; Modha et al., 2018), identifying toxic comments on forums (Wulczyn et al., 2017) and offensive language identification (Wiegand et al., 2018; Zampieri et al., 2019). While most of the work in identifying abusive on social media is predominantly studied for English social media posts some of the latest work include study on German (Wiegand et al., 2018), Italian (Bosco et al., 2018) and Mexican Spanish (Álvarez-Carmona et al., 2018).

Some of the early methods on identifying abusive text used word n-gram, part-of-speech (POS) tagging (syntactic features), manually created profanity lexicons or stereotypical words, TF-IDF features along with sentiment and contextual features

and trained supervised classifiers such as support vector machines (Yin et al., 2009; Warner and Hirschberg, 2012). Waseem (2016) studied character n-grams, skipgrams, brown clusters and POS tag based features for identifying hatespeech. Waseem and Hovy (2016) studied usefulness of various socio-linguistic features such as gender, location, word-length distribution, Author Historical Salient Terms (AHST) features in identifying hatespeech.

Some of the recent work compared efficiency of both character n-gram based models as inputs to logistic regression and multi-layer perceptron models (Wulczyn et al., 2017). Nobata et al. (2016) showed that character n-grams features alone can perform well and can efficiently model noisy text. They also showed off-the-shelf word embeddings can be used to identify abusive text.

Pavlopoulos et al. (2017) used deep-learning based models specifically they employed RNN with a novel classification-specific attention mechanism and achieve state-of-the-art results on identifying attack and toxic content in Wikipedia comments. Badjatiya et al. (2017) investigated three different neural networks for hatespeech detection: (i) Convolutional neural network (inspired by CNN's for sentiment classification by Kim (2014)) (ii) Long short-term memory networks (LSTM) to capture long range dependencies and (iii) FastText classification model that represents document by averaging word vectors that can be fine-tuned for the hatespeech task.

While Badjatiya et al. (2017) analyzed various architectures to encode text for hatespeech detection, we are not aware of any work that studied various word decomposition models for identifying abusive language in text. Recent work on identifying offensive language in text include fine-tuning large pretrained langueqe model BERT which use subword units to encode text (Zampieri et al., 2019; Zhu et al., 2019). For the SEMEVAL-2019 task of offensive language identification 7 out of top 10 submissions used BERT finet tuning. Zampieri et al. (2019) highlighted that 8% of 104 systems participated in the shared task used BERT based fine-tuning.

In this work, we analyze the effectiveness of different ways of learning representations with character-based models, subword or BPE based models and word features based models. We also combine these with well known pre-trained word embeddings and very large pretrained language models for fine-tuning and detecting abusive language in text. In Section 3 we describe the datasets that we study in this work for hatespeech and abusive detection.

3 Datasets

We experiment with three datasets: Twitter dataset (Waseem and Hovy, 2016), Personal Attack and Toxicity datasets from Wikipedia Talk dataset (Wulczyn et al., 2017) that covers sexism/racism, personal attack and toxicity aspects of abuse in user generated text online.

3.1 Twitter Dataset

We use the hatespeech Twitter dataset (Hatespeech) provided by Waseem and Hovy (2016). This dataset was created from a corpus of 136k tweets collected from Twitter by searching for commonly used racist and sexist slurs on various ethnic, gender and religious minorities over a two-month period. The original data had 16,907 tweets corresponding to sexist, racist and neither labels (3378, 1970 and 11559 respectively). However, we could only retrieve 11170 of the tweets (2914: sexism, 17: racism and 8239: neither) with python's Tweepy library. Similar issue of missing tweets has been reported by Mishra et al. (2018). However, the percent of tweets we lost are much higher than theirs and most of the tweets lost are for the *racism* label. We have lost majority of the tweets corresponding to sexism label. Since we lost large chunk of tweets we conduct our experiments on cross validation of 5 splits and report scores on all of the 5 splits.

3.2 Wikipedia talk page

We use the personal attacks (W-ATT) and toxicity (W-TOX) datasets that were randomly sampled from 63 Million talk page comments from the public dump of English Wikipedia by Wulczyn et al. (2017). Each comment in both the datasets were annotated by at least 10 workers and we use the majority label as its gold label. Overall, we have 115.8k comments in W-ATT dataset (69.5k, 23.1k and 23.1k in train, dev and test splits respectively) and 159.6k comments in W-TOX dataset (95.6k, 32.1k and 31.8k in train, dev and test splits). Similar to hatespeech dataset both the W-ATT and W-TOX datasets also have skewed distribution of labels having 13.5% and 15.3% of them labeled as abusive.

4 Methods

In this section, we present various word decomposition methods and modeling architectures we analysed for studying Twitter and Wiki Talk page W-ATT and W-TOX comment datasets.

4.1 Word-based Model

As a baseline, we adpot the fastText (Grave et al., 2017) classification algorithm. The fastText algorithm performs mean pooling on top of the word embeddings w_i^{emb} to obtain a document representation. This document representation is passed through a Softmax layer to obtain classification scores. The embeddings can either be learned or can be initialized with pre-trained embeddings and fine-tuned during training. We run multiple variants of fastText in our experiments.

4.2 Subword-based Model

Subwords are formed by concatenating all the characters of a particular length within a word boundary. Addition of subwords gives the model ability to learn words which are misspelled such as *emnlp* and *emnnlp* are similar. A pure word based model would consider *emnnlp* as out-of-vocabulary (OOV) word, if not seen in training set, but a subword model would decompose *emnnlp* into "emn" and "nlp", and train subword embeddings w_{sub}^{emb} for each of these subwords. We take subword variant of fastText model to incorporate subword context into the model. The algorithm considers all subwords of varying lengths within the boundary of a word.

4.3 Joint Word and Character Embedding Model

Our joint word and character embedding based model is adapted from Kim (2014) and Peters et al. (2018). We refer to Kim (2014) as TextCNN going forward.

Let x_i be the input word and c_0^n be its character representation, where n is the number of characters in the word. We transform c_0^n representation by passing through a character embedding layer, which is a n-gram Character-CNN similar to (Peters et al., 2019). The output of the n-gram CharacterCNN is concatenated with the word's corresponding pretrained embedding to obtain w_{full}^{emb} as described in 1(a) Character-level features are concatenated with w_i^{emb}, the word embedding of word i, to form w_{full}^{emb}, the full set of word-level input

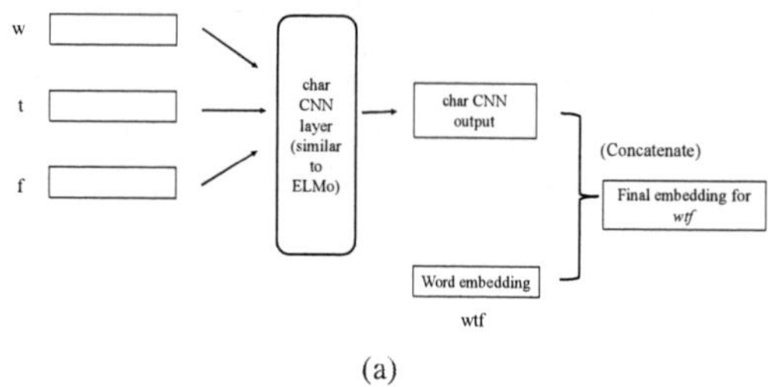
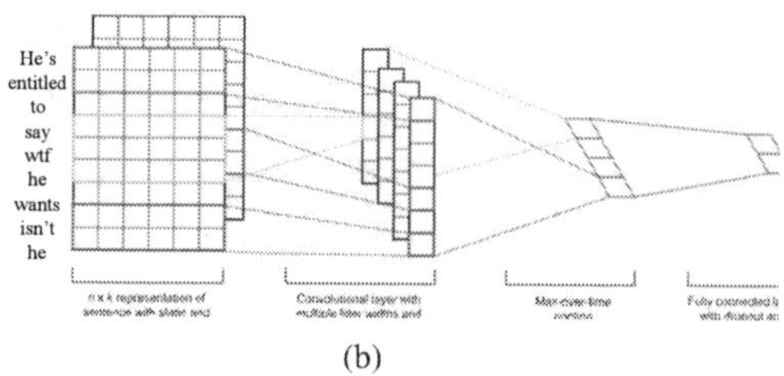

Figure 1: Architecture for model described in 4.3. In Figure 1(a), we present an example of for obtaining a word embedding by concatenating character embeddings with the embedding of the word itself. These final embeddings are then fed into the non-static variant of the Kim2014 (Kim, 2014) architecture (shown in Figure 1(b)). The layers of Kim2014 model alongwith the character CNN layer are updated during training.

features:

$$w_{full}^{emb} = (w_i^{char}; w_i^{word})$$

We randomly replace singleton words with special [UNK] (unknown) tokens for obtaining its w_i^{emb}, and also apply dropout (Srivastava et al., 2014) on w_{full}^{emb}. The input word embeddings w_{full}^{emb}, in a sentence with l tokens and convolutional window size h, $w_{i:i+h}^{emb}$ is transformed through a convolution filter w_c:

$$c_i = f(w_c.w_{i:i+h-1}^{emb} + b_c)$$

where b_c is a bias term and f is a non-linear function (ReLU). This produces a feature map c, on-top of which we apply a global max-over time pooling.

$$c` = max(\mathbf{c})$$

This process for one feature is repeated to obtain m filters with different window sizes h. The resulting filters are concatenated to form TextCNN document representation. The document representation is passed through Softmax layer to obtain classification predictions. We also experiment with original version of TextCNN, which is a pure word based model, without the character embedding variant.

4.4 End-to-end Character Embedding Model

To understand the potential of end to end character based models in dealing noisy text, we use Very Deep Convolutional Neural Network (VDCNN) architecture proposed by Conneau et al. (2017) that operates at character level by stacking multiple convolutional and pooling layers that sequentially extract a hierarchical representation of the text. This representation is fed into a fully connceted layer which is trained to maximize the classification accuracy on training data.

4.5 Byte Pair Encoding + Word + Char embedding models

We train a Byte Pair Encoding(BPE) based model introduced by Sennrich et al. (2016) on the given training corpus. We use this trained BPE model on training data to tokenize/encode our documents in training, validation and test data and use each BPE unit as a word to learn embeddings. We perform $30,000$ merge operations on each training dataset to learn subword or BPE units.

4.6 Pretrained Language Models

Recent liteature have shown that transferring knowledge from large pre-trained language models could benefit various NLP tasks either by adding a task specific architecture or by fine-tuning the language model for the end task (Peters et al., 2018; Devlin et al., 2018; Peters et al., 2019). In this work, we use $BERT$ model and we fine-tune the model for each of our train datasets.

5 Experiments

In this section, we present different variants of the models described in Section 4 presented in Table 1.

fastText: We use multiple variants of fastText model. Our fastText$_{ngrams=1}$ uses embeddings learned for each unigram. We treat this as our baseline model without any preprocessing of the text. Our fastText$_{ngrams=2}$ model also uses bigrams along with unigrams as independent tokens to learn embeddings. All pairs of bigrams are chosen wtihout ant frequency threshold. Our fastText$_{ngrams=2}$ + subword $(2-6)$ also uses all subwords within a word boundary within the range of $2-6$. All our models are trained with learning rate of 0.5 and for 5 epochs.

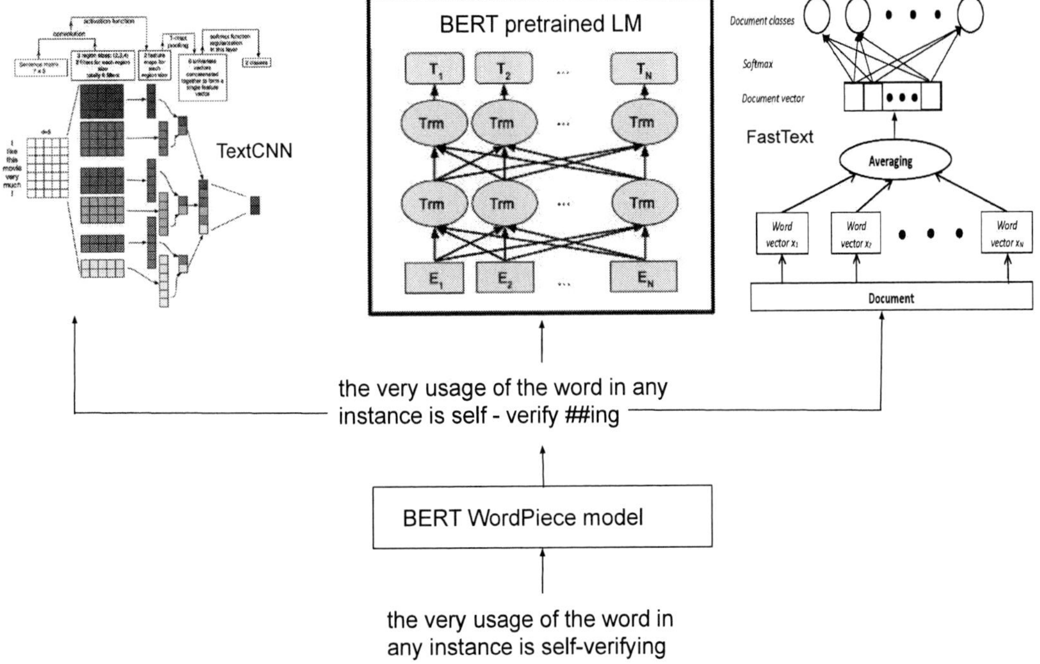

Figure 2: We present the approach discussed in 5.1. The Input text for a document is tokenized via the BERT Wordpiece tokenized model pretrained on GoogleNews and Wikipedia. This tokenized text is fed as input to the word based models which aids in forming representations from a more informative subword split as an independent unit.

TextCNN (Kim, 2014): We run the TextCNN for classification in non-static mode, with learning rate of 0.0001, dropout of 0.5 for 50 epochs. We have used default kernel window sizes $N_f = (3, 4, 5)$ with $m = 100$ filters. We initialize the embeddings layer with word2vec pretrained embeddings[1] publicly available from google. We used the non-static variant of TextCNN, with pretrained embedding initialization for word embedding layer.

TextCNN + char n-grams: The word embedding layer is constructed for this approach as mentioned in 1(b). The kernel window sizes h for character tokens are $N_f = (1, 2, 3, 4, 5, 6)$ with $m = (32, 32, 32, 64, 64, 64)$ filters respectively. Increasing the number of filters further to match those of parameters in Peters et al. (2018) for character tokens led to overfitting on our datasets, and hence we reduced the parameters. All the layers are allowed to be tuned while training. The character embeddings CNN layer is initialized randomly with Xavier initialization (Glorot and Bengio, 2010). We set the character embedding layer output to 300, upon concatenation the word embedding w_{full}^{emb}

length would be 600. This model is trained in exactly similar settings as the above mentioned word based TextCNN model.

Fully Character Embeddings Model: We run VDCNN (Conneau et al., 2017) with 9 convolution layers with learning rate of 0.0001 reducing the learning rate by hald every 15 intervals for 100 epochs. We use a batch size of 64 and use stochastic gradient descent (SGD) as optimizization function with 0.9 momemtum.

BERT: For our BERT experiments we use the $BERT_{base}$ (uncased) model. $BERT_{base}$ model consists of 12 Transformer layers with 12 self-attention heads with 768 hidden dimensions and consists of 110 M total parameters. This model is trained in BookCorpus and English Wikipedia corpus. We attach a linear layer on top of $BERT_{base}$ model and the [CLS] token representation is fine-tuned on the training set. We use a binary cross-entropy loss to fine-tune BERT for our datasets. The fine tuned model is evaluated on the test set. We experimented with dropout values set at $(0.1, 0.2)$ between the transformer encoder layers. We achieved best results at dropout of 0.2, which

---

[1] https://code.google.com/archive/p/word2vec/

Model	pre	sword	Tok	Hatespeech					W-ATT	W-TOX
				0	1	2	3	4		
fastText$_{ngrams=1}$	N	N	N	69.7	71.8	84.2	95.5	82.2	93.3	95.6
fastText$_{ngrams=1}$	Y	N	N	69.6	74.8	84.5	95.7	79.5	93.5	95.6
fastText$_{ngrams=1}$ + BERT tokentization	N	Y	Y	71.2	**83.0**	83.0	95.2	83.4	94.5	96.1
fastText$_{ngrams=1}$ + Custom BPE	N	Y	Y	66.3	72.0	74.8	73.2	72.4	81.5	84.6
fastText$_{ngrams=2}$ + subword $(2-6)$	N	Y	N	64.3	71.2	75.9	92.2	85.7*	93.1	95.8
fastText$_{ngrams=2}$ + subword $(2-6)$ + BERT tok	N	Y	Y	64.1	66.7	75.1	93.4	85.3	93.9*	95.7
fastText$_{ngrams=2}$ + subword $(2-6)$ + BERT tokentization + preE	Y	Y	N	**71.5**	76.9	**87.9**	93.2	75.7	93.4	95.8*
TextCNN (Kim, 2014)	N	N	N	69.8	76.9	85.3	95.7	**85.9**	92.8	95.6
TextCNN + Character n-grams	N	N	N	70.6	78.1	87.1	96.3	**85.9**	93.2	95.9
TextCNN + BERT tokenization	N	N	Y	**71.6**	76.8	84.2	96.6	85.2	94.1	96.2
VDCNN (9 layers)	N	N	N	65.3	71.6	80.7	89.3	85.9	91.6	93.9
BERT (dropout = 0.2)	N	N	N	72.2	80.1	85.2	**97.0**	78.2	**95.7**	**96.8**

Table 1: We report Weighted F1-scores for the different models on the Hatespeech, W-TOX and W-ATT datasets.

we report in our experiments.

5.1 BERT Wordpiece Tokenizer Model with Word models

We use Wordpiece (BPE) model of BERT (Devlin et al., 2018) pretrained on BooksCorpus and English Wikipedia, produced using 30000 merge operations. BERT uses this model as precursor before encoding the text through transformer. We try to examine the benefit of the wordpiece text encoding vs the benefit we obtain from fine-tuning the pretrained LM. We hypothesize that pretrained BPE model splits a word into most frequent subwords found in the wikipedia corpus, which can help in mining the informative subwords. The informative subwords might prove very beneficial in noisy settings where we observe missing spaces and typos. In order to achieve this, we use this pretrained BPE model for encoding the document text before inputing to our word based models, TextCNN and fastText word variant. This is demonstrated in Figure 2. We have tried following variants with BERT Wordpiece tokenization as preprocessing step.

BERT Tokenizer with fastText$_{ngrams=2}$ TextCNN Word model: We preprocess the given dataset text using pretrained BPE model, and run a fastText bigram classification model on the preprocessed output. We also evaluate the TextCNN word model with the preprocessed text as input.

BERT Tokenizer with fastText subword: The preprocessed dataset with BERT trained BPE for training fastText subword model as described in Section 5.

Custom BPE model on the dataset: We also tried to examine if we would get a similar performance boost we obtained from BERT Wordpiece model by encoding text via a custom wordpiece model trained on the text. This helps us differentiate if the gains are from training a wordpiece model on a large text or if the gains are from using subword splitting. We used 30,000 number of merge operations for the custom BPE model, which is the same as in BERT BPE to aim for a meaningful comparison. We have also tried other values of merge operations from the custom BPE model, but none have yielded substantially better performance.

6 Results and Analysis

Table 1 presents the Weighted F1 score based on the support of each of the classes in the test set for our classification task. For a classification problem with N samples in the test set and C classes, Weighted F1 score [2] is defined as

$$\frac{1}{N} \sum_{i=1}^{C} n_i * F_i \qquad (1)$$

---

[2]we use sklearn library for computing macro and weighted f1 scores in the paper `https://scikit-learn.org/stable/modules/generated/sklearn.metrics.f1_score.html`

Technique	PROCESSED DOC
Original	a complaint about your disruptive behavior here
	: https : / / en . wikipedia . org / wiki / wikipedia : administrators
	% 27 _noticeboard / incidents # disruptive_users_vandalizing_article_about_spiro_koleka
Custom BPE	complain about your disruptive behavior here
	: https : / / en . wikipedia . org / wi@ @ ki / wikipedia : administrators
	% 27 _noticeboard / incidents # disrup@ @ ti@ @ ve_@ @ user@ @ s_@ @
	vandali@ @ z@ @ ing_@ @ article_@ @ about_@ @ spi@ @ ro@ @ _@ @ ko@ @
	le@ @ ka
BERT token-ization	complain about your disrupt @ @ive behavior here
	: https : / / en . wikipedia . org / wiki / wikipedia : administrators
	% 27 _ notice @ @board / incidents # disrupt @ @ive _ users
	_ van @ @dal @ @izing @ @_ article @ @_ about @ @_ sp @ @iro @ @_ ko @ @le
	@ @ka

Table 2: Sample document split created by BERT BPE tokenizer, Custom BPE tokenizer

Model	W-ATT	W-TOX
WS (Mishra et al., 2018)	84.4	85.4
CONTEXT HS + CNG (Mishra et al., 2018)	87.4	89.3
fastText(ngrams=2)	85.2	86.8
fastText(ngrams=2, BERT BPE)	85.9	88.6
fastText(ngrams=2, BERT BPE, PreE)	**86.8**	88.6
Kim2014	82.7	88.4
Kim2014 (BERT BPE)	83.4	**89.3**
BERT (dropout = 0.2)	**89.5**	**90.6**

Table 3: Macro F1 average on the W-TOX and W-ATT datasets.

where n_i denotes the number of samples in class i. We have reported weighted F1 as the twitter data we obtained had only 17 samples for racism, with stratified CV split having only 4 samples on average. As the results on this label could be very random and prone to lot of variance due to very little number of samples in the train and test set, we choose to use weighted $F1$ over macro $F1$. We also have observed very high variance among performance in different CV splits, hence report the numbers separately on each of them.

Table 1 also mentions if each of the experiment involves using word splitting via BPE, either by pretrained BERT Wordpiece tokenization model, or by training a custom BPE model on our given dataset. We have also highlighted the individual best performance from a modeling architecture with a $*$.

Table 2 presents the Macro $F1$ score on W-ATT and W-TOX datasets. Macro $F1$ score is defined as :

$$\frac{1}{C} \sum_{i=1}^{C} F_i \qquad (2)$$

We have picked the best performing models from 1 for macro $F1$ comparison. We have also compared to previous approaches that have achieved best performance on these datasets. Mishra et al. (2018) reported Macro F1 on both validation and test data together. From their work it is unclear if the model is tuned on validation, and same data was used along with test to report numbers. Hence, we only use their number as reference. The main conclusions of these experiments are fourfold:

1. Pretrained BPE models transfer well: Pretraining a Wordpiece model on a large general corpus like wikipedia, and using this for encoding input text by splitting words has shown significant improvements for all the word based models. The fastText word model with bigrams (row 3 in table 1) trained with BERT tokenization achieves the best performance on 1st split of the hatespeech data, and also shows improvement over the native fastText bigrams model on Wiki-ATT dataset. The same observation can be made with TextCNN word model with preprocessing by pretrained BERT Wordpiece tokenization model(row 11 in Table 1). However, we have either noticed a slight degradation or an insignificant improvement by applying BPE encoding with fastText subword based model. This is expected as breaking the informative subwords from BERT into much smaller units might result in lot of noisy updates.

Predicted Label	Technique	Text
not_attack	Original	believe that he was the greatest mother-fucker in the world
*attack**	BPE	believe that he was the greatest mother## -## fuck## er in the world
not_attack	Original	many thanks for your leaving all edits alone in future with such idiotic diatribes
*attack**	BPE	many thanks for your leaving all edit## s alone in future with such idiot## ic## dia## tri## bes

Table 4: Qualitative samples from original text, and BERT Wordpiece model text. Actual label is marked with an asterisk. We can observe that BERT BPE model can effectively mine informative subwords as observed in general domain wikipedia

2. Fine tuning pretrained language models: We observe that fine-tuning large pretrained language models achieve best performance on toxicity dataset. BERT with dropout=0.2 achieves the best performance on most of the datasets and splits. It achieves better or at par performance over any word based model. Only fastText subwords and textCNN/fastText word based model trained on BERT Wordpiece tokenization preprocessing achieve higher performance compared to BERT finetuning. The gains from BERT Wordpiece tokenization model encoding to fastText word model outperforms performance of BERT model itself. We leave it as future work to further investigate the contribution from BPE Wordpiece tokenization to other classification tasks.

3. End to End Char models arent as effective as subword or word + char models: Adding character based embedding to aid word embedding based models, and subword models enhance the performance over their pure word based modeling baselines. This proves the hyptohesis of modeling at subword level definitely is beneficial for detecting abusive language. Interestingly, end to end character models arent as effective, which demonstrates the basic fact knowledge of word leads to a powerful representation, and word boundary information is still informative in noisy settings.

4. State-of-the-art performance on W-TOX and W-ATT with BERT finetuning: Table 3 shows the results for Macro $F1$ score of our models in comparison to previous approaches that have achieved best performance on these datasets. Mishra et al. (2018) reported Macro F1 on both validation and test data together. From their work it is unclear if the model is tuned on validation, and

same data was used along with test to report numbers. Hence, we only use their number as reference. We have also observed better numbers with their approach. We have achieved state of the art macro $F1$ score on W-ATT and W-TOX datasets with BERT finetuning. We have also added performance of BERT Wordpiece tokenized text with word based models for comparison, with their numbers running really close to those of BERT.

5. Effect of custom BPE model trained on the dataset: We have noticed significant performance degaradation as reported in Table 1, by tokenizing the text with custom BPE model trained on the W-ATT and W-TOX corpus, in comparison to using the original text or the BERT BPE encoded text. It's interesting to notice the text tokenized by BERT yields very informative subwords, that can help the word based model in comparison to subwords yielded by custom BPE model, even though the vocabulary size of both the models is very similar. Table 4 presents a qualitative example on how the BERT BPE mines informative subwords compared to the custom BPE model. One can note that BERT BPE model clearly splits the text on underscores extracts stem of the word in few cases.

7   Qualitative Analysis

Table 4 represents couple of examples from W-ATT dataset, where the pure word based model has failed to detect abusive language, but the model trained and tested on BERT Wordpiece tokenized text is able to detect the *attack*. As we can see, Wordpiece model trained on large wikipedia text with 30k operations(BERT) doesnt merge or create relatively uncommon word like *idiotic* from *idiot* and *ic*. This helps the model to just learn about *idiot* clearly from training set, and later use this for clear demarcation.

8 Acknowledgements

We would like to thank Kasturi Bhattacharjee and Faisal Ladhak for the time they spent in reviewing our work, and their valuable feedback and comments.

9 Conclusion and Future Work

Existing literature has shown the importance of using finer units such as character or subword units to learn better models and robust representations for identifying abusive language in social media. In this work, we explore various combinations of such word decomposition techniques and present experiments that bring new insights and/or confirm previous findings. Additionally, we study the effectiveness of large pretrained language models trained on standard text in understanding noisy user generated text. We further investigate the effectiveness of subword units ("wordpieces") learned for unsupervised language modeling can improve the performance of bag-of-words based text classification models such as fastText. We evaluate our models on Twitter hatespeeech, Wikipedia toxicity and attack datasets.

Our experiments demonstrate that encoding noisy text via BERT wordpiece tokenization model before passing it through word-based models (fastText and TextCNN) can boost the performance of word-based models and achieve state-of-the-art performance. Based on our experiments, we conclude that subword models perform competitively with character-based models and occasionally outperform them. We observe that adding character embeddings to TextCNN model can slightly boost the performance compared to word-CNN models.

Our experiments on fine-tuning BERT show improvements on both Wikipedia toxicity and attack datasets. We observe that BERT can effectively transfer pretrained information to classifying tweets and user comments despite the domain shift of pre-training on BookCorpus, Wikipedia Text . Future work in this direction could include pretraining BERT on huge collection of social media text, which might further enhance the performance of identifying abusive language on social media text. Recent work by Wiegand et al. (2019) highlights that most of the datasets that study abusive language are prone to data sampling bias and abusive language identification on realistic scenario is much harder with higher percentage of implicit content. A potential future direction would be to explore how pretrained models on generic text could incorporate or handle implicit abuse.

References

Miguel Á Álvarez-Carmona, Estefanıa Guzmán-Falcón, Manuel Montes-y Gómez, Hugo Jair Escalante, Luis Villasenor-Pineda, Verónica Reyes-Meza, and Antonio Rico-Sulayes. 2018. Overview of mex-a3t at ibereval 2018: Authorship and aggressiveness analysis in mexican spanish tweets. In *Notebook Papers of 3rd SEPLN Workshop on Evaluation of Human Language Technologies for Iberian Languages (IBEREVAL), Seville, Spain*, volume 6.

Segun Taofeek Aroyehun and Alexander Gelbukh. 2018. Aggression detection in social media: Using deep neural networks, data augmentation, and pseudo labeling. In *Proceedings of the First Workshop on Trolling, Aggression and Cyberbullying (TRAC-2018)*, pages 90–97.

Pinkesh Badjatiya, Shashank Gupta, Manish Gupta, and Vasudeva Varma. 2017. Deep learning for hate speech detection in tweets. In *Proceedings of the 26th International Conference on World Wide Web Companion*, pages 759–760. International World Wide Web Conferences Steering Committee.

Cristina Bosco, Dell'Orletta Felice, Fabio Poletto, Manuela Sanguinetti, and Tesconi Maurizio. 2018. Overview of the evalita 2018 hate speech detection task. In *EVALITA 2018-Sixth Evaluation Campaign of Natural Language Processing and Speech Tools for Italian*, volume 2263, pages 1–9. CEUR.

Justin Cheng, Cristian Danescu-Niculescu-Mizil, and Jure Leskovec. 2015. Antisocial behavior in online discussion communities. In *Ninth International AAAI Conference on Web and Social Media*.

Alexis Conneau, Holger Schwenk, Yann LeCun, and Loïc Barrault. 2017. Very deep convolutional networks for text classification. In *Proceedings of the 15th Conference of the European Chapter of the Association for Computational Linguistics, EACL 2017, Valencia, Spain, April 3-7, 2017, Volume 1: Long Papers*, pages 1107–1116.

Thomas Davidson, Dana Warmsley, Michael Macy, and Ingmar Weber. 2017. Automated hate speech detection and the problem of offensive language. In *Eleventh International AAAI Conference on Web and Social Media*.

Jacob Devlin, Ming-Wei Chang, Kenton Lee, and Kristina Toutanova. 2018. Bert: Pre-training of deep bidirectional transformers for language understanding. *arXiv preprint arXiv:1810.04805*.

Maeve Duggan. 2017. Online harassment 2017.

Xavier Glorot and Yoshua Bengio. 2010. Understanding the difficulty of training deep feedforward neural networks. In *Proceedings of the thirteenth international conference on artificial intelligence and statistics*, pages 249–256.

Edouard Grave, Tomas Mikolov, Armand Joulin, and Piotr Bojanowski. 2017. Bag of tricks for efficient text classification. In *Proceedings of the 15th Conference of the European Chapter of the Association for Computational Linguistics, EACL 2017, Valencia, Spain, April 3-7, 2017, Volume 2: Short Papers*, pages 427–431.

Yoon Kim. 2014. Convolutional neural networks for sentence classification. *arXiv preprint arXiv:1408.5882*.

Ritesh Kumar, Atul Kr Ojha, Shervin Malmasi, and Marcos Zampieri. 2018. Benchmarking aggression identification in social media. In *Proceedings of the First Workshop on Trolling, Aggression and Cyberbullying (TRAC-2018)*, pages 1–11.

Irene Kwok and Yuzhou Wang. 2013. Locate the hate: Detecting tweets against blacks. In *Twenty-seventh AAAI conference on artificial intelligence*.

Pushkar Mishra, Helen Yannakoudakis, and Ekaterina Shutova. 2018. Neural character-based composition models for abuse detection.

Sandip Modha, Prasenjit Majumder, and Thomas Mandl. 2018. Filtering aggression from multilingual social media feed. In *Proceedings of the First Workshop on Trolling, Aggression and Cyberbullying (TRAC–1), Santa Fe, USA*.

Chikashi Nobata, Joel Tetreault, Achint Thomas, Yashar Mehdad, and Yi Chang. 2016. Abusive language detection in online user content. In *Proceedings of the 25th international conference on world wide web*, pages 145–153. International World Wide Web Conferences Steering Committee.

John Pavlopoulos, Prodromos Malakasiotis, and Ion Androutsopoulos. 2017. Deep learning for user comment moderation. *arXiv preprint arXiv:1705.09993*.

Matthew Peters, Sebastian Ruder, and Noah A Smith. 2019. To tune or not to tune? adapting pretrained representations to diverse tasks. *arXiv preprint arXiv:1903.05987*.

Matthew E Peters, Mark Neumann, Mohit Iyyer, Matt Gardner, Christopher Clark, Kenton Lee, and Luke Zettlemoyer. 2018. Deep contextualized word representations. *arXiv preprint arXiv:1802.05365*.

Björn Ross, Michael Rist, Guillermo Carbonell, Benjamin Cabrera, Nils Kurowsky, and Michael Wojatzki. 2016. Measuring the Reliability of Hate Speech Annotations: The Case of the European Refugee Crisis. In *Proceedings of NLP4CMC III: 3rd Workshop on Natural Language Processing for Computer-Mediated Communication*, volume 17 of *Bochumer Linguistische Arbeitsberichte*, pages 6–9.

Magnus Sahlgren, Tim Isbister, and Fredrik Olsson. 2018. Learning representations for detecting abusive language. In *Proceedings of the 2nd Workshop on Abusive Language Online (ALW2)*, pages 115–123.

Haji Mohammad Saleem, Kelly P. Dillon, Susan Benesch, and Derek Ruths. 2017. A web of hate: Tackling hateful speech in online social spaces. *CoRR*, abs/1709.10159.

Andrew Schrock and Danah Boyd. 2011. Problematic youth interaction online: Solicitation, harassment, and cyberbullying. *Computer-mediated communication in personal relationships*, pages 368–398.

Rico Sennrich, Barry Haddow, and Alexandra Birch. 2016. Neural machine translation of rare words with subword units. In *Proceedings of the 54th Annual Meeting of the Association for Computational Linguistics, ACL 2016, August 7-12, 2016, Berlin, Germany, Volume 1: Long Papers*.

Nitish Srivastava, Geoffrey Hinton, Alex Krizhevsky, Ilya Sutskever, and Ruslan Salakhutdinov. 2014. Dropout: a simple way to prevent neural networks from overfitting. *The Journal of Machine Learning Research*, 15(1):1929–1958.

Robert S Tokunaga. 2010. Following you home from school: A critical review and synthesis of research on cyberbullying victimization. *Computers in human behavior*, 26(3):277–287.

Fabio Del Vigna, Andrea Cimino, Felice Dell'Orletta, Marinella Petrocchi, and Maurizio Tesconi. 2017. Hate me, hate me not: Hate speech detection on facebook. In *Proceedings of the First Italian Conference on Cybersecurity (ITASEC17), Venice, Italy, January 17-20, 2017.*, pages 86–95.

William Warner and Julia Hirschberg. 2012. Detecting hate speech on the world wide web. In *Proceedings of the Second Workshop on Language in Social Media*, pages 19–26. Association for Computational Linguistics.

Zeerak Waseem. 2016. Are you a racist or am i seeing things? annotator influence on hate speech detection on twitter. In *Proceedings of the first workshop on NLP and computational social science*, pages 138–142.

Zeerak Waseem and Dirk Hovy. 2016. Hateful symbols or hateful people? predictive features for hate speech detection on twitter. In *Proceedings of the NAACL student research workshop*, pages 88–93.

Michael Wiegand, Josef Ruppenhofer, and Thomas Kleinbauer. 2019. Detection of Abusive Language: the Problem of Biased Datasets. In *Proceedings of the 2019 Conference of the North American Chapter of the Association for Computational Linguistics: Human Language Technologies, Volume 1 (Long and Short Papers)*, pages 602–608.

Michael Wiegand, Melanie Siegel, and Josef Ruppenhofer. 2018. Overview of the germeval 2018 shared task on the identification of offensive language.

Nancy E Willard. 2007. *Cyberbullying and cyberthreats: Responding to the challenge of online social aggression, threats, and distress.* Research press.

Ellery Wulczyn, Nithum Thain, and Lucas Dixon. 2017. Ex machina: Personal attacks seen at scale. In *Proceedings of the 26th International Conference on World Wide Web*, pages 1391–1399. International World Wide Web Conferences Steering Committee.

Dawei Yin, Zhenzhen Xue, Liangjie Hong, Brian D Davison, April Kontostathis, and Lynne Edwards. 2009. Detection of harassment on web 2.0. *Proceedings of the Content Analysis in the WEB*, 2:1–7.

Marcos Zampieri, Shervin Malmasi, Preslav Nakov, Sara Rosenthal, Noura Farra, and Ritesh Kumar. 2019. Semeval-2019 task 6: Identifying and categorizing offensive language in social media (offenseval). *arXiv preprint arXiv:1903.08983.*

Jian Zhu, Zuoyu Tian, and Sandra Kübler. 2019. Umiu@ ling at semeval-2019 task 6: Identifying offensive tweets using bert and svms. *arXiv preprint arXiv:1904.03450.*

A Platform Agnostic Dual-Strand Hate Speech Detector

Johannes Skjeggestad Meyer and **Björn Gambäck**
Department of Computer Science
Norwegian University of Science and Technology
NO–7491 Trondheim, Norway
johannes@skmeyer.com, gamback@ntnu.no

Abstract

Hate speech detectors must be applicable across a multitude of services and platforms, and there is hence a need for detection approaches that do not depend on any information specific to a given platform. For instance, the information stored about the text's author may differ between services, and so using such data would reduce a system's general applicability. The paper thus focuses on using exclusively text-based input in the detection, in an optimised architecture combining Convolutional Neural Networks and Long Short-Term Memory-networks. The hate speech detector merges two strands with character n-grams and word embeddings to produce the final classification, and is shown to outperform comparable previous approaches.

1   Introduction

An increasing number of online arenas are becoming available for users worldwide to publish their opinions, from Internet fora and blogs, to microblog services like Twitter and social media such as Facebook and MeWe, and various chat rooms. However, in all arenas that are open to user generated content, there is a risk of some people misusing this opportunity to purposefully insult others, or even to convey hateful messages. This is often in breach of the given arena's terms and conditions, and sometimes, in some countries, illegal. Hence, there is a need for automatic detection of these messages across a multitude of online arenas, but without depending on any information specific to a given forum, so that the systems can be used across platforms without being changed.

Notably, information about the text's author, such as their usage history or their social network and activities, have been shown to be useful when categorising hate speech (Qian et al., 2018; Unsvåg and Gambäck, 2018; Mishra et al., 2018).

In particular, on some occasions, an author belonging to an exposed group may use language that would normally be considered hateful towards that group, without the statement coming through as hateful. In such cases, disregarding user information may lead to misclassifications. However, what user metadata is stored may differ between services, and so using such information reduces the general applicability of a system. The research in this paper therefore aims at avoiding any such information, using exclusively text-based input in the detection. This is accomplished through a deep learning-based architecture combining Convolutional Neural Networks and Long Short-Term Memory-networks, and by utilising both character n-grams and word embeddings as input in a dual-strand methodology.

The rest of the paper is structured as follows: Section 2 describes prior work on hate speech detection. Section 3 then introduces the data set used in the experiments and Section 4 the proposed architecture. Section 5 presents experiments and results, while Section 6 discusses those results. Finally, Section 7 concludes and presents ideas for future exploration.

2   Related Work

Research on hate speech detection has attempted many kinds of input features, and many different classification methods. In the early research, the input types used were highly language dependent, utilising specific syntax features and the presence of certain words. Later, these kinds of features were exchanged for more general text representations. Specifically, the approaches got more directed towards word- and character models, and in various alternations. Some researchers, such as Gambäck and Sikdar (2017), used both types at the same time, while others, e.g., Waseem and Hovy

Proceedings of the Third Workshop on Abusive Language Online, pages 146–156
Florence, Italy, August 1, 2019. ©2019 Association for Computational Linguistics

(2016) and Pavlopoulos et al. (2017), used only one of the types. Each kind of feature has its own advantage. The character n-gram approach is relatively resilient against misspellings, while word embeddings allow related words to produce similar output. In Mehdad and Tetreault (2016), word and character n-grams were used separately, in order to compare their performance, showing character n-grams to be more effective. Some systems, like that of Founta et al. (2018a), also apply various metadata and information about the author of the text. However, as the aim of this paper is to achieve classification more independent of the origin platform of the texts, such platform-dependent systems will largely be disregarded here.

Early research used traditional machine learning approaches, e.g., Support Vector Machines (SVMs) (Yin et al., 2009) and Naïve Bayes-based classifiers (Razavi et al., 2010). Some more recent research has also used traditional machine learning approaches, such as Logistic Regression (Waseem and Hovy, 2016). However, most recent work has focused on Deep Learning approaches: Gambäck and Sikdar (2017) and Park and Fung (2017) used Convolutional Neural Networks (CNNs), while Pavlopoulos et al. (2017) used Recurrent Neural Networks (RNNs) with Gated Recurrent Units (GRUs). Others have combined neural network-types, with Zhang et al. (2018) utilising a CNN followed by a GRU-based RNN, and Founta et al. (2018a) a two-part approach, with one part using word embeddings fed into an RNN-layer consisting of GRU-nodes, and the other, parallel part taking metadata as input to a feed-forward network.

Others have tried combining deep learners with more traditional methods: Badjatiya et al. (2017) tested both a CNN-based and a Long Short-Term Memory (LSTM)-based system (Hochreiter and Schmidhuber, 1997), in combination with Gradient Boosted Decision Trees (GBDT), while Gao et al. (2017) also used an LSTM, but running in parallel with logistic regression. In the SemEval 2019 OffensEval shared task (Zampieri et al., 2019b), the best performing systems utilised pretrained contextual embeddings such as BERT (Bidirectional Encoder Representations from Transformers; Devlin et al. 2018) and ELMo (Embeddings from Language Model; Peters et al. 2018), in essence focusing on word-level n-grams (or *word pieces* as defined in BERT).

Several hate speech detection systems have been tested on the data set from Waseem and Hovy (2016) and can thus be compared more directly. Although the SVM-Naïve Bayes classifier of Mehdad and Tetreault (2016) outperformed their RNN-based system, deep learners seem to in general perform better than purely traditional machine learning classifiers on this dataset, with the CNN-based system of Gambäck and Sikdar (2017) outperforming the Logistic Regression-based system of Waseem and Hovy (2016).

Notably, Badjatiya et al. (2017) claimed outstanding results for a hybrid system combining an LSTM with a GBDT. However, other researchers have failed to reproduce the experiments by Badjatiya et al., with Fortuna et al. (2019) indicating that Badjatiya et al.'s stated results rather were due to a faulty cross-validation process and with Mishra et al. (2018) noting that Badjatiya et al.'s decision tree-boosted version was tested on instances that the LSTM already had been trained on, leading to over-fitting.

3   Data Set

The largest data set used in research on inappropriate language is the one in Pavlopoulos et al. (2017), with 1.6 million comments from the Greek sports site *Gazzetta*. However, the labels in this data set are based on which comments the site's moderators found to be inappropriate in some way, including, but not restricted to, hate speech.

The Twitter data set from Davidson et al. (2017) is also reasonably large and could have been an interesting option, but also somewhat lacks justifications for how each sample has been labelled: Davidson et al. attempted to differentiate between hate speech and other offensive content, but relied heavily on the crowd-sourced (CrowdFlower) annotators to make the distinction.

On the other hand, Zampieri et al. (2019a), Golbeck et al. (2017), Founta et al. (2018b), and Waseem and Hovy (2016), all used extensive sets of rules when labelling their data. However, the first of those is aimed at offensive language, while the second is not straight-forwardly available.

Furthermore, although the data set of Founta et al. (2018b) is substantially larger, the older one by Waseem and Hovy (2016) has been used in more previous research, and was thus taken as the basis here, too, for reasons of easier comparison to previous results.

Version	Neutral	Racist	Sexist	Total
Original	11,559	1,972	3,383	16,914
Available	10,913	1,924	3,097	15,934

Table 1: Size of the Waseem and Hovy (2016) data set

The data set of Waseem and Hovy (2016) originally contained 16,914 tweets labelled for racism and sexism. However, 980 of these tweets had been deleted by the time the data were collected, leaving 15,934 samples. As Table 1 shows, most of the deleted tweets were from the neutral group. As this is the largest group, it is also where the impact of deletion is the smallest. The smallest group, on the other hand, is where the loss is the lowest; more than 97% of the racist-labelled tweets were still available. The group with the greatest loss relative to size, is the sexist. Even here, though, more than 91% of the tweets still remained. In total, the loss constitutes less than 6% of the original tweets.

An issue with the data set is its representativeness. One aspect of this is the relatively high percentage of hate speech, at about 30%. In the data set of Pavlopoulos et al. (2017), too, about 30% of the samples were considered inappropriate, but there the 'positive' label was not restricted to just hate speech. In contrast, a study on the Facebook-pages of two Norwegian TV channels showed that every 10th comment was hateful (Bjurstrøm, 2018), even after the media outlets had had 12 hours to moderate the debate. Similarly, Burnap and Williams (2015) found that 11% of tweets gathered in relation to a particularly hate-inducing event included offensive or antagonistic content, while Davidson et al. (2017), with a somewhat stricter definition, found 5% of their data to contain hate speech. This means that the propensity of hate speech is higher in the training data than what the system would face in real use. Furthermore, the Waseem and Hovy (2016) data was collected using bootstrapping, in particular of tweets related to an Australian TV cooking show, which could affect the results when applying a system trained on the data to arbitrary tweets.

4   Architecture

As discussed above, the input forms that have proven best for hate speech identification are word embeddings and character n-grams. Hence, the system described here uses both forms as input.

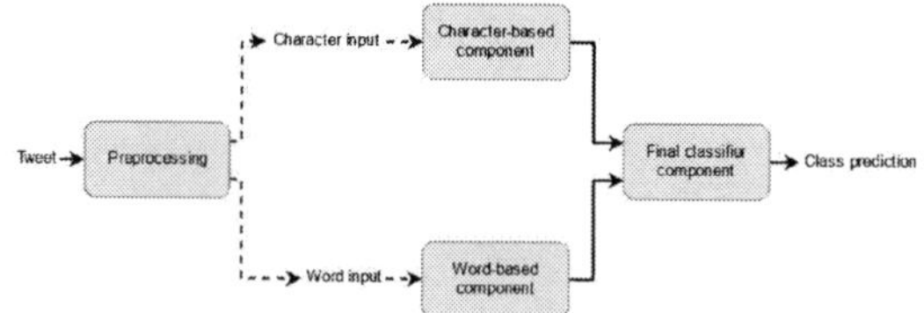

Figure 1: High-level architecture of the system

However, the character- and word-based inputs are initially treated separately, in a dual-strand approach. Specifically, the system consists of a preprocessor and three main components. Two of those work in parallel, operating on the word and character-based inputs, respectively. The last component determines the final classification by combining the output of the previous two. The high-level architecture of the system is illustrated in Figure 1. Apart from the preprocessing, the system is implemented using TensorFlow.[1]

4.1   Text Preprocessing

The text samples (tweets) are first divided into mini batches, normally containing 20 samples each. Each tweet is then treated in two disjoint ways; one to create character representations, the other to create word representations. In both cases, Özcan's *tweet-preprocessor*[2] is used.

In the character-based preprocessing, each tweet is first cleared of emojis and lowercased, with each character transformed into a one-hot vector representation (a vector of length 31, with one slot each for the 26 letters of the English alphabet, four for space, number, '#', and '@', and one slot for any character that does not fall into any of the other categories). The samples of each mini batch are then zero-padded (post-data padded with only zero-valued vectors) to the length of the longest sample of that mini batch.

In the word-based preprocessor, emojis, URLs and Twitter-mentions are replaced with placeholders. Then hashtags are split into single words at capital letters, and the texts are lowercased, with punctuation and other symbols removed, and with all symbols that are not alphanumeric replaced by a space. The tweets are tokenised by splitting on whitespaces and the remaining words are transformed into their word embedding representations, with the batch samples zero-padded.

---

[1] www.tensorflow.org
[2] pypi.python.org/pypi/
tweet-preprocessor

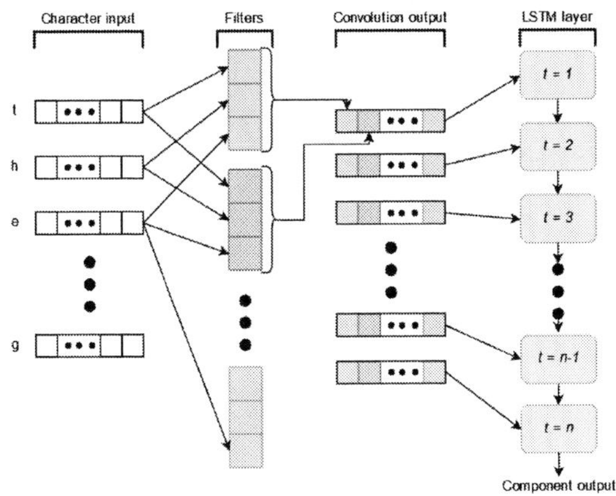

Figure 2: Character-handling component

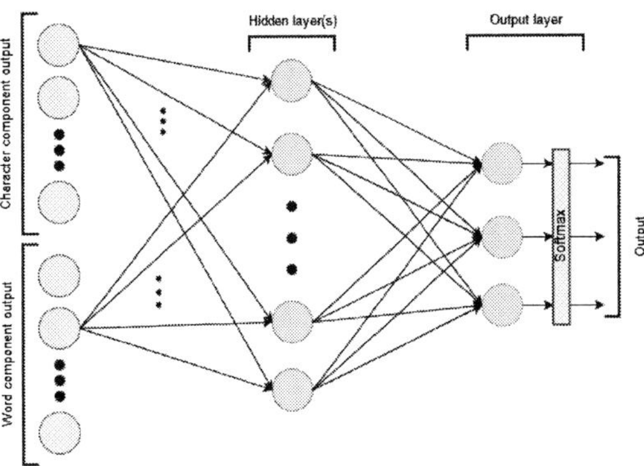

Figure 3: Architecture of the final classifier

The word embeddings used here are pretrained on external data sets, so as to avoid an additional source of overfitting due to the relatively small size of the Waseem and Hovy (2016) data set. Two different kinds of embeddings were used, word2vec (Mikolov et al., 2013) and GloVe (Pennington et al., 2014). The word2vec-embeddings have a dimensionality of 300 and were trained on about 100 billion words from the Google News data.[3] The GloVe-embeddings on the other hand, were trained on Twitter, using 2 billion tweets.[4] The highest available dimensionality, 200, was used. Out of Vocabulary words were given a random value of corresponding dimensionality.

4.2 Word Input Component

The part of the system working on the word-based input, i.e., on word embeddings, is in the form of a Long Short-Term Memory (LSTM) network. The architecture allows for both unidirectional and bidirectional LSTM. The component's output for each sample should be the output state of the LSTM at the sample's last *relevant* (non-zero) time step. This is extracted by finding the non-padded lengths of the different samples, and collecting the LSTM-output at the time step corresponding to the last element.

4.3 Character Input Component

The character-based portion of the system is divided into two parts; one convolutional and one recurrent, as shown in Figure 2. The architecture is inspired by that of Zhou et al. (2015) in how it combines these two elements.

---

[3]`code.google.com/archive/p/word2vec/`
[4]`nlp.stanford.edu/projects/glove/`

The first part takes the input and performs a 1-dimensional convolution, using multiple filters of size n, essentially treating the input as character n-grams. The output of this convolution is sorted by locations in the input, so that results of different filters at any given location appear together. This way, the results of the convolutions imitate the time steps of an LSTM. The architecture allows for several layers of convolution.

In the second part of the component, the results of the convolution are input to an LSTM. The sample lengths of the LSTM are calculated from the output of the convolutions and used to extract the component output.

4.4 Final Classifying Component

Since different input samples vary in length, the above two components have to treat irregularity in input size, but the final component requires fixed-size inputs. Consequently, the outputs at the last relevant (last non-zero) time step for each of the first two components are combined by merging the two output vectors of each sample, with the result fed into a fully connected, feed-forward network, as Figure 3 shows. Note that the input layer simply provides data for subsequent layers, without applying any activation function.

In the output layer, the network has one node for each possible label (sexist, racist and neutral). The hidden nodes use Rectified Linear Unit (ReLU) as activation, but the output layer uses linear activation, with the weighted sum of a node's inputs used directly as output. This is run through a softmax layer, returning a probability distribution on which class a sample belongs to.

4.5 Training

The classification error of a sample during system training is calculated using cross entropy. The gradients of each weight's contributions to these losses are then calculated. After this, the gradients of the entire mini batch are accumulated, and used to update the system's weights according to the Adam optimiser (Kingma and Ba, 2014).

In order to avoid overfitting the network to the training data, some regularisation is necessary. The primary means of regularisation in this system is dropout (Srivastava et al., 2014), which is applied to the dense layers of the final component, as well as the LSTMs of the character- and word-based components. In the LSTMs, the dropout nodes vary from one time step to the next, and no dropout is applied to the states of the LSTM. In addition, the system uses L^2-regularisation, with the L^2-penalty calculated using all non-bias weights in the system, then added to the cross entropy classification error. Furthermore, the system uses early stopping, so that the training does not continue for too long. Combined, these three regularisers reduce overfitting in the system, thus increasing its general applicability.

In the experiments below, the hyperparameters of the Adam optimiser had the values suggested by Kingma and Ba (2014). The probability of "switching off" nodes due to dropout was set to 0.5, in accordance to the suggestions of Srivastava et al. (2014). All experiments were run using 10-fold cross validation, with stratified folds and size 20 mini batches.

5 Experiments and Results

To determine the optimal configurations of the system described above, experiments were carried out with varying layer sizes of the neural networks, as well as varying *number* of layers used in the different components. In addition, the system was tested using both bidirectional and unidirectional LSTMs.

In order to evaluate the effects of the variations consistently, the sizes of the word-based and the character-based components were changed separately. That is, when the sizes of the character-based component were changed, the word-based part was kept constant, and vice versa. This was done so that the best configuration of each component could be found independently, reducing the number of configurations to explore.

As for variations in the number of layers, these were, for similar reasons, also made independently by component. Furthermore, in the character-based component, the number of convolutional and LSTM layers were changed separately. In the experiments with changes to the convolution, variations in the length of the convolutional filters were also made.

In addition, the system was tested using only character-based input, in order to evaluate the effectiveness of the CNN-LSTM combination on the character input. For comparative purposes, only using word-based input was also tested, disabling the character-based component.

Beyond varying the setup configurations of the network itself, the effects of using different word embeddings were explored.

5.1 System Configuration Experiments

The first experiments separately tested variations to the components, with the unmodified part forming a baseline setup. In the first half of these experiments, each kind of nodes had one layer. Hence, the character-based component had one convolutional layer, followed by one LSTM layer; the word-based component had one LSTM layer; and the dense, feed-forward part had one hidden layer.

In the baseline system, the word-based component had one layer of 150 LSTM nodes. This dimensionality was chosen because it reduces the number of dimensions from the word embeddings, going down to half the size in the case of word2vec, without decimating the information carried through.

The convolutional layer in the character-based part had 64 filters of length 3. The filter length here denotes the n in the character n-grams. This was set to 3 as trigrams have proven useful in prior work (Waseem and Hovy, 2016; Mehdad and Tetreault, 2016). 64 convolution filters were used since 64 is a power of 2 approximately twice the length of the character vectors. As such, it is significantly greater than the character vector size, while at the same time smaller than the size of each filter (i.e., 3×31).

The character-based component's LSTM layer had 100 nodes, a number chosen to balance the impact of the word- and character-based components on the final classifier, and since it should not be too much higher than the dimensionality of the convolution output (i.e., the number of filters used

Character		Word	Unidirectional LSTM			Bi-LSTM
Filters	LSTM	LSTM	P	R	F_1	F_1
64	100	150	79.12	**75.87**	**77.46**	**77.46**
100	100	150	79.06	74.90	76.93	77.08
50	50	150	79.42	74.94	77.11	77.31
512	256	150	79.59	75.24	77.35	77.06
64	100	50	**79.87**	74.58	77.13	77.11
64	100	100	79.30	74.67	76.92	77.04
64	100	200	79.10	75.38	77.20	77.21
64	100	250	79.24	74.67	76.89	77.10

Table 2: System configuration experiments.

Layer 1		Layer 2		P	R	F_1
Filters	Length	Filters	Length			
64	3	—	—	79.50	77.33	78.40
64	4	—	—	80.53	76.03	78.22
64	3	64	3	80.45	76.18	78.26
64	3	128	3	79.88	76.58	78.19
128	3	64	3	79.40	76.75	78.05
64	3	64	4	80.01	76.93	78.44
64	3	128	4	79.71	76.20	77.92
128	3	64	4	80.00	76.07	77.98
64	4	64	3	80.51	**77.73**	**79.10**
64	4	128	3	80.35	76.88	78.58
128	4	64	3	80.48	76.12	78.24
64	4	64	4	**80.57**	76.34	78.40
64	4	128	4	79.72	76.89	78.28
128	4	64	4	79.55	76.84	78.17

Table 3: Varying the convolutional segment of the character-based component. The setup columns show the number of filters at each consecutive layer, along with their corresponding filter lengths.

in the convolution). Hence, the final component had 250 input elements (150 from the word-based part and 100 from the character-based) and three output nodes; one for each class. Basheer and Hajmeer (2000) suggest that the number of nodes in a hidden layer should be between the numbers of input and output nodes. While such rules are not entirely reliable, the hidden layer size was set to 120; near the average of the input and output sizes.

In addition, the bidirectional version of this baseline configuration was tested, with each direction of the LSTMs having the dimensionality described above, thus giving the input to the final component twice the number of dimensions of the unidirectional case, so the hidden layer dimensionality was doubled.

The system was then tested with varying configurations in the character-based component, using 100 convolutional filters along with the 100 dimensions of the character LSTM. Then, the size was first cut down to 50 for both number of filters and LSTM layer size, and then increased to 512 filters and an LSTM layer size of 256. Finally, experiments were performed where the dimensionality of the word-based component was changed, while the character-based part had the default configuration, running the system with word-LSTM sizes of 50, 100, 200 and 250, respectively.

The results are shown in Table 2, for both the uni- and bidirectional configuration versions (only unidirectional precision and recall values are displayed, since the Bi-LSTM performance did not vary substantially). As the table shows, the baseline setup (row 1) worked best in terms of both recall and F_1-score. Several other configurations had better precision, such as the version where the word-based, unidirectional LSTM had a layer size of 50, but the corresponding recall values were comparatively lower than in the baseline setup.

In these first experiments, the coefficient restricting the impact of the L^2-regularisation was given the commonly used value 0.001. However, the experiments showed that smaller values gave better results, so later experiments used a value of 0.0002 for this coefficient.

5.2 Convolution Experiments

In the next group of experiments, shown in Table 3, variations were made to the convolutional part of the character-based component (hence only unidirectional LSTMs were used, not bidirectional). Specifically, the system performance with filter length 4 was tested; then, an extra layer of convolution was added, with combinations of length 3 and length 4 filters being used. The standard number of filters in these experiments was 64, with the layers using a higher number having 128 filters. Next, the same three experiments were performed with the first convolutional layer using filters of length 3, and the second layer length 4. Then, the order was reversed, with the first layer filters having length 4 and the second layer length 3. Finally, the experiments were run with both layers using length 4 filters.

Since these experiments used a smaller value for the coefficient controlling L^2-regularisation, the first row of Table 3 reports a different baseline performance than row 1 in Table 2. The baseline setup still had the second highest score on recall, outperformed only by the best setup in these experiments. This configuration, with two layers of 64

Setup	P	R	F_1
Baseline setup	79.50	**77.33**	**78.40**
Two character-LSTM layers	80.21	76.20	78.15
Two character-LSTM layers, bidirectional	79.73	76.59	78.13
Two word-LSTM layers	79.61	76.31	77.92
Two word-LSTM layers, bidirectional	79.69	76.38	78.00
Two convolutional layers ($64 \times 3, 64 \times 3$) and two character-LSTM layers	79.39	76.09	77.71
Two convolutional layers ($64 \times 4, 64 \times 3$) and two character-LSTM layers	**80.29**	76.36	78.27
Two LSTM layers each	79.40	76.38	77.86

Table 4: Using multiple LSTM layers

Setup	P	R	F_1
Baseline setup	79.50	77.33	78.40
Baseline, characters only	**81.38**	77.18	**79.23**
Two conv. layers ($64 \times 4, 64 \times 3$)	80.51	77.73	79.10
Two conv. layers ($64 \times 4, 64 \times 3$), char. only	80.23	**77.84**	79.01
Baseline, words only	79.99	77.07	78.50

Table 5: Using only character or only word input

convolutional filters where the first layer's filters were of length 4, and the second layer's of length 3, had a substantially better performance than the rest of the setups.

5.3 Two-layer LSTM Experiments

In addition to multilayer convolution, configurations using two-layer LSTMs were tested, with two same-sized layers in the LSTM part of the word- and character-based components, respectively. First, the character-based component's LSTM was given two layers of size 100, with the rest of the system having the settings of the baseline configuration. Then two 150-dimensional LSTM layers in the word-based component were used, reverting the character-based component back to the baseline.

Further, the system was tested with both two convolutional layers *and* two LSTM layers in the character-based part, trying two settings of the convolutional section, one 'baseline-like' with the two convolutional layers each having 64 filters all of length 3, and the other version being the one which performed best in the convolution experiments above, i.e., two layers of 64 convolutional filters, with the first layer's filters having length 4, and the second layer's length 3.

Finally, the baseline configuration was expanded to two LSTM layers in each of the system components holding LSTMs.

Table 4 shows the results and also includes the performance of the baseline setup, for comparison. Using two unidirectional LSTM layers in the character-based component of the baseline system setup and on the optimal convolution configuration (i.e., with filters of length 4 in the first convolutional layer) showed marked precision increases. However, recall in those cases was significantly weaker than in the baseline setup. Similar results, but with less marked precision increase,

were found when using two LSTM layers in the word-based part, as well as in the bidirectional setup versions, and the equivalent two-character LSTM. Using two convolutional layers with all filters at length 3 and using two LSTM layers in each of the system components, gave lower precision than the baseline.

5.4 Single Component Experiments

Finally, the baseline setup was used, with one convolutional layer and one LSTM layer, but with the word-based LSTM removed and the dense layer reduced to 50 nodes. Then the equivalent was done using the best-performing configuration above, the system having two convolutional layers of 64 filters each, with lengths 4 and 3. For comparison, the system was then tested using just the word-based input. Here, too, the baseline setup was used as the starting point, meaning one LSTM layer of size 150.

The results are shown in Table 5. Interestingly, both of the character-only systems outperformed the baseline. Furthermore, the characters-only version of the baseline setup showed the highest precision of all the experiments in this research. As for the characters-only version of the configuration with two convolutional layers, the recall was higher than in the version including word-based input, but the precision was lower. Notably, it still outperformed the word-inclusive baseline setup on all measures. The word-only configuration was outperformed by the character-only systems, but still performed better than the baseline using all inputs.

All the above experiments utilised pretrained word2vec embeddings. For comparison, the baseline and optimal configurations were also evaluated using GloVe embeddings. In terms of F_1-score, both of the tested configurations improved when changing to GloVe. The baseline setup improved on all measures, though the improvement in precision was very slight. In the configuration with two convolutional layers, the precision got worse when changing to GloVe-embeddings. However, the recall of this setup using GloVe was the highest recorded throughout this research (78.28), outperforming the second best (the same configuration with the word-based component disabled) by more than 0.4%. In addition, the precision, while lower than the equivalent word2vec-performance, was still acceptably high (80.22). Hence, the resulting macro average F_1-score was 79.24 (84.14 micro average), which is higher than any other configuration in these experiments.

6 Discussion

The experimental results showed several consistencies. Notably, the recall values of all system configurations were lower than the corresponding precision. Furthermore, the recall had much greater variations between the different classes. Specifically, all the setups had the best performance on the recall of neutral samples, and the worst on sexist. The recall of sexist samples was also where the main difference from the change in value of the L^2-coefficient occurred. Using the original value of this coefficient, the recall on sexist samples was mostly in the range 53–58%, whereas with a lower coefficient value, the averages were mainly in the range 60–65%.

In general, the performance on neutral samples was the most stable. The performance on the sexist class was mainly higher than on the racist one, although they tended to display opposite variations, so that when one class performed better, the other performed worse.

As Table 5 shows, using only one type of input in the default setting improved performance compared to using both. This is likely due to a difference in convergence rates between the two strands of the system, similar to the findings of Founta et al. (2018a). Word embeddings are inherently more informative than the one-hot vectors used for character input, and so the word-based strand is likely to have a significantly higher convergence rate than the character-based one. Such a discrepancy in convergence rates may cause one of the strands to dominate the other, hampering the training and resulting in an overall suboptimal performance. This issue may also have affected the experiments on variations in layer sizes and number of layers, as changes in the size of a system component will change its rate of convergence. These variations would work to the advantage of some

	System	P	R	F_1
macro avg	64×4, 64×3, GloVe	80.22	**78.28**	**79.24**
	Waseem and Hovy (2016)	72.87	77.75	73.89
	Waseem (2016), multiclass	—	—	53.43
	Waseem (2016), binary	—	—	70.05
	Gambäck and Sikdar (2017)	**85.66**	72.14	78.29
	Fortuna et al. (2019)	—	—	78
weighted / micro avg	64×4, 64×3, GloVe	**84.14**	84.14	**84.14**
	Zhang et al. (2018)	—	—	82
	Park and Fung (2017)	82.7	82.7	82.7
	Founta et al. (2018a)	84	83	83
	Badjatiya et al. (2017)	83.9	84.0	83.9
	Mishra et al. (2018) (WS)	82.86	83.10	82.37
	Mishra et al. (2018) (LR)	84.07	**84.31**	83.81
	Mishra et al. (2018) (HS)	83.50	83.71	83.54

Table 6: System performance comparison

configurations and the disadvantage of others. The results indicate that this may be the case. However, they are not sufficient to draw a conclusion.

The difference in performance between using word2vec- and GloVe-embeddings may to some extent be explained by the fact that the word2vec-embeddings were trained after removing stop words from the training data. Hence, in word2vec-embeddings, the stop words were considered Out of Vocabulary terms and given a random value. With the average number of words in the samples being 15, the impact of not having a meaningful representation of stop words could be significant. GloVe-embeddings, on the other hand, include representations of typical stop words, and thus have an advantage in the classification.

Several other researchers have tested their hate speech detection systems on the Waseem and Hovy (2016) data set. Table 6 shows the performance of some of these. Note though that Waseem (2016) introduced another, but related, data set, which Gambäck and Sikdar (2017) used, while Park and Fung (2017) combined both data sets.

A problem with the results shown in Table 6 is that different papers have used different methods to calculate the performance, with some using micro averaging (or weighted macro averaging) and others macro averages. Hence, Table 6 includes both the macro and micro averaged performance of the optimal configuration found in Section 5 (GloVe-embeddings and two convolutional layers with 64 filters of lengths 4 and 3, respectively).

As the macro averaged performance (upper part of Table 6) shows, the system using the optimal configuration with two convolutional layers and

GloVe-embeddings outperformed the Waseem and Hovy (2016) system, and also had a higher performance, in terms of F_1-score, than the system of Gambäck and Sikdar (2017). However, since that paper utilised a slightly different data set, the comparison is not entirely valid. In the case of the system introduced by Waseem (2016), the approach described in Section 4 performed significantly better, particularly compared to the multiclass version — although these results are not for the primary data set of Waseem (2016), which had markedly higher performance.

Based on micro averaged performance values, the system clearly outperforms those of Zhang et al. (2018) and Park and Fung (2017). It also outperforms the system of Founta et al. (2018a), when this is restricted to using text as input, and the best non-GBDT version reported by Badjatiya et al. (2017). However, since Badjatiya et al.'s GBDT performance and cross-validation have been found to be questionable, the row labelled Fortuna et al. (2019) gives the macro average results Fortuna et al. reported obtaining using the Badjatiya et al. (2017) system with decision tree boosting.

Furthermore, Mishra et al. (2018) reimplemented three other systems in order to use as baselines for testing the improvements that could be obtained when utilising author profiling features. Hence, Mishra et al. (2018) (WS; "word-sum") is essentially a reproduction of Badjatiya et al.'s results, but with a slightly different setup, while Mishra et al. (2018) (LR) reproduces the LR-based approach taken by Waseem and Hovy (2016), and Mishra et al. (2018) (HS, "hidden-state") is their implementation of the RNN approach used by Pavlopoulos et al. (2017).

7 Conclusion and Future Work

The dual-stranded CNN-LSTM combination for hate speech detection outlined here, which uses both word embeddings and character n-grams as input, performed relatively well on the Waseem and Hovy (2016) data set. Specifically, the system did well when using two layers of convolution on the character input, with diminishing filter lengths, combined with single layer LSTMs in both strands. Using multiple layers of LSTMs, on the other hand, actually reduced performance. With a macro averaged F_1-score of 79.24, the architecture performed better than all comparable, state-of-the-art systems on the data set.

It is possible that the different convergence rates in the architecture's word-based and character-based components may have reduced performance. A way to avoid this could be to train the system using an interleaving technique, as done by Founta et al. (2018a) — or take the similar multitask learning approach suggested by Waseem et al. (2018) — so that only one of the two parallel system components is trained at any given time.

Another idea for further research would be to test the impact of using the architecture described here in combination with other top-level classifiers, such as the Gradient Boosted Decision Trees used by Badjatiya et al. (2017). It could also be interesting to investigate utilising dynamic convolutions for classifying hate speech, since Wu et al. (2019) report those as out-performing approaches based on self-attention, such as BERT (Devlin et al., 2018), on some other language processing tasks.

Acknowledgements

Thanks to Zeerak Waseem and Dirk Hovy for providing the data set used here — and to all other researchers and annotators who contribute publicly available data.

Thanks also to all the anonymous reviewers for many useful comments, and to Elise Fehn Unsvåg, Vebjørn Isaksen, Steve Durairaj Swamy, Anupam Jamatia, and Amitava Das for many insightful discussions and experiments on hate speech detection approaches, features and data sets.

References

Pinkesh Badjatiya, Shashank Gupta, Manish Gupta, and Vasudeva Varma. 2017. Deep learning for hate speech detection in tweets. In *Proceedings of the 26th International Conference on World Wide Web Companion*, pages 759–760, Perth, Australia. International World Wide Web Conferences Steering Committee.

Imad A. Basheer and Maha Hajmeer. 2000. Artificial neural networks: Fundamentals, computing, design, and application. *Journal of Microbiological Methods*, 43(1):3 – 31.

Hanne Bjurstrøm. 2018. Hatefulle ytringer i offentlig debatt på nett (Hateful utterances in public debates on the Internet). Likestillings- og diskrimineringsombudet, Norwegian Government, Oslo, Norway.

Pete Burnap and Matthew L. Williams. 2015. Cyber hate speech on Twitter: An application of machine classification and statistical modeling for policy and decision making. *Policy & Internet*, 7(2):223–242.

Thomas Davidson, Dana Warmsley, Michael W. Macy, and Ingmar Weber. 2017. Automated hate speech detection and the problem of offensive language. In *Proceedings of the 11th International Conference on Web and Social Media*, pages 512–515, Montréal, Québec, Canada. AAAI Press.

Jacob Devlin, Ming-Wei Chang, Kenton Lee, and Kristina Toutanova. 2018. BERT: pre-training of deep bidirectional transformers for language understanding. *CoRR*, abs/1810.04805.

Paula Fortuna, Juan Soler-Company, and Nunes Sérgio. 2019. Stop PropagHate at SemEval-2019 Tasks 5 and 6: Are abusive language classification results reproducible? In *Proceedings of the 13th International Workshop on Semantic Evaluation (SemEval)*, pages 741–748, Minneapolis, Minnesota, USA. ACL.

Antigoni-Maria Founta, Despoina Chatzakou, Nicolas Kourtellis, Jeremy Blackburn, Athena Vakali, and Ilias Leontiadis. 2018a. A unified deep learning architecture for abuse detection. *CoRR*, abs/1802.00385.

Antigoni-Maria Founta, Constantinos Djouvas, Despoina Chatzakou, Ilias Leontiadis, Jeremy Blackburn, Gianluca Stringhini, Athena Vakali, Michael Sirivianos, and Nicolas Kourtellis. 2018b. Large scale crowdsourcing and characterization of Twitter abusive behavior. In *Proceedings of the 12th International Conference on Web and Social Media*, pages 491–500, Stanford, California, USA. AAAI Press.

Björn Gambäck and Utpal Kumar Sikdar. 2017. Using convolutional neural networks to classify hate-speech. In *Proceedings of the 1st Workshop on Abusive Language Online*, pages 85–90, Vancouver, Canada. ACL.

Lei Gao, Alexis Kuppersmith, and Ruihong Huang. 2017. Recognizing explicit and implicit hate speech using a weakly supervised two-path bootstrapping approach. In *Proceedings of the 8th International Joint Conference on Natural Language Processing*, volume 1: Long Papers, pages 774–782, Taipei, Taiwan. AFNLP.

Jennifer Golbeck, Zahra Ashktorab, Rashad O. Banjo, Alexandra Berlinger, Siddharth Bhagwan, Cody Buntain, Paul Cheakalos, Alicia A. Geller, Quint Gergory, Rajesh Kumar Gnanasekaran, Raja Rajan Gunasekaran, Kelly M. Hoffman, Jenny Hottle, Vichita Jienjitlert, Shivika Khare, Ryan Lau, Marianna J. Martindale, Shalmali Naik, Heather L. Nixon, Piyush Ramachandran, Kristine M. Rogers, Lisa Rogers, Meghna Sardana Sarin, Gaurav Shahane, Jayanee Thanki, Priyanka Vengataraman, Zijian Wan, and Derek Michael Wu. 2017. A large labeled corpus for online harassment research. In *Proceedings of the 2017 ACM on Web Science Conference*, pages 229–233, Troy, New York, USA. ACM.

Sepp Hochreiter and Jürgen Schmidhuber. 1997. Long short-term memory. *Neural Computation*, 9(8):1735–1780.

Diederik P. Kingma and Jimmy Ba. 2014. Adam: A method for stochastic optimization. *CoRR*, abs/1412.6980.

Yashar Mehdad and Joel Tetreault. 2016. Do characters abuse more than words? In *Proceedings of the 17th Annual Meeting of the Special Interest Group on Discourse and Dialogue*, pages 299–303, Los Angeles, California, USA. ACL.

Tomas Mikolov, Kai Chen, Greg Corrado, and Jeffrey Dean. 2013. Efficient estimation of word representations in vector space. *CoRR*, abs/1301.3781.

Pushkar Mishra, Marco Del Tredici, Helen Yannakoudakis, and Ekaterina Shutova. 2018. Author profiling for abuse detection. In *Proceedings of the 27th International Conference on Computational Linguistics*, pages 1088–1098, Santa Fe, New Mexico, USA. ACL.

Ji Ho Park and Pascale Fung. 2017. One-step and two-step classification for abusive language detection on Twitter. In *Proceedings of the 1st Workshop on Abusive Language Online*, pages 41–45, Vancouver, Canada. ACL.

John Pavlopoulos, Prodromos Malakasiotis, and Ion Androutsopoulos. 2017. Deep learning for user comment moderation. In *Proceedings of the 1st Workshop on Abusive Language Online*, pages 25–35, Vancouver, Canada. ACL.

Jeffrey Pennington, Richard Socher, and Christopher D. Manning. 2014. GloVe: Global vectors for word representation. In *Proceedings of the Conference on Empirical Methods in Natural Language Processing*, pages 1532–1543, Doha, Qatar. ACL.

Matthew E. Peters, Mark Neumann, Mohit Iyyer, Matt Gardner, Christopher Clark, Kenton Lee, and Luke Zettlemoyer. 2018. Deep contextualized word representations. In *Proceedings of the 2018 Conference of the North American Chapter of the Association for Computational Linguistics: Human Language Technologies*, volume 1 (Long Papers), pages 2227–2237, New Orleans, Louisiana, USA. ACL.

Jing Qian, Mai ElSherief, Elizabeth Belding, and William Yang Wang. 2018. Leveraging intra-user and inter-user representation learning for automated hate speech detection. In *Proceedings of the 2018 Conference of the North American Chapter of the Association for Computational Linguistics: Human Language Technologies*, volume 2 (Short Papers), pages 118–123, New Orleans, Louisiana, USA. ACL.

Amir H. Razavi, Diana Inkpen, Sasha Uritsky, and Stan Matwin. 2010. Offensive language detection using multi-level classification. In *Advances in Artificial Intelligence: Proceedings of the 23rd Canadian Conference on Artificial Intelligence, Canadian AI 2010*, pages 16–27, Ottawa, Canada. Springer.

Nitish Srivastava, Geoffrey Hinton, Alex Krizhevsky, Ilya Sutskever, and Ruslan Salakhutdinov. 2014. Dropout: A simple way to prevent neural networks from overfitting. *The Journal of Machine Learning Research*, 15(1):1929–1958.

Elise Fehn Unsvåg and Björn Gambäck. 2018. The effects of user features on Twitter hate speech detection. In *Proceedings of the 2nd Workshop on Abusive Language Online*, pages 75–85, Brussels, Belgium. ACL.

Zeerak Waseem. 2016. Are you a racist or am I seeing things? Annotator influence on hate speech detection on Twitter. In *Proceedings of the First Workshop on NLP and Computational Social Science*, pages 138–142, Austin, Texas, USA. ACL.

Zeerak Waseem and Dirk Hovy. 2016. Hateful symbols or hateful people? Predictive features for hate speech detection on Twitter. In *Proceedings of the 2016 Conference of the North American Chapter of the Association for Computational Linguistics*, pages 88–93, San Diego, California, USA. ACL.

Zeerak Waseem, James Thorne, and Joachim Bingel. 2018. Bridging the gaps: Multi task learning for domain transfer of hate speech detection. In Jennifer Golbeck, editor, *Online Harassment*, pages 29–55. Springer, Cham, Switzerland.

Felix Wu, Angela Fan, Alexei Baevski, Yann N. Dauphin, and Michael Auli. 2019. Pay less attention with lightweight and dynamic convolutions. *CoRR*, abs/1901.10430.

Dawei Yin, Brian D. Davison, Zhenzhen Xue, Liangjie Hong, April Kontostathis, and Lynne Edwards. 2009. Detection of harassment on Web 2.0. Paper presented at the 'Content Analysis for the Web 2.0' Workshop at the 18th International World Wide Web Conference, WWW2009, Madrid, Spain.

Marcos Zampieri, Shervin Malmasi, Preslav Nakov, Sara Rosenthal, Noura Farra, and Ritesh Kumar. 2019a. Predicting the type and target of offensive posts in social media. In *Proceedings of the 2019 Conference of the North American Chapter of the Association for Computational Linguistics: Human Language Technologies*, pages 1415–1420, Minneapolis, Minnesota, USA. ACL.

Marcos Zampieri, Shervin Malmasi, Preslav Nakov, Sara Rosenthal, Noura Farra, and Ritesh Kumar. 2019b. SemEval-2019 Task 6: Identifying and categorizing offensive language in social media (OffensEval). In *Proceedings of the 13th International Workshop on Semantic Evaluation (SemEval)*, pages 75–86, Minneapolis, Minnesota, USA. ACL.

Ziqi Zhang, David Robinson, and Jonathan Tepper. 2018. Detecting hate speech on Twitter using a convolution-GRU based deep neural network. In *European Semantic Web Conference*, Lecture Notes in Computer Science, pages 745–760, Heraklion, Greece. Springer.

Chunting Zhou, Chonglin Sun, Zhiyuan Liu, and Francis C. M. Lau. 2015. A C-LSTM neural network for text classification. *CoRR*, abs/1511.08630.

Detecting Aggression and Toxicity using a Multi Dimension Capsule Network

Saurabh Srivastava
TCS Research
Noida, India
`sriv.saurabh@tcs.com`

Prerna Khurana
TCS Research
Noida, India
`prerna.khurana2@tcs.com`

Abstract

In the era of social media, hate speech, trolling and verbal abuse have become a common issue. We present an approach to automatically classify such statements, using a new deep learning architecture. Our model comprises of a Multi Dimension Capsule Network that generates the representation of sentences which we use for classification. We further provide an analysis of our model's interpretation of such statements. We compare the results of our model with state-of-art classification algorithms and demonstrate our model's ability. It also has the capability to handle comments that are written in both Hindi and English, which are provided in the TRAC dataset. We also compare results on Kaggle's Toxic comment classification dataset.

1 Introduction

Many people refrain from expressing themselves or giving opinions online for the fear of harassment and abuse. Twitter admitted that such behavior is resulting in users quitting from their platform and sometimes they are even forced to change their location. Due to this, combating hate speech and abusive behavior has become a high priority area for major companies like Facebook, Twitter, Youtube, and Microsoft. With an ever-increasing content on such platforms, it makes impossible to manually detect toxic comments or hate speech.

Earlier works in Capsule network based deep learning architecture to classify toxic comments have proved that these networks work well as compared to other deep learning architectures (Srivastava et al., 2018). In this paper, we investigate the performance of a multi-dimension Capsule network as opposed to using a fixed dimension Capsule network for capturing a sentence representation and we shall discuss how well it captures features necessary for classification of such sentences. For our experiments we have taken up two different datasets, namely, TRAC-1, which has comments in Hindi and English both scraped from Facebook and Twitter and, Kaggle's Toxic Comment Classification Challenge which is a multi-label classification task. In our experiments, we discovered that our model is capable of handling transliterated comments, which is another major challenge in this task. Since one of the datasets we used, TRAC-1, was crawled from public Facebook Pages and Twitter, mainly on Indian topics, hence there is a presence of code-mixed text. This type of data is more observed in a real-world scenario.

2 Related Work

Numerous machine learning methods for detection of inappropriate comments in online forums exist today. Traditional approaches include Naive Bayes classifier (Kwok and Wang, 2013)(Chen et al., 2012)(Dinakar et al., 2011), logistic regression (Waseem, 2016) (Davidson et al., 2017) (Wulczyn et al., 2017) (Burnap and L. Williams, 2015), support vector machines (Xu et al., 2012) (Dadvar et al., 2013) (Schofield and Davidson, 2017), and random forests. However, deep learning models, for instance, convolutional neural networks (Gambäck and Sikdar, 2017) (Potapova and Gordeev, 2016) and variants of recurrent neural networks (Pavlopoulos et al., 2017) (Gao and Huang, 2017)(Pitsilis et al., 2018) (Zhang et al., 2018), have shown promising results and achieved better accuracies. Recent works in Toxic comment classification (van Aken et al.) compared different deep learning and shallow approaches on datasets and proposed an ensemble model that outperforms all approaches. Further, work done by (Nikhil et al., 2018) (Kumar et al., 2018) proposed LSTMs with attention on TRAC dataset for bet-

Proceedings of the Third Workshop on Abusive Language Online, pages 157–162
Florence, Italy, August 1, 2019. ©2019 Association for Computational Linguistics

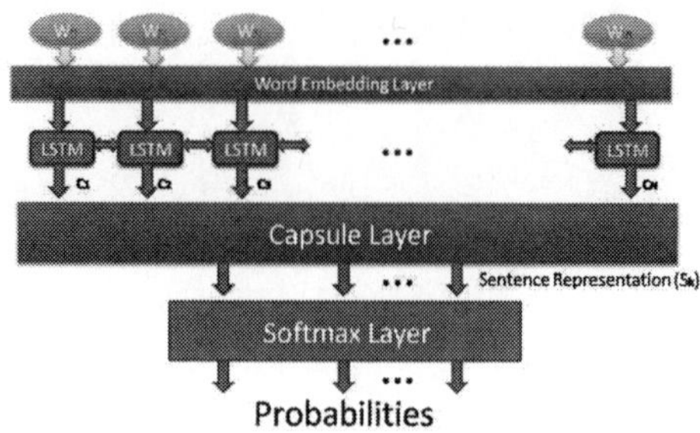

Figure 1: Multi Dimension Capsule Network

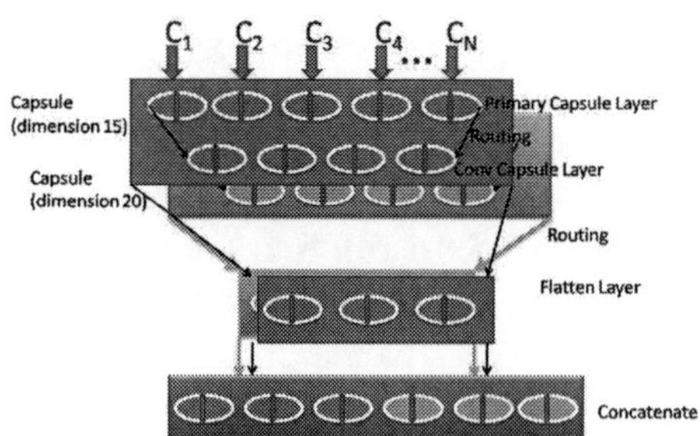

Figure 2: Capsule Layers

ter classification. Capsule networks have shown to work better on images (Sabour et al., 2017), also recently these networks have been investigated for text classification (Yang et al., 2018). (Srivastava et al., 2018) proposed a Capsule Net based classifier for both the datasets used in this study, and showed that it works better than the previous state-of-art methods. We propose to extend this work by modifying it into a multi-dimension Capsule network, taking inspiration from Multi filter CNNs (Kim, 2014a).

3 Multi Dimension Capsule Net for Classification

We describe our multi-dimension Capsule Net architecture in this section which consists primarily of 5 layers as shown in Fig 1. To get initial sentence representation, we concatenated individual word representation obtained from pretrained fast-Text embeddings (Joulin et al., 2016). The sentence representation is then passed through a feature extraction layer which consists of BiLSTM units to get a sentence representation. This representation is then passed through the Primary and Convolutional Capsule Layer to extract the high-level features of a sentence. Finally, the features are then passed through a classification layer to calculate the class probabilities.

Word Embedding Layer: To get initial sentence representation, we used a weight matrix $\mathbf{W} \in \mathbb{R}^{d_w \times |V|}$ where, d_w is the fixed vector dimension and $|V|$ is vocabulary size. The vector in column $\mathbf{w_i}$ of $\mathbf{W}$ represents lexical semantics of a word w_i obtained after pre-training an unsupervised model on a large corpus (Mikolov et al., 2013), (Pennington et al., 2014), (Joulin et al., 2016).

Feature Extraction Layer: This layer consists of BiLSTM units to capture the contextual information within words of a sentence. As proposed in (Schuster and Paliwal, 1997), we obtained both the forward and backward context of a sentence. The layer outputs $\mathbf{C_i} = [\overrightarrow{c_i}; \overleftarrow{c_i}] \in \mathbb{R}^{2 \times d_{sen}}$ for a word w_i where, $\overrightarrow{c_i}$ and $\overleftarrow{c_i}$ are forward and backward contexts (hidden activations), and d_{sen} is number of LSTM units. Finally, for all the N words, we have $\mathbf{C} = [\mathbf{C_1}, \mathbf{C_2}, ..., \mathbf{C_N}] \in \mathbb{R}^{N \times (2 \times d_{sen})}$. We have used BiLSTMs for feature extraction as opposed to CNNs which have been used as a feature extraction layer for capsules in (Yang et al., 2018) and (Sabour et al., 2017), as CNNs put forward a difficulty of choosing an optimal window size (Lai et al., 2015) which could introduce noise.

Primary Capsule Layer: In (Sabour et al., 2017) authors proposed to replace singular scalar outputs of CNNs with highly informative vectors which consist of "instantiation parameters". These parameters are supposed to capture local order of word and their semantic representation (Yang et al., 2018). We have extended the model proposed in (Srivastava et al., 2018) to capture different features from input by varying the dimension of capsules. As proposed in (Kim, 2014b). having different window size can allow us to capture N-gram features from the input, we hypothesize that by varying dimension of capsules we can capture different instantiation parameters from the input. For context vectors $\mathbf{C_i}$, we used different shared windows refer Fig 2, $\mathbf{W_b} \in \mathbf{R}^{(2 \times d_{sen}) \times d}$ to get capsules $\mathbf{p_i}$, $\mathbf{p_i} = g(\mathbf{W^b C_i})$ where, $\mathbf{g}$ is non-linear *squash* activation (Sabour et al., 2017), d is capsule dimension and d_{sen} is the number of LSTM units used to capture input features. Factor d can be used to vary a capsule's dimension which can be used to capture different instantiation parameters. The capsules are then stacked together to create a capsule feature map, $\mathbf{P} = [\mathbf{p1}, \mathbf{p2}, \mathbf{p3}, ..., \mathbf{pC}] \in \mathbb{R}^{(N \times C \times d)}$ consisting of total $N \times C$ capsules of dimension d.

Dynamic Routing algorithm was proposed in

(Sabour et al., 2017) to calculate agreement between capsules. The routing process introduces a **coupling effect** between the capsules of level (l) and (l+1) controlling the connection strengths between child and parent capsules. Output of a capsule is given by

$$\mathbf{s_j} = \sum_{i=1}^{m} \mathbf{c_{ij}} \hat{\mathbf{u}}_{j|i}; \; \hat{\mathbf{u}}_{j|i} = \mathbf{W_{ij}^s} \mathbf{u_i}$$

where, $\mathbf{c_{ij}}$ is the coupling coefficient between capsule i of layer 1 to capsule j of layer (l+1) and are determined by iterative dynamic routing, $\mathbf{W^s}$ is the shared weight matrix between the layers 1 and l+1. The routing process can be interpreted as computing soft attention between lower and higher level capsules.

Convolutional Capsule Layer: Similar to (Sabour et al., 2017) and (Yang et al., 2018), the capsules in this layer are connected to lower level capsules. The connection strengths are calculated by multiplying the input with a transformation matrix followed by the routing algorithm. The candidate parent capsule $\hat{\mathbf{u}}_{j|i}$ is computed by $\hat{\mathbf{u}}_{j|i} = \mathbf{W_{ij}^s} \mathbf{u_i}$ where, $\mathbf{u_i}$ is the child capsule and $\mathbf{W^s}$ is shared weight between capsule i and j. The coupling strength between the child-parent capsule is determined by the routing algorithm to produce the parent feature map in r iterative rounds by $\mathbf{c_{ij}} = \frac{\exp(\mathbf{b_{ij}})}{\sum_k exp(\mathbf{b_{ik}})}$. Logits $\mathbf{b_{ij}}$ which are initially same, determines how strongly the capsules j should be coupled with capsule i. The capsules are then flattened out into a single layer and then multiplied by a transformation matrix $\mathbf{W^{FC}}$ followed by routing algorithm to compute the final sentence representation ($\mathbf{s_k}$). The sentence representation is finally passed through the softmax layer to calculate the class probabilities.

4 Datasets

4.1 Kaggle Toxic Comment Classification

In 2018, Kaggle hosted a competition named Toxic Comment Classification[1]. The dataset is made of Wikipedia talk page comments and is contributed by Conversation AI. Each comment has a multi-class label, and there are a total of 6 classes, namely, toxic, severe toxic, obscene, threat, insult and identity hate. We split the data (159571 sentences) into training (90%), validation (10%) and 153164 test sentences.

[1]https://www.kaggle.com/c/jigsaw-toxic-comment-classification-challenge/data

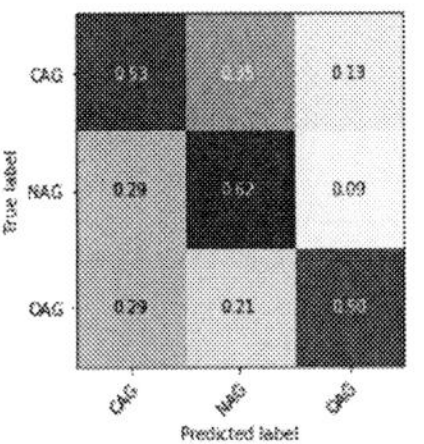

Figure 3: Confusion matrix for TRAC dataset

4.2 TRAC dataset

It is a dataset for Aggression identification[2], and contains 15,000 comments in both Hindi and English. The task is to classify the comments into the following categories, Overtly Aggressive (OAG), Covertly Aggressive (CAG), and Non-aggressive (NAG). We used the train, dev and test data as provided by the organizers of the task.

5 Experiments

As a preprocessing step, we performed case-folding of all the words and removal of punctuations. The code for tokenization was taken from (Devlin et al., 2018) which seems to properly separate the word tokens and special characters.

For training all our classification models, we have used fastText embeddings of dimension 300 trained on a common crawl. For out of vocabulary (OOV) words we initialized the embeddings randomly. For feature extraction, we used 200 LSTM units, each for capturing forward and backward contexts (total of 400). We used 20 capsules of dimension 15 and another 20 of dimension 20 for all the experiments. We kept the number of routings to be 3 as more routings could introduce overfitting. To further avoid overfitting, we adjusted the dropout values to 0.4. We used cross-entropy as the loss function and Adam as an optimizer (with default values) for all the models. We obtained all these hyperparameters values by tuning several models on the validation set and then finally selecting the model with minimum validation loss.

6 Results and Analysis

We have reported the results on a total of 3 datasets, two of which belong to TRAC-1 dataset. Our evaluation metric for TRAC-1 is F1 score, while for Kaggle dataset is ROC-AUC. We performed better for all the datasets except for TRAC Twitter data, in which our model could not beat the previous Capsule Network. We have used very

[2]https://sites.google.com/view/trac1/shared-task

Model	Kaggle Toxic Comment Classification (ROC-AUC)	TRAC Twitter English (F1-Score)	TRAC Facebook English (F1-Score)
Vanilla CNN	96.615	53.006	58.44
Bi-LSTM	97.357	54.147	61.223
Attention Networks (Raffel and Ellis, 2015)	97.425	55.67	62.404
Hierarchical CNN (Conneau et al., 2017)	97.952	53.169	58.942
Bi-LSTM with Maxpool (Lai et al., 2015)	98.209	53.391	62.02
Bi-LSTM and Logistic Regression	98.011	53.722	61.478
Pretrained LSTMs (Dai and Le, 2015)	98.05	53.166	62.9
CNN-Capsule (Yang et al., 2018)	97.888	54.82	60.09
LSTM-Capsule (Srivastava et al., 2018)	98.21	**58.6**	62.032
Our Model	**98.464**	57.953	**63.532**

Table 1: Results Of various architectures on publicly available datasets

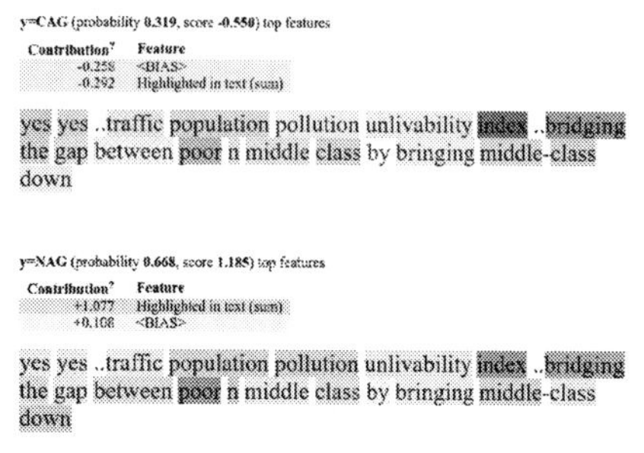

Figure 4: CAG comment predicted as NAG comment

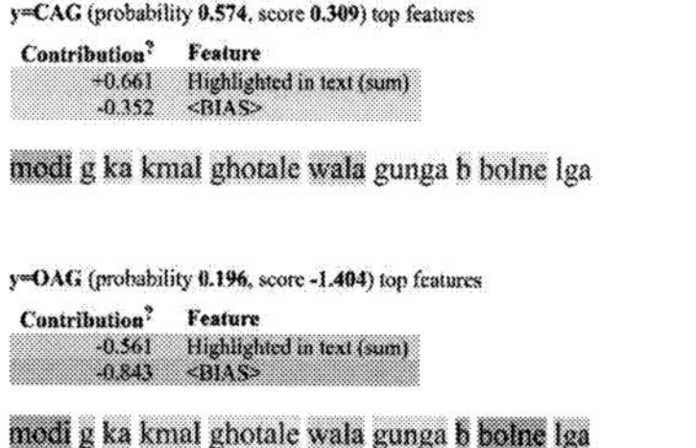

Figure 5: OAG comment predicted as CAG comment

strong and some recent baseline algorithms for comparing our results. We shall now analyze examples for which our model is making mistakes, we will pick samples from TRAC Facebook English dataset. For analysis, we use LIME (Ribeiro et al., 2016), which performs some perturbations on the input data to understand the relationship between input and the output data. It uses a local interpretable model to approximate the model in question and tries to create certain *explanations* of input data.

From the confusion matrix, we can observe that the model gets most confused by predicting CAG comments as NAG. This can be because the words used in the sentence might not sound aggressive and the model labels them as neutral sentences. However, in reality, the sentence as a whole is a sarcastic one. For example, refer to Fig 4 which goes wrong because the words it is focussing on, are all neutral words, but when combined, it is sar-

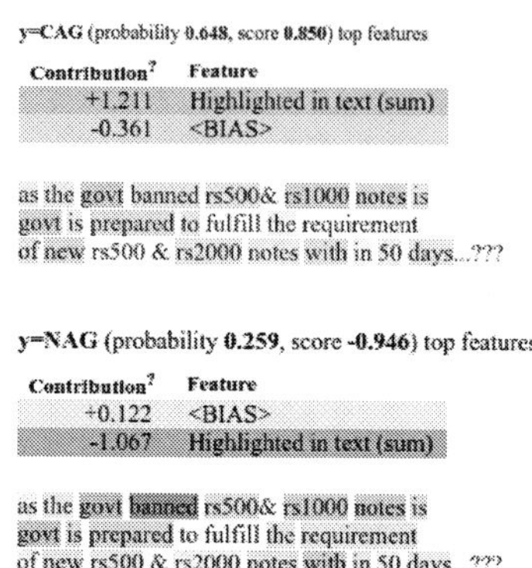

Figure 6: NAG comment predicted as OAG comment

casm on bridging the gap the between the poor and the middle class.

Secondly, the model is also incorrectly predicting NAG and OAG comments as CAG equally, this is because there are certain comments against the government which are mostly present in CAG class. Refer to Fig 6 and Fig 4, in these comments, the government or some government official is being criticized, the attack is not directly pointed and there is hidden aggression.

7   Conclusion and Future Work

We reported our results on several obvious state-of-the-art deep learning architectures and reported better results on Capsule network. We also analyzed some misclassifications made by the model and tried to reason them as well using heatmap of the weights obtained from the model. For future work, as mentioned in (Sabour et al., 2017), there can be several methods to train capsules hence, we would like to explore these methods. We also want to try different loss functions like spread loss, focal loss and margin loss. We would also like to explore competency of capsules on different NLP tasks and explore their working using different investigation techniques seen in (Yang et al., 2018).

References

Betty van Aken, Julian Risch, Ralf Krestel, and Alexander Löser. Challenges for toxic comment classification: An in-depth error analysis. In *Proceedings of the 2nd Workshop on Abusive Language Online (ALW2)*.

Pete Burnap and Matthew L. Williams. 2015. Cyber hate speech on twitter: An application of machine classification and statistical modeling for policy and decision making: Machine classification of cyber hate speech.

Ying Chen, Yilu Zhou, Sencun Zhu, and Heng Xu. 2012. Detecting offensive language in social media to protect adolescent online safety. In *2012 International Conference on Privacy, Security, Risk and Trust and 2012 International Confernece on Social Computing*, pages 71–80. IEEE.

Alexis Conneau, Douwe Kiela, Holger Schwenk, Loic Barrault, and Antoine Bordes. 2017. Supervised learning of universal sentence representations from natural language inference data. *arXiv preprint arXiv:1705.02364*.

Maral Dadvar, Dolf Trieschnigg, Roeland Ordelman, and Franciska de Jong. 2013. Improving cyberbullying detection with user context. In *Proceedings of the 35th European Conference on Advances in Information Retrieval*, ECIR.

Andrew M Dai and Quoc V Le. 2015. Semi-supervised sequence learning. In *Advances in Neural Information Processing Systems*, pages 3079–3087.

Thomas Davidson, Dana Warmsley, Michael W. Macy, and Ingmar Weber. 2017. Automated hate speech detection and the problem of offensive language. In *ICWSM*.

Jacob Devlin, Ming-Wei Chang, Kenton Lee, and Kristina Toutanova. 2018. Bert: Pre-training of deep bidirectional transformers for language understanding. *arXiv preprint arXiv:1810.04805*.

Karthik Dinakar, Roi Reichart, and Henry Lieberman. 2011. Modeling the detection of textual cyberbullying. In *fifth international AAAI conference on weblogs and social media*.

Björn Gambäck and Utpal Kumar Sikdar. 2017. Using convolutional neural networks to classify hate-speech. In *Proceedings of the First Workshop on Abusive Language Online*. Association for Computational Linguistics.

Lei Gao and Ruihong Huang. 2017. Detecting online hate speech using context aware models. In *Proceedings of the International Conference Recent Advances in Natural Language Processing, RANLP 2017*.

Armand Joulin, Edouard Grave, Piotr Bojanowski, and Tomas Mikolov. 2016. Bag of tricks for efficient text classification. *arXiv preprint arXiv:1607.01759*.

Yoon Kim. 2014a. Convolutional neural networks for sentence classification. In *Proceedings of the 2014 Conference on Empirical Methods in Natural Language Processing (EMNLP)*, Doha, Qatar. Association for Computational Linguistics.

Yoon Kim. 2014b. Convolutional neural networks for sentence classification. *arXiv preprint arXiv:1408.5882*.

Ritesh Kumar, Guggilla Bhanodai, Rajendra Pamula, and Maheshwar Reddy Chennuru. 2018. Trac-1 shared task on aggression identification: Iit(ism)@coling'18. In *Proceedings of the First Workshop on Trolling, Aggression and Cyberbullying (TRAC-2018)*, Santa Fe, New Mexico, USA. Association for Computational Linguistics.

Irene Kwok and Yuzhou Wang. 2013. Locate the hate: Detecting tweets against blacks. In *Twenty-seventh AAAI conference on artificial intelligence*.

Siwei Lai, Liheng Xu, Kang Liu, and Jun Zhao. 2015. Recurrent convolutional neural networks for text classification. In *AAAI*, volume 333, pages 2267–2273.

Tomas Mikolov, Ilya Sutskever, Kai Chen, Greg S Corrado, and Jeff Dean. 2013. Distributed representations of words and phrases and their compositionality. In *Advances in neural information processing systems*, pages 3111–3119.

Nishant Nikhil, Ramit Pahwa, Mehul Kumar Nirala, and Rohan Khilnani. 2018. Lstms with attention for aggression detection. In *Proceedings of the First Workshop on Trolling, Aggression and Cyberbullying (TRAC-2018)*.

John Pavlopoulos, Prodromos Malakasiotis, and Ion Androutsopoulos. 2017. Deep learning for user comment moderation. In *Proceedings of the First Workshop on Abusive Language Online*. Association for Computational Linguistics.

Jeffrey Pennington, Richard Socher, and Christopher Manning. 2014. Glove: Global vectors for word representation. In *Proceedings of the 2014 conference on empirical methods in natural language processing (EMNLP)*, pages 1532–1543.

Georgios K. Pitsilis, Heri Ramampiaro, and Helge Langseth. 2018. Detecting offensive language in tweets using deep learning.

Rodmonga Potapova and Denis Gordeev. 2016. Detecting state of aggression in sentences using CNN.

Colin Raffel and Daniel PW Ellis. 2015. Feedforward networks with attention can solve some long-term memory problems. *arXiv preprint arXiv:1512.08756*.

Marco Tulio Ribeiro, Sameer Singh, and Carlos Guestrin. 2016. Why should i trust you?: Explaining the predictions of any classifier. In *Proceedings of the 22nd ACM SIGKDD international conference on knowledge discovery and data mining*, pages 1135–1144. ACM.

Sara Sabour, Nicholas Frosst, and Geoffrey E Hinton. 2017. Dynamic routing between capsules. In *Advances in Neural Information Processing Systems 30*, pages 3856–3866.

Alexandra Schofield and Thomas Davidson. 2017. Identifying hate speech in social media.

Mike Schuster and Kuldip K Paliwal. 1997. Bidirectional recurrent neural networks. *IEEE Transactions on Signal Processing*, 45(11):2673–2681.

Saurabh Srivastava, Prerna Khurana, and Vartika Tewari. 2018. Identifying aggression and toxicity in comments using capsule network. In *Proceedings of the First Workshop on Trolling, Aggression and Cyberbullying (TRAC-2018)*, Santa Fe, New Mexico, USA. Association for Computational Linguistics.

Zeerak Waseem. 2016. Are you a racist or am i seeing things? annotator influence on hate speech detection on twitter. In *Proceedings of the first workshop on NLP and computational social science*, pages 138–142.

Ellery Wulczyn, Nithum Thain, and Lucas Dixon. 2017. Ex machina: Personal attacks seen at scale. WWW.

Jun-Ming Xu, Kwang-Sung Jun, Xiaojin Zhu, and Amy Bellmore. 2012. Learning from bullying traces in social media. In *Proceedings of the 2012 Conference of the North American Chapter of the Association for Computational Linguistics: Human Language Technologies*, NAACL HLT.

Min Yang, Wei Zhao, Jianbo Ye, Zeyang Lei, Zhou Zhao, and Soufei Zhang. 2018. Investigating capsule networks with dynamic routing for text classification. In *Proceedings of the 2018 Conference on Empirical Methods in Natural Language Processing*, Brussels, Belgium. Association for Computational Linguistics.

Ziqi Zhang, D Robinson, and Jonathan Tepper. 2018. Detecting hate speech on twitter using a convolution-gru based deep neural network.

An Impossible Dialogue! Nominal Utterances and Populist Rhetoric in an Italian Twitter Corpus of Hate Speech against Immigrants

Gloria Comandini
Dipartimento di Lettere e Filosofia
Università degli Studi di Trento, Italy
`gloria.comandini@unitn.it`

Viviana Patti
Dipartimento di Informatica
Università degli Studi di Torino, Italy
`patti@di.unito.it`

Abstract

The paper proposes an investigation on the role of populist themes and rhetoric in an Italian Twitter corpus of hate speech against immigrants. The corpus has been annotated with four new layers of analysis: *Nominal Utterances*, that can be seen as consistent with populist rhetoric; *In-out-group* rhetoric, a very common populist strategy to polarize public opinion; *Slogan-like nominal utterances*, that may convey the call for severe illiberal policies against immigrants; *News*, to recognize the role of newspapers (headlines or reference to articles) in the Twitter political discourse on immigration featured by hate speech. The results show that populist themes compose 1/3 of the hate speech, displaying not only In-Out-group rhetoric, but also authoritarianism, mostly carried by Slogan-like nominal utterances. It also appears that news don't convey much hate speech, while they compose almost half of the non hateful tweets.

1 Introduction

Political populism is a pervasive phenomenon observed in several different world regions and ages, but it recently gained increasing attention due to the growing electoral consensus around populist parties in many countries. Even if it is difficult for scholars to converge on a precise definition of populism, a phenomenon which is intrinsically featured by an ever-shifting nature, multifaceted national varieties and unexpected electoral trajectories (Mazzoleni, 2014), most scholars agree in defining it as an ideology considering society to be separated into two homogeneous and antagonistic groups, *the pure people* versus *the corrupt élite*, and arguing that politics should be expression of the "general will" of the people (Mudde, 2004). However, "the people" is a vague concept denoting an artificial group: on one hand, everyone can identify themselves, projecting their identity on it

(Reinemann et al., 2016; Sauer et al., 2018), on the other hand anyone can be the enemy of "the people", as they just need to be presented as hostile, dangerous and foreign to an apparently homogeneous people group. Populist rhetoric heavily relies on these themes and can be empirically understood through its communicative strategies (Kriesi, 2014). Usually, it is based on "dividing people according to national, ethnic, religious belonging or according to their gender and sexual orientation into 'good/'bad, 'us/'them or 'the élite'/'the people (Sauer et al., 2018). Thus, it is featured by an *in/out-group* rhetoric (Sauer et al., 2018), where the out-group is perceived as uniform and depicted as a threat, being also regarded as inferior (Mazzoleni and Bracciale, 2018).

Such rhetorical strategy has been observed by scholars in several political debates in different word regions and languages, from US to Italy, where political leaders exploit such dichotomy to polarize public opinion, using a repetitive discourse, simple syntax and vernacular lexicon (Wodak, 2018).

Another worrying aspect which is featuring the political discourse on social media is hate speech. Hate speech dehumanize its targets, reinforcing the sense of identity of the haters (Gagliardone, 2014). This places hate speech near the rhetorical strategies of populism: in fact, we can recognize an in-group (haters) and an out-group (hated) in hate speech too. Moreover, when hate speech is produced by leaders of populist parties, it targets a very specific group of people in order to create a scapegoat, see for instance the case of *immigrants*, having a role in several contemporary political debates.

Given such theoretical framework from social sciences, this work proposes an extension of the Italian Twitter corpus of Hate Speech (HS) against immigrants (Sanguinetti et al., 2018). This new

Proceedings of the Third Workshop on Abusive Language Online, pages 163–171
Florence, Italy, August 1, 2019. ©2019 Association for Computational Linguistics

extension, named POP-HS-IT, is oriented to offer a new dimension of analysis to understand how the political discourse on immigrants and hate speech convey populist views (RQ1), how it is conveyed by the spontaneous writings of individual citizens or by the reference to newspapers (RQ2), or eventually through slogan-like nominal utterances (RQ3).

The paper is organized as follows. In Section 2, we will present some background studies on populism and hate speech in social media and on nominal utterances. In Section 3, we will describe the *Italian Twitter Corpus of Hate Speech against Immigrants*, its original annotation scheme and the sample we analyzed, POP-HS-IT. In Section 4, we will illustrate the new annotation layers we used to investigate the relationship between populism and hate speech in POP-HS-IT, describing every layer individually and reporting information on the inter-annotator agreement. In Section 5, we will present and discuss the results of the annotation, analyzing the presence of *news* and nominal utterances, then focusing on the role of slogan-like nominal utterances and, in the end, on the dualistic constructions of *in/out-group rhetoric*. In the Conclusions results are summarized in the light of the initial RQs and some proposals of future works are discussed.

2 Background

Populism and hate speech in social media. Although there are many definitions of hate speech, for the current study we will refer to it as a language *"that is abusive, insulting, intimidating, harassing, and/or incites to violence, hatred, or discrimination. It is directed against people on the basis of their race, ethnic origin, religion, gender, age, physical condition, disability, sexual orientation, political conviction, and so forth* (Erjavec and Kovai, 2012).

In the last years, in many countries Twitter has become a very prominent online space for sharing knowledge and opinions, becoming a privileged medium also for political communication, and a powerful tool in the hands of populist leaders. In fact, social networks like Twitter are, on the one hand, "distributed, non-hierarchical and democratic" and, on the other hand, an alternative to the mainstream media, which many supporters of populist parties strongly distrust (Bartlett, 2014).

Thus, Twitter is a good ground for observing populist rhetoric, and therefore populism-driven hate speech (Mazzoleni and Bracciale, 2018). But even without populist themes, xenophobic hate speech against immigrants is consistent on Twitter. When we focus on Italy, as described in (Sanguinetti et al., 2018), in the *Italian Twitter Corpus of Hate Speech against Immigrants* 13% of the tweets have been annotated as hate speech. The phenomenon is monitored daily on the `http://mappa.controlodio.it/` platform, where its diffusion can be observed at different geographic levels of granularity (entire Italian territory, regions, provinces) (Capozzi et al., 2018).

Nominal utterances. For the annotation of nominal utterances, we will use the definition and the annotation framework of a specialistic corpus, COSMIANU (Corpus Of Social Media Italian Annotated with Nominal Utterances) (Comandini et al., 2018).

Nominal utterances (NUs), intended as syntactic declarative constructions built around a nonverbal head, are a very ancient and a very common linguistic phenomenon. In fact, we can find NUs in many ancient and current Indo-European, Slavic and Semitic languages (such as Latin, English, Spanish, French, Italian Hebrew, Arabic and Russian) as well as in Finno-Ugric and Bantu languages (Benveniste, 1990; Simone, 2013).

Some past investigations (Cresti, 1998; Landolfi et al., 2010; Garcia-Marchena, 2016) have shown that NUs occur with a moderately high frequency in spoken language. Moreover, it has been proved that NUs are very common in journalistic writings (especially in the headlines) (Mortara Garavelli, 1971; Dardano and Trifone, 2001) and in social media texts, (Ferrari, 2011; Comandini et al., 2018), which are a fertile ground for NUs. Indeed, the informal and fast nature of this kind of communication media probably makes the expression via short messages, often without any explicit hierarchical relationship, preferable.

A first experiment on the annotation of NUs in an Italian computer-mediated communication dataset is presented in (Comandini et al., 2018) and resulted in the development of the COSMIANU corpus, with 20,6% of the sentences containing an NU. A set of preliminary experiments on automatic NUs identification has been performed relying on this corpus, using an SVM classifier.

The best configuration of features analyzed (two-word window context, tokens, lemma and Part-Of-Speech) provided results that, in terms of *Precision*, *Recall*, and *F1* (79.80, 67.96, 73.40), outperformed the baseline by over 43 points (33.80, 27.13, 30.10) (Comandini et al., 2018).

Analyzing the hate speech on a Twitter corpus with NUs should provide more information about the way in which aggressive messages are conveyed by an economical, sharp and fast linguistic phenomenon. In fact, with their simple syntactic form and their inclination to assemble cumulative expressions, NUs can be seen as consistent with populist rhetoric. In this way, we could investigate the relationship between populist themes/rhetoric strategies and hate speech, identifying stylistic feature that could be useful for hate speech detection, and for the comprehension of hate speech's underlying connection with populist political discourse. This seems to be a new a new approach to hate speech's study and we are not aware of other similar researches.

3   Hate Speech Corpus Description

Our starting point is the *Italian Twitter Corpus of Hate Speech against Immigrants* (HSC henceforth) described in (Sanguinetti et al., 2018) and recently exploited in the Hate Speech Detection shared task proposed at the Evalita 2018 evaluation campaign (Bosco et al., 2018). The dataset includes Twitter messages gathered with a classical keyword-based approach by filtering the corpus using neutral keywords related to three social groups deemed as potential HS targets in the Italian context: immigrants, Muslims and Roma. The corpus has been manually annotated partly by experts and partly by Figure Eight contributors and consists of 6,928 tweets. The main feature of this corpus is its annotation scheme, designed to encode a multiplicity of factors contributing to the definition of the hate speech notion. The scheme includes, besides HS tags (no-yes), also HS intensity degree (from 1 to 4 if HS is present, and 0 otherwise), the presence of *aggressiveness* (no-weak-strong) and *offensiveness* (no-weak-strong), as well as *irony* and *stereotype* (no-yes). All the information about the inter-annotator agreement concerning these tags can be found in (Sanguinetti et al., 2018).

Sample Analyzed To investigate the role of NUs in Twitter racist hate speech and to study the re-lationship between hate speech, populist rhetoric and NUs, we selected, annotated and analyzed a sample of tweets from HSC. This sample (named POP-HS-IT henceforth) includes all the messages that convey hate speech in HSC, for a sum of 794 tweets, which has been complemented by a random selection of a proportional number of non hateful messages (949) from the same corpus, as in Figure 1 (left).

4   The New Annotation Layers

Starting from the conviction that when we study the hate speech against immigrants on Twitter, we need also to analyze its relationship with populist rhetoric, we aim at investigating, on the one hand, the general behavior of NUs in POP-HS-IT. Furthermore, since we are observing a solid presence of newspapers headlines on the tweets in POP-HS-IT, we will enrich the annotation to investigate how much of Twitter's communication about immigrants is conveyed and refers to newspaper's articles and headlines, with the twofold aim to study the way populist press is presenting these themes, and to reflect on how different communication channels interact in the discourse on immigration featured by hate speech. On the other hand, we intend to study the use of the in-group - out-group dichotomy, in order to see how populist themes are expressed in the informal written production of Twitter users and also how this relates with the expression of hate.

In order to investigate on the role of populism and nominal utterances on hate speech, in POP-HS-IT we added four new layers of analysis (*news, nominal utterances, in-group - out-group, slogans*) to those already existing (*hate speech, aggressiveness, offensiveness, irony, stereotype, intensity*). All of these novel annotations have been applied manually by at least two expert annotators (linguists, different genders) according to the scheme described below[1].

4.1   Nominal Utterances

This layer of annotation has been applied to the whole sample of tweets. It shows if a tweet contains at least one NU; thus it has a binary value (*yes* or *no*), in which *no* reveals a tweet without NUs. The tweet marked as *yes* are also annotated with

---

[1]The new guidelines for the annotation of *news, in-group - out-group* rhetoric, *slogans* and NUs can be found here: `https://github.com/GloriaComandini/Corpora`

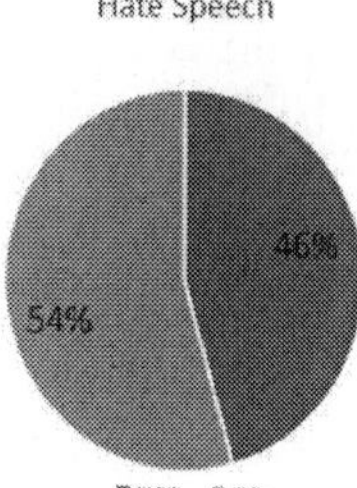

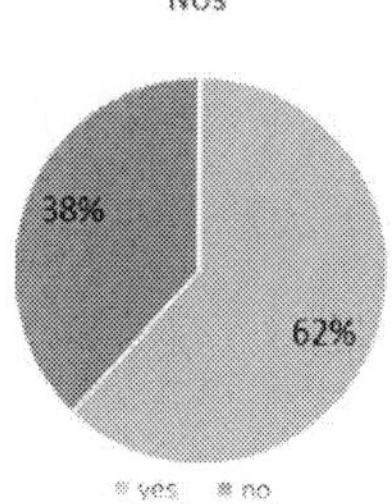

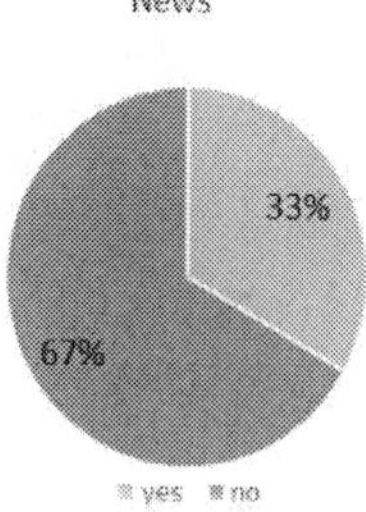

Figure 1: Distribution of hate in the initial dataset (left), including a subset of tweets from the Hate Speech Corpus (Sanguinetti et al., 2018). Distribution of the tags related to the presence of *News* (right) and *Nominal Utterances* (NUs, center) in the final version of the POP-HS-IT corpus.

the following information: number of their NUs and number of their NUs that convey hate speech.

For the annotation of NUs in the POP-HS-IT corpus, we mostly referred to the annotation framework provided for COSMIANU (Comandini et al., 2018).

However, the peculiar Italian's variety found in Twitter, non-standard and heavily filled with hashtags, links and other unique strategies of communication, made clear that some adjustments were needed.

First of all, we needed to decide how and if links, hashtags and strategies to address other users (like the use of @ + username) should have been included in the NUs. Since some links, hashtags and username addressed are an important part of the message, but without any explicit syntactical connection to the rest of the tweet, in cases like (1) and (2), they were excluded from the NU.

> (1)   #agorarai   <NU>Cavolo! </NU>[...] <NU>O solo gli italiani? </NU>@gennaromigliore
>
> (*#agorarai Heck! [...] Or only Italians? @gennaromigliore*)
>
> (2) <NU>Manco allo zoo dai </NU>https://t.co/GkkqViN7wN
>
> (*Not even at the zoo, come on https://t.co/GkkqViN7wN*)

On the contrary, hashtags well integrated in the syntactic structure of the sentence were included in the NU, as in (3).

> (3) <NU>#Roma, avviato l'iter per il superamento dei campi #rom </NU>
>
> (*#Rome, started the practice for the overcoming of #Roma's camps*)

The annotation strategy applied on POP-HS-IT is for the most part the same as in COSMIANU. We marked as NU every utterance whose main clause is non-verbal, that is to say an utterance whose main clause doesn't have a verb in a finite form. The major difference with COSMIANU's annotation framework is the treatment of subordinate clauses with a verb in a finite form: where in COSMIANU they were excluded from the extension of the NU, in this study we included them in the NU, as in (4). In fact, while in a specific study of NUs the exclusion of the verbal subordinate may be useful to an automatic recognition of NUs, in this research being able to read the full length of a NU is important for a faster comprehension of hate speech and the role of NUs in hate speech.

> (4) <NU>Un sottilissimo filo che separa una "goliardata" dal #razzismo </NU>
>
> (*A very thin line that separates a joke from racism*)

Verbal and non-verbal clauses with a coordination relation to the NU are treated in the same way as in COSMIANU, with verbal coordinates separated from the NU (see (5)) and non-verbal coordinates included in the NU (see (6)).

> (5) <NU>Casa popolare assegnata all'inquilina, </NU>ma una rom incinta la occupa...
>
> (*House for working class people assigned to the tenant, but a pregnant Roma woman occupies it...*)
>
> (6) <NU>4 nomadi arrestati per furti, colpito anche il Vicentino </NU>

(4 nomads arrested for thefts, damaged also the Vicentino)

4.2 News

This layer of annotation has also been applied to the whole sample of POP-HS-IT's tweets. Annotators had to distinguish tweets written by private users with spontaneous comments, from tweets reporting news from newspapers; thus, it has a binary value (*no- yes*). A tweet from a newspaper (or that is just the retweet of a newspaper headline), usually presents the title of the newspaper and/or a very recognizable structure, as for instance in (7):

(7) Corriere: Tangenti per gli appalti nei campi rom: chiesto il rinvio...

([The] Courier: Bribes for contracts in Roma's camps: requested the indictment)

4.3 In-group vs Out-group

This annotation has been applied only to tweets featured by hate speech. Indeed it is meant to isolate the most common theme of populism, since we assumed it was also present in hate speech. This layer has a binary value (*no-yes*), where *yes* is typical of messages like (12):

(8) L'Italia e gli italiani prima di tutto. L'Europa si faccia carico degli immigrati. L'Italia ha altri problemi da risolvere

(Italy and Italians first. It's Europe that should take on immigrants. Italy has other problems to solve)

4.4 Slogan

Also this last layer has been applied only on hate speech tweets with at least one NU, since we were interested in analyzing how NU in hate speech can convey populist slogans and a sharp adherence to a point of view, that the writer doesn't want to question or discuss (see (13)). This layer has a binary value (*no-yes*). The slogans are always NUs.

(9) <NU>RIMPATRII IMMEDIATI FORZATI </NU>

(FORCED IMMEDIATE REPATRIATIONS)

4.5 Annotation process and inter-annotator agreement

All of these novel annotations have been applied manually to the data by an expert annotator (Italian native speaker, linguist). A second independent annotation has been applied to the data for the *news* and *in-group - out-group* labels. The resulting inter-annotator agreement in terms of Cohen's kappa is 0.98 for both *news* and *in-group - out-group*. Moreover, as explained in Section 4.1, we modified the guidelines for NUs' recognition with respect to the ones used in (Comandini et al., 2018)[2]. Thus, for this task we applied a second human annotation to the 30% of the POP-HS-IT dataset. Three expert annotators were employed on different slices of the data. The resulting agreement in terms of Cohen's kappa are 0.96, 0.90 and 0.88, respectively. Disagreement has been solved by fact-checking (for the *news*) and by constructive discussion among the annotators. Figure1 shows the final distributions of the labels for the *NUs* (center) and *News* (right) annotation layers in POP-HS-IT. When we focus only on *hateful tweets* in POP-HS-IT, the final result concerning all the annotation layers applied is summarized in Table 1. Discussion of results follows.

Table 1: Distribution of the labels (*NUs*, *News*, *Slogans* and *In/Out-group* rhetoric) in the hateful tweets of the POP-HS-IT corpus. Slogans are a sub-set of NUs.

	Hateful tweets
NUs (all)	415
NUs (only slogans)	*136*
no NUs	379
New	93
no News (personal comments)	701
In-out group rhetoric	165
no In-out group rhetoric	629

5 Results and Discussion

Firstly, the investigation of the reference to newspaper's articles showed us that they compose the 33% of POP-HS-IT, as showed in Figure 1 (right). More exactly, news are remarkably prominent in non hateful tweets, while they are only a minor part of the hateful messages.

---

[2]For an in-depth description of this framework, see the annotation guidelines (in Italian) available here: `http://tiny.cc/auhvvy`

In fact, the non hateful sample (949 tweets) contains 484 news (51%) and 465 comments from single users (49%), while the hateful sample (794 tweets) exhibit only 93 news (11,71%) and 701 comments from single users (88,29%), as showed in Table 1.

So, of course in the non hateful discourse about immigration the spontaneous opinion of the single user is still very consistent, but the percentage of headlines shows us that Twitters communication on this subject is considerably featured by publishing or re-tweeting newspapers articles or headlines. On the contrary, it seems that hate speech is not particularly conveyed by references to newspaper's articles, or at least newspaper's headlines are perceived as more neutral and less hateful.

The presence of NUs is consistent in both the hateful sample and the non hateful sample, emerging in 62% of POP-HS-IT, as shown in Figure 1 (middle). However, it appears that hate speech has less NUs than non hate speech.

In references to newspaper's articles, both hateful and non hateful, NUs play a significant role. Non hate speech news (484) have 425 (87,8%) tweets with NUs and 59 (12,2%) tweets without NUs, for a total NU's number of 668 and an average of 1,57 NUs for each tweet. Similarly, hate speech news (93) (see Table 1) have 72 (77,42%) tweets with NUs and 21 (22,58%) tweets without NUs, for a total NU's number of 111 and an average of 1,54 NUs for each tweet. This results are not surprising, because NUs have already been know to be very common in newspaper's articles, and even more in articles headlines (Mortara Garavelli, 1971); but we are not aware of any other corpus-based studies on the matter.

Users' comments, both hateful and non hateful, have less NUs than newspaper's articles, and hateful comments have less NUs than non hateful comments. Non hateful tweets from single users are 465 and have 238 (51%) tweets with NUs and 227 (49%) tweets without NUs, for a total NU's number of 298 and an average of 1,31 NUs for each tweet. Hateful comments from single users are 701 (see Table 1) and have 343 (48,93%) tweets with NUs, and 358 (51,07%) tweets without NUs, for a total NU's number of 463 and an average of 1,35 NUs for each tweet.

This distribution of NUs probably means that this linguistic phenomenon is merely very common in Twitter's Italian discourse about immigration, and possibly in Twitter's Italian in general, while Italian hate speech about immigrants on Twitter doesn't rely heavily on NUs as we expected.

5.1 Nominal Utterances and Hate Speech against Immigrants

As expressed in the previous paragraphs, NUs are a stable characteristic of Twitter's Italian discussion about immigrants, and especially they are typical of newspaper's headlines (contained often in both hateful and not hateful tweets). Even if their presence is not higher in hateful tweets, still, NUs convey a significant part of hate speech: of 570 total NUs, 329 (57,72%) convey hate speech (see (10)), while 241 NUs (42,28%) convey other, non hateful meanings (see (11)). Therefore, most of the NUs in hate speech are the focus of the hateful message of the tweet. We can find these hateful NUs in 270 tweets (the 34% of all hate speech tweets) for an average of 1,21 NUs for each tweet.

(10) <NU>vivere in sicurezza senza la feccia di questi IMMIGRATI e rom impuniti che gira in ITALIA </NU>

(*Living safely without this scum of unpunished IMMIGRANTS and Roma who goes around in ITALY*)

(11)   <NU>Aumento   casi   morbillo?   </NU><NU>Ok. </NU></NU>Colpa   dei   vaccini? </NU>

(*Increase of measles cases? Ok. Vaccines' fault?*)

These hateful NUs have a close relationship with slogans. 124 (37,38%) of them can be classified as slogans. Slogans' numbers amount to 136 (see Table 1), so the 91,17% of them are composed by hateful NUs (see (12)), while only 12 (8,83%) of them don't convey hateful messages (see example (13)).

(12) <NU>tutti fuori clandestini e rom ! </NU>

(*illegal immigrants and Roma people, all out!*)

(13) <NU>w l'Italia!! </NU>

(*go Italy!!*)

Slogans are an interesting investigation's subject, because they are brief and concise formulae, easy to memorize and with high expressive value. Thus, it is interesting to notice that most of these slogans are used to convey an hateful message, making it the most highlighted and emphatic part of the tweet.

Of these slogans, 45 (33,33%) are calls to action for expelling immigrants from Italy (see (14)), and almost all them (33) have an Intensity of 3, while 4 have an Intensity of 1, 6 have an Intensity of 2 and 2 have an Intensity of 4. The other slogans vehemently ask for the killing or the imprisonment of immigrants (see (15)), while slogans with Intensity 1 are usually more descriptive, than exhortatory (see (16)).

(14) <NU>RIMPATRII IMMEDIATI di clandestini rom e stranieri criminali tutti!!! </NU>

(*IMMEDIATE REPATRIATION of illegal immigrants Roma people foreigners criminals everyone!!!*)

(15) <NU>pena capitale x tutti musulmani in Europa immediatamente! </NU>

(*death penalty for all the Muslims in Europe immediately!*)

(16) <NU>SUBIRE e essere islamizzati </NU>

(*ENDURING and being Islamized*)

Collectively, these slogans convey a particular way to express the populism's in-group - out-group way of thinking called *authoritarianism*, that is the call for "severe political measures or illiberal policies against those who threaten the homogeneity of the people" (Mazzoleni and Bracciale, 2018).

5.2 In-group and Out-group: Dualistic Constructions

The annotation of in-group - out-group rhetoric shows us that tweets with this dichotomy are not as recurring as we thought. In fact, only 165 (20,15%) of the hate speech comments have a in-group - out-group rhetoric, as showed in Table 1.

This dualistic construction mostly shows an opposition between Italians, often described as poor and abandoned by the government, and immigrants, depicted as privileged and protected by the leftist government (see (17)). Thus, unsurprisingly, the analysis' dimension of stereotypes exhibit a noteworthy score in these tweets: 138 of them (83,63%) display a stereotyped point of view (see (18)).

(17) Neanche dopo i disastrosi sismi in Centro Italia, Renzi blocca i clandestini per devolvere i soldi risparmiati agli Italiani #migranti

(*Not even after the disastrous earthquakes in Central Italy, Renzi stops illegal immigrants to hand over the saved money to Italians #migrants*)

(18) Gli immigrati africani in Italia, invece, sono ospitati a oziare in alberghi a 3-4 stelle. Bella differenza.

(*Instead, African immigrants in Italy are hosted to laze in 3-4 stars hotels. Nice difference.*)

In 16 cases, this rhetoric is also conveyed by newspaper's headlines, illustrating many kinds of Italians' struggles caused by immigrants (see (18)).

(18) #Libero: "Dieci milioni di euro buttati per i rom. Schiaffo all'Italia: guardate questi numeri

(*#Libero: "Ten millions of Euros throwed away for Roma people. A smack for Italy: look at these numbers*)

It is interesting to see that 75% of these dualistic tweets contain at least one NU, for a total of 127 NUs, 77 (60,62%) of which convey hate speech. This means that, even with a small number of newspaper's articles in their ranks, tweets with in-group - out-group rhetoric are a very fertile ground for NUs.

Still, these tweets don't contain slogans very often: only 26 tweets exhibit both slogans and dualistic rhetoric, see for instance (19):

(19) Vergogna, prima pensare agli italiani

(*Shame, first think of Italians*)

This could mean that this rhetoric doesn't tend to use slogan-like constructions. Instead, it seems to rely on more diverse syntactic structures, even if their lexicon is remarkably limited and with an hammering repetition of "Italians" and "Italy", while the out-group tends to be mentioned exploiting a slightly wider variety of terms (e.g., foreigners, illegal immigrants, immigrants and so on). This high repetitiveness is also typical of populist rhetoric.

Still, populist slogans and dualistic tweets, together, reach a sum of 262 populist hate speech's tweet (i.e., 33% of the entire POP-HS-IT). Therefore, we can say that populism in Twitter's hate speech is present, but it tends to acquire more than one form and to convey non only in/out-group rhetoric, but also authoritarianism rhetoric.

6 Conclusions and Future Work

In this paper we proposed a novel study of an *Italian Twitter Corpus of Hate Speech against Immigrants* (HSC) extended with four new levels of annotations: nominal utterances, in/out-group rhetoric, slogans and role of news. We named this new sample of HSC enriched with new annotation layers POP-HS-IT. Our goal was to investigate how the political discourse on immigrants and hate speech convey populist views (RQ1), how these populist views are impacted by newspaper's articles (RQ2) or by the spontaneous writings of single users, and how these populist views are conveyed through slogan-like nominal utterances (RQ3). The following answers emerge from our analysis.

Populist views are present in Twitter's hate speech against immigrants (RQ1), but they are not the majority of it; still, with a total of 257 populist hate speech's tweet, populist slogans and in/out-group dualistic tweets compose a third of the hate speech in the corpus. They also display the two most frequent populist themes of Twitter's hate speech against immigrants: in/out-group rhetoric that puts Italians against immigrants, and authoritarianism that calls for violent and illiberal actions against immigrants.

The reference to newspapers articles is very frequent in POP-HS-IT, but they are not perceived as bearer of hate speech, and therefore they are less represented also in slogans and in/out-group rhetoric (RQ2).

Slogan-like NUs are not the majority of the NUs in the corpus, but most of them convey hateful contents and are the semantic and pragmatic focus of the tweet. Also, they exhibit the populist rhetoric of authoritarianism, often with a medium-high level of hateful incitement, due to their nature of violent calls to action (RQ3).

For a complete analysis of this matter it is necessary to investigate more populist themes and the role of NUs in populist rhetoric. Still, this research starts to shed some light on the role of populist themes in hate speech: populist themes are remarkably present in hate speech against immigrants, and they need to be investigated to understand and challenge hate. Moreover, these populist themes are likely present in the rhetoric of populist politicians from all over the world as suggested in (Mazzoleni and Bracciale, 2018). Thus, the annotation framework of POP-HS-IT can be used to study the relationship between populism and hate speech in different social media corpora and in many languages. In fact, we plan to apply our analysis also on different available corpora in several languages (Basile et al., 2019; Waseem and Hovy, 2016), in order to study differences and commonalities in different cultures and domains.

Finally, the preliminary analysis of annotation results proposed opens new perspectives for the exploitation of the data set and of the new annotation layer for the development of HS detection systems, which is matter of future investigations.

Acknowledgements

We would like to thank the anonymous reviewers for their insightful comments. We are also grateful to our colleagues for their valuable help in annotating the corpus. The work of Viviana Patti was partially funded by Progetto di Ateneo/CSP 2016 (*Immigrants, Hate and Prejudice in Social Media*, S1618_L2_BOSC_01).

References

Jamie Bartlett. 2014. *Populism, Social Media and Democratic Strain*, pages 99–116. Fores.

Valerio Basile, Cristina Bosco, Elisabetta Fersini, Debora Nozza, Viviana Patti, Francisco Manuel Rangel Pardo, Paolo Rosso, and Manuela Sanguinetti. 2019. SemEval-2019 task 5: Multilingual detection of hate speech against immigrants and women in Twitter. In *Proceedings of the 13th International Workshop on Semantic Evaluation*, pages 54–63, Minneapolis, Minnesota, USA. ACL.

Émile Benveniste. 1990. *Problemi di linguistica generale*. Mondadori, Milano, Italia.

Cristina Bosco, Felice Dell'Orletta, Fabio Poletto, Manuela Sanguinetti, and Maurizio Tesconi. 2018. Overview of the Evalita 2018 Hate Speech Detection Task. In *Proceedings of the Sixth Evaluation Campaign of Natural Language Processing and Speech Tools for Italian. Final Workshop (EVALITA 2018) co-located with the Fifth Italian Conference on Computational Linguistics (CLiC-it 2018), Turin, Italy, December 12-13, 2018.*, volume 2263 of *CEUR Workshop Proceedings*. CEUR-WS.org.

Arthur T. E. Capozzi, Viviana Patti, Giancarlo Ruffo, and Cristina Bosco. 2018. A data viz platform as a support to study, analyze and understand the hate speech phenomenon. In *Proceedings of the 2Nd International Conference on Web Studies*, WS.2 2018, pages 28–35, New York, NY, USA. ACM.

Gloria Comandini, Manuela Speranza, and Bernardo Magnini. 2018. Effective communication without verbs? sure! identification of nominal utterances in italian social media texts. In *Proceedings of the Fifth Italian Conference on Computational Linguistics (CLiC-it 2018), Torino, Italy, December 10-12, 2018.*, volume 2253 of *CEUR Workshop Proceedings*. CEUR-WS.org.

Emanuela Cresti. 1998. Gli enunciati nominali. In *Atti del IV convegno internazionale SILFI (Madrid 27-29 giugno 1996)*, pages 171–191, Pisa. Franco Cesati Editore.

Maurizio Dardano and Pietro Trifone. 2001. *La nuova grammatica della lingua italiana*. Zanichelli, Milano, Italia.

Karmen Erjavec and Melita Poler Kovai. 2012. you dont understand, this is a new war! analysis of hate speech in news web sites comments. *Mass Communication and Society*, 15:899–920.

Angela Ferrari. 2011. Enunciati nominali. *Enciclopedia dell'Italiano*. `http://www.treccani.it/enciclopedia/enunciati-nominali_(Enciclopedia_dell'Italiano)/`.

Iginio Gagliardone. 2014. Mapping and analysing hate speech online. *SSRN Electronic Journal*.

Oscar Garcia-Marchena. 2016. Spanish Verbless Clauses and Fragments. A corpus analysis. In *CILC 2016. 8th International Conference on Corpus Linguistics*, volume 1 of *EPiC Series in Language and Linguistics*, pages 130–143. EasyChair.

Hanspeter Kriesi. 2014. The populist challenge. *West European Politics*, 37(2):361–378.

Annamaria Landolfi, Carmela Sammarco, and Miriam Voghera. 2010. Verbless clauses in Italian, Spanish and English: a Treebank annotation. In S. Bolasco, I. Chiari, and L. Giuliano, editors, *Statistical Analysis of Textual Data. Proceedings of the 10th International Conference on Statistical Analysis of Textual Data (JADT 2010)*, pages 450–459. LED, Milan.

Gianpietro Mazzoleni. 2014. Mediatization and political populism. In Frank Esser and Jesper Strömbäck, editors, *Mediatization of Politics: Understanding the Transformation of Western Democracies*, pages 42–56. Palgrave Macmillan UK, London.

Gianpietro Mazzoleni and Roberta Bracciale. 2018. Socially mediated populism: the communicative strategies of political leaders on facebook. *Palgrave Communications*, 4(1):1–10.

Bice Mortara Garavelli. 1971. Fra norma e invenzione: lo stile nominale. In Accademia della Crusca, editor, *Studi di grammatica italiana*, volume 1, pages 271–315. G. C. Sansoni Editore, Firenze, Italia.

Cas Mudde. 2004. The Populist Zeitgeist. *Government and Opposition*, 39(4):541563.

Carsten Reinemann, Toril Aalberg, Frank Esser, Jesper Strmbck, and Claes de Vreese. 2016. *Populist Political Communication: Toward a Model of Its Causes, Forms, and Effects*, page 1225. Routledge.

Manuela Sanguinetti, Fabio Poletto, Cristina Bosco, Viviana Patti, and Marco Stranisci. 2018. An Italian twitter corpus of hate speech against immigrants. In *Proceedings of the 11th Language Resources and Evaluation Conference*, Miyazaki, Japan. European Language Resource Association.

Birgit Sauer, Anna Krasteva, and Aino Saarinen. 2018. *Post-democracy, party politics and right-wing populist communication*, pages 14–35. Routledge.

Raffaele Simone. 2013. *Nuovi fondamenti di linguistica*. McGraw-Hill, Milano, Italia.

Zeerak Waseem and Dirk Hovy. 2016. Hateful symbols or hateful people? predictive features for hate speech detection on twitter. In *Proceedings of the NAACL Student Research Workshop*, pages 88–93, San Diego, California. Association for Computational Linguistics.

Ruth Emily Wodak. 2018. From hate speech to hate tweets. In M. Pajnik and B. Sauer, editors, *Populism and the Web. Communicative Practices of Parties and Movements in Europe*, pages xvii–xxiii. Routledge, New York.

"Condescending, Rude, Assholes":
Framing gender and hostility on Stack Overflow

Siân Brooke
Oxford Internet Institute
University of Oxford
United Kingdom
sian.brooke@oii.ox.ac.uk

Abstract

The disciplines of Gender Studies and Data Science are incompatible. This is conventional wisdom, supported by how many computational studies simplify gender into an immutable binary categorization that appears crude to the critical social researcher. I argue that the characterization of gender norms is context specific and may prove valuable in constructing useful models. I show how gender can be framed in computational studies as a stylized repetition of acts mediated by a social structure, and not a possessed biological category. By conducting a review of existing work, I show how gender should be explored in multiplicity in computational research through clustering techniques, and layout how this is being achieved in a study in progress on gender hostility on Stack Overflow.

1 Introduction

The binarization of gender in computational studies often does not sit well with critical theorists. Treated as the ultimate and most simple categorical variable, 0 = Female and 1 = Male is hardcoded into quantitative approaches from the first introductory text. In contrast, critical scholars see gender as social structure, arguing that it creates opportunities and constraints based on a sex-category. From this standpoint, the so called differences between men and women are entirely social conventions and the male-female binary is a fallacy. From Butler's (1990) work, scholars have understood gender as performative and existing as a stylized repetition of acts rather than an intense adherence to two distinct classifications. Yet, Butler's (1990) stylized acts and gendered self are limited by the recursive processes inherent in

gender as a stratification. Risman (2004) argues gender is a social structure, having consequence on the individual level in the development of the self, in interaction, and institutional domains. This paper focuses on the consequences of gender social structures in computational cultures, forming the groundwork of a larger doctoral project into how culture and role-based identities intervene in women's participation and legitimate interaction in informal coding cultures.

The title for this paper originates from the most common words that women used to describe Stack Overflow, the world's largest programming forum. In their annual survey in 2019, Stack Overflow asked just under 80,000 users what aspects of the platform they would most like to change – which showed some interesting gender disagreements. The words most likely to differentiate men included "official, complex, algorithm", whilst the words that differentiated women painted a quite different picture; "condescending, rude, assholes" (Stack Overflow, 2019). This gender difference in participation and perception of the Stack Overflow community is the basis of the project outlined in this paper, showing how hostility in 'condescension' and 'rudeness' deters women from taking part in programming.

In presenting the findings of this year's Stack Overflow Developers Survey these results where weighted by gender for the first time. Far from demonstrating an understanding of prejudice and hostility on the platform, the weighting was justified by "characteristics of [the] data" to "correct for demographic skew" (Stack Overflow, 2019). The lack of women in computational cultures is not a simple sampling error or a characteristic of data, but an active gender filter that deters women from taking part. I support a move in data science to infuse computational techniques with the capacity to reflect gendered power relations, moving beyond data based

172

Proceedings of the Third Workshop on Abusive Language Online, pages 172–180
Florence, Italy, August 1, 2019. ©2019 Association for Computational Linguistics

dismissals. In justifying my stance, I will first outline scholarship on the merits of studying identity and gender within a social context and how research design should acknowledge stereotypes. Next, I will show how women's participation in computational culture effects and is affect by anonymity. Thirdly, I will discuss the difficulties of operationalizing gender and the potential benefits of complicating the binary model. Finally, I will show how clustering has shown to be a promising technique to account for gender structures in online forums and my own proposed study. Overall, this paper argues for complicating the gender binary, forgoing predictive accuracy for representative and messy modelling.

2   Identity in Context

Early studies of the Internet heralded its disembodying attributes as liberating and a precursor of equality. It was proposed that anonymity can subjugate gender hierarchies, allowing for free and unhindered expression (Allen, 1995). However, as we make sense of identity online, we often round to the most common attributes, and thus anonymity serves to homogenize participants in online forums as belonging to a singular group. This group is college educated, white, and male (Kendall, 2011; Massanari, 2015). The prevailing voice here amplifies the discourse of an apparently neutral meritocracy – hiding the inequalities of race and gender.

Critical research has a long history of investigating gender, inequality, and interaction. Whilst the principles of social structures are pertinent across contexts, their exact form can change with social locale (Bucholtz & Hall, 2005; Risman, 2004). Wenger & Lave (1991) propose that researchers of such collective identities should focus on communities of practice (CoP) in which members are drawn together by a common interest or that are created deliberately with the goal of gaining knowledge in a certain field. This conception has since been expanded to include virtual communities of practice (VCoP), to show the extension of this anthropological phenomenon online. Stack Overflow can count as one such VCoP, as individuals come together to solve their programming woes. In such communities, Bucholtz (2005) argues that a situational and context-based methodology is fundamental to understanding the gendered social meaning that is

attributed to practices by individuals and cultures. Moreover, the representation of identity in speech should be conceptualized in terms of *communities* of as identity, not collections of individuals (or observations) as the bestowing of agency cannot be segregated from culture. In this manner, one's identity and behavior towards others is shaped by the community in which one participates and interacts – even online.

3   Gender in Context

In the initial scholarly discussion of identity formation and interaction, Lakoff (1973) first proposed that men and women differ in how they use words. Whilst gendered meaning necessitates difference, a difference in speech does not directly imply gendered meanings. A man's speech being different to women's means little without context. To ascertain if gendered differences carry meaning one must look at the interrelated layers of the interaction, such as what it means for a woman to be a speaker in this particular scenario (Needle & Pierrehumbert, 2018). What does it mean to be a woman to correct a man in computer science classroom? What does it mean for a man to fail a mathematics class but excel in a gender studies course? Such identity struggles are visible in discourse, or how knowledge creates meaning in interaction as a consequence of social structure (Risman, 2004). It is thus is necessary to consider the social context when considering how gender may be presented.

Gender can alter how a community talks about itself and its members. In using the sociolinguistic framing of gender and local context, feminist linguists have pointed to how normative discourse can represent gendered power structures and the male-centric nature of language (Lamerichs & Te Molder, 2003; Tanczer, 2015). This is particularly apparent in the use of 'guys' as a collective. As we move online, the physical markers of gender are invisible in anonymous forums, and male-centricity is amplified to male-by-default (Tanczer, 2015). As a space becomes more masculine and the in-group becomes male, women are framed in terms of stereotypes and identity tropes (Tanczer, 2015). In computational cultures, this communication process cultivates a femininity of technological incompetence and juvenile 'girlness' (Nic Giolla Easpaig & Humphrey, 2016; Shifman & Lemish, 2011). A male dominated masculine space can therefore lead to understanding women only in terms of the outsider.

There are consequences to stereotypes as they are relational. Gender stereotypes can be internalized and influence the manner in which one conceives of their own abilities and those of others. Risman's (2004) conception of gender as a encompassing social structure permeates online and offline interaction. As gender shapes interactions due to cultural expectations it also shapes one's identity, and there are consequences for institutional domains and technological cultures. As gender power relations are evident in self-presentation and interaction, this in turn affects opportunities in formal settings as stereotypes dictate expectations of others and ourselves (Adams et al, 2006). A popular theory in social psychology, *stereotype threat* refers to being at risk of confirming, as a self-characteristic, a negative stereotype about one's social group (Steele & Aronson, 2000). When one's self is viewed in terms of a salient group membership, performances can be undermined because of concerns about confirming negative stereotypes of one's group. In other words, telling women they can't code because they are women becomes a self-fulfilling prophesy - a false definition of the situation evokes new behavior, which makes the original false conception come true. Ergo, women can't code so there are few women in programming, from here we have 'proof' of the original stance that women can't code.

4   Girls can't code

In negotiating identity in masculine or nerd dominated spaces on, women may purposefully obscure their gender to participate in the social structures of a technical setting. The prominence of stereotypes and the belief that "girls can't code" means that women who show they are women in programming forums often face hostility and harassment (Ford et al., 2016). Nonetheless, Terrell et al (2017) found that women's contributions of code to the repository GitHub were approved at a higher rate than code written by men. In fact, women's contribution acceptance rates were higher than men for every programming language in the top 10 on the GitHub platform (Terrell et al 2017). However, when women's gender was identifiable on their GitHub profile, their acceptance rate dropped to significantly lower than

the average for men (Terrell et al., 2017). This shows not only do women obscure their gender in order to participate, but they are penalised when their gender is known, dropping below the level of men.

Looking to Stack Overflow, Ford et al. (2016) found that impersonal interactions were the main factor that discouraged women from contributing. The women (N = 22) interviewed for the study cited three features of the platform that deterred them from contributing: (1) anonymity was seen to contribute to blunt and argumentative responses on posts, (2) invisibility of women leads to the site feeling like a 'boy's club' full of 'bro humor' (Ford et al., 2016, p. 6), and (3) large communities are intimidating, and not possible in the same way offline. On Stack Overflow we can see a continuation of the theory that anonymous spaces lead to male-by-default interactions. The affordances of anonymity in Computer Mediated Communication (CMC) are evidently more beneficial to an ingroup, and attributes (or language) that might work for a majority group can be barriers for identifying with a community. Building on this, Ford et al. (2017, p. 1) conducted a second study where they developed the concept of *peer parity*: having similar individuals to compare oneself to in a space. The study found that the presence of female-identifying usernames on a thread increased the likelihood that a woman would engage actively with the Stack Overflow community (Ford et. al., 2017). When taken together, Terrell (2017) and Ford (2016; 2017) show that women hide their gender to participate, but this contributes to perceptions of a male-dominated space. This in turn deters women from participating as they do not see anyone like themselves. For women, stereotype threat creates a cyclical self-fulfilling prophesy, as does anonymity in not seeing *someone like me* in technical spaces.

5   Unlikely Allies

The disparity of women's representation in technical culture extends to those capable of computational methods, as only 15% of Data Scientists and computational researchers are women (Miller & Hughes, 2017). Comparatively, and estimated 75% of sociologists who focus on Gender are women (ASA, 2015). There are a number of notable exceptions to the trend, but this does not mean that the overall picture is endangered (See Ford 2016; 2017 as an example).

Whilst Data Science may dismiss inequality and women's lack of representation as a characteristic of the data, those who may provide insight are frequently not in the invited into the conversation. For Data Scientists, perchance it is not only the stereotype that girls can't code, but maybe also gender theorists.

Research has shown how valuable the social science lens is to computational fields (Kokkos & Tzouramanis, 2014; Nguyen, Doğruöz, Rosé, & de Jong, 2016; Otterbacher, 2013). Researchers at this intersection are aware of the tension between the theoretical framing and empirical methods of their work. Yet, whilst theory must begin with human-orientated ideas, these notions are only valuable if they are confirmed through empirical methods. Far from incompatible, the value placed on creativity and predictive accuracy in computational fields is well matched to the esteemed validity and reliability of the social sciences (Nguyen et al, 2016). This exciting and novel modus operandi is beginning to flourish in examining a range of inequalities online.

In computational sociolinguistics text is social data, and the choice of language used signals a performed identity (Nguyen et al., 2016). In a traditional sociological framing, agency occurs in linguistic symbols as social currency. A struggle is evident here, as the parsimonious causality prized by quantitative and computational approaches meets the messiness of the social world. In computational sociolinguistics a balance needs to be sort between language reflecting additional social structures, and language arising from speaker agency (Nguyen et al., 2016). Put simply, not everyone writes in a way that reflects their biology, and thus the agency of speakers should be acknowledged in interpreting findings.

As a case that exemplifies this argument, Otterbacher et al. (2013) examined the anonymous review site Internet Movie Database (IMDb) and found that women's reviews were weight as having less utility than men's. They also found that highly rated woman authors would exhibit "male" characteristics in their writing, such as less pronouns, complexity, and vocabulary richness (Otterbacher, 2013). The agency of the speakers is shown in the increased 'maleness' of language, as well as methodological evidence against biological determinism. Here, reputation voting systems of IMDb meant that female-based writing was downvoted. The reputation system acts as a gender filter, in which the gender-majority dictates success (Herring et al, 2002). Gender structures clearly mediate online interactions even in contexts that are far less heavily associated with masculine stereotypes that computational cultures.

The proposed study applies this conception that the male-majority dictates the identity performance required to succeed in a given social context and institutional setting (Risman, 2004). Looking to Stack Overflow, we propose that an estimated 89-94% male majority fosters masculine linguistic repertories where those who don't conform are punished with invisibility – colloquially referred to as being "downvoted into oblivion" (Clark-Gordon et al, 2017). As Hogan (2013) points out, conforming to a male-voice in order to successfully participate in a space is not a characteristic unique to computational culture or online forums. Take for instance the use of male pen names, the Brontë sisters were Currer, Ellis, and Acton Bell and Mary Ann Evans who used the guise of George Eliot (Hogan, 2013). The implication here is that computational methods allow for the mapping of such phenomena. However, before introducing the proposed study, we must first consider how feminine and masculine speech used by both male and female authors complicates the simple binary understanding of gender operationalized in many computational studies.

6   The trouble of operationalization

In applying computation, it is crucial that the research design is aptly framed to not recreate inequalities. As noted earlier, gender is often treated as a latent attribute – a implicit assumption that linguistics choices are associated with distinct categories of people (Needle & Pierrehumbert, 2018). The generalization of gender norms in computational research has been shown to contribute to stereotypes – seeing gender as something that people 'have' (not 'do'), neglecting agency to mask ones gender. In defending the binary classification to gender it is important to note that statistical definitions of the accuracy of predicative modelling does not mean that the picture is not oversimplified (Nguyen et al., 2016). Incorporating more critical understandings of gender may decrease predictive accuracy, but as it would include an understanding of socials structures the reproducibility of results may benefit. As gender social structures have consequences in interactions and infrastructure, a critical approach may not overfit a model to gender in a particular context. To build on the aphorism of the statistician George Box, if 'all models are wrong', can adding critical gender theory make them more useful?

In discussing the apparently conflict paradigms of social theory and computational methods, Nguyen et al. (2016) point to the value placed on of construct validity in more critical approaches. For the uninitiated, construct validity is "extent to which the experimental design manages extraneous variance effectively" (Nguyen et al., 2016). This can be particular important in how gender is conceived of within a study. As we saw with Otterbacher et al.'s (2013) study into linguistic gender on IMDb, women who exhibited "maleness" in there speech were more highly rated. This shows that whilst a platform appears to be numerical equal, it can still be performatively and legitimately masculine. In not paying due attention to such confounding factors of gender social structures, may leave the results of an investigation to be weak, regardless of the number associated with predictive accuracy. Indeed, the social word is far messier than many predictive models may lead us to believe.

Whilst computational studies into gender differences do valuable work to highlight the dearth of women in technical spaces, they can be guilty of perpetuating the underrepresentation. It can be dangerous to qualify contextual legitimacy or success in terms that are intrinsically gendered. In examining the open source development platform GitHub, Vedres and Vasarhelyi (2018) found that 'disadvantage is a function of gendered behavior'. In the study the variable of femaleness was qualified by professional ties, level of activity (push/pull requests), and areas of specialization (Vedres & Vasarhelyi, 2018). The study argues that measures of reputation ('success' – as starred repositories) and survival ('time account active') on the platform were adversely affected by femaleness rather than by categorical discrimination. They found that not only was this true for women, but men and users with unidentifiable gender are also likely to suffer for exhibiting behavior that demonstrated femaleness. The findings of Vedres and Vasarhelyi (2018) are valuable as they show that behavior classified as feminine adversely effects one's status (in their defined terms), not just listing 'female' on a profile.

Nonetheless, as is typical of gender classification studies, the 'behavioral' aspect was built from an extrapolation of categorical gender. That is, the features that are defined as 'femaleness', are built from behavior associated with a 'female' (categorically defined) account. Thus, the causality of gendered performance versus identification is unclear, and not supported by critical studies. The assertion made here that "women are at a disadvantage because of what they do, rather than because of who they are" (Vedres & Vasarhelyi, 2018) oversimplifies acting as a women and being a women into discrete and mutually exclusive categories. Nevertheless, that study shows that the default masculinity is ratified through behavior that generates contextual 'success', rather than by the overt presence of men. Vedres & Vasarhelyi's (2018) project reflects one of the significant challenges of critical research with computational methods: the operationalization of gender as a variable in manner that does conflate masculinity with community's definition of success.

7 Beyond the binary

As illustrated above, gender as a binary can miss some vital aspects of community functioning and belonging. As interactions dictate how men and women can act even in identical structural positions, gender can define the capacity for action in a given environment. For instance, Cheryan et al. (2009) found that exposure to stereotypical masculine computer science environments actively deters women from participating, even when the space was populated by women. Extending this, work by Ford and Wajcman (2017) & Schwartz and Neff (2019) shows that the social structures of gender permeate online spaces, as technology's design and use draws on the cultural and institutional repertoires in a male dominated space.

Whilst incorporated in many traditionally critical gender studies, going beyond a binary understanding can prove challenging to quantitative and computational research. How can gender be operationalized into a variable that accounts for a myriad of gender performances? Much work relies on the idea that the majority of individuals consider gender a binary, so therefore it is binary in studying the social phenomena in which said individuals participate. Whilst there is merit to this rationale, there are simple computational methods that can be used to negate a constrained and binary understanding of gender. A promising technique is that of Cluster Analysis. In clustering observations are grouped based on similarity, and to show the difference between different groups. Clustering is an unsupervised Machine Learning technique commonly used to gain valuable insights for patterns in data.

In their study into gender, networks, and linguistic style on Twitter, Bamman et al (2014) propose a more nuanced approach to quantitative work on gender. They point to how measures of predictive accuracy do not mean that the model does not distort the social world. Building on Butler's (1990) casting of gender, they take a two step approach to modelling gender.

Step 1: Predict gender with a Logit model using lexical features (i.e. Dictionary words, slang, taboo, hashtags)

Step 2: Group authors by similarity in word usage and look at the gender breakdown of each cluster.

By looking at which words and lexical features are most associated with users that profile states their gender in Step 1, Bamman et al (2014) take a situated approach to meaning. The stylized reputation of acts that are make up a gender performance vary by context. For instance, if a individual swears, the way that profanity is received by a audience will depends on the characteristics of the speaker (gender, ethnicity, age) and the context in which they are speaking (with friends, family dinner, classroom) and the role they are acting (policeman, mother, priest). As such, a perspective that incorporates situated meaning is the only way to understand the relationship between gender and language. In Step 2 of Bamman et al's (2014) study, Twitter users were grouped by similarities in word usage. Using a clustering algorithm based on the Expectation-Maximization framework, the clusters were built without considering gender yet had strong gender majorities. This approach to clustering allowed for multiple expressions of gender, which the authors speculate may be related to an interaction between age or ethnicity (Bamman et al., 2014). Conducting research in this manner, with gender not treated as the response variable, allowed for findings that were unexpected. For example, whilst taboo terms were generally shown to be preferred by men, several male-associated cultures reversed this trend

(Bamman et al., 2014). Overall, the clustering methodology of this study incorporates the social relation of "male" and "female" categories, going beyond descriptive understandings and acknowledging the normative gender performances that define inclusion and exclusion. Whilst this is not a perfect approach, it does highlight the possibility of clustering to examine how social identity can be evident in data without being determined by demographic markers. However antithetical they may seem, critical gender studies and computational methods can be unlikely, and valuable, allies.

8   **Stack Overflow:** A Research Agenda

Often referred to as the 'programmer's paradise', Stack Overflow is the largest online community of coding knowledge, boasting 9.9 million registered users and 50 million monthly visitors, of whom 21 million are professional developers and university-level students (Ford et al., 2016). Yet, with an estimated population of only 6-11% women, the popular platform is only paradise for some. The approach uses on Butler's conception of gender as enacted, incorporating situational meaning (Lea and Spears' 1991) and considering discourse-in-context, as argued for by Needle and Pierrehumbert (2018), Buckoltz (1999) and Lamerichs & Te Molder (2003). Building on the work of Adam (2003), Edwards (2003), Tanczer (2015), and Sollfrank (1999, 2002), this study examines the visibility of gender in accessible technical spaces. Through a twostep process of Natural Language Process, Machine Learning (*sklearn*), and Cluster Analysis (*Expectation-Maximization framework*), as used by Bamman et al (2014), I will analyse linkages between masculine-linguistic practise and reputation building.

A significant portion of the contribution of the study will be methodological, as I aim to provide a simple road map by which critical research can be conducted with computational methods, accounting for levels of gender visibility. In exploring this, I ask how visible gender is on Stack Overflow, and what situational meaning imbues text with hostility.

8.1 Data Collection

In first setting out the data for analysis, I will use the Stack Overflow data dump, hosted on Google BigQuery. Separated into different tables, the information available is posts, users, votes, comments, posts history, and post links. Updated on a quarterly basis, the BigQuery dataset includes an archive of Stack Overflow's user-contributed content, including posts, votes, tags, and badges. This dataset is updated to mirror the Stack Overflow content on the Internet Archive and is also available through the Stack Exchange Data Explorer. Inherent in this data are several challenges of working with big data (~180GB), such as different features of a post stored in separate tables (i.e. 'tags', accepted answers, post content). The Data Dump also contains substantial metadata, meaning data that provides a description of information in the dataset, such as suggested edits and location of users. Datasets such as this provide a wealth of information and contextual CMC that is underutilized in social science research. I will use the location of users to narrow my population to the USA and UK. Whilst this does lead to a Western-focused dataset, it also means that I am not homogenizing gender performances across cultural contexts.

8.2 Rudeness and Offence

On the Stack Overflow dataset, I propose to examine how visible gender and what forms hostility can take in context. Informing my analysis with Meta Stack Overflow, I will examine what practices are considered hostile and reduce the visibility (*peer parity* – Ford et al, 2016) of women on the platform. In taking a local and contextual approach to hostile behavior on Stack Overflow candidate features for inclusion were informed by the results of the 2019 Developers Survey and a forum dedicated to studying the research site, Meta Stack Overflow. I will incorporate formal/structural measures of hostility, such as the "Offensive Comment" tag. I will additionally include a subtler element in ascertaining what terms and practices are most associated with this tag. Contextual features that have so far emerged form a reading of Meta Stack Overflow include ratio of code to text, and references to "reading the documentation" in short answers or "not doing your homework for you", and similar sentiments.

The candidate features for inclusion thus reference local and contextual understandings of hostility.

8.3 Gender as Tiers

In examining gender as a social structure, I propose to account for both those who clearly identify their gender on their profile as well as those who purposefully obscure it to participate without facing gendered social sanctions. I propose three-tier classifications of gender to map onto the results of the cluster analysis.

(1) **Self-identified Male or Female:** Identified as a man/woman clearly through their profile (Gender, About Me, Name),
(2) **Linguistically Masculine or Feminine:** Estimated through a bag-of-word approach using the posts/comments associated with tier 1
(3) **Neutral:** Unidentified profiles (those users who fall under the conventionally defined 0.8 confidence of tier 2)

Through this distinction, my investigation will not conflate those who identify a gender, with those who perform it. As Otterbacher et al. (2013) show, "maleness" characteristics in speech does not mean that the speaker identifies as a man. This differentiation between claiming and hiding a gender identity in technical cultures will not only be beneficial in terms of building a representative model, but also in not seeing unidentified data as just noise, but rather a potentially purposeful act. These gender classifications will be mapped onto hostility and reputation to see the relationship between gender identification, linguistic-gender and legitimate participation.

Therefore, I will use NLP and clustering techniques to ascertain the gender dimensions of hostile behavior on Stack Overflow, and how this can lead to women's lack of participation. The output of the study will be a categorization of gendered behaviors that mark the space as masculine and create cultural barriers for women's entry into coding forums, even in the anonymous space of programmer's paradise.

Bibliography

Adams, G., Garcia, D. M., Purdie-Vaughns, V., & Steele, C. M. (2006). The detrimental effects of a suggestion of sexism in an instruction situation. *Journal of Experimental Social Psychology, 42*(5), 602–615.

https://doi.org/10.1016/j.jesp.2005.10.004

Allen, B. J. (1995). *Gender and Computer-Mediated Communication. Sex Roles* (Vol. 32).

ASA. (2015). ASA Sections: Membership by Gender | American Sociological Association. Retrieved June 2, 2019, from https://www.asanet.org/research-and-publications/research-sociology/trends/asa-sections-membership-gender

Bamman, D., Eisenstein, J., & Schnoebelen, T. (2014). *Gender identity and lexical variation in social media 1. Journal of Sociolinguistics* (Vol. 18).

Bucholtz, M. (1999). " Why be normal ?" Language and identity practices in a community of nerd girls Answer the following questions in small groups. *Language in Society, 28*, 203–223.

Bucholtz, Mary, & Hall, K. (2005, October 1). Identity and interaction: A sociocultural linguistic approach. *Discourse Studies.* SAGE PublicationsLondon, Thousand Oaks, CA and New Delhi. https://doi.org/10.1177/1461445605054407

Butler, J. (1990). *Gender Trouble: Feminism and the Subversion of Identity.* New York: Routledge. https://doi.org/10.1057/fr.1991.33

Cheryan, S., Plaut, V. C., Davies, P. G., & Steele, C. M. (2009). Ambient Belonging: How Stereotypical Cues Impact Gender Participation in Computer Science. *Journal of Personality and Social Psychology, 97*(6), 1045–1060. https://doi.org/10.1037/a0016239

Clark-Gordon, C. V., Workman, K. E., & Linvill, D. L. (2017). College students and yik yak: An exploratory mixed-methods study. *Social Media and Society, 3*(2). https://doi.org/10.1177/2056305117715696

Edwards, P. (2003). Nerd Worlds: Computer hackers, unofficial culture and mascu line identities, [unpublished paper]. *Program in Science, Technology and Society, Sta Nford University, Stanford, CA.*

Ford, D., Smith, J., Guo, P. J., & Parnin, C. (2016). Paradise unplugged: identifying barriers for female participation on stack overflow. In *Proceedings of the 2016 24th ACM SIGSOFT International Symposium on Foundations of Software Engineering - FSE 2016* (pp. 846–857). New York, New York, USA: ACM Press. https://doi.org/10.1145/2950290.2950331

Ford, H., & Wajcman, J. (2017). 'Anyone can edit', not everyone does: Wikipedia's infrastructure and the gender gap. *Social Studies of Science, 47*(4), 511–527. https://doi.org/10.1177/0306312717692172

Herring, S., Job-Sluder, K., Scheckler, R., & Barab, S. (2002). Searching for Safety Online: Managing "Trolling" in a Feminist Forum. *The Information Society, 18*(5), 371–384. https://doi.org/10.1080/01972240290108186

Hogan, B. (2013). Pseudonyms and the Rise of the Real-Name Web. In *A Companion to New Media Dynamics* (pp. 290–307). Blackwell Publishing Ltd. https://doi.org/10.1002/9781118321607.ch18

Kendall, L. (2011). "White and Nerdy": Computers, Race, and the Nerd Stereotype. *Journal of Popular Culture, 44*(3), 505–524. https://doi.org/10.1111/j.1540-5931.2011.00846.x

Kokkos, A., & Tzouramanis, T. (2014). A robust gender inference model for online social networks ad its application o LinkedIn and Twitter. *First Monday, 19*(9). https://doi.org/10.5210/fm.v19i9.5216

Lamerichs, J., & Te Molder, H. F. M. (2003). *Computer-mediated communication: from a cognitive to a discursive model* (Vol. 5).

Lave, J., & Wenger, E. (1991). *Situated learning : legitimate peripheral participation.* Cambridge University Press.

Lea, M., & Spears, R. (1991). Computer-mediated communication, de-individuation and group decision-making. *International Journal of Man-Machine Studies, 34*(2), 283–301. https://doi.org/10.1016/0020-7373(91)90045-9

Massanari, A. L. (2015). *Participatory Culture, Community, and Play: learning from reddit.* Oxford: Peter Lang.

Miller, S., & Hughes, D. (2017). *The Quant Crunch: How The Demand for Data Science Skills Is Disrupting the Job Market. BurningGlass, IBM* (Vol. 41). https://doi.org/10.1177/0032258x6804100305

Needle, J. M., & Pierrehumbert, J. B. (2018). Gendered associations of English morphology. *Laboratory Phonology: Journal of the Association for Laboratory Phonology, 9*(1), 1–23. https://doi.org/10.5334/labphon.134

Nguyen, D. ., Doğruöz, A. S. ., Rosé, C. P. ., & de Jong. F. . (2016). Computational sociolinguistics: A survey. *Computational Linguistics, 42*(3), 537–593. https://doi.org/10.1162/COLI_a_00258

Nic Giolla Easpaig, B., & Humphrey, R. (2016). "Pitching a virtual woo": Analysing discussion of sexism in online gaming. *Feminism & Psychology, 0*(0), 1–9. https://doi.org/10.1177/0959353516667400

Otterbacher, J. (2013). Gender, writing and ranking in review forums: a case study of the IMDb. *Knowledge and Information Systems, 35*(3), 645–664. https://doi.org/10.1007/s10115-012-0548-z

Risman, B. J. (2004). Gender as a social structure: Theory wrestling with activism. *Gender and Society.* https://doi.org/10.1177/0891243204265349

Robin, L. (1973). Language and Woman ' s Place. *Cambridge University Press, 2*(1), 45–80. https://doi.org/10.1017/S0047404500000051

Schwartz, B., & Neff, G. (2019). The gendered affordances of Craigslist "new-in-town girls wanted" ads. *New Media & Society,* 146144481984989. https://doi.org/10.1177/1461444819849897

Shifman, L., & Lemish, D. (2011). "Mars and venus" in virtual space: Post-feminist humor and the internet. *Critical Studies in Media Communication, 28*(3), 253–273. https://doi.org/10.1080/15295036.2010.522589

Sollfrank, C. (1999). Women Hackers: A report from the mission to locate subversive women on the net. *Cyberfeminist International.*

Sollfrank, C. (2002). Not every hacker is a woman. Retrieved April 28, 2017, from http://www.obn.org/reading_room/writings/html/notevery.html

Stack Overflow. (2019). Stack Overflow Developer Survey 2019. Retrieved May 10, 2019, from https://insights.stackoverflow.com/survey/2019

Steele, C. M., & Aronson, J. (2000). Stereotype threat and the intellectual test performance of African Americans.

Tanczer, L. M. (2015). Hacktivism and the male-only stereotype. *New Media & Society,* 1–17. https://doi.org/10.1177/1461444814567983

Terrell, J., Kofink, A., Middleton, J., Rainear, C., Murphy-Hill, E., Parnin, C., & Stallings, J. (2017). Gender differences and bias in open source: pull request acceptance of women versus men. *PeerJ Computer Science, 3,* e111. https://doi.org/10.7717/peerj-cs.111

Vedres, B., & Vasarhelyi, O. (2018). *Gendered behavior as a disadvantage in open source software development.*

Online aggression from a sociological perspective:
An integrative view on determinants and possible countermeasures

Lea Stahel
University of Zurich
Department of Sociology
Andreasstrasse 15, CH-8003 Zurich
stahel@soziologie.uzh.ch

Sebastian Weingartner
University of Zurich
Department of Sociology
Andreasstrasse 15, CH-8003 Zurich
weingartner@soziologie.uzh.ch

Abstract

The present paper introduces a theoretical model for explaining aggressive online comments from a sociological perspective. It is innovative as it combines individual, situational, and social-structural determinants of online aggression and tries to theoretically derive their interplay. Moreover, the paper suggests an empirical strategy for testing the model. The main contribution will be to match online commenting data with survey data containing rich background data of non-/aggressive online commentators.

1 Introduction

In the past years, online aggression in social media has attracted a lot of attention not only in the broader public but also in academia (e.g. Cicchirillo et al. 2015; Sydnor 2018). Studies show that offending, defaming, or threatening online comments posted by Internet users fundamentally negatively affect the targeted persons' well-being, social harmony, and democratic outcomes (e.g. Anderson et al., 2014; Bauman, 2013; Kwon and Gruzd, 2017). Accordingly, knowing why people aggress online is the first step to counter it. Although previous research on online aggression has been successful in suggesting and explaining single determinants driving aggressive online commenting (see studies in the *State of Research* below), (1) their interplay has hardly been studied due to the lack of an overarching theoretical framework and (2) socio-structural determinants have been largely ignored so far. Moreover, from a methods point of view, (3) there are no studies that systematically link digital commenting data to offline information on adult aggressors from the wider population.

Hence, the present paper introduces a theoretical model that relates several determinants of online aggression to each other in a more general framework of sociological explanation. Based on the model, we aim to answer the following research questions: (1) Which individual determinants, situational determinants, and social-structural determinants drive online aggression? (2) How do various determinants relate to each other when producing aggressive online behavior? (3) Are there differences in online aggression between social-structural groups?

Answering such questions requires a specific empirical strategy. We intend to conduct a large-scale quantitative survey in German-speaking Switzerland, including aggressive and non-aggressive online commentators. They are drawn from a large population of commentators having submitted to online commentary sections of a large Swiss media organization. We match their survey information with their commenting behavior, ranging from non-aggressive to frequently aggressive (this classification emerges from human/automated content analysis).

We will elaborate on the theoretical model and the planned empirical strategy in the following sections. First, however, we will describe in more detail the current state of online aggression (OA in the remainder of the paper) research.

2 State of research

In the literature so far, determinants of OA are explored primarily from three different perspectives: the individual-psychological, the situational, and the social-structural. All three perspectives are shortly reviewed here, from the fields of psychology, political science, and communication.

2.1 Psychological-individual determinants

From a psychological-individual perspective, OA can on the one hand be motivated by relatively stable psychological traits ("aggressors as

Proceedings of the Third Workshop on Abusive Language Online, pages 181–187
Florence, Italy, August 1, 2019. ©2019 Association for Computational Linguistics

antisocial individuals"). The underlying theory proposes that each individual has a unique personality and that associated traits motivate behavior and thus (online) aggression. For example, online aggressors score relatively higher in narcissism, psychopathy, and Machiavellianism (e.g. Abell and Brewer, 2014), might lack empathy (Steffgen et al., 2011), may be less open, low in self-control, and impulsive (Peterson and Densley, 2017), but also more depressive and shy (Bauman, 2013).

On the other hand, OA can be motivated by less stable individual emotions, beliefs, and goals ("aggressors as venting, convinced Internet activists"). For example, people in negative mood may troll (Cheng et al., 2017), being angry at unfair negotiators motivates to digitally aggress (Johnson et al., 2009), and car drivers vent their rage (Stephens et al., 2016). Also, online aggressors belief that they do not get caught and that their online con-ent is not permanently stored (Wright, 2013). Further, people participating in collective online outrage are motivated by moral heuristics and moral beliefs (e.g. based on moral disengagement theory by Faulkner and Bliuc, 2016) and punishing violators of social norms (based on social norm theory; Rost et al., 2016). Finally, online aggressors have goals. They spread political ideologies, seek thrill and fun, draw attention to social in-justice (Erjavec and Kovačič, 2012), or seek social standing, status, and recognition (e.g. Ballard and Welch, 2017).

2.2 Situational determinants

Research on situational determinants suggests that online aggressive individuals are influenced by properties of the digital media environment and the surrounding social and situational context ("aggressors as ordinary people, but situationally-driven"). The psychological-communicative Reduced cues approach (Sproull and Kiesler, 1986) argues that properties of online environments may cause toxic online disinhibition (Suler, 2004): people feel less restraint because of the absence of social-context cues, anonymity, invisibility, asynchronicity, or minimization of authority. This is explained either by deindividuation theories (Diener, 1980) or by the social identity model of deindividuation effects (SIDE) which argues that deindividuation triggered by reduced social cues and anonymity in online settings boosts the salience of individuals'

social identity relative to their personal identity. Thus, if a group norm is salient (e.g. in an online forum), commentators will conform to it rather than engage in uncontrolled aggressive behavior (Reicher et al., 1995). SIDE is empirically supported in several settings (e.g. Hmielowski et al., 2014).

OA is also explained by social learning theories and situational social control. For example, perceiving flaming norms socializes people into flaming (Cheng et al., 2017). Also, people more likely aggress online if informal social controls from an effective community policy and peer pressure are lacking, predicted by routine activity theories of crime (Navarro and Jasinski, 2012), deterrence theory (Xu et al., 2016), or social norms (Álvarez-Benjumea and Winter, 2018). Similarly, people more likely aggress if they have become cyber-victims themselves (Quintana-Orts and Rey, 2018), receive comments challenging their beliefs (Hutchens et al., 2015) or threatening their face (Masullo Chen and Lu, 2017), or if public actors misbehave (Johnen et al., 2017; Rost et al., 2016). Finally, legal frameworks, ethical guidelines, and moderation strategies set up by online (news) platforms may be situationally influential (Ksiazek, 2015).

2.3 Social-structural determinants

Research on social-structural determinants is very scarce. It includes socio-demographics, social group memberships, and structural positions and relations. Accordingly, OA may differ by cultural and national backgrounds (Shapka et al., 2018), gender (Ballard and Welch, 2017; Bauman, 2013; Shapka et al., 2018), and age (Bauman, 2013; Shapka et al., 2018). Also, incivility on Twitter is higher in areas of low socioeconomic status (SES), low social capital potential (i.e. potential for interconnected citizen networks), and low in-district partisan polarization (Vargo and Hopp, 2017). Finally, (few) structural and sociodemographic factors are considered in the social media cyberbullying model (SMCBM) model by (Lowry et al., 2016).

2.4 Gaps

Reviewing the literature on OA, several gaps emerge. Theoretically, there is, first, no overarching theoretical framework integrating the determinants suggested. Accordingly, theoretical approaches to cyberbullying are "sparse and piecemeal" (Espelage et al., 2012: 49) and „have received scant conceptual development" (Runions, 2013: 751). Hence, a major task of future research is to develop "a comprehensive theoretical model that might ground the conversation about cyber aggression and violence" (Peterson and Densley, 2017: 197). At best, such a model addresses the "interaction between micro, meso, and macro levels of explanation" in order to overcome research's current lack of "continuity and coherence" (Peterson and Densley, 2017: 197).

Second, there is a need to relate OA more systematically to social-structural factors. Up to now, information on aggressors and their aggression-benefiting circumstances is limited (Coe et al., 2014: 675; Peterson and Densley, 2017:195). Especially with regard to potential "civility divides" (Vargo and Hopp, 2017: 26), exploring socio-demographic and socio-economic determinants (such as gender, age, education, or prestige) enables to empirically test whether "those equipped with economic and social privilege in the off-line realm may disproportionally gain value from online deliberation, while those with diminished economic and social resources may interact in a hostile, uncivil, (…) strata of the Internet" (Vargo and Hopp, 2017: 24; also see Cicchirillo et al., 2015).

Third, there are no studies that systematically link digital commenting data to offline information in a large sample of adult aggressors. Most studies only use natively online data. If offline in-formation is collected at all, then it is linked to OA intentions, self-reports, or experimental triggers, at best.

3 Theoretical model

Here, we introduce an integrative model that relates a multitude of determinants to each other in a general framework of sociological explanation, also explicitly theorizing social-structural determinants. This model builds on the ideas of structural individualism (Coleman, 1994) and the model of frame-selection (Esser, 2001; Kroneberg, 2011).

Basically, structural individualism aims at dissecting social phenomena into its constitutive parts, that is meaningful decisions of individual actors. These decisions, however, are embedded in a configuration of social structures and institutions. This social context, in turn, affects (if correctly perceived) actors' goals, beliefs, and opportunities, which then guide their behavior (Maurer and Schmid, 2010; Udehn 2001). From this perspective, OA comments are defined as individual decisions (actions) which are in a first step explained by both characteristics of the individual (e.g. beliefs) and situational parameters (e.g. others' behaviors). In a second step, individual determinants are related to social-structural background. The relationship between these two sets of determinants can be thought of in several ways: social context conditions may structure the set of behavioral alternatives available, the behavioral costs, and an individual's preferences, attitudes, and body of knowledge. Theoretically, this can be explained by learning theories (Bandura 1977) or social production function theory (Ormel et al. 1999).

It needs to be specified, then, how individual decisions come about. This is important because the theory of action chosen has an impact on which individual and situational determinants can be taken into account. Instead of relying on a rather simple rational-choice approach for explaining individual decisions, we opt for the more elaborate model of frame-selection (MFS) as introduced by Kroneberg (2011, 2014). In classical rational-choice theory (Opp, 1999), it is assumed that actors choose those behavioral alternatives which they expect to best fulfill their preferences given certain behavioral constraints. Thus, behavior is a function of individual goals (evaluative beliefs, including egoistic just as prosocial goals), beliefs about the consequences of decisions, and behavioral constraints (the latter two are often summarized as descriptive beliefs). However, rational-choice theory is silent about which descriptive and evaluative beliefs are active in a specific decision situation. Therefore, MFS explicitly incorporates the process of the definition of the situation (Esser, 1996). In this process, actors subjectively define which kind of situation they are actually facing (which may – in contrast to rational-choice theory – deviate from "objective" situational requirements). They do so by synchronizing given situational cues with internalized knowledge about typical situations (frames). Hence, descriptive and evaluative beliefs guiding behavior are not taken for granted but depend on actors' subjective perceptions of the situation. This means that behavioral differences between (groups of) actors do not simply result from individual or situational differences, but from interactions between individual and situational characteristics.

Based on these theoretical considerations, we propose the following explanatory model of OA (Figure 1):

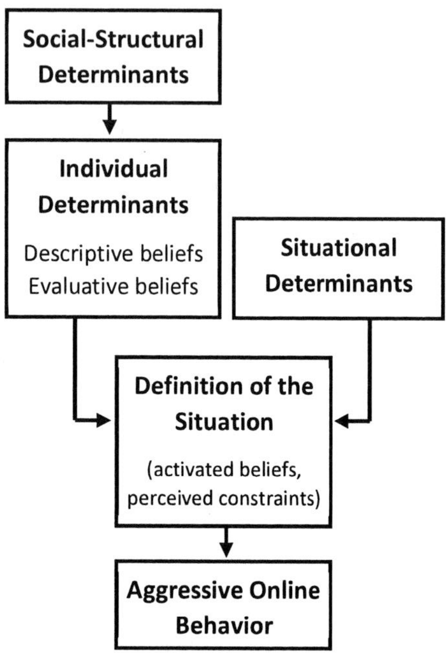

Fig 1: Explanatory model of aggressive online behavior.

In this model, OA behavior results from individuals' definitions of potential online commenting situations. Such definitions represent a situation's general meaning and thus determine which individual beliefs are activated and which situational constraints are perceived by the actor. How situations are defined depends on two sets of factors: (1) situational determinants comprise all relevant characteristics of the situational context and thus are in principle identical for all actors in the same situation (but still differently perceived). (2) individual determinants comprise all descriptive (representations of current states of the world) and evaluative beliefs (representations of desired states of the world) of an individual and thus do not vary across situations for a specific actor. The interactive relationship between individual and situational determinants can be understood in two ways. Straightforwardly, it means that those individual beliefs (and opportunities) guide behavior which are activated by certain situational cues. This differs according to the overall set of beliefs internalized by the individual. However, if some descriptive or evaluative beliefs are strongly internalized and thus chronically active, they can prompt a certain definition of the situation (and thus action) irrespective of the situational conditions given (possible misperception). As mentioned above, we assume descriptive and evaluative beliefs to be tied to social-structural determinants. In accordance with structural individualism, sociological factors such as socio-economic or demographic attributes are reflected in individual determinants. Hence, social-structural groups are expected to be similar in terms of certain beliefs. Overall, the model emphasizes that OA does neither result from characteristics of the individual, nor from characteristics of the situation, but rather from the interplay of these two.

4 Empirical approach

The empirical study seeks to collect data on individual, situational, and social-structural determinants of OA behavior. Therefore, we intend to conduct an online survey in German-speaking Switzerland with four different groups: frequent OA commentators, occasional OA commentators, non-OA commentators, and non-commentators. Group-differences in determinants, then, allow to assess determinants' relative effect on OA behavior. However, sampling OA commentators is not easy because it is a relatively rare behavior. Thus, we apply an elaborate, two-step sampling strategy: First, in order to sample OA and non-OA commentators, we use the unique opportunity to collaborate with a large Swiss media corporation. We will use a large dataset of news comments submitted to its website (including meta-data such as time of submission). The dataset includes moderated comments: comments considered as being non-aggressive by moderators (and were published in the commentary section) and comments considered as aggressive (and were not published). By employing human/automated content analysis of all comments, we identify the following groups and assign all commentators to one of them: frequently aggressive commentators, occasionally aggressive commentators, and non-aggressive commentators. From each group, we invite around 1500 people to participate in the survey. Second, in order to sample persons who do not engage in online commenting at all (non-commentators), we use a random sample of the resident population of German-speaking Switzerland.

Particular attention is given to data protection and the ethics of recruiting. First, all the comments and meta data received by the Swiss media corporation is principally public data, thus principally searchable and retrievable. This is because commentators submit their comments to news platforms in the knowledge that their comments get principally published (even in cases where comments are ultimately not published by moderators). Beyond, this data set is given to us in an anonymized form. Thus, privacy concerns can be excluded. Second, not the authors but the Swiss media corporation invites the commentators to participate in the survey (as the e-mail addresses of commentators are only available to the corporation but not to us). Third, by forming groups of commentators (see above) whereby individuals in each group receive group-specific online surveys, the survey data of individuals will only be connected to the affiliation to these groups but at no time to individual comments or commentators. This makes it impossible to identify single individuals in the resulting data set. Fourth, an ethics approval will be sought in the process of designing the survey.

Our approach of matching online data with survey data allows to combine behavioral data with a broad range of – so far scarcely collected – individual, social-structural, and situational determinants of OA. While individual and social-structural determinants will mainly be measured in the survey, most situational determinants will be measured through aggregating user-generated comments and meta-data.

5   Conclusion

The preceding paper introduced a novel, sociologically informed theoretical framework integrating a broad set of determinants of aggressive online commenting behavior. Furthermore, it suggested an empirical strategy allowing to disentangle the effects single determinants by matching online data with survey data.

References

Abell, L., Brewer, G., 2014. Machiavellianism, self-monitoring, self-promotion and relational aggression on Facebook. *Computers in Human Behavior* 36, 258–262.

Álvarez-Benjumea, A., Winter, F., 2018. Normative Change and Culture of Hate: An Experiment in Online Environments. *European Sociological Review* 29, 1–15.

Anderson, A.A., Brossard, D., Scheufele, D.A., Xenos, M.A., Ladwig, P., 2014. The "nasty effect: " Online incivility and risk perceptions of emerging technologies. *Journal of Computer-Mediated Communication* 19 (3), 373–387.

Ballard, M.E., Welch, K.M., 2017. Virtual warfare: Cyberbullying and cyber-victimization in MMOG play. *Games and Culture* 12 (5), 466–491.

Bandura, A. (1977). *Social learning theory.* Englewood Cliffs NJ: Prentice Hall.

Bauman, S., 2013. Cyberbullying: What does research tell us? *Theory into practice* 52 (4), 249–256.

Cheng, J., Bernstein, M., Danescu-Niculescu-Mizil, C., Leskovec, J., 2017. Anyone can become a troll: Causes of trolling behavior in online discussions. arXiv preprint arXiv:1702.01119.

Cicchirillo, V., Hmielowski, J., Hutchens, M., 2015. The mainstreaming of verbally aggressive online political behaviors. *Cyberpsychology, Behavior, and Social Networking* 18 (5), 253–259.

Coe, K., Kenski, K., Rains, S.A., 2014. Online and uncivil?: Patterns and determinants of incivility in newspaper website comments. *Journal of Communication* 64 (4), 658–679.

Coleman, J.S., 1994. *Foundations of social theory.* Harvard University Press, Cambridge.

Diener, E., 1980. Deindividuation: The absence of self-awareness and self-regulation in group members. The psychology of group influence 209242.

Erjavec, K., Kovačič, M.P., 2012. "You Don't Understand, This is a New War!: " Analysis of Hate Speech in News Web Sites' Comments. *Mass Communication and Society* 15 (6), 899–920.

Espelage, D.L., Rao, M.A., Craven, R.G., 2012. Theories of cyberbullying. Principles of cyberbullying research: Definitions, measures, and methodology, 49–67.

Esser, H., 2001. *Soziologie. Spezielle Grundlagen.* Band 6: Sinn und Kultur. Campus, Frankfurt a. M.

Esser, H., 1996. Die Definition der Situation. *Kölner Zeitschrift für Soziologie und Sozialpsychologie* 48 (1), 1–34.

Faulkner, N., Bliuc, A.-M., 2016. 'It's okay to be racist': moral disengagement in online discussions of racist incidents in Australia. *Ethnic and Racial Studies* 39 (14), 2545–2563.

Hmielowski, J.D., Hutchens, M.J., Cicchirillo, V.J., 2014. Living in an age of online incivility: Examining the conditional indi-rect effects of online discussion on political flaming. *Information, Communication & Society* 17 (10), 1196–1211.

Hutchens, M.J., Cicchirillo, V.J., Hmielowski, J.D., 2015. How could you think that?: !?!: Understanding intentions to engage in political flaming. *New Media & Society* 17 (8), 1201–1219.

Johnen, M., Jungblut, M., Ziegele, M., 2017. The digital outcry: What incites participation behavior in an online firestorm? *New Media & Society*, 1461444817741883.

Johnson, N.A., Cooper, R.B., Chin, W.W., 2009. Anger and flaming in computer-mediated negotiation among strangers. *Decision Support Systems* 46 (3), 660–672.

Kroneberg, C., 2011. *Die Erklärung sozialen Handelns: Grundlagen und Anwendung einer integrativen Theorie.* VS-Verlag, Wiesbaden.

Ksiazek, T.B., 2015. Civil interactivity: How news organizations' commenting policies explain civility and hostility in user comments. *Journal of Broadcasting & Electronic Media* 59 (4), 556–573.

Kwon, K.H., Gruzd, A., 2017. Is aggression contagious online?: a case of swearing on donald trump's campaign videos on youtube. Proceedings of the 50th Hawaii International Conference on System Sciences, 2165–2174.

Lowry, P.B., Zhang, J., Wang, C., Siponen, M., 2016. Why do adults engage in cyberbullying on social media?: An integration of online disinhibition and deindividuation effects with the social structure and social learning model. *Information Systems Research* 27 (4), 962–986.

Masullo Chen, G., Lu, S., 2017. Online political discourse: Exploring differences in effects of civil and uncivil disagreement in news website comments. *Journal of Broadcasting & Electronic Media* 61 (1), 108–125.

Maurer, A., Schmid, M., 2010. *Erklärende Soziologie: Grundlagen, Vertreter und Anwendungsfelder eines soziologischen Forschungsprogramms.* VS-Verlag, Wiesbaden.

Navarro, J.N., Jasinski, J.L., 2012. Going cyber: Using routine activities theory to predict cyberbullying experiences. *Sociological Spectrum* 32 (1), 81–94.

Opp, K.-D., 1999. Contending conceptions of the theory of rational action. *Journal of Theoretical Politics* 11 (2), 171–202.

Ormel, J., S. Lindenberg, N. Steverink, et al. (1999). Subjective well-being and social production functions. *Social Indicators Research* 46(1): 613–90.

Peterson, J., Densley, J., 2017. Cyber violence: What do we know and where do we go from here? *Aggression and violent behavior* 34, 193–200.

Quintana-Orts, C., Rey, L., 2018. Forgiveness and cyberbullying in adolescence: Does willingness to forgive help minimize the risk of becoming a cyberbully? *Computers in Human Behavior* 81, 209–214.

Reicher, S.D., Spears, R., Postmes, T., 1995. A social identity model of deindividuation phenomena. *European review of social psychology* 6 (1), 161–198.

Rost, K., Stahel, L., Frey, B.S., 2016. Digital social norm enforcement: Online firestorms in social media. *PLoS One* 11 (6), e0155923.

Runions, K.C., 2013. Toward a conceptual model of motive and self-control in cyber-aggression: Rage, revenge, reward, and recreation. *Journal of youth and adolescence* 42 (5), 751–771.

Shapka, J.D., Onditi, H.Z., Collie, R.J., Lapidot-Lefler, N., 2018. Cyberbullying and Cybervictimization Within a Cross-Cultural Context: A Study of Canadian and Tanzanian Adolescents. *Child development* 89 (1), 89–99.

Sproull, L., Kiesler, S., 1986. Reducing social context cues: Electronic mail in organizational communication. *Management science* 32 (11), 1492–1512.

Steffgen, G., König, A., Pfetsch, J., Melzer, A., 2011. Are cyberbullies less empathic?: Adolescents' cyberbullying behavior and empathic responsiveness. *Cyberpsychology, Behavior, and Social Networking* 14 (11), 643–648.

Stephens, A.N., Trawley, S.L., Ohtsuka, K., 2016. Venting anger in cyberspace: Self-entitlement versus self-preservation in# roadrage tweets. *Transportation research part F: traffic psychology and behaviour* 42, 400–410.

Suler, J., 2004. The online disinhibition effect. *Cyberpsychology & behavior* 7 (3), 321–326.

Sydnor, E. (2018). Platforms for incivility: Examining perceptions across different media formats. *Political Communication* 35(1): 97–116.

Udehn, L. (2001). *Methodological individualism: Background, history and meaning.* London: Routledge.

Vargo, C.J., Hopp, T., 2017. Socioeconomic status, social capital, and partisan polarity as predictors of political incivility on Twitter: a congressional district-level analysis. *Social Science Computer Review* 35 (1), 10–32.

Wright, M.F., 2013. The relationship between young adults' beliefs about anonymity and subsequent cyber aggression. *Cyberpsychology, Behavior, and Social Networking* 16 (12), 858–862.

Xu, B., Xu, Z., Li, D., 2016. Internet aggression in online communities: a contemporary deterrence perspective. *Information Systems Journal* 26 (6), 641–667.

Author Index